PEMAQUID, MAINE →

L.I.

SALEM

BOSTON

DELAWARE RIVER

Varkens Kill

ATLANTIC OCEAN

ted
undary

SLAND

NCE
E TR:

S
CE
UCK R

PLYMOUTH

Taunton

MARTHA'S
VINEYARD

NANTUCKET

e New England
Confederation, 1643-64

0   20   40   60

Scale of Miles

Mass. [   ]   Ply. [   ]

Conn. [   ]   N.H. [   ]

Dutch-Swedish [   ]

The United Colonies
of New England—1643-90

by

HARRY M. WARD

VANTAGE PRESS

New York   Washington   Hollywood

To

NAN NAN

FIRST EDITION

Copyright, 1961, by Harry M. Ward

Published by Vantage Press, Inc.
120 West 31st Street, New York 1, N. Y.

Manufactured in the United States of America

Library of Congress Catalog Card Number: 60-15581

First Stripes of American Union: a flag of four red stripes flown from a coastal trading vessel, probably from across the Sound from New Haven Colony. New Amsterdam Harbor, 1647. (See Ch. 4.)

TABLE OF CONTENTS

                                                          Page

PREFACE   7

ABBREVIATIONS   9

Chapter

    I. DETERMINING INFLUENCES   11

   II. GENESIS OF UNION   24

  III. ARTICLES OF CONFEDERATON   49

   IV. A STRUCTURAL VIEW   60

    V. GREAT EXPECTATIONS   90

   VI. QUEST FOR INDIAN POLICY 118

  VII. NABOTH'S VINEYARD 136

 VIII. THE EAGLE AND THE "BEETLE FLY" 157

   IX. CONSTITUTIONAL CRISES OF 1653-5 178

    X. A TIME FOR FALLING OUT 201

   XI. CEMENT OF THE UNION 230

  XII. NEW WINE INTO OLD BOTTLES 259

 XIII. TRIUMPH OF MILITARY EXPEDIENCY 278

  XIV. DOMINION INTERLUDE 312

   XV. REMNANTS OF CONFEDERATION 342

  XVI. A LEGACY FOR AMERICA 370

APPENDICES

A. Articles of Confederation, 1643 384

B. Articles of Confederation, 1672 391

C. Meetings of the Commissioners of the
   United Colonies 398

D. The Commissioners of the United Colonies 400

BIBLIOGRAPHY 412

INDEX 427

PREFACE

This is a study of intercolonial cooperative action among the New England colonies from their beginnings to the New York Conference of 1690. The towering experiment of the period was the Confederation of four New England colonies, which served a practical purpose for nearly fifty years and was destined to implant in the minds of the colonists the idea of federal union and to serve as a precedent for the later American Union.

The United Colonies of New England was the acorn from which the mighty oak sprang. The seedling may appear at times tender and frail—in such terms as population and resources—when compared to a modern age, but it is the lesson of history that great events have small beginnings. The American Revolution, one of the most far-reaching events of all time, was accomplished in an arena of a scattered and not always sympathetic populace numbering less than the present state of Guatemala. As a prime mover of the Puritan Confederation expressed it: "Small things in the beginning of natural or politic bodies are as remarkable as greater in bodies full grown."

A word may be said about the transcribing of seventeenth century script. Until recently it was the fashion to transfer literally the many contemporary abbreviations and signs when making direct quotations, as if this method would better preserve the quaintness of the period. But such frill-like writing was nothing more than a shorthand method and does not therefore depict the actual spelling of the words intended. Thus, in quotations an attempt is made to spell out the words beyond the shorthand used, according to the spelling intended. Also, for the sake of readability, certain letterings are sometimes changed, for example: substituting the letter "u" for the words beginning with "v" (e.g., "united Colonys") and "v" for "u" in such words as "have."

Dating presents a problem. In Great Britain and the American colonies of the seventeenth century the Old Style method of reckoning time was used—thus a date in the seventeenth century is ten days earlier than that reckoned by the present Gregorian calendar (e.g., May 19 becomes May 29). The first day of the year was March 25, with March considered as the first month. The matter is further complicated in that the Dutch, with whom the Commissioners of the United Colonies had many dealings, dated their correspondence according to the New Style method (present time) and that historians have not been consistent in their methods of dating (often mixing in dates of both calendars—rather than using one or the other). In this study a compromise method has been devised, which it is hoped will give the reader the benefit of present dating and at the same time will remain true to the sequential thinking of the period. Thus in the text all specific dates are reckoned according to the modern calendar, while in the footnote references the actual date in the source is given.

Because the purpose of this study is to present an administrative and constitutional history it must be selective. In areas of economic, social, and church history or in the development of Puritan thought the reader may well consult a number of able studies, which need not be duplicated here.

The United Colonies of New England of 1643-90 is a subject too long neglected in our history. It cannot be dismissed on the grounds that it endured sporadically as a mere league and was not strong enough to last until the forming of our present government. The New England Confederation was the first full-scale attempt at federation. It provided a half-century of unity for the New England colonies, far outliving its successor, the Confederation of 1781; and considering that it was the product of colonists on their own in search of principles of government independent of the mother country, it ranks as one of the most noble political experiments of all time.

I wish to express my indebtedness and gratitude to Professor Richard B. Morris of Columbia University, who first suggested a study of the Confederation and guided it during the early stages. I am also indebted to Mr. Lawrence Phelps Tower, who has greatly contributed to this study by making available his research findings on the origins of the American flag. Professor Ralph Curry of Georgetown College offered many suggestions which have improved the literary quality of the book. The committee report of the Institute of Early American History on the original manuscript has enabled the author to make needed revisions. I wish to thank Mr. and Mrs. Leo Flaherty of the Massachusetts Archives and collectively the efficient and personable staffs of the Massachusetts Historical Society, the Connecticut State Library, and other libraries visited or where information was sought.

ABBREVIATIONS

(Abbreviations needing explanation not in this list may be found in the Bibliography.)

AASP	American Antiquarian Society Proceedings
DHR	Dedham Historical Register
CCR	Connecticut Colony Records
CHSC	Collections of the Connecticut Historical Society
JHUS	Johns Hopkins University Studies in History and Political Science
MCR	Massachusetts Colony Records
MHSC	Collections of the Massachusetts Historical Society
MHSP	Proceedings of the Massachusetts Historical Society
NEQ	New England Quarterly
NHCR	New Haven Colony Records
NYHSC	Collections of the New York Historical Society
PCR	Plymouth Colony Records
PCSM	Publications of the Colonial Society of Massachusetts
PPS	Publications of the Prince Society
RICR	Rhode Island Colony Records
RIHSC	Collections of the Rhode Island History Society
BPL	Boston Public Library
CA	Connecticut Archives
CHS	Connecticut Historical Society
MA	Massachusetts Archives
MHS	Massachusetts Historical Society
NYHS	New York Historical Society
NYPL	New York Public Library
RIA	Rhode Island Archives
RIHS	Rhode Island Historical Society

CHAPTER I

Determining Influences

The Puritan founders of the first intercolonial league in America drew upon their common heritage—in thought and in practical experience. They profited from the lessons of history. The leaders in the Puritan migration were highly articulate: as exponents of a Bible Commonwealth they were well educated for the task ahead of them; and many, as members of the gentry or the rising merchant class, could have well worn the robes of religious and political authority had they not been denied them by arbitrary policies at home.

The New England settlers transplanted local political institutions known to them in the mother country. But, in casting about for an inspiration of a "confederate" union of autonomous states, they were most impressed by the Dutch "United Provinces." Many of the leaders of the emigration to New England had lived under this league during the peak of its effectiveness. Englishmen also were familiar with the Dutch league through trade or through communities in England that had undergone a high influx of Dutch refugees the preceding generation. The inspiration which the Dutch Union afforded the early colonists of New England, when added to the firm planting of English local institutions, gave rise to the dichotomy of state and national powers later characteristic of American federalism. But behind the desire of the New England Puritans to establish a confederation of the colonies are various factors that shaped their political thinking.

Calvinism provided the basis for many of the Puritan notions of church and state. Those fit to govern were to come from the "elect." For salvation man cooperates with God. In some respects the church government in Calvinism was democratic. There was less distinction between clergy and laymen than among the Lutherans or Roman Catholics; elders could preach or administer the sacraments. Ministers were chosen by local congregations. Elders and deacons were elected by the congregation as

11

a whole. The highest authority in a church was that of a congregation, and this authority could be delegated to representatives of the local churches meeting in an assembly, or synod.
Democracy in America owes much to the Calvinist form of
church government.

The writings of the Puritan leaders in the settlement of America reveal a familiarity with other leagues in history, particularly those of the Israelites, Greeks, and the Swiss. Though
congregationalists, the Puritans admired the solidarity and unity
of ancient Zion. The best known to the Puritans of the ancient
Greek confederacies was the Achaian League of 281-146 B. C.
Like other leagues of the time, the Achaian League was a loose
gathering of city-states for the purposes of defense. It did reach
the stage of a federal assembly wherein all citizens of the member city-states could attend and vote. Greek federations adopted
the principle of appointing a board of delegates from the various states on the basis of equal representation of the states—thus
setting the precedent for later confederations. Democracy in its
purest form worked within the individual city-states, but it was
found that representative government worked best on the interstate level.

The Union of the Swiss Cantons was a precedent frequently
cited by the Commissioners of the United Colonies during the
constitutional debates of 1653-5. Formed in 1291 of three forest
cantons, this league through a long and turbulent history
emerged in the sixteenth century with thirteen cantons. Although
the Swiss Confederation provided a central diet for conducting
foreign affairs, levying war, and arbitrating interstate disputes,
it fell into the same pitfalls that were to harass the New England
Confederacy by not providing enforcement machinery for the
central government.

The Romans appear to have had an unconscious influence on
Puritan ideas of government. It was chiefly confined to the Roman influence on English institutions. But it was the example of
Rome the Puritans sought to avoid. Nothing was more inimical
to the Puritan mind of New England (though many of their
brethren in Cromwellian England had different views) than
dictatorship from the military arm.

The Puritans in New England also knew of the medieval
Hanseatic League, which had demonstrated the advantages of
a trading union. A union of city republics for defense and promot-

ing commercial activity and colonization, it was mercantile rather than political. Like the later confederations of the Dutch and the Puritans it was to suffer from the aggrandizement of the leading province over the lesser states.

Although an attempt has been made to trace Dutch influences upon local government in New England,[1] which is at most minimal in view of early Anglo-Saxon origins, the Dutch Republic nevertheless made a great single contribution in its experiment in union. The Union of Utrecht, 1579, "ever regarded as the foundation of the Netherlands Republic," had many features appearing in the New England Confederation. Though the Union of Utrecht was a "living example of the perils besetting a Confederacy which dared not become a Union,"[2] the founders of the New England Confederation after their migration to the New World were too concerned with their own problems to learn any lessons from the bickerings and strife in the Dutch Union. But they did keep in mind the early Dutch experiment in union. The twenty-six articles of the Union provided that a governor-general under the archduke should be the nominal executive. However, there was no provision for a central executive department. Envoys from the individual provinces served as a quasi-legislature, and, as in the Confederation, there were no provisions for a supreme judicial authority. The Union of Utrecht, though it proved to be a temporary government, was that under which the Pilgrims lived for eleven years before migrating to the New World.

The "political impressions of the Puritans," which can only be assumed from circumstantial evidence, indicates the Union of Utrecht as the "forerunner and prototype of the New England Confederacy."[4] Although such evidence is not necessary to prove that the United Netherlands had a profound effect upon the formation of the New England Confederation—a comparison of the Articles of the two unions warrants this assumption—it does offer insight. For instance, many of the founders of the Confederation had Dutch contacts. Hooker spent a sojourn in Amsterdam.[5] Theophilus Eaton was a close friend of John Davenport who had lived in Holland. Thomas Dudley resided at one time in Holland. Three of the twelve signers of the Articles of Confederation knew life first hand in the United Provinces.[6] The arduous experience of the Leyden flock served as an elementary education for the tasks of living together and carving a home out of the wilderness.

At the beginning of the seventeenth century, Holland and not England was the center of Puritanism in Europe. This was the reason the Pilgrims sought refuge in Holland. The Pilgrim community in Holland acquired a spirit of toleration that was carried to the New World, where this spirit later contrasted with the haughty Puritanism of the Bay Colony. Although fear of assimilation of the less strict ways of Dutch living was the main reason given for their removal to the New World, the Pilgrims, nevertheless, had found some security in their Dutch home, as the words of the Leyden pastor attests: "We are well weaned from the delicate milk of our mother country, and inured to the difficulties of a strange and hard land, which yet, in great part, we have by patience overcome."[7] The contact with the Dutch Union was a contributing factor to the New England Union.

Although the New England colonists looked to the Dutch for a precedent for union, their own homogeneity made union possible. Alike in language, religion, customs, geographical origins, and motivation, it was natural in the wilderness for the New England colonies to overlook petty differences and band together for mutual protection and welfare.

The quest for union among the New England settlements in the seventeenth century began a long time before colonists sought a federal relationship with the mother country. Moreover, it was a time when the "sad distractions" of civil war made it impossible to work out an imperial policy. All governmental influence from England on the early colonies, therefore, was limited to previous contact with local institutions in the homeland and through these institutions with the crown. The gradual development of the English Constitution brought forth the king as supreme landlord and preserver of the peace. Thus, in the English mind there was appearing a sense of duality—though not federal itself, it gave rise to federal thinking—wherein an Englishman was subject to local authority and common law, but could seek equity from the crown. The English sovereign of the seventeenth century was very different from that of today, enjoying powers of administration not subject to the purview of Parliament. Not only did this dualism of local and national or king and Parliament serve to create a climate for federal thinking, but it also accentuated the principle of representative government, a prerequisite for establishing federal government.

The Puritans could not rely upon English political theory,

still in its infant stages; the great days of the Putney debates, Hobbes, Harrington, Milton, and Locke lay ahead. Moreover, the New England Puritans, being practical men, cared little for political theory as such. In the New World, they were imbued with Calvinistic self-reliance and the spirit of vigorous self-government; the latter, whether directly or indirectly, was the chief contribution of England in this period to the cause of American federalism. There is little value in calling attention to the various theories on the origins of self-government in America —for example, the "Germanic theory," the "primordial germ theory," or the "Massachusetts charter theory"—except to point out that the elements of local self-government transferred from England regained a new vitality in the wilderness soil of the New World.

Contributing to Puritan ideas of confederation was their "federal" way of thinking. The federal theology, a preoccupation of the divines, sought to work out a compromise between the Covenant of Works and the Covenant of Grace. Two aspects of this "federal" thinking are of particular importance.

The first is that of thinking in both general and particular terms. This method of thinking led to the acceptance of the paramountcy of the individual churches in matters of local concernment and to the attempt to seek the general will through synods and consociations. Examples of this dualism in reasoning are found throughout the writings of the Saints. Thus, Hooker's famous inquiry into the nature of the soul begins with the declaration of method: first "we will open it in general," and then "we will discover the parts of it."[8] Or take John Davenport's pamphlet against arbitrary church government: "the Power of every particular Church is chiefe in its own particular matters ...as a Synod hath the chiefe power, in things that are common to many Churches;"[9] or Winthrop's "General Observations" and "Particular Considerations" in weighing the problem of migrating to America.[10] This disposition to categorize reasoning on two different planes—the general and the particular—helped to provide an intellectual climate favorable for experimentation in federalism.

A second aspect of Puritan thought influencing the Puritan mind toward the idea of federalism in government was the emphasis upon the covenant, which extended from the realm of theology into ideas of church and state. By 1640, the covenant idea in the Massachusetts and New Haven colonies had achieved a prominence unlike anywhere else.[11] Believers in congregations bound themselves together first in churches of Christ and then in government by making a solemn covenant with God and each other. The ideal society was that of a confederation of congregations supported by a sympathetic state.

The sovereignty of God, as it was in Calvinism, was the basic tenet of Puritan theology, and it belonged to the true believer to be "joyned to the Lord" in "one Spirit." The power to take new members into communion with the Godhead belongs to God himself:

> ... as you see sometimes great Princes will take in a neighbour Nation into league with them and not tell them of it; he maketh a Covenant with Christ, and taketh us into that Covenant ... for we are not able to give ourselves unto him till he first take us.[12]

The Covenant of Works was the Law of Nature God undertakes for man, with man as peer; but since man is not actually a peer it was necessary to form a new covenant of grace based on faith.[13] As Cotton put it, God contracted with Abraham to be God and Abraham "to be a People unto himself," with Jesus Christ under the new covenant the "Mediator or Surety of this Covenant between them both." This, according to Cotton, was the "sum of the Articles, and of the Confederates."[14] The idea of covenant relationship between God and man and man and society runs throughout all New England literature of the time.[15] The covenant theory was the way of reconciling theological views of predestination with the rising social and economic demands for freedom.[16]

The Covenant of Grace was extended to the visible church. The true church consists of believers united with Christ as a political body of Saints, with the pastor as chief officer and the elders seeing to it that true policy is carried out.[17] But the Church was to be more than a union of Saints—it had a mission to spread the Gospel throughout the world. In order to spread the Word of Christ and to establish the true belief for churches of like faith there was need for a consociation of churches. As an early writer put it, "let ... Churches be ... neither National nor Provinciall, but gathered together in covenant ...."[18] But a covenant of churches

was not to be hierarchical or to compel member churches
to endorse policy set forth by a consociation.[19] The principle of
independency was to be preserved. Each church was a complete
unit in itself, subject only to the authority of the Bible. Consociations and synods were a sort of brotherhood—"a superstructure
after covenant"—whose purpose was to advise and counsel the
various churches, but with no powers of excommunication, only
to refuse fellowship with them.[20] The fundamental unit of church
government was the covenant of the people of a congregation
with God, and no "Oaths or Covenants of God's People are
against Christ, but in subordination to him, and to the advancement of his Kingdom."[21] The covenant of the first Puritan church
in Salem set the pattern for succeeding church covenants:

> We Covenant with the Lord and one with another; and doe
> bynd ourselves in the presence of God, to walke together
> in all his waies, according as he is pleased to reveale him-
> self unto us in his Blessed word of truth.[22]

Thus, in the words of Thomas Hooker, "Visible Saints are the
only true and meet matter, whereof a visible Church should be
gathered, and confoederation is the form."[23]

The covenant idea was put to use by the Puritans of New
England to explain the nature of the State. As in theology—
man accepts divine grace in return for his obedience to the
sovereign God and for performance of the duties of a Christian
—man surrenders certain of his powers to a body politic to preserve the liberties and rights of all belonging to the covenant.
The covenant idea, which has become a "conspicuous principle
of American constitutionalism,"[24] was the basis of the political
institutions of the early settlements. Winthrop believed that his
Company had entered into a covenant with each other; and the
settlers of Plymouth, without authority from the home government,

> solemnly and mutually in the presence of God, and one of
> another, covenant and combine our selves togeather into a
> civill body politick ... to enacte, constitute, and frame such
> just and equall lawes, ordinances, actes, constitutions, and
> offices, from time to time, as shall be thought most meete
> and convenient to the generall good of the Cononie, unto
> which we promise all due submission and obedience.[25]

Herein lies the beginning of the compact theory in America and a fundamental principle of American federalism.

Thus were the two main contributions of the Puritan mind to the idea of federalism in America: reasoning in general and particular terms and the covenant idea. Other phases of Puritan thought and Congregationalism contributed to a lesser degree. There are the Providential interpretation of history, a respect for fundamental law, a desire for uniformity in religion and politics, and a Puritan conscience that sought justification for acts of great moment (such as war)—all of which were thought better served by confederation. The emphasis in Congregationalism upon local autonomy was a primary factor in creating a loose league of states instead of a consolidated union.

Another contributing factor to the Puritan idea of government is found in the governmental experience of the colonists. The beginnings of government in New England helped to mold the pattern of intercolonial union. The earliest form of government in New England was the trading corporation, of which Massachusetts affords the most significant example. A General Court of freemen was created by the stockholders of the Company to govern the settlements. The Board of Assistants of the Company, elected by the freemen, did not develop into an independent council, like the southern colonies, but remained a part of the General Court. With the transfer of the seat of government of the Company to Massachusetts, the colony became a corporate body in itself and with ultimate power lodged in the colony's General Court. The Plymouth settlement, after buying out the merchant adventurers at home, proceeded along similar lines. When the colonies were ready for confederation, they treated with one another through envoys dispatched from the General Courts of distinct corporate bodies.

The joint-stock agreement, wherein members sharing in the risks reaped profits in proportion to their investments, was common in New England, and was an influence upon the idea of confederation. Even when whole towns broke off from the older settlements, they migrated not as towns but as companies. The towns as they branched off into new settlements were incorporated by the Colony court, and in such instances as Rhode Island, Connecticut, and New Haven, the original colony was a confederation of towns, setting up a central court by mutual agreement. Each colony was a union of incorporated towns, as the New England Confederation was to become a union of independent colonies. The confederation of the New Haven towns into a colony occurred simultaneously with the forming of the New England Confederation—in order to secure representation in the league these settlements had to be united into a single political body. The story of the combining of the New England towns, whether within an established colony or as independent city-states entering into a league, is a story told in the many histories of the period. Suffice it here to say this affinity for union gave evidence of a "synthetic unionist movement which, allied or opposed to the analytic and disruptive movement, makes or destroys empires."[26]

The experience of the colonists in working out their own affairs of government in town and colony gave rise to many forms adaptable to the growth of American federalism. The most important was the principle of representative government. Originally the freemen sat in the legislative bodies of the colonies, but with the expansion of freemanship, it became more convenient to send deputies from the towns to the General Courts rather than having the freemen attend in person. Even the annual courts of election, which elected the assistants and the magistrates, who actually formed the upper house of the General Courts, gave way to votes by proxy. This absenteeism, coming as it did with the expansion of the suffrage, brought the control of the government more to the people at large; but this movement was tempered by conditions for the self-perpetuation of the magistrates, whose conservatism sought to check any excesses of the people. The emerging principle of balanced government—harmonizing the voice of the people and conservative interests—was to appear in the Constitution of 1787. But this principle did not find its way into the New England Confederation, whose inherent weakness was that the Commissioners of the United Colonies were ambassadors of the General Courts (in most instances selected by the Courts from the magistrates) and not elected by the people.

Committees were the favorite means of New England democracy in doing the work of a community. The committee system was prolific. Committee heads were drawn from leading citizens, whether selectmen, deputies, magistrates, or elders, to serve in posts ranging from "Commissioner for small causes," which abound in the records of the time, to the high post of Commissioner for the United Colonies. The importance of allotting work to committees should not be underestimated in accounting for the rise of American federalism. The New England Confederation had many features of a standing committee for intercolonial defense and mutual concernment, and it might be noted that the Continental Congress was the outgrowth of committees of correspondence and safety. Also in the eighteenth century standing committees gave rise to the executive departments of the National Government, which was to make the difference between Federal Union and Confederation.

Allied to the growth of the committee system was the appearance of the council. The council was more than a standing committee, for it was recognized as having executive powers not always amenable to a legislative body. Councils were resorted to in order to fill the interims between regular government, such as during the time between adjournment and reconvening of the General Court or for matters requiring continual supervision (e.g., during time of war). The Massachusetts Council served as an important arm of government in that colony. Formed for the purpose of transacting business of the colony that could not wait until the reconvening of a session of the General Court, the Council was expected to afford continuity in government much as was expected of the ill-fated Committee of States of 1784. This standing council in Massachusetts, composed of all the assistants and the Governor, gradually enhanced its position until the coming of the provincial government in 1692. With the Court of Assistants assuming judicial power and the legislative functions residing with the General Court, the Council came the closest to exerting executive powers[27] during this time. The very fact that an extra-charter Council was permitted to develop pointed to the need for oversight and administration by a board outside the arena of the legislature. The Commissioners of the United Colonies themselves, with similar powers on an intercolonial level and drawn from the leading men of the colonies, may be viewed as an extension of the colonial councils.

The councils of war of both the town and colonial levels had a marked influence on the New England Confederation. The Council of War in Plymouth, the product of a long and continuous development, was the counterpart of the Massachusetts Council. During the time of Indian hostilities the councils of war exerted for the sake of expediency almost unboundless authority

in the theaters of war. It was the peculiar characteristic of the
New England Puritans to go all out to meet a situation, and when
the emergency was met, to return without the blink of an eye
to their normal affairs. Though local governments could easily
recuperate from the strains of war, the New England Confederation could not rebound from the military role cast upon it. As
a Council of War it was an anomaly in peace-time. Indeed, the
course of intercolonial cooperative action was doomed for nearly
a century to progress no further than the confines of the war-
council.

From four directions the Puritans in New England were influenced in their conception of intercolonial confederation: from
the Continent, England, Puritan thought, and the experience of
the colonies. The Saints in the wilderness would assemble this
driftwood and build a structure of intercolonial government.
This would not be an easy task because the sands of time and
experience were not yet firm.

---

[1] E.g., in the northern Dutch provinces, where the Pilgrims spent their stay
and where "English Puritans swarmed," there were Germanic influences in the
township, broad suffrage, common lands, and the written ballot. Because of the
Dutch contact, as one author holding this view in the last century has put it, the
local institutions of New England and the Southern colonies developed along
different courses. (See Douglas Campbell, *The Puritan in Holland, England,
and America* (New York: 1892), II, 428-39.

[2] John L. Motley, *History of the United Netherlands* (New York: 1868),
IV, 539; also *The Rise of the Dutch Republic* (New York), II, 567.

[3] Lucy M. Salmon, "The Union of Utrecht," *Annual Report of the AHA*
(1893), I, 137-148. This study compares similarities in the Union of Utrecht
and the New England Confederation.

[4] *Ibid.* According to this vigorous spokesman for the case of Dutch influence
on American federalism: though American union was inevitable it was "impossible that one so perfect as was the confessedly imperfect one of the New England Confederation should have been evolved from the inner consciousness of
its framers." Thus, one has to look to the experience of the settlers, which
extends only as far back as the Dutch Republic—all other federations being too
remote, or, in the case of Switzerland, too fundamentally different from the
course of American union. Nevertheless, contrary to this view, the founders of
the Confederation were aware of the European precedents in union.

[5] See George L. Walker, *Thomas Hooker,* (New York: 1891).

[6] Salmon, *loc. cit.*

[7] John Robinson and William Brewster to Sir Edwin Sandys, quoted in Asbel
Steele, *Life and Times of William Brewster* (Philadelphia: 1857), pp. 193-4.

The Pilgrims in the *Mayflower* rejected an autocratic system and substituted instead a "democratic federative principle much after the pattern which they had experienced in the Federative Republic of the United Netherlands." (D. Plooij, *The Pilgrim Fathers from a Dutch Point of View* New York: New York University Press, 1932), p. 16.

[8] Thomas Hooker, *The Soules Ingrafting into Christ* (London: 1637), pp. 1-3.

[9] John Davenport, "A Just Complaint Against an Unjust Doer," (1634), transcribed from the original in the British Museum by H. M. Dexter, Yale University Library.

[10] *Winthrop Papers*, II, 119ff.

[11] Champlin Burrage, *The Church Covenant Idea*, (Philadelphia: American Baptist Public Society, 1904), p. 88.

[12] John Cotton, *A Treatise of the Covenant of Grace*, (London: 1659), pp. 13, 29.

[13] Daniel A. White, *New England Congregationalism*, (Salem: 1861), p. 261.

[14] John Cotton, *op. cit.*, p. 3.

[15] Perry Miller, *The New England Mind*, (New York: The Macmillan Co., 1939), p. 504.

[16] See *ibid.*, pp. 399, 400, 430.

[17] Ezra H. Byington, *The Puritan in England and New England*, (Boston: Roberts Bros., 1897), p. 23; Henry M. Dexter, *Congregationalism*, (New York: Harper and Bros., 1880), pp. 448ff; Herbert W. Schneider, *The Puritan Mind*, (New York: Henry Holt and Co., 1930), p .19.

[18] Edward Johnson, "Wonder-Working Providence," *Original Narratives of Early American History*, ed. by J. F. Jameson (New York: Charles Scribner's Sons), p. 140.

[19] In Holland, the Pilgrims refused to accept "the system of church government" dictated by the Synod of Dort (W. C. Martyn, *The Pilgrim Fathers of New England*, (New York: 1867), and in the New World the Cambridge Synod allowed that there should be no attempt to enforce new standards until they had been approved by the churches. (John W. Platner, "The Congregationalists," in the *Religious History of New England* (Cambridge: Harvard University Press, 1917), p. 20).

[20] Miller, *op. cit.*, p. 169; Walker, *Hooker, op. cit.*, pp. 143-5.

[21] John Eliot, "The Christian Commonwealth," *MHSC*, 3: IX: 140.

[22] Quoted in Burrage, *op. cit.*

[23] Walker, *op. cit.*, p. 144.

[24] Andrew C. McLaughlin, *The Foundations of American Constitutionalism*, (New York: New York University Press, 1932), p. 29. This study has a chapter titled "The Foundations of Federalism," but hardly dips back before the Revolutionary period. Typical of the bypassing of historians of the New England Confederation is his statement: "The New England Confederation, which lasted for some fifty years, probably had influence on the later plans for organizing the American Union." (p. 136).

[25] The Mayflower Compact, printed in Azel Ames, *The May-Flower and Her Log*, (New York: Houghton, Mifflin and Co., 1901), pp. 335-6.

[26] A. Wyatt Tilby, *The American Colonies, 1583-1763*, Vol. I of *The English People Overseas*, (New York: Houghton, Mifflin and Co., 1912), pp. 82, 84.

[27] It is the author's assumption that executive powers are the inherent part of any government operating on people, whether exercised singly or collectively. A different view holds that there was no such thing as "executive" power in Massachusetts in the early seventeenth century, only "consultive" power. See Ellen E. Brennan, "The Massachusetts Council of the Magistrates," *NEQ*, IV (Jan.-Oct., 1931), 54-93.

CHAPTER II

Genesis of Union

The Union of 1643 was a number of years in the making. Along the winding perimeter of choppy coasts and inward valley plains, English settlements sprang up almost overnight. The lure of the cod, beaver, and fertile lands proved irresistible to distressed Puritans in England, and for those already in New England there was plenty of room for expansion. On the north, the fingers of settlement reached beyond the Piscataqua, and, southward, English eyes turned to Long Island Sound and on hopes of cutting into the Dutch fur trade. The opening of the Connecticut Valley, with its rich lands and strategic position for the Indian trade, allured settlers from the older colonies. Harkening to the call of the horn of plenty, God's chosen people sought to possess all of New Canaan. But a wilderness could not be won in a day—there must be hardship, dedication, and on occasion, joint effort.

The people of New England were a homogeneous lot. Alike not only in language, national stock, customs, and institutions, they also possessed sensitively a common religious mission. Through banding together they might consolidate the position they had already hewn for their faith and better spread the Gospel. As the colonists came face to face with the emboldened red man and began knocking on the doors of the outlying Dutch and French settlements, they learned that their purposes could best be served through united action. The need for union was also felt through the want of a permanent board to arbitrate intercolonial disputes, to regulate trade, and in the case of war to determine and guide intercolonial participation. In these days before the formulating of English colonial policy, the colonists became increasingly aware of the need for some form of union in order to survive in the wilderness and to facilitate cooperation among themselves. The road to a confederation of the four Puritan colonies—Plymouth, Massachusetts, Connecticut, New Haven—began soon after the founding of the Bay

24

Colony. However, before union could be effected, the colonists had to learn the lessons of experience and acquire the habits of working together. There were also the intricacies of diplomacy.

Plymouth and Massachusetts were early inclined toward cooperative action. Though founded on different religious principles, both colonies followed the paths of Congregationalism. The relationship between these two settlements was cordial, and the governors of the two colonies occasionally exchanged visits.[1] These were the days before Massachusetts far outstripped its less fortunate neighbor on the Cape.

Late in the fall of 1632 came distressing news to the Massachusetts authorities. A pirate by the name of Dixy Bull with a band of freebooters was causing havoc on the Piscataqua settlements. A meeting of the Council was hastily held, which resulted in the sending out immediately of a small ship with twenty men "to join with those of Pascataquack, for the taking of the said pirates." But the expedition was delayed because of the severe winter. In the meantime, the Piscataqua settlements sent their own expedition north to ferret out Dixy Bull. Except for the capturing and execution of an Indian murderer, this expedition failed to run down the pirates. The pirates, however, fearing that a joint expedition would be sent against them in the spring, renounced any further intentions of ravaging the English settlements, and wrote the governors of the colonies that they were "resolved to sink themselves rather than be taken." In the spring, a pinnace was finally sent from Massachusetts, but after two months, the search for the pirates was abandoned. Dixy Bull was thought to have gone to the French. Though rudimentary, this action may be regarded as the first joint naval expedition of the colonies and the starting point of cooperative action among the colonies.[2]

In an effort to check Dutch commercial expansion, the Governor of Plymouth, Edward Winslow, and William Bradford visited Massachusetts during the summer of 1633. The purpose of the visit was to negotiate the erection of a joint trading post on the Connecticut River. The presence of "three or four thousand warlike Indians" in the vicinity of the proposed truck-house, however, deterred the Bay Colony from giving its assistance. Nevertheless, Plymouth went it alone; and, although not having similar success against the French,[3] the Plymouth post was able to hold off Dutch encroachments.[4]

As small pox raged throughout the land and visited heavily upon the Indian tribes, intercolonial strife appeared. Roger Williams drew censure from Massachusetts when he declared Plymouth Colony was founded on lands outside of the king's grant.[5] About the same time, a trader by the name of Hocking from a Massachusetts plantation on the Piscataqua attempted to set up a trading post in territory claimed by Plymouth on the Kennebec River. During an argument, Hocking and one of the Plymouth traders were killed. Shortly thereafter, John Alden, a witness to the shooting, went to the Bay Colony on business and was seized by the Massachusetts authorities.[6] Plymouth then sent Captain Standish to Boston "to give them true information" and to procure Alden's release. After Alden was let go, a meeting was arranged for representatives from the Piscataqua settlements, Boston, and Plymouth to "consulte and determine" the question with "full power to order and bind" their respective jurisdictions. No delegates came from the Piscataqua settlements, and the other commissioners, falling into "fair debating," concluded that the absentees were the ones to blame.[7] It was necessary to deal firmly with such acts of violence—otherwise, as Winthrop saw it, there would be occasion for the king to send over a governor-general. Also there was no need to bring "us all and the gospel under a common reproach of cutting one another's throats for beaver."[8]

Another controversy arose in 1635 when settlers from Dorchester moved into the Connecticut Valley near the Plymouth trading house. The Plymouth authorities charged that these settlers from Massachusetts, "hereing of the fame of Conightecute River," waited until the Indians were swept away by disease, and then claimed the territory as their own because it was the "Lords wast" and "voyd of inhabitants." Plymouth defended her claim to the land because it had been purchased from the Indians and she had since provided for its upkeep. The pressure from Massachusetts, however, proved too great, and Plymouth yielded this territory to her larger neighbor for "as good termes" as could be obtained—to "make any forcible resistance was farr from their thoughts." In the treaty between the two colonies, Massachusetts recognized Plymouth's prior rights, but the Plymouth settlers were to retain only their houses and one sixteenth of all the lands purchased from the Indians.[9] This rough handling from the Bay Colony injured the Pilgrim pride, and Governor

Bradford made the most of it by fully airing his thoughts. Thus began a deep-seated resentment of Plymouth towards the haughty spirit of her superior neighbor, which, though often concealed, was to last as long as Plymouth remained a colony.

The time arrived for the subjugation of the Canaanites. The once powerful Pequots, decimated by disease and warfare with the Dutch, were now desperate. Everywhere the English were crowding them out. In a death struggle with the English, the Pequots could not hope to hold their own unless aided by the other New England tribes. But this was not a very likely eventuality since the Pequots had won the lasting enmity of many of the neighboring tribes, whom they had once kept in vassalage. Yet, by merely provoking the settlers instead of attacking them outright, the Pequots might lure the settlers into an indiscretion that "a good Indian was a dead Indian" and thereby arouse the fury of all the tribes. It was worth a risk.

The Pequot War grew out of a series of murders by the Indians beginning as early as 1634 and coming to a climax in 1637 when nine were killed and several women kidnapped. The harboring of the murderers of John Oldham, a respected Indian trader and explorer, in 1636 helped to add fuel to the demands for a punitive expedition against the Pequots. Governor Vane sent a party of ninety men under John Endicott to attack the Pequots. An assault was made on the Pequots on Block Island, but since the Indains would not do battle nor treat with the English, Endicott rashly ordered the burning of homes and crops of the Indians. A brief encounter with a Pequot war party made further hostilities inevitable. It soon became unsafe for an Englishman to venture from the frontier settlements for fear of being cut down by savages waiting in ambush.[10]

A full-scale attack by the Pequots, especially if supported by the Narragansett tribes, could completely erase from the map the infant settlements on the Connecticut River. Before the next English offensive could get underway, these settlements, with permission from Massachusetts, formed a new colony and in May, 1637, a General Court was convened. The Connecticut settlers could now more effectively treat with the other two colonies for cooperative action against the Indians.

Endicott's fiasco on Block Island was condemned by both the Plymouth and Connecticut General Courts as an arbitrary action not taking into consideration the interests of the two lesser colonies.[11] The next move against the Pequots would be better planned. It would be designed to secure the joint efforts of the colonies and to rally other Indian tribes against the Pequots. Already Massachusetts, though not first seeking the advice of the other colonies, had concluded with the powerful Narragansett tribes

> A firm peace between us and our friends of other plantations, (if they consent,) and their confederates, (if they will observe the articles, etc.,) and our posterities.[12]

In the meantime, the Pequots began harassing the Connecticut settlements, though not openly. An army under Captain John Mason was raised from the three river towns[13] for the purpose of taking the field.[14] Sixty Mohegans, who had been driven from their homes by the Pequots,[15] and some four hundred assorted Narragansetts and Nyantics[16] joined forces with the English. The spirit of cooperation prevailed between Massachusetts and Plymouth after petty differences had been ironed out.[17] Captain John Underhill, recently returned from his adventures in the Dutch army, led a contingent of twenty Massachusetts men, joining Mason's motley force for a surprise assault on the Pequot stronghold on the Mystic River. Massachusetts ordered the raising of one hundred and sixty additional troops,[18] but the Pequots were in the meantime crushed, mercilessly at the first bloody Swamp fight in New England's history. Since we are not concerned here with the story of the Pequot War—it has found its place in the lore of early New England—but rather with the cooperation of the colonies, we will not go into the circumstances of this slaughter of the Pequots. Suffice it to mention that over seven hundred of the enemy were either killed or taken prisoners, while the English counted only sixteen lost.[19] A Plymouth force of fifty men was raised too late to see action against the enemy.[20]

The Pequot War had drawn the military cooperation of the three New England colonies. Although Connecticut had borne the brunt of the war, the ambitious Puritan colonies of New England sensed the potential military power that could be accomplished through synchronized cooperation.

The fruits of victory belonged to those who shared in the

conquest. As soon as the war was over, the Massachusetts General Court declared that the Pequot lands, obtained through the subjugation of the Indians with the help of their "assotiats," now belonged in "just right and title" to themselves and their "assotiats upon Conecticot."[21]

Later, when settlers from the different colonies poured into these lands, the question of jurisdiction posed a sore problem for the Confederation.

A "Tripartite Treaty" was concluded at Hartford in 1638 between the English, Mohegans, and Narragansetts. The two hundred surviving Pequots were put under the protection of three Indian sachems: eighty under Miantinomo and twenty under Ninigret, both Narragansett chiefs; and one hundred under Uncas of the Mohegans. An annual tribute was to be collected from these chiefs for keeping the remnant Pequots, and the English were to arbitrate any dispute arising among them.[22] The treaty was doomed from the start because no provision was made for enforcement machinery.

Another factor disposing the New England colonies toward union was a constant fear that the king would send over a governor-general for the colonies.[23] In 1637, Sir Ferdinando Gorges was given the empty title of governor-general over all New England, and in the same year a copy of a commission was received from England ordering the incumbent magistrates in New England to continue in office. This action was resented by Massachusetts because of the implication that no "lawful authority" was in force in the colonies before the sending of this commission.[24] Such a commission may have resulted from the efforts of Edward Winslow of Plymouth, who, in 1635, had petitioned the crown for a special warrant authorizing the colonies to defend themselves. It is possible that Winslow had in mind at this early date to lay the groundwork for a confederation of the New England colonies.[25] Nevertheless, it was feared by many that the king was now attempting to inaugurate a policy of direct supervision over New England affairs. The Puritan colonies wanted to work out their own policy without interference from abroad. In union they could speak in a firm tone to the mother country. But events in England prevented any immediate supervision from the crown.[26]

To the movement toward union was added perhaps its most

vital force: the threat of aggrandizement from the French and
Dutch in the New World. The French, pressing on the Plymouth
trading posts in the north, had already captured the post at
Penobscot. The captors immediately fortified this post, which
discouraged the dispatching of a Plymouth force to retake it.[27]
An internecine struggle in New France[28] provided opportunity
for driving a wedge of Puritan power against the extension of
Catholicism. As the English settlements came into increased
contact with the French and Dutch in the New World, it became
evident that any friction might lead to a disastrous war, especially if the enemy combined forces with the Indians. As early
as 1635, Governor Bradford expressed the fear of war with the
French: they "incroach more and more upon the English, and
fill the Indeans with gunes and munishtion, to the great deanger
of the English," and "if these things be not looked to, and remady
provided in time, it may easily be conjectured what they may
come toe."[29] The encroachments of the Dutch were becoming
irritable to Connecticut,[30] and Edward Hopkins was ordered to
see what he could do about the situation during his visit to
England.[31] At home, the Connecticut magistrates were empowered to negotiate any of the problems with the Dutch, providing
the Dutch were willing.[32]

The year 1637 was a providential year. The victory over the
Pequots was considered the handiwork of the Lord, "who would
have his people know their work was his, and he onely must order
their Counsels."[33] Now was the time to consolidate the gains in
the new Canaan. A grateful people would condemn religious
error and order their counsels toward closer union. In the summer, a great synod of leading churchmen from all New England
was convened at Newton (Cambridge). For over three weeks,
the divines sweltered in the August heat, debating over the
vagaries of the Gospel as manifested by the Antinomian and
Baptist heresies and seeking to erase errors and to advance the
"Unity in the true worship of God."[34] Eighty "erroneous opinions"
—"some blasphemous, others erroneous, and all unsafe"—were
blacklisted from the doctrines of New England Puritanism by
the overwhelming vote of the assembly.[35] The forces of consolidation and "true union with Christ" were on the march. The
colonists had come into the new world to hew out a Christian
Commonwealth; by banding together for religious polity they
could point out religious error and nip subversion in the bud.

To the north or south, or which way you'll wind
Churches now are spread, and you'll pasture find
Many men of worth, for learning and great fame
Grave and godly, into these parts here came.

A prudent Magistracy here was placed
By which, the Churches defended were and graced;
And this new commonwealth in order held,
And sin, that foul iniquity, was quell'd.[36]

Governor Winthrop of Massachusetts was so pleased at the
outcome of the general assembly of 1637 that he sought to put
this synod of churches on a permanent basis by providing for
regular annual meetings.[37] Though the enthusiasm of Winthrop
for annual conventions did not spread among the rest of the
Saints, the principle of collective action among the colonial
churches in matters of general concernment was established.
The Lord had safely guided the people of New England through
the wilderness; henceforward, His chosen people would be left
on their own feet.[38] The Churches of New England, as "Legall
Synagogues" holding "Union with Christ,"[39] should render themselves

> serviceable for the Common good of these plantations as
> well as of those: which the Divine providence hath com-
> bined together in as strong a bond of Brotherly affection,
> by the sameness of theyre condition, as Joab and Abishai
> were, whose severall armyes did mutually strengthen them
> boath against severall enimyes.[40]

A confederation of the churches, or "consociation," in the form
of synods was considered

> lawfull and in some cases necessary; as namely in things
> that are not peculiar to one Church, but common to them
> all ... all churches have right of Government within them-
> selves, but some had need of counsell and advice of others.[41]

The acceptance of the Puritans of the principle of uniformity
in matters of faith and doctrine was a triumph for an emerging
conservatism. From their basic tenet of the sufficiency of the

Scriptures, the Puritans were now retreating to the Anglican "distaste for unauthorized interpretation."[42] A consociation of churches provided a safeguard for maintaining orthodoxy in Congregationalism.[43] However, before another synod could be held in New England a political intercolonial union was to emerge—a chief end of which would be to preserve the hegemony of the Church and to open new ground for the planting of the Gospel.

The Synod of 1637 is important in the road to union not only because it brought the churches together and stressed their common mission in the New World, but it also provided a sounding board for proposals for confederation of the colonies.

Because of the meager records of the time, it is difficult to ascertain from what source the Confederation was first proposed. Perhaps the distinction belongs to Plymouth at the beginning of the Pequot War in 1637 when she came forth with a proposal that touched upon permanent union. Plymouth consented to join Massachusetts in a pact, to give Massachusetts aid on the condition of a reciprocal guarantee for "all like occasions." Though the Bay Colony had originally solicited the aid of Plymouth forces, it now refused to enter such an agreement, giving as the reason that "as we now deale with you as a free people, and at libertie, so as we cannot draw you into this warr with us, so we desire we may at the like freedome, when any occasion may call for help from us."[44] Plymouth undoubtedly had other motives behind this proposal than mutual protection against the Indians—the founders of the colony had lived for over a decade under the Dutch Union and knew that confederation was a means of preserving territorial and political integrity.

But it was during the course of the synod in the late summer of 1637 that the Confederation was seriously broached. At that time some of the magistrates and ministers of Connecticut met with the Massachusetts General Court at Boston, whereupon a "day of meeting" was appointed to "agree upon some articles of confederation," notice being given to Plymouth "that they might join in it." The Plymouth General Court, however, did not receive sufficient notice in advance to send commissioners to this meeting.[45] The articles discussed at this meeting—it may be assumed from the scant records[46]—were similar to the articles ratified in 1643. After the synod broke up, it was nearly a year before negotiations, again between Connecticut and Massachusetts, were resumed.

On June 8, 1638, Roger Ludlow, on the behalf of the Connecticut General Assembly, wrote to the Massachusetts Court that Connecticut was "desirous to reteine that old love and familiarity which formerly wee enjoyed," and, stressing the points which the two colonies had in common, suggested that they might "combine and unite." Only by this means could the "Common Cause" be maintained and their "priviledges and freedomes" be defended "against all opposers." It was proposed, therefore, that some "Rules Articles and agreements" be established by which they "may have recourse as the bottom uppon which our Peace and loue may be anchored" as "evidence to each in case either should goe aboute through any Corruption to make a breach."[47] John Haynes, William Pynchon, and John Steele were then appointed delegates to the Massachusetts General Court to negotiate an union, wherein they were empowered "to conclude in wrytinge of such thinges as are agreed on by both sides."[48]

The meeting in Boston was marked by continual strife. Massachusetts took advantage of the opportunity to advance her claim to Agawam (Springfield). Finally, the Connecticut delegation, one of whom resided in Springfield, consented to allow Springfield to come under the Massachusetts jurisdiction, but this was not enough for the Bay Colony, which wanted the assent of the General Court at Hartford. This, of course, the Connecticut Court refused to allow,[49] and the question of which colony should exercise authority over this most northerly of the river towns was to pass into the era of the Confederation. Massachusetts was learning that to achieve union she could not name a price, but had to treat her neighbors at the conference table as equals. Governor Winthrop wrote of this meeting in Boston that the differences "between us and those of Connecticut were divers; but the ground of all was their shyness of coming under our government," although "we never intended to make them subordinate to us."[50]

There was one other storm of controversy. The real obstacle to union, a point of contention in the making of all federations, involved the surrender of sovereign powers of the individual colonies. The source of the disagreement stemmed from the interpretation of a clause in the proposed articles which called for arbitration of intercolonial disputes by commissioners appointed by the colonies. The clause on which the two colonies could not agree stated

> That, upon any matter of difference, two, three, or more commissioners of every of the confederate colonies should assemble, and have absolute power (the greater number of them) to determine the matter . . . if they could agree, so: if not, then to report to their several colonies, and to return with their advice, and so to go on till the matter might be agreed.[51]

The Connecticut delegates were accused of altering this article "in the most material point" by proposing that differences should be referred to the churches when they could not be settled by the commissioners. To the Massachusetts delegates this procedure would cause unnecessary trouble and expense, and still might leave an issue unresolved.[52] According to Winthrop, the "Articles of Confederacy" were practically agreed upon when they were "throwen aside" by Connecticut. A new "frame" later submitted to the Bay Colony "utterly neglected" the "mayne end" of confederation.[53]

That irrepressible democrat on the river who had only recently departed with his flock from the Bay fold, Thomas Hooker, reported the proceedings of the Boston meeting differently from that of Governor Winthrop. To Hooker, both sides had agreed that the article concerning the commissioners exceeded the "lymitts of that equity which is to be looked at in all combinations of free states"; and another way, which would "breed or occasion lesse heart burning, was attended and mutually assented to on all sydes."[54] Hooker pointed out to the Massachusetts Governor that he did not understand "how a serious consideration of articles propounded in a way of love," wherein "nothing was faulted," can be "judged a throwing away of articles, and sending a new forme." On the question of referring civil controversies to the churches, Hooker felt that a larger question was involved: whether the church and state should be "combined one with another or severed each from other." But Hooker did agree that commissioners should be chosen as "counsellours" and, in matters of "Judicature," as judges for the people. To refer questions from the civil arena to church elders would be

John Winthrop

merely to remove the question a step, and for that matter such a process could go on *ad infinitum*. Simply what was needed was a set of rules for the commissioners to follow, and for "safety" a "multitude of counsellors." Hooker, thus going along vaguely with the need for commissioners but at the same time implying that they in some way should be amenable to the people, differed with Winthrop's aristocratic view that a majority vote of a select intercolonial board should have "absolute power" in determining controversies. On one point Hooker was certain: the Connecticut delegates at Boston did not have power to bind Connecticut to an intercolonial board of arbitration.[55] Thus the negotiations for union were again doomed to lag.

Whatever may be said of the generalities of Hooker's famous discourse, he gave voice to two doctrines later written into the American constitution: the separation of church and state and the separation of powers. Furthermore, with modern scholarship pointing to Hooker as well as Williams as a forerunner of American political democracy, his insistence of the people having a direct voice in the affairs of government should be noted. Thus the first serious attempt at confederation raised more questions than it answered, but it nevertheless brought the idea of confederation to the forefront and chartered the obstacles that had to be overcome.

Upon the adjourning of the Boston meeting Connecticut consented to reply to the Bay Colony within three months concerning further plans for union. This, however, was not done. Winthrop then wrote to Hooker in the spring of 1639, stating that though the three months had long been past it would be "no hard taske to reconcile us."[56] This letter was amusingly vague, proposing that there should be a rule for deciding differences, such as "Thou shalt bringe it to the Judges, if thore bo none competent, then thou shalt set up Judges." If this suggestion was too "public and too violent a remedye in our Case," then it should be that "you should yield in some things and we in the rest," but "you may prescribe some other."[57]

Connecticut now took up the initiative in attempting to bring about confederation. The Dutch threat appeared greater now with a new governor who was "more discreet and sober than the former."[58] Because the Dutch were also getting too inquisitive about the relations between Connecticut and Massachusetts, it was important, therefore, that the "Dutch might not take notice of any break or alienation between them."[59] On August 15, 1639, it was ordered that the governor write a letter to Governor Winthrop of Massachusetts to the effect that the Connecticut General Court was "very ready and willing to entertaine a firme combination for a defensive warr and other mutuall offices of love and friendshipp, according to the propositions formerly agreed." George Fenwick, who had recently started a settlement in the Warwick patent at Saybrook at the mouth of the river, was consulted, and his approval for further negotiations for union was obtained.[60] Even New Haven, which was in direct competition with the Dutch on the Sound, began to sense the advantages of the combined military strength that could be mustered by union.[61]

During a "season" of earthquakes in New England,[62] Governor John Haynes and Thomas Hooker of Connecticut visited the Bay Colony for the purpose of resuming negotiations for erecting a confederacy.[63] It may be assumed that, during their stay for nearly a month, there was a thorough discussion of the problems confronting an intercolonial league. A product of this meeting was an agreement on the main purpose of confederation: the prevention of further "alienation" of religion.[64] But, as to the actual proceedings of this conference, the early records are strangely quiet. More than two years were to pass before the Connecticut General Court again ordered its delegates, this time in the persons of George Willis and Edward Hopkins, "if they have an opportunity, to further the league of Unity with the Bay."[65]

Why was the league between the two colonies not consummated at this time? More time was needed to bring in the two smaller colonies of New Haven and Plymouth; and, perhaps, all of Puritan New England could be brought into one grandiose Bible Commonwealth—a bulwark in the New World against the enemies of Puritanism.[66] There were the intercolonial rivalries, such as disputes over new lands or competition for the beaver trade.[67] There was need for a compromise spirit rather than the dogged self-righteousness especially on foot in the Bay. Massachusetts's insistence on governing Agawam, the refusal of Connecticut to be bound by a treaty made by Massachusetts with the Narragansett Indians on the eve of the Pequot War, and the suspicion of Connecticut that Massachusetts was hindering emigration to Connecticut[68] are examples of the obstinacy that had to be overcome before confederation could be achieved.

Although the time in 1639 was not yet ripe for union, a few years would completely change matters. The forces of expansion and consolidation were at work. The Bay Colony soon extended its jurisdiction over the Piscataqua settlements, which took in the Mason and most of the Gorges patents.[69] Thus, there was need to defend the expanded boundaries—the claims to outlying territories would receive strong sanction with the support of the united Puritan colonies. Connecticut and New Haven, rapidly expanding on the Sound, were coming into constant conflict with the Dutch. These colonies, therefore, could also use the aid of a united New England in support of their claims. Plymouth Colony would gladly condescend to become an equal partner with the larger colonies—there was no better way to insure her territorial integrity. A few years would also make a difference in the strength of the Puritan settlements. Weak and scattered in the '30's, these settlements in the succeeding decade emerged as strong and independent colonies, each with a vital corporate government. The river towns, having entered into "Combination and Confederation togather" by the famous Fundamental Orders of 1639, had officially assumed the status of colony. The plantations about New Haven, seeking the protection afforded by union, confederated with the town of New Haven, bringing forth another distinct colony.[70] Thus, by 1643, there were four distinct Puritan colonies in New England. Through confederation, these colonies could promote their common mission and at the same time through cooperation preserve their particular interests. Each colony recognized the colonial status of the other colonies, thus providing a basis for fruitful negotiations. The continual expansion of territorial limits indirectly worked against the rigid conformity of the original settlements.[71]

England was virtually on the brink of civil war, and for nearly a decade would not be able to maintain a formal governmental connection with her colonies. The Puritan colonies were accustomed to fending for themselves, and they would continue to do so. As one of the leading exponents of union put it: "If we in America should forbear to unite for offence and defence against a common enemy till we have leave from England our throats might be all cut before the messenger would be half sent through."[72]

Throughout history, leagues—whether economic, military, or political—have been formed primarily for defensive reasons. Military expediency has often played a dominant role. This has been especially true in the whole development of federalism in America. The Continental Congress was called into being in order to defend the liberties of Englishmen in America, and the Federal Government of 1789 received effective powers to hold its own as an independent nation. Moreover, the giant strides in the maturing of American federalism since the forming of the Union have resulted from the government facing the great crises in our history. When a people are squarely faced with a problem and are aroused to the impending evils that may result from inaction, no time is wasted in reaching a solution, whether or not the decision is a wise one. The people of New England might have dallied with the idea of Confederation for many more years had not their fears of foreign and Indian aggression been intensified. The New England Confederation, despite many high-sounding phrases of its Puritan founders depicting a religious mission, was primarily a league of defence for better employing the military arm of the colonies.

In 1642, a fearful rumor spread throughout the scattered settlements that the savages lurking among the New England hills would soon let loose legions of destruction. Every Algonquin tribe in the vicinity of New Amsterdam was on the warpath.[73] The powerful Connecticut tribes were thought to be uniting in a general confederacy to drive out the English.[74] The Narragansetts were particularly suspected because of their default in the paying of tribute according to the Tripartite Treaty of 1638.[75] Preparations for war were made by the colonies.[76] Plymouth Colony, thoroughly alarmed because of her weak position and the possibility of facing an Indian uprising alone, took advantage of the general alarm to send a commission into the Bay Colony. It was ordered in September, 1642, that

> Mr. Edward Winslow, Mr. Timothy Hatherly, and Captaine Miles Standish are deputed and authorized by the Generall Court, this day, to treate and conclude with such commissioners as the Governor and Court of Massachusetts shall appoynt for that purpose, upon such heads and propositions as the Lord shall direct them for our combineing together mutually in a defensive and offensive warr for our

present defence against the intended surprisall of the natives; and also to treate and conferr with them about a
further combination and league to be concluded betwixt
us for future tymes...

The Plymouth and Massachusetts commissioners were to conduct negotiations concerning the handling of war preparations
between the two colonies. One clause, which became a factor
in delaying ratification of the Confederation, provided that whatever should be agreed upon had to receive confirmation by the
General Court.[77] Thus, Plymouth was now joined with Connecticut in actively working for confederation. A war scare had led
Plymouth to seek again a defensive league, as during the Pequot
War, and it was this fear of Indian hostilities which, in the words
of Governor Bradford, "made them enter into this more nere
union and confederation."[78]

Although the groundwork for confederation was being laid,
thorns in intercolonial relations still remained. In 1638, Winthrop wrote that "another plot the old serpent had against us, by
sowing jealousies and differences between us and our friends at
Connecticut, and also Plymouth."[79] The dispute with Connecticut as to the jurisdiction over Springfield, already mentioned,
was a barrier in the early negotiations for union. The Plymouth
controversy, though producing ill feeling with the Bay Colony,
however, had a more positive effect.

The settlements around Boston constantly sought new lands.
A new settlement on the south, at present-day Hingham, contested with Scituate, a Plymouth town, for four or five miles of
undivided salt marshes lying between the two towns. Much
correspondence passed between the two colonies attempting to
settle the jurisdiction of this area.[80] The dispute was intensified
when an attempt was made to run a boundary between Scituate
and Hingham. The Plymouth claim was based upon three
grounds: an "anciente compacte" with the Indians, their patent,
and by actual possession and maintenance.[81] The Bay Colony,
which "desired only so much of the marshes there, as might
accommodate Hingham," surveyed the line at the Charles River
and found "it come so far southward as would fetch in Scituate
and more."[82] Not to be outdone, a survey by the Plymouth
authorities conversely took in all of Hingham. Neither side would
give in, and in the terse commentary of William Bradford:

So as now ther grue great differance betweene these 2. townships, about their bounds, and some meadow grownds that lay betweene them. They of Hingham presumed to alotte parte of them to their people, and measure and stack them out. The other pulled up their stacks, and threw them. So it greu to a controversie between the 2. governments, and many letters and passages were betweene them about it; and it hunge some 2. years in suspense.[83]

Surprisingly, the controversy was successfully settled by arbitration in 1640. Each of the general courts had selected two commissioners, invested with "full and absolute power to agree and settle the bounds betwene them" and their decision was to stand "irrevocably."[84] The success of this arbitration encouraged the idea for a permanent body in the future to handle similar problems; and the impetus toward confederation was such that the first item in the records of the Commissioners of the United Colonies was the settlement of this boundary dispute.[85]

About the time that the Plymouth delegates were sent into the Bay to negotiate a union because of the Indian situation, a new set of proposals from Connecticut was read in the General Court at Boston. This assembly added "some few cautions and new articles,[86] and for the taking in of Plymouth (which were now willing) and Sir Ferdinando Gorges' province." The Articles were then returned to Connecticut "to be considered upon against the spring, for winter was now approaching, and there could be no meeting before."[87] But the urgency of the need to meet the Indian threat remained, and the General Court sitting in Boston found it necessary to order that

the magistrates in and neare Boston, with the deputies of Boston, Charlestowne, Cambridg, Watertowne, Roxberry, Dorchester, or the greater part of them, are appointed to be a comitte to treate with any comissioners from Plimoth, Conectecot, or Newe Haven, about the union, and concerning avoyding any danger of the Indians, and to have power to do hearin what they shall find need full for comon safety and peace, so as they enter not into an offencive warr without order of this courte.[88]

The report of this special committee of the Massachusetts General Court must have been favorable towards union, for the other three colonies made arrangements to send delegates into the Bay to treat with the Massachusetts committee for general union. For the first time in six years since the negotiations had begun, all four Puritan colonies were ready for confederation. With the colonies agreeing to meet each other on equal terms and with intercolonial cooperative action already an established fact among the Puritan colonies, some form of union was inevitable.

In March, 1643, William Collier and Edward Winslow, magistrates of Plymouth, were impowered to go to Massachusetts to "treate about the combination" at the meeting to be held in May.[89] However, nothing was said concerning the clause in the instructions to the Plymouth delegates in 1642, which stated that the final determination of the Articles belonged to the General Court. For the May meeting, Connecticut on April 6, 1643, selected John Haynes, Edward Hopkins, and George Fenwick to "Prosecute the combination," with "full power if they have opportunity to conclude the same."[90] Thus, Connecticut was to be represented by the Governor, Deputy Governor, and, in order to encourage the coming of Saybrook into the Connecticut fold, George Fenwick, the founder of Saybrook.

Ten days after the appointing of the Connecticut delegates, Theophilus Eaton and Thomas Gregson were named commissioners from New Haven for the Boston meeting, with powers to conclude "a Generall combination for all the plantations in New England" for the "exalting of Christs ends and advanceing the publique good in all the plantations." To the recently confederated towns on the Sound the step towards larger union was an act of divine Providence, and before the New Haven delegates were permitted to leave

> Mr. Goodyare, our pastor, the fower deputyes, together with Georg Lamberton, Robert Newman and Thomas Fugill shall meete and advise with them before they goe, the better prepare them for thatt great and weighty business.[91]

Anyone else with "anything of weight" to suggest to the commissioners was invited to "repaire to the committee." By the sixth of May the "whole Court seemed to rest satisfied in the wisdome and faithfullnes of those which they had chosen and intrusted for thatt great business."[92]

The Commissioners, as mentioned above, from the four colonies met at Boston on May 29, 1643. After several meetings, all being "desirous of union and studious of peace, they readily yielded each to other, in such things as tended to the common good."[93] The Articles of Confederation drawn up were signed outright by the commissioners from the three colonies who had plenary power to do so. It was expected that the Plymouth commissioners, whose instructions did not permit them to bind the colony at this time, would have such authority from the General Court at the first regular meeting in September. [94]

The New England Confederation of 1643 united English settlements along the coasts and rivers from Long Island to present-day New Hampshire. An estimate of the rapid growing population at this time has been estimated at 24,000.[95] The eastern settlements were not brought into the Confederation because Massachusetts did not wish to recognize them as being outside of the Bay's jurisdiction.[96] On the outskirts of the confederated colonies was the Gorges province of Maine, which was considered too much a thorn in the flesh to be brought into the union. As Winthrop puts it

> they ran a different course from us both in their ministry and civil administration; for they had lately made Acomenticus (a poor village) a corporation, and had made a taylor their mayor, and had entertained one Hull, an excommunicated person and very contentious, for their minister.[97]

The mission of the United Colonies is best expressed in an election sermon of later years: "God sifted a whole nation that He might send choice grain into the Wilderness."[98] It was only natural, therefore, that the orthodox colonies of the Confederation should form a bulwark against the liberalism represented by Rhode Island. That Rhode Island should be excluded from the Confederation was a foregone conclusion. It was believed that its government was anarchical,[99] and "Mrs. Hutchinson and those of Aquiday island broached new heresies every year."[100] Although the colony of Providence Plantations was incorporated in the fall of 1643 and a charter was obtained from the king, there were attempts from time to time to bring dissident parts of the colony into the Confederation. The Coddington faction of Aquidneck, at odds with the Williams group at Providence, on several occasions sought entrance into the Confederation by joining with Plymouth or Massachusetts.[101] But as the government of the colony became more closely knit, Aquidneck (Portsmouth) was forced to yield to the will of the other three towns, whose bitter experience with the Puritan colonies in matters of religion and land controversies precluded their giving in under any circumstances. The Commissioners of the United Colonies held out hope that the inhabitants of Rhode Island would join one of the Puritan colonies because of the "confusion and Danger haveing much Disturbance amongst your selves and noe security from the Endians."[102] But the United Colonies guessed wrong. Fortified with a royal charter, Rhode Island would indeed become more of a sore spot to the United Colonies than her liberal infections might have caused as an equal partner in the league of the New England colonies.

The New England Confederation was the culmination of efforts at intercolonial cooperative action and negotiations for union. Conceived from "one blood"[103] with a common mission[104] to hew out a Christian Commonwealth from the wilderness and faced with the common dangers of a strange world—not able to turn to the mother country because of the "sad distractions"— such a union was inevitable. But what of this union? What had God wrought into One from the imperfect clay?

---

[1] John Winthrop, *Journal,* ed. by James K. Hosmer, (New York: Charles Scribner's Sons, 1908), I, 94, 103.

[2] Winthrop, *Journal,* I, 95,96, 101-2; Howard M. Chapin, *The First Century of Amer. Colonial Privateering, 1625-1725,* (Toulon, France: 1926), pp. 17-8.

[3] Winthrop, *Journal,* I, 13.

[4] William Bradford, *History of Plimouth Plantation* (Boston: 1898), pp. 370-75; Edwin M. Bacon, *The Connecticut River* (New York: G. P. Putnam's Sons, 1906), pp. 16-23; Winthrop, *Journal,* I, 103. Seventy men in "warrlike manner" had been sent from Manhattan to dislodge the Plymouth post, but wishing to avoid bloodshed they returned.

[5] Winthrop, *Journal,* I, 116-7.

[6] Bradford, *op. cit.,* pp. 377-8.

[7] *Ibid.,* pp. 382-3.

[8] Winthrop, *Journal,* I, 124.

[9] Bradford, *op. cit.,* pp. 405-8.

[10] For the account of the Pequot War thus far see Chapin, *op. cit.,* "Memoir

of the Pequots," from the Stiles MSS, *MHSC*, 1:X101; John Mason, "Hist. of the Pequot War," *MHSC*, 2:VIII, Introd. by T. Prince, pp. 122-3; Bacon, *op. cit.*; John G. Palfrey, *Hist. of New England* (Boston: 1853), I, 458ff.

[11] Winthrop, *Journal*, I, 194; Winthrop to Bradford, 20May37, *Winthrop Papers*, III, 417-9; Bacon, *op. cit.*, p. 96. Winthrop told Bradford that "Ill consequences may follow" from "ill thoughts."

[12] Winthrop, *Journal*, I, 193-4.

[13] As the settlements of Windsor, Hartford, and Wethersfield are commonly called.

[14] John Mason, "History of the Pequot War," *MHSC*, 2:VIII:122-3.

[15] Underhill's "History of the Pequot War," *MHSC*, 3:IV:11-28.

[16] Palfrey, *op. cit.*, p. 465.

[17] Winslow was sent from Plymouth to the Bay concerning Plymouth sending military aid, but the talks bogged down when Massachusetts refused to send aid against the French at the Kennebec trading post belonging to Plymouth. *(PCR*, I, 60; Bradford, *op. cit.*, 419-23; *MCR*, I, 192.) Winthrop wrote Bradford that although the French designs on the Kennebec post were a different case, "yet we cannot wholy excuse our failing in that matter." (Letter of 20May37, *op. cit.)*

[18] Winthrop, *Journal*, I, 218.

[19] "A True Relation of the Late Battel Fought in New England," *MHSC*, 3:V:40.

[20] Bradford, *op. cit.*, p. 424.

[21] *MCR*, I, 216.

[22] *PCR*, IX, 51.

[23] Jeremy Belknap, *The History of New-Hampshire*, (Dover, N. H.: 1862), III, 40-41; Joseph B. Felt, *The Ecclesiastical History of New England*, (Boston: 1855), I, 208. For fear of a ship bringing a commission for a governor-general, no one could board a ship without a permit until the ship had been docked twenty-four hours.

[24] Winthrop, *Journal*, I, 221, 224.

[25] Jacob B. Moore, *Lives of the Governors of New Plymouth and Massachusetts Bay*, (Boston: 1851), p. 119.

[26] Even in Cromwell's time, one author has observed, it "was a *new* England, not New England" that was furthermost in Cromwell's thoughts. Henry S. Burrage, *The Beginnings of Colonial Maine*, 1602-58, (Portland: 1914), pp. 287-9.

[27] Felt, *op. cit.*, pp. 243-6.

[28] For the course of the D'Aulnay-La Tour rivalry as it affected New England, see Chapter 5.

[29] Bradford, *op. cit.*, p. 401.

[30] *CCR*, I, 565.

[31] *Ibid.*, p. 68.

[32] *Ibid.*, p. 72.

[33] Johnson's *Wonder Working Providence*, *op. cit.*, p. 168.

[84] *Ibid.*, p. 171.

[85] Winthrop, *Journal*, I, 232.

[86] "A descriptive and Historical Account of New England in verse," *MHSC*, 1:III:79-80.

[87] Winthrop, *Journal*, I, 235.

[88] Kenneth B. Murdock, "William Hubbard and the Providential Interpretation of History," *AASP*, LII (1942), 33.

[89] John Cotton, *Way of the Churches Cleared,* (London: 1648), Columbia University Library, p. 54.

[40] John Davenport and Theophilus Eaton to Gov. and Gen. Ct. of Mass., 12Mar38, in Isabel M. Calder, ed., *Letters of John Davenport,* (London: 1937), p. 67.

[41] Richard Mather, *Church-Government and Church-Covenant,* (London: 1643), pp. 64-5.

[42] G. P. Gooch, *The History of English Democratic Ideas in the Seventeenth Century,* (Cambridge: University Press, 1898), p. 78.

[43] Perry Miller, "Thomas Hooker and the Democracy of Early Connecticut," *NEQ*, IV (Oct., 1931), 672.

[44] Bradford, *op. cit.,* p. 421.

[45] Winthrop, *Journal*, I, 231-2.

[46] In the words of Winthrop, the articles proposed in 1637 "was concluded after" (1643). *Ibid.,* p. 232.

[47] Roger Ludlow, in behalf of the Conn. Gen. Assembly to the Governor and Assistants of Mass., 29May38, *Winthrop Papers,* IV, 36-7.

[48] *Ibid.,* p. 37.

[49] Isabel M. Calder, *The New Haven Colony,* Vol. XXVIII of Yale University Historical Publications (New Haven: Yale University Press, 1934), p. 111.

[50] Winthrop, *Journal*, I, 287-8.

[51] *Ibid.*

[52] Winthrop's Summary of his Letter to Hooker, *Winthrop Papers,* IV, 53.

[53] Hooker to Winthrop, Dec38, *ibid.,* pp. 79-82, *CHSC*, I, 8-12.

[54] *Ibid.*

[55] *Ibid.;* Felt, *op. cit.,* p. 405; John Brown, *The Pilgrim Fathers of New England* (New York: 1897), pp. 331-2. Hooker's views were similar to the Separatist views of Samuel Eaton of the New Haven Colony, who held that proprietors of a plantation might delegate authority, but they reserved the right to take it back into their own hands. (Edward E. Atwater, *History of the Colony of New Haven* (Meriden, Conn.: 1902), pp. 94-5.)

[56] Winthrop to Hooker, Mar39, *Winthrop Papers,* IV, 100.

[57] *Ibid.*

[58] William Hubbard, *A General History of New England, MHSC* 2: V and VI, 465-6.

[59] *Ibid.*

[60] *CCR,* I, 31.

[61] John Davenport and Theophilus Eaton to the Gov. and Gen. Ct. of Mass.,

12Mar38/9, *MHSC* 3:III:167. Gov. Kieft of New Amsterdam had put a stop to English trade at the fort of Good Hope, which was located next to the English settlement at Hartford, and also protested against the English settling at Quinnipiack (New Haven). Because of this threat of the Dutch, a committee from Connecticut, consisting of Deputy Governor Ludlow, Thomas Welles, and Hooker, went to Saybrook to secure Fenwick's approval on the proposed articles of confederation. (See Benjamin Trumbull, *A Complete History of Connecticut*, (New Haven: 1818), I, 114. Fenwick wrote to Winthrop (7Oct39, Winthrop Papers, IV, 141-2) that "what soever tends to mutuall defence and shall conduce to the setling and mentaineing unfained love, yow may expect from me and all those who are interested in this place."

[62] Winthrop, *Journal*, I, 292.

[63] *Ibid.*, 301-2; Hubbard, *op. cit.*

[64] Felt, *op. cit.*, p. 406.

[65] *CCR*, I, 68.

[66] Winthrop speaks of "our combination to resist any authority, that should come out of England against us." (Winthrop, *Journal*, I, 285). Attempts at this early date to vacate the Mass. Charter on account of subversion were actually initiated before the Privy Council. (See C. F. Adams, "Sir Christofer Gardiner, Knight," *Harper's New Monthly Magazine*, LXVI(1883), 586-97.)

[67] See C. H. McIlwain, ed., Peter Wraxall's *An Abridgement of the Indian Affairs, 1678-1751*, Vol. XXI of the Harvard Historical Series, (Cambridge: 1915), xiv.

[68] Calder, *op. cit.*

[69] C. W. Tuttle, *Historical Papers*, (Boston: 1889), p. 179.

[70] By the time the Confederation was formed, Stamford and Southold (L. I.) had been incorporated into New Haven Colony. Guilford's joining was a condition upon New Haven entering the Confederation.

[71] E.g., Mass. in annexing the New Hampshire towns in 1641-3 found it necessary to relax its policy of requiring religious conformity as a basis for citizenship.

[72] Quoted in John Fiske, *The Beginnings of New England*, (Cambridge: 1902), p. 193.

[73] Maud W. Goodwin, *Dutch and English on the Hudson*, Vol. VII of the Chronicles of America Series, Allen Johnson, ed., (New Haven: Yale University Press, 1921), p. 64.

[74] Winthrop, *Journal, II*, 6.

[75] *CCR*, I, 62; Winthrop, *Journal*, II, 6; Bradford to Winthrop, 29Jun40, *Winthrop Papers*, IV, 258-9.

[76] Bradford to Winthrop, 16Aug40, *Winthrop Papers*, IV, 275.

[77] *PCR*, 46-7; Ebenezer W. Peirce, *Civil, Military and Professional Lists of Plymouth and Rhode Island Colonies, 1621-1700*, (Boston: A. Williams and Co., 1881), pp. 84-5.

[78] Bradford, *op. cit.*, p. 496.

[79] Winthrop, *Journal*, I, 287.

[80] E. V. Bigelow, *A Narrative History of the Town of Cohasset*, (Boston: Usher Press, 1898), pp. 120-8.

[81] Bradford to Winthrop, 11Apr38, *Winthrop Papers*, IV, 23.

[82] Winthrop, *Journal*, I, 287.

[83] Bradford, *op. cit.*, p. 439.

[84] *Ibid.*, p. 440.

[85] *PCR*, IX, 1-2. Massachusetts received the marshes on the Cohasset River adjacent to Hingham, while those on the Scituate side were awarded to Plymouth. Massachusetts, nevertheless, still reaped an advantage by retaining sixty acres at the south of the river.

[86] With the addition of these articles and the one providing for the entry of Plymouth (Article 13), it may be assumed that this was close to the final form adopted in May.

[87] Winthrop, *Journal*, II, 82.

[88] *MCR*, II, 31.

[89] *PCR*, II, 53.

[90] *CCR*, I, 82.

[91] *NHCR*, I, 87.

[92] *Ibid.*

[93] Hubbard, *op. cit.*, p. 467. In this spirit only could a union be "formed or preserved." (R. C. Winthrop, *Life and Letters of John Winthrop*, (Boston: Little, Brown & Co., 1869), II, 306.)

[94] *PCR*, IX, 8. At the September meeting Winslow and Collier signed for Plymouth, and the commissioners from the other three colonies signing again were John Winthrop and Thomas Dudley for Massachusetts; George Fenwick and Edward Hopkins for Connecticut; Theophilus Eaton and Thomas Gregson for New Haven.

[95] Franklin P. Dexter, "The Early Relations Between New Netherland and New England," *Papers of the NHCHS*, III, 467. For a recent work which uses new methods for estimating the population of the time, though arriving at about the same estimate as Dexter, see Bowen, Richard L., *Early Rehoboth*, (Rehoboth: 1945), I, *passim*.

[96] Arbita D. Parker, *A History of Pemaquid*, (Boston: MacDonald and Evans, 1925), p. 100.

[97] Winthrop, *Journal*, II, 99. In 1642 Gorges had given Agamenticus a second charter changing it from a borough to a city, giving it the name of Gorgeana. Henry S. Burrage, *The Beginnings of Colonial Maine, 1602-58*, (Portland: 1914), 319-20.

[98] Q. in J. H. Tuttle, *Massachusetts and her Royal Charter*, Boston: 1924), p. 16.

[99] Winthrop, *Journal*, II, 81.

[100] *Ibid.*, p. 39.

[101] John A. Goodwin, *The Pilgrim Republic*, (Boston: 1888), p. 416; James Ernst, *Roger Williams*, (New York: The Macmillan Co., 1932) pp. 269, 317, 515.

[102] *PCR*, IX, 110.

[103] Hubbard, *op. cit.*, pp. 465-6.

[104] "Although providence had cast them into four several colonies, yet Religion had already united them, coming over all for one and the same end." (Johnson's *Wonder Working Providence, op. cit.*, p. 219.)

CHAPTER III

Articles of Confederation

It was hardly to be expected that the new constitution of the Puritan colonies would be greeted with the huzzas and booming of cannon that ushered in the government under the Constitution of 1787. The Puritan character precluded any sudden, joyous burst of emotionalism. Though the Confederation, long bathed in prayer and counsel of the elders, was now an actual fact, to give in vain rejoicing over a creation of mortal hands might lead to divine displeasure—should the hand of Providence rest upon the Confederation in times of momentous events, then would be the time for rejoicing. The Puritan oligarchy had given to the settlers of America the first intercolonial constitution—an act in itself an assertion of independence and an establishment of a Law of the Land.

The Articles of Confederation were not ratified according to any prescribed procedure. The Commissioners from Connecticut and New Haven at the May meeting in Boston already had ample authority from their general courts to conclude an agreement. Signing for Massachusetts was Edward Rawson, Secretary for the General Court. Nevertheless, it was decided to submit the Articles for ratification to all four of the general courts.

The Massachusetts General Court, in adjournment from May 20 to September 17, had already taken the necessary action to ratify the Articles—even before agreed upon the 29th of May. On the day before adjournment

> The Court voted and expressed their consent to the articles between us, Conectecot, Newehaven, and Newe Plimoth, if they consent to them, and appointed them to bee transcribed and subscribed by the Secretary.[1]

The General Court apparently made no provision before its adjournment to elect its two Commissioners either for the May meeting or for the first session of the Confederation in the fall.

This undoubtedly explains Rawson's signing for Massachusetts in May. The records of the Commissioners for the first session, September 17, indicate that "it appears" John Winthrop and Thomas Dudley were named Commissioners by the General Court. Yet, the General Court did not reconvene until the day of the first meeting of the Confederation. It is, therefore, unlikely —though possible—that a commission for Winthrop and Dudley was drawn up the last minute and transmitted between the two groups then meeting in the Town House. But, if such hasty proceedings did not take place, then the authority for Winthrop and Dudley to fix their signatures to the Articles at the September meeting must have been derived from the order of the Court of May 20, which established a committee of six to "treate with our brethren and confederates of Conectecot and Newehaven."[2] Thus, it is probable the two ranking members of this committee, Governor Winthrop and Deputy Governor Dudley, automatically became the representatives for the colony at the final signing of the Articles because of their position in the colony or because of an order of the Massachusetts Council. Regardless of the method used, both men were magistrates, thus more fittingly representing the Council than the General Court. The Confederation may then be regarded as an extension of the colonial councils. This is further borne out by the fact that during the course of the Confederation there was a preponderance of magistrates as Commissioners.

Though there is no record of ratification by the Connecticut General Court, the Commissioners' orders to attend the September meeting were issued July 15, 1643. Perhaps the method was the same as that of the New Haven General Court on July 16, 1643, which had the Articles read, approved them by a "whole Court," and then ordered the Articles entered into the record.

On June 16, 1643, the Articles were read in the Plymouth General Court, and Edward Winslow and William Collier were granted "full commission and authoryty, in name of the whole Court, to subscribe the articles of confederation" and to "affix the comon seale of the government." The official date of ratification was given by Plymouth as September 8, 1643. Although all the Commissioners were to sign the Articles as their first act in September, the date of the Plymouth ratification marks the beginning of the Articles as binding upon all four colonies.

The Articles of Confederation of 1643 became a cherished document. During the life of the Confederation, each Puritan colony dared not take on the sole responsibility of breaching this compact. The Articles are found in many of the early writings and histories of the colonial period. It can be assumed these Articles of Confederation were consulted in the drawing up of later plans for colonial union.

Form the time of the adoption of the Articles of Confederation in 1643, writes an author only a generation removed from the Confederation period, "we are to look upon the 4 Colonies of *New-England*, as *one Body*, with Regard to all the public Transactions with their Neighbours, tho' the private Affairs of each Province were still managed by Magistrates and Courts of their own."[3] To that spokesman of Puritan orthodoxy, Cotton Mather, the colonies of New England, with the signing of the Articles of Confederation, "became in *fact*, as well as *name*, UNITED COLONIES," with "full powers from the General Courts in each, to concert and conclude matters of general concernment for *peace* or *war* of the several colonies thus *confederated*."[4] The combining of the four New England colonies was a unique move in American history, and the Articles of Confederation is a unique document.

The lengthy paragraph which forms the Preamble of the Articles emits the spirit of independence in which the Confederation was formed. True to the Puritan penchant for justification of all acts, the reasons for confederating are carefully stated. First, there is the desire to preserve the "puritie" of their religion and to worship safe from outside interference. The need for cooperation of the colonies is cited since the colonies could not be consolidated into one government because they were further "dispersed" than originally intended. Furthermore, a combination of the colonies could afford more strength in meeting the threats of the French, Dutch, and the Indians.

The Puritans undoubtedly felt that the time for the Confederation was opportune: it was their "bounden dutye" to proceed "without delay." One can read between the lines when a reason for the Confederation is given as the "sad distractions in England" by which they were hindered "from that humble way of seekeing advise, or reapeing those comfortable fruits of protection which at other tymes we might well expecte." The Confederation would probably have been formed in any event, but with civil war in the mother country, they had the perfect excuse for taking intercolonial polity into their own hands. An interesting change in this phrase, when the colonies had reason to fear imperial policy, was made when the Articles were revised in the 1670's. By way of illustrating the independent attitude of the colonists in 1643, the same phrase in the revised Articles moderately reads: "and seing by reason of distance from our Deare Native Country wee are hindered both from a humble way of seeking advise and reaping those comfortable fruites of Protection which otherwise wee might well expect." Although recognizing the similarities of the colonies in "Nation and Religion," the Articles acknowledge no higher earthly authority than those Articles of union.

The form of union was to be similar to the Church government: a "Consotiation." As the New England churches refused to adopt the Presbyterian system, so in the civil government, the superstructure of Confederation was not to be regarded as another step in hierarchy, but as a means for "mutuall help and strength in all our future concernements." The purposes of the Confederation were to promote the Congregational Way and to better survive in the wilderness, and for these ends, therefore, borrowing from the title of the Dutch League[5] and anticipating the more famous Unions of 1781 and 1789, the confederation of the New England colonies was to be known as "The United Colonies of New England."

Before considering the substance of the enumerated Articles, it is well to point out that even in the Preamble there occurred a phrase that could be twisted to serve the particular interests of the colonies and could be wielded as a defensive weapon by a recalcitrant member of the Confederation. This stipulation was that the confederates should continue "One according to the tenor and true meaneing of the ensuing Articles." This phrase appears in all the debates among the confederates, and in a Massachusetts copy of the Articles it was underlined.[6] The Massachusetts General Court certainly did not hesitate to fall back on it. Without a supreme judicial authority to interpret the "true meaneing" of the Articles and without coercive powers in the Confederation, each colony could interpret the Articles to its liking. Thus, during the course of the Confederation, the Puritan colonies, to their amazement, on occasion found themselves in good faith on opposite sides of the fence.

In a poetical tribute to one of the founders of the Confederation, a contemporary author voices what may be considered a summary of the Preamble and a cautionary note for the times ahead:

> Our State affaires thy will repaires, assistant thou hast bin
> Firm league to make, for Gospels sake, four Colonyes within;
> With Sweads, French, Dutch, and Indians much, Gods peoples peace this bred
> Then Eaton ... remember ... the Child that's yet unfed.[7]

The United Colonies of New England pledged themselves, as did their posterity well over a century later,[8] "joyntly and severally" to "enter into a firme and perpetuall league of frendship and amytie for offence and defence, mutuall advice and succour upon all just occations both for preserueing and propagateing the truth and liberties of the Gospell and for their owne mutuall safety and wellfare." The colonies, therefore, regarded their confederation as a league, and since they did not claim themselves a nation as did the Confederacy of 1781, there was no need to live up to such a reputation. Strong national government and confederation, in the strict sense, are incompatible. Therein lies the reason for the brief duration of the Confederation of 1781-89 and the long expanse of the New England Confederation.

The Articles of Confederation was a treaty between individual governments; it was never questioned that the final authority did not rest with the General Courts, and it was expected that the Commissioners to the Confederation would function much as ambassadors from independent states. The Union was indeed "an international league of Independent Commonwealths, without the baubles of a crown or a mitre."[9] Yet, real power was surrendered to the Board of Commissioners in matters relating to arbitration and military preparations. The Commissioners were also impowered to levy defensive war. Though in theory seeming to surrender vague judicial and executive powers to the Board of Commissioners for the colonies, the founders of the Confederation in fact allowed only consultive powers to develop. The intentions of the founders are not clear on this fundamental question whether or not sovereignty in special jurisdictions was conferred upon the Confederation. For a while, during the first decade of the Confederation, it looked as if the lesser members sought to promote the conception that a super-government transcending the General Courts in special areas was the intention of the founders. Whatever would be the interpretation of the Articles, the Confederation without coercive powers was not destined to become more than a league. Because it was a league (with a governing board), however, does not subtract from its value, as the modern reader, who is accustomed to thinking in terms of strong government, is apt to conclude, for the New England Confederation in many of its long years was potent and effective—accomplishing as a league the broad aims to which it was dedicated.

By the third Article the members of the Confederation agreed not to admit new members into the Confederation without the consent of all the members. The present territorial limits of each colony were guaranteed and the political integrity of each was to be preserved. (*Cf.*, Art. IV, Sec., 3 of the Constitution.)

The military nature of the Confederation, hinted at in the Preamble, appears strongly in Article Four. The burdens of all war measures, whether falling upon the colonies singly or collectively, were to be borne by all the colonies in proportion according to the means of each colony. The Commissioners were charged with accounting for the number of males in their respective colonies who were between the ages of sixteen and sixty. The "service of men and all charges of the warr" were to be levied according to the "Poll"; but each colony was permitted to pursue its own course performing its share. As the colonies were to share in the burdens of war, so they would proportionately reap their share of the spoils. A distinction was made between offensive and defensive wars, but each colony was required to contribute in all wars deemed "just." At whose discretion circumstances would be deemed justifiable for war measures was not specified, and when compared with the course of American Constitutional history, this was indeed a serious omission. We have since, through such media as the militia acts of our early government and Supreme Court decisions such as Martin *v.* Mott, Luther *v.* Borden, and the Prize Cases—to mention a few examples—tipped the scales in favor of the Presidency; but the New England Confederacy had no lines on which to develop such powers, being without an arm of government separate and distinct from the individual colonies. Thus, when faced with the determination of war, the grounds of which were questioned by members of the Confederation, the Commissioners were committed to follow the course of their General Courts, which in disagreement weakened the prestige of the Confederacy.

The Fifth Article sought further to define the role of the confederated colonies in war-time. In case of invasion of one of the colonies, three magistrates of the colony invaded were authorized to call upon the other colonies to send aid according to the following proportion: Massachusetts, 100 armed men; the other colonies, forty-five each or less if their proportion was under this amount. Whenever the Commissioners of the United Colonies should meet, it would fall to them to go into the cause of such an invasion. If the colony invaded was at fault then it was to return the aid given it and to make amends to the "Invaders." This, of course, was an impotent clause and an example of the Puritan affinity for hair-splitting. It has already been pointed out that for the Commissioners to pass upon the justifiability of war was an empty clause in the face of ultimate powers residing with the general courts, and now to compel one of their own members to give up to an enemy when that member was found in the wrong was absurd.

Beginning with Article Six, the Articles of Confederation gets into the structure of the Confederation and rules of procedure which will be treated more extensively in the next chapter. Eight Commissioners were to be chosen annually, two from each colony. The only qualification for a Commissioner was that he be in "church fellowship" and bring "full power" from his general court. Thus only one party was recognized, that of church members, and this clause would make it unconstitutional to bring in as an equal member of the Confederation the colony of Rhode Island or the eastern settlements.

The war powers of the Commissioners were extended from merely deciding the "justice" of a war and to levy the proportionate charges of a war to include the sole power to determine whether the colonies could enter offensive war. This was the most far-reaching power invested in the Commissioners, for no colony could legally enter an offensive action without the approval of the other colonies. By this provision the Commissioners would exercise a vital restraint upon any rash and bellicose factions, which unfortunately plague all societies, from stampeding the colonies into war. In effect, the Articles conferred on the Commissioners full powers to make war or peace. How such powers were to fare in actual fact is part of the story that follows.

Besides their war powers the Commissioners were to "frame and establish agreements and orders in general cases of a civil nature" which would be of interest to all the colonies. In intercolonial disputes the Commissioners were to serve as a board of arbitration. Specific powers included the establishing of an Indian policy so that the Indians "neither grow insolent nor be injured without due satisfaction, lest warr break in upon the Confederates through such miscarryages." The Massachusetts General Court, which was somewhat wary of the possibility of the three smaller colonies using the Articles to dominate her, in the copy of the Articles which was ratified by the Court, underlined this phrase regarding the Indians.[10] Perhaps the Bay Colony feared that the other three colonies, with settlements scattered all along the frontier, might easily seize upon friction with the Indians over lands to stir up an Indian war in which Massachusetts would not want any part. That justice in the treatment of the Indians should be written into the Articles was to illustrate in the time of the Confederation, as it did under the Confederation of 1781 and the early National Government, that a well-meaning policy of a weak central government could not cope with swarms of land hungry settlers.[11] Unlike the Constitution, which provided for the regulation of commerce with the Indians, though not to the extent of managing Indian Affairs as did the Confederation of 1781, the Commissioners were thus charged with formulating Indian policy.

The Commissioners were also given the power of making regulations concerning runaway servants and the extradition of criminals. Upon certificate from a magistrate (two in the case of criminals) of the jurisdiction from which a servant had fled (in the Constitution, from the executive authority of the state), a fugitive found to be in any of the confederate colonies was to be returned. Thus in the New England Confederation was the first fugitive slave law.

Meetings of the Commissioners of the United Colonies were to be held annually on the first Thursday in September. Extraordinary sessions might be called by three magistrates from any one of the jurisdictions. Again note the relation of the Commissioners to the council of magistrates. A President was to be chosen from among the Commissioners to preside over the meetings, but his powers as President were procedural and re sembled that of a modern chairman of the board. Meetings were to run in five year cycles as follows: Boston—Boston—Hartford—New Haven—Plymouth. No provisions were made for the number to establish a quorum, and it seems to have been expected that all the Commissioners would always attend. Nevertheless, Massachusetts was forced to give an important concession, in that all business could be transacted with the approval of six of the eight Commissioners, and four Commissioners "shall have power to direct a warr which cannot be delayed." Thus the two Massachusetts Commissioners could vote against a measure sponsored by the three smaller colonies, and yet not exercise a veto. When six Commissioners could not agree, however, then the general courts were to decide. Whether Massachusetts was aware of the implications of not having a veto power at this time is difficult to ascertain, but she would learn during the crises of the Confederation the sting that could be dealt by three aggressive little colonies.

The Articles of Confederation was a sacred document to the Puritans. No form of human action was regarded higher than the act of entering into a covenant. As pointed out in the first chapter, the covenant relationship was everywhere in Puritan thought. The Articles was the highest political covenant that they had as yet entered into among themselves, and there was no reason to question the good faith of the contracting parties. The Articles could not be violated; and in the different interpretations that were to develop, they were never breached. Secession simply was not allowed. But if an act of the Confederation was interpreted by any of the Confederates as injurious or a "breach of agreement," the Commissioners were expected to try to work out a solution, so that "both peace, and this present confederation may be entirely preserved without violation." Thus, it was implied that whenever a burden upon a colony should become so intolerable as to lead to secession, the other colonies, in order to preserve the Union, should permit the interpretation given by the offended colony to stand. Nullification was allowable, not secession.

The final clause of the Articles provided for ratification, as did the two Constitutions of the 1780s. The only colony actually affected by this clause was Plymouth. The delegates from the other colonies had been given power from their general courts to conclude the Articles at the May meeting.

The Articles of Confederation of 1643 was entered upon as a treaty—an alliance of the colonies by which the ablest men were to come together to direct matters of intercolonial interest and to make recommendations. As for war powers and arbitration of intercolonial disputes, the Confederation, through a board of Commissioners, was to take on the semblance of central government. An important reservation was held by the Massachusetts General Court. The instructions of the Court had stipulated to the committee negotiating the Confederation in the fall of 1642 that the colony could not be bound to any agreement calling for joint participation in "offensive war" without the consent of the General Court.

The defects of the Articles of Confederation were many. As the "Body of Liberties" two years before sought to enhance the position of the church in New England affairs, so the Confederation on the intercolonial level represented primarily the interests of the Puritan oligarchy. Although the colonies were to contribute proportionately to the war measures of the Confederation, no adequate system was provided for requisitioning supplies and levying taxes. A central fiscal agency was lacking—for that matter there were no provisions for any political machinery other than the Commissioners. During the seventeenth century, Americans had little conception of supreme judicial authority. Each colony was to interpret the meaning of the Articles for itself.

There was want of an appeal to the patriotic sense. No oaths of allegiance to the United Colonies were required; nor was there any specification as to what might constitute treason against all the colonies. Means of enforcing the decisions of the Commissioners were lacking, and the Commissioners as a governing body —though regarded above the individual colonies—were at the same time officials of the particular colony they represented. For a truly central government there was need to separate from each other the officers of the central government and the colonial governments. Nevertheless, the Articles of Confederation of 1643 was to serve as the basis for the longest lasting interstate Confederation in American history.

---

[1] *MCR*, II, 36.

[2] *Ibid.*, p. 38. Members of the committee were Winthrop, Dudley, and Bradstreet of the magistrates, and Gibbons, Tyng, and Hathorne of the deputies.

[3] Daniel Neal, *The History of New-England to 1700*, (London: 1720), p. 211.

[4] Cotton Mather, *Magnalia Christi Americana*, ed. by Thomas Robbins and L. F. Robinson, (Hartford: 1855), I, 160.

[5] The United Provinces of the Netherlands.

[6] Misc. MSS, I, MHS, 19May43.

[7] Johnson's *Wonder Working Providence, op. cit.*, p. 178.

[8] A passage from the Articles of Confederation, which went into force in 1781, bears a striking resemblance to the passage in the New England Articles quoted above. In the later document: "The said states hereby severally enter into a firm league of friendship with each other, for their common defence, the security of their Liberties, and their mutual and general welfare, binding themselves to assist each other, against all force offered to, or attacks made upon them, or any of them, on account of religion, sovereignty, trade, or any other pretence whatever." (Article III.)

[9] John W. Thornton, *The Historical Relation of New England.*

[10] Misc. MSS, I, MHS, 19May43.

[11] I refer especially to the policy of the Confederation Government (1781-9) and our early National Government, which, through the War Department sought ineffectively to keep settlers from crossing into Indian territory and government reservations by stringing a line of forts on the Ohio.

CHAPTER IV

A Structural View

The structure of the Confederation and the methods of its operation may be seen in the examination of five topics: the amending process; the Commissioners of the United Colonies; the meetings of the Commissioners; administrative functions; and attributes of sovereignty.

The Commissioners in their deliberations proceeded much as a legislative body. Each colony possessed an equal vote in its two Commissioners. True legislative powers could not develop beyond the point of recommendation and oversight of administration unless means of giving sanction could be found. Such a development might have arisen from the war powers invested in the Commissioners or through usage. But because of the bickerings of the Confederates and because ultimate power resided with the general courts, there was little room for the emergence of legislative power. The Articles of Confederation was to remain the sole point of law binding the four colonies. It is then in the Articles of Confederation as law that we must look for the federal law. Where statutory law failed to develop, the loose constitutional link of the Articles remained. The Articles of Confederation was flexible and could be jostled about to meet the needs of the changing times. Its pliability would add momentum to the Confederacy.

The amending process was very broad. The Articles did not specify any means for formal amendment, and the twelfth article even stated that the "treaty" should "continue firme and stable without alteration." But, if there were a breach of agreement or an injury committed against any one colony, the Commissioners from the other colonies could take measures to ease the difficulty so that "both peace and this present confederation may be entirely preserved without violation."

Without prescription for formal amendment, amending the Articles of Confederation was to occur chiefly in four ways: interpretation by the Commissioners; deference to the interpretations of the general courts; addition or subtraction from the jurisdiction of the Commissioners; and disregard of the Articles, which, when permitted to go too far, made the revision of the Articles necessary.

To cite a single example of the first method is the Commissioners' interpretation of Article Nine, which stated the Commissioners should meet and decide on the justification of a war before levying a charge on the colonies. Later, however, the "greater part of Comissioners conceived that till warr be begunn upon some one of the Colonies by an Actuall Assault, no charge shalbe expected from the rest of the Jurisdictions."[1]

The Commissioners were constantly subjected to pressure from their general courts. Subsequent chapters will show how the general courts on the chief issues influenced the course of the Confederation. It was often customary in Massachusetts to refer the report of her Commissioners to a mixed committee of magistrates and deputies, who reported on the Commissioners' findings with recommendations to be endorsed by the General Court.[2] The courts also took it upon themselves to give precise definition to the Articles. One example was the Commissioners' acceptance of the Massachusetts Court's narrow construction of "safety" in the second article as meaning safety only from an enemy and not from famine and pestilence.[3]

The scope of the Articles was also changed as the Commissioners took on more and more duties. The best example in the course of the Confederation is seen in the administration of Indian affairs. For example, appointing Indian governors became a duty of the Commissioners—also, providing instruction for the Indians and collecting tribute. The supervision of Indian missionary work[4] came to assume such proportions that the second Articles of Confederation (1672) included a special clause stating that it was the Commissioners' responsibility to dispose of the goods donated for promoting the Gospel among the Indians.

Finally, a means of changing the Articles was the occasional ignoring of the Articles. When there might be inconvenience or difficulty in following the provisions of the Articles, they were, by mutual consent, circumvented. Such an example may be found in 1647 and 1649 when no regular meetings in September were held because the emergency sessions during the summers of these years thoroughly exhausted the business at hand.

Several attempts were made by the general courts to amend

the Articles outright. The most notable attempt occurred in 1648 when the Massachusetts General Court appointed a committee to look into the acts "that have passed the commissioners which may seeme either to confound the power of our Generall Courts, or so interfere with it as may in a short time prove not onely prejudiciall, but exceedingly uncomfortable."[5] Among the changes proposed by this committee, designed to permit Massachusetts to go her own way in case she was overborne by the other three colonies, were: (1) in want of agreement of six Commissioners a matter could be referred to the four general courts and any three of them could then determine the question; (2) the meetings should be triennial, except when required sooner; and (3) Massachusetts should have at least one more Commissioner.[6] The Commissioners, however, turned down these proposals for amendment because of the "feare that any of the Alterations mentioned would prove daingerous and Inconvenient to all or som of the Colonyes."[7]

Since the formal amending process was to break down and the general courts were not able to get together and push through amendments, the only direct way to institute a revision in the Articles was to dissolve the Confederation and begin anew. Thus, when the king's commissioners toured New England, critically eyeing colonial affairs, and New Haven Colony was incorporated into Connecticut, the Confederation for all practical purposes ended; yet, it was never admitted to be defunct, and at the first opportunity a new set of Articles replaced the original Articles.[8] Thus, without means to make statutory revisions and with the inability to amend the basic law, except to stretch and interpret its clauses, the Articles of Confederation could not be substantively amended.

The method of selecting the Commissioners was left to each general court. The Commissioners at their meetings were the judges of the elections of their members only in so far as to require each Commissioner to bear a commission stamped with the approval of his colony.

After the Confederation was under way, Massachusetts and Plymouth followed the practice of choosing Commissioners at the annual courts of election held in the spring. Connecticut and New Haven, although often following the same practice, occasionally left the election of the Commissioners to a regular session of the General Court. The magistrates, from whom most of the Commissioners were drawn, were elected at these annual courts of election. When the freemen started staying home instead of attending this court they won the right to vote by proxy. One system of voting in Massachusetts was the use of Indian beans: white meant yea, black, nay. Eventually, Indian corn, sealed up in a paper bearing the name of each candidate, could be forwarded to Boston on election day.[9] The Commissioners were regarded as general officers. A Commissioner was a leading officer of the general court he represented—namely, Governor, Deputy Governor, Secretary, magistrate, or, rarely, a deputy who held a commanding position such as Speaker of the House of Deputies. There is little record on the selection of the Commissioners. However, certain procedural patterns are perceptible in each of the colonies.

The Plymouth combination of Commissioners consisted usually of the governor and one of the assistants (the name for magistrates, used by three of the colonies by the time of the revised Confederation). After 1670, one Commissioner was always the governor. Commissioners were chosen annually until 1691—the only exception being the years 1685 and 1687-8, when none were chosen. In 1651, the Commissioners, along with the governor, assistants, and treasurer could be elected by proxy: freemen could give their votes to the deputies, who brought them to the general court where they were to be opened.[10] Two years later:

> in case two commissioners bee chosen and that through age enabilitie for Travell sicknes or the like they can not appeer at the time and place appointed for that end; That then the next in nomination shall serve upon order from the Governor.[11]

Thus, the filling of a vacancy was not unlike the procedure today in many states where the governor is permitted to make interim appointments to the United States Senate.

That Plymouth consistently chose the governor as a Commissioner may have been due to the increasing awareness that she was fast becoming the "meanest and weakest least able to stand" of the confederated colonies,[12] sending the most important personage available in order to lend weight in preserving the integrity of Plymouth in the Confederation. In any event, the choosing of the governor as Commissioner was a foregone conclusion, as the election of 1672 shows:

> The severall townes of this government, not knowing that the comissioners for the United Collonies were to sitt att Plymouth this yeare, did omitt the sending of their voates for our honored Governor to be comissioner in the first place, soe that it fell out that Mr. Hinckley had more written voates then hee; but the oversight being espyed att the instant of election, and the freemen for the most parte then present did vote via vose for the Governor to be the first in our choise.[13]

New Haven consistently chose its governor as one of the Commissioners of the United Colonies. Theophilus Eaton held the post until the year of his death in 1657, and was followed by Governors Newman and Leete. At the first meeting after New Haven ceased to be a separate colony, Leete, perhaps as payment for his support of Connecticut's claim to New Haven, became one of the Commissioners from Connecticut. It was the custom in New Haven to choose two alternate delegates.

In Massachusetts, the election of the Commissioners became enmeshed between two contending political factions: the conservative group of original freemen and those who sought extension of the suffrage. For the first two years the Commissioners were named in the regular sessions of the General Court. But, in 1646, the freemen challenged the right of the Court to choose the Commissioners, whom they regarded as general officers of the Colony.[14] The privilege of freemanship consisted of the right to vote for the general officers of the Colony, such as the Governor, in the annual Court of Election, much on the same principle today that the election of the President devolves upon all the people. In 1644, the conservatives appeased the Essex faction by naming William Hathorne, a deputy, to the commissionership. Thus, fear arose that the magistrates and deputies from the rival towns of Boston and Salem would act jointly in the General Court and attempt to control patronage. Liberalism triumphed and the freemen of the colony had their way. Beginning in 1646, the Massachusetts Commissioners were chosen at the annual Court of Elections. Until 1675 at least one of the Commissioners or a reserve Commissioner was a military man;

from that time on, however, Commissioners were chosen annually until 1684, and in 1689 no military man appears as a
Commissioner.

Since the Connecticut Commissioners were first elected in a
regular session of the general court in July, 1643, this practice
continued for several years each July. But Connecticut experienced the same revolution as the Bay Colony, and from 1646
on, the Commissioners from the River Colony were elected at
the annual Court of Elections, except when the freemen voted
that the General Court or the General Assembly "should have
power to chuse Comissioners for the ensuing year."[15] On June
12, 1647 the first provision for a reserve Commissioner ordered

> that in case Mr. Whiting, being at present uppon a voyadge
> att sea, be by Providence prevented of his intended returne,
> then Capten Mason to be on of the Commissioners of the
> United Colonyes, in the Bay or elswher, at the tyme or
> tymes appointed.[16]

The tradition of long terms of service for the colonial officials
of Connecticut began with Edward Hopkins, who as either
governor or deputy governor served as a Commissioner from
1643 to 1651. John Talcott, however, later served fifteen terms.
Rarely did a deputy take a seat as Commissioner. In Connecticut, the offices of Secretary and Treasurer were more exalted
than in Massachusetts. The Secretary, unlike the Massachusetts
system, came from the magistrates. It is not surprising, therefore,
to find the secretary and the treasurer frequently filling the
post of Commissioner.

Occasionally in Connecticut the selection of a Commissioner
was highly irregular, but nevertheless expedient. Thus in 1672,
when the governor was neither a Commissioner nor a reserve:

> The Governors occasion calling him forth of this Colony
> about the time of the meeting of the Commissioners in
> September next, this Court lookes at it as inconvenient in
> this juncture of time that the Governor and Deputy Gov-
> ernor should be both absent at the same time and therefore
> request and impower the Governor to attend as Commis-
> sioner in the roome of the Deputy Governor at the next
> meeting in Plimouth.[17]

By this action it was seen fit to dispatch Governor John Winthrop, Jr., to the intercolonial meeting, probably both on account of his enormous prestige and his failing health. Thus the elder statesman would also be spared the grueling tasks of the governorship in heading off the inevitable Indian holocaust. Again, in 1675, the Secretary was "discharged from his attendance" as a Commissioner for the meeting in Boston, and the aged and venerable Governor substituted in his place. This was done because of the recent trouble with the Indians and "it was judged requisit that as many of the Assistants as can with convenience doe continue at Hartford, to assist in the management of the occasions of the Colony."[18] Commissioners were chosen annually until 1684 and in 1686 and 1689.[19]

The men who served as Commissioners of the United Colonies, we have seen, were the most important men in the colonies. Working their way up to the ranks of the magistry and often the governorship, they were men of seasoned political experience. Though the qualification of church membership remained, they were practical men and wished to improve their worldly affairs —seldom does a minister appear among the Commissioners. Commercial and landed interests were the major personal concern of most of the Commissioners. New England shipping interests were championed by such men as Hopkins and Goodyear, the latter even going to the extent of having dual citizenship in New England and New Amsterdam. The conservatism of the Commissioners may in part be seen in the fact that most were elder statesmen, tired from the forays of the political arena and past the prime of life—Simon Bradstreet, for example, was an octogenarian at the time of his final service to the Confederation. Many of the Commissioners were related directly or through marriage. A son sometimes followed in his father's footsteps—father and son combinations included the Winslows, Winthrops, Bradfords, Allyns, and the Dudleys. The Winthrop family was represented by three generations: John, John, Jr., and Wait. Indeed, the closely knit group of Commissioners, having much in common and representing the conservatism of the magistrates, may have aided that feeling of complacency working its way into New England Puritanism. A magistrate of Connecticut soon after the founding of the Confederation wrote: "how comfortable the state of things are with us in regard of that late confederation between all the united Collonies."[20]

Commissioners of the United Colonies in their exalted position in the Colony felt keenly their Puritan sensitivity to criticism. In 1677, one John Jones was hailed into court, charged with intentionally trying to run over Commissioner Thomas Danforth of Massachusetts. Jones was also heard to say bitterly that "it was noe matter if Mr. Danforth and Major Gucking [Gookin] were both hanged."[21] Simon Bradstreet on another occasion sought an indictment against a Boston apothecary "for his Injurious and reflective speeches."[22]

The Commissioners represented the only party in power, the church party. Yet, occasionally a wave of liberalism challenged the policies of the die-hards. The Plymouth Commissioners, John Brown, James Cudworth, and Josiah Winslow, would not condone the harsh policy of persecuting the Quakers. Cudworth was for a time ousted from office in Plymouth. One of the most respected men of seventeenth century New England, John Winthrop, Jr., while Commissioner, stood alone in not signing the act of the Commissioners recommending the death penalty for Quakers who might return from banishment. A political division in the Confederation was evident in the stand of the small colonies against the hegemony of Massachusetts. Differences arose concerning military and Indian policies. Even the administration of the funds for the spreading of the Gospel among the Indians was questioned. In Massachusetts, party controversy centered around the "outs" of Essex County and the "ins" of Boston. A reform movement led by the Essex group succeeded in trimming the arbitrary power of the Winthrop faction.[23] However, an attempt to retire the two oldest magistrates failed—thus leaving the Winthrop forces intact. Nevertheless, the unpopularity of Winthrop was abetted by his inadequate handling of foreign affairs and by aggressive critics, such as William Hathorne, a newcomer to the General Court from Salem. Possibly, for political expediency, the Essex faction was bought off with the offices of Commissioners for the United Colonies—indeed, most of the Massachusetts Commissioners came from Essex County.[24] The divisions in the Confederation itself, however, usually followed the positions of the particular general courts which the individual Commissioners represented.

A special form was to be used by the general courts in issuing commissions to their Commissioners:

These: are to certify

That all adjournd Courts houlden att plimouth for the jurisdiction of plimouth the first day of the fourth month 1647 Mr William Bradford and Mr John Browne wore chosen Commissioners for this jurisdiction for suche and somesuch occasions or exigents, may requine, and pertiuclerly for the next yearly meeting att plimouth the first thursday in September 1647: and wore Invested with full power and authority to treate of and Conclude of all things according to the tanure and true meaning of the articles of Confederation for the united Colonys of New England Concluded att boston the 29 of may 1648:

Myres Standish

Dollier

William Thomas

Att a Generall Court held at Hartford the 14th of May 1668, John Winthrop Esq. or Gouernor, & Wm Leet Esqr, were chosen Comissrs For this Colony, for one full & Compleat yeare, & partiuclerly for the next Meeting at Boston, the first Thursday In Sept Enext. & were invested with full power, & Authority, to treat of, & conclude of all things according to the Articles of Confederation, —

John Allyn Secretary of
the Colony of Conecticutt

Two commissions for the Commissioners of the United Colonies from Plymouth (see text) and Connecticut, 1647 and 1668, resp.

At a generall Court holden at   for the Jurisdiction of the   day   A. and B. were chosen Comissioners for this Jurisdiction for a full and compleat yeare as any occation or exigents may require and particulerly for the next yearely meeting at the first Thursday in September   And were invested with full power and authoryty to treate of and conclude...[25]

There was little variation from this procedure by the general courts. A typical commission is as follows:

These are to Certifye
Thatt Att A Generall Court houlden Att Plimouth For the Jurisdiction of Plimouth, the first Day of the fourth Moneth 1647. Mr. William Bradford; and Mr. John Browne weare Chosen Commissioners for this Jurisdiction; or exigent, may Require, And particulerly for the next yearly meeting Att Plimouth the first Thursday in september 1647; And were intrusted With full power And Authoritye; to treat of; And Conclude of All Things According to the Tenure, And true meaning of the Artickles of Confederation for the United Collonyes of New England Concluded Att boston the 29 of May 1643.

Myles Standish
William Collier
William Thomas[26]

Reimbursing the Commissioners for expenses incurred in office varied according to the individual colonies. At first, Massachusetts provided two troopers and four horses for the Commissioners to make the trip to the meetings.[27] Later this means was thought to be detrimental to the troopers. An annual allotment of forty pounds was then granted—twenty pounds per Commissioner.[28] No other colony appears to have awarded an annual sum to her Commissioners, although occasionally compensation was made. In 1664, Plymouth ordered the "sume of six pounds" towards her Commissioners' "expence of time and other troubles and inconveniencyes by them sustained in theire late journey to Conecticott."[29] In 1689, ten pounds was allotted from the "proffit of fishing at the Capte this year."[30] The host colony took extreme care in providing for the accommodation of the visiting Commissioners. In 1664, Connecticut ordered that

> Mr. Steele, Andrewe Bacon and James Boosy are to order and appoynt some convenient howse in Hartford, for the comly and suitable meeteing of the Comissioners in September next, wherein they may agitate the affairs of the Combination.[31]

Massachusetts for the meeting in Boston in 1657 specified

> that the present secretary shall and heerby is authorized and appointed to take due care...for the intertayning of the honnored comissioners for the United colonyes, theire servants, etc. and that the marshall generall, besides our comissioners owne attendents, shall waite on them, and see that all things are carried honnorably and orderly.[32]

For this meeting, Secretary Rawson, some months afterwards, was ordered to draw bills upon the Treasurer of the Colony for the Commissioners' accommodations.[33] Only several Commissioners could afford to cover their own expenses. At least one New England Commissioner possessed two Negro slaves.[34]

Although the Commissioners were "invested with full power and authority to treat of and conclude of all things, according to the true tenor and meaning of the articles"[35] or "to agitate such occatyons as concerne the united Collonyes,"[36] these powers carried no sanction. The Commissioners more often than not acquired control over certain functions through default of the general courts. For example, in 1646, Massachusetts ordered that the Colony Secretary should cease sending warrants to the constables compelling them to bring in a count of all males within the towns between the ages 16-60. Instead, the Commissioners should "send forth their own warrants to the cunstables for the same purpose, that this Courte may not be troubled therewith, nor the service neglected."[37] Nevertheless, largely because of the prestige of the men who were selected as Commissioners, the recommendations of the Commissioners were taken seriously. The "returnes" of the Commissioners were read in the general courts and often referred to committees for action.[38] Except in rare cases which fomented constitutional crises, all acts of the Commissioners were considered binding upon all the colonies.[39]

A third feature of the Confederation considered in this chapter is the meeting of the Commissioners. Meetings were held annually in September as prescribed by the Articles of Confederation —the exceptions being 1657, 1649, and during the lapse of the Confederation in the late 1660's. The triennial meetings under the second Articles were also held in September but were often adjourned to a later time.[40] The place of the meetings was at the seat of government of the colonies or in the vicinity. The meeting place in Boston, the site for most of the sessions, was the famous Town House,[41] where for more than half a century the affairs of town and colony were transacted. Nothing was lacking in atmosphere at the Town House: the ground floor, resembling Faneuil Hall in a later period, was leased to shopkeepers; in its confines were stored arms and public grain; it was a place for town festivities and for the drilling of the Ancient and Honorable Artillery Company; public preaching and prayer resounded from its walls; and from the prison yard was cast the grim shadow of the gallows. One can also imagine the savage grandeur of visiting Indian sachems who were summoned from time to time before the Commissioners. With the bustling activity at all levels of government, the Town House must have indeed provided a stimulating atmosphere for the Commissioners of the United Colonies.

At one time, three of the general courts consented to give the Commissioners the right to forgo the September meetings, provided there would still be an annual meeting.[42] Massachusetts, however, instead of endorsing this proposal, counteracted it with a much more drastic one—that the meetings be triennial, except when required during the interval because of an emergency, with the Commissioners having the power to put off even the triennial meetings.[43] This reaction of Massachusetts to the other proposals was probably brought about by suspicions of the rider attached to them:

> that when any meetinge is agreed upon ... if no more than 6. come they may meete consult, and in (case they all agree) conclude such things as concerne the severall Colonies, as if the whole number were togeither.[44]

It was during this period that the two annual September meetings were not held. After the airing of Massachusetts's position in 1649, the regular time for the meetings was strictly followed. The first and fifth meetings were held in Boston—the intervening meetings in Hartford, New Haven, and Plymouth, respectively. During the first Confederation, Massachusetts called five extraordinary sessions, all of which were held in Boston, the regular meeting places losing their turn.[45] The getting together of several Commissioners for such matters as transacting the "Indian Worke" or meeting with Cromwell's representatives was not considered an official meeting of the Commissioners. Yet, apparently some official meetings were not entered in the records of the Confederation. For example, the eight Commissioners met the last day of August, 1650, in Plymouth,[46] but a week later they reconvened in Hartford, with four new Commissioners in attendance. The August meeting must have been held in order to give Plymouth the feeling of not being bypassed[47] and to prepare an agenda for the regular meeting.

No meetings were held in 1665 and 1666. At Hartford, in 1667, plans were discussed for amending the Articles.[48] The new Articles were drawn up at a session in 1670, and on September 15, 1672, the first regular meeting of the new Confederation was held.[49] An extraordinary session was called by Connecticut in 1673;[50] regular September sessions were held in 1675, 1678, 1681, and 1684. The next regular meeting would have taken place in 1687, but because of the establishment of the Dominion of New England in 1686 this meeting was not held. In an attempt to revive the Confederation after the fall of the Andros government, a meeting was held in 1689.

On several occasions the legality of a meeting was questioned. The meeting in 1649 was considered "frustrate" by Massachusetts because no regular session was held that year.[51] The meeting in 1652 at Plymouth was also declared "frustrate" by the Commissioners who were present because three Commissioners were missing. Although two of the missing Commissioners showed up the evening of the first day of business, the session was still considered illegal. The reasons given were: (1) the day appointed by the Articles was past; (2) the number of Commissioners, as called for by the Articles for the annual meeting, was not complete nor was likely to be; and (3) a dangerous precedent might be established. Nevertheless the Plymouth meeting continued in session, although its actions were considered not binding.[52] In May, 1653, a session was declared "dissolved" upon the expiration of the terms of two Commissioners, but the meeting continued while a messenger was dispatched to bring back "speedily" the new commissions.[53] Although only five Commissioners were present for the meeting in Boston, 1675, the meeting was declared "lawfull" and was held despite Winthrop's motion for adjournment and the condemnation of Connecticut for the "absolute violation of the maine ends of the Articles of Confederation" in not sending a second Commissioner.[54]

Several Plymouth meetings may have been held in the town of Rehoboth. In 1654, the Plymouth General Court requested the Commissioners from the colony to seek a "constant meeting place," such as Boston or Rehoboth.[55] In 1660, the Commissioners agreed

> that the next meeting which should bee holden att Plymouth shalbee held att Rehoboth a towne in that Jurisdiction unlesse their Generall Courts or any of them; shall before the end of May next give notice to the contrary to the Secretarys of all the other Jurisdictions.[56]

There is no other indication that Plymouth meetings may have been held in Rehoboth. Intercolonial correspondence continually sought out the possibilities of holding extraordinary sessions.[57]

The first day of each session began with the reading of the Articles of Confederation, followed by the presentation and reading of the commissions of the Commissioners. A president was then chosen from the delegation of the colony where the meeting was being held—there were exceptions to this rule, such as the several times when Theophilus Eaton was president at meetings in Hartford. The main order of business was then considered, undergoing full[58] and serious[59] debate, becoming at times "most uncomfortable."[60] The meetings appear to have been busy affairs, especially those held during the first decade—witness the numerous Indian hearings and the voluminous correspondence with the Dutch. Although a file of letters and official papers was kept,[61] there is no indication to whom this responsibility was entrusted. As a matter of fact, a characteristic of the Commissioners' work was the minimum involvement with red tape.

The Commissioners followed the practice of putting their findings and recommendations in writing—each Commissioner attached his signature at the end of the complete record. Massachusetts wanted the privilege of signing first, but the Commissioners from the smaller colonies would not grant Massachusetts this recognition of pre-eminence. However, it was agreed upon that the principle in signing should be that order followed at the signing of the Articles—namely, Massachusetts-Plymouth-Connecticut-New Haven.[62] Each colony received a copy of the Acts of the Commissioners—witness Winthrop's statement that "the names of the Commissioners and all their proceedings are at large set out in the books of their records, whereof every colony hath one."[63] The Plymouth copy was primarily in the handwriting of Secretaries Nathaniel Morton or Nathaniel Souther.[64] Secretary Allyn of Connecticut, long in office, signed the official correspondence of the Colony; and Secretary Rawson, performing the same role in Massachusetts, also played a prominent part in the Confederation by keeping the Indian accounts and writing much of the correspondence to the Dutch.[65] Probably, the secretary for each colony was the one responsible for recording the minutes of the Confederation—original minutes being taken at the home session and at the same time those records of previous sessions incorporated in the colony records. As a matter of convenience, the Secretary for the Colony of Connecticut was frequently appointed Commissioner from that colony.

Certain aspects of administrative machinery should be discussed. The primary role of the Commissioners was to serve as ambassadors to a central agency for coordinating the efforts of the several colonies with common policy. As "super-ambassadors" the Commissioners represented the colonies in foreign affairs. In intercolonial disputes the Commissioners served as a board of mediation and arbitration; in affairs of religion and education they frequently performed as a board of trustees. The judicial role of the Commissioners varied from the setting up of uniform standards in the probating of wills[66] to joining with William Pynchon of Springfield, as Assistant of the Bay Colony, in order to form a court "to hear and determine all cases both, civill, criminal."[67] Because of the absence of an admiralty court in the four colonies, the Commissioners temporarily took upon themselves admiralty jurisdiction. In Indian affairs they constituted a regular "Bureau of Indian Affairs." The Commissioners of the United Colonies, therefore, were entrusted with a wide range of responsibilities, which in the later evolution of American government became departmentalized.

As a central agency for the colonies the Commissioners soon developed a small staff of their own, though it was rudimentary. Although the Articles of Confederation provided for no other persons than the Commissioners, several persons came into the employ of the Confederation. Daniel Gookin, though owing his appointment to the Massachusetts General Court, superintended Indian affairs for the Confederation and also brought the Gospel to the Indians. Other employees of the Confederation were a variety of interpreters, whose wide range of duties included running messages and collecting tribute from the Indians. The most notable of the interpreters was Thomas Stanton, who became a regular handyman for the Confederation. Besides his normal duties as an interpreter, Stanton served as an envoy to the Dutch, helped in the printing of the Indian catechisms, and supervised Indian instruction. It was Stanton's house that served as the place of rendezvous for the 1654 expedition against the Niantic Indians. An interpreter's job, such as Stanton's, proved to be quite dangerous; it was no easy task to remind a Narragansett sachem of a breach of covenant or, if the Indians were reluctant in paying tribute that was due, to seize "soe much more of the said Sachems estate as may make meet satisfaction to themselves soe as noe unnecessary disturbance or damage bee put upon the Indians therby."[68] In recognition for his services, Stanton was awarded thirty pounds as an annual salary,[69] which was increased to fifty pounds by the Corporation.[70] Stanton's commission of 1650 best sums up his role in the Confederation:

And for the pequats that are with the Narriganssets Nianticks Mohegans or any others; Thomas Stanton is desired and appointed to demaund and Receive the same and to give an account at the meeting of the Commissioners what hee hath Recovered and who they are that Refuse and upon what grounds hee is also to attend the Constant yearly meetings of the Commissioners or any other extreordinary meeting upon Convenient notice to interpret and performe such other service...in Reference to the Indians....[71]

Edward Rawson was appointed a "steward or agent for the Receiving and disposing" of goods and commodities from the Corporation for Promoting the Gospel.[72] Edward Winslow served as an agent in England for the Commissioners in helping to carry out the work of the Corporation. Hezekiah Usher was appointed to draw bills of exchange upon the Corporation.[73] John Eliot and Thomas Mayhew were the most prominent of those engaged in Indian missionary work by the Confederation.

When in session the Commissioners were apparently accessible to any who had advice to give. In 1653, Massachusetts appointed a committee "to Joyne with such of the Commissioners of the United Collonies as they shall please to nominate to draw up the case respecting the Duch and Indians if they please."[74]

A commander-in-chief was added to the staff of the Confederation in time of war emergency, but this office gradually slipped away from the control of the Commissioners. This tendency is evidenced by the fact that, in 1645, the Commissioners chose Major Gibbons directly for an expedition against the Narragansetts;[75] while in 1654 the Commissioners selected three men, leaving it to Massachusetts to make the choice of one, but because all three were unavailable, Massachusetts used her own judgment in making a selection; and in 1675 the only attempt to force a commander upon the colonies was the compromise agreement that the "Commander in Cheiffe of the forces of that Collonies; where the seate of warr shall happen to be, shalbe the Cheiffe over the whole."[76]

The Commissioners followed closely what procedure was set forth by the Articles, and added immensely to it as the Confederation faced different problems. The general courts, which had direct control over the Commissioners both in their selection and as officials of the colonies, set up many of the methods of procedure. The general courts, however, followed a day-to-day procedure in activities relating to the Confederation, and any consistency grew out of custom.

The greatest procedural defect, as was the substantive, was that the Commissioners could not pass legislation binding on the general courts. The general courts retained the power to make and enforce laws even though the Commissioners were invested with "full power" to settle certain questions. The Confederation existed more in the realm of theory than actuality, and the failure to work out adequate particulars of procedure left it rigid and immobile.

To what extent, if any, did the New England Confederation exercise sovereign powers? To John Quincy Adams, the Confederation was the "exercise of sovereign power in its highest attributes";[77] whereas historians, such as Herbert L. Osgood, have generally pointed out that the "right to interpret the Articles of Confederation" rested "finally with the general courts of the colonies themselves."[78] To the Puritans sovereignty was a "high and tremendous attribute, being an ocean that has neither bank nor bottom" and could not "lightly be launched."[79] In order to examine the question of sovereignty, two aspects must be considered: the relation of the colonies to the mother country, and the relation of the Confederation to the general courts.

There is no doubt that the New England colonies, with the exception of Rhode Island, from 1643 to the Restoration, considered themselves largely independent of the mother country. To the Puritan mind it was "a sin to refuse an oath touching any thing that is good and just, being lawfully imposed by authority."[80] Yet in this early period of our history, the settlers of the new Zion took pains to avoid recognizing the home government as the supreme authority.

By order of the same general court in which Massachusetts sent Commissioners to the Confederation in 1643, the phrase "You shall bear true faith and allegiance to our sovereign Lord King Charles" was omitted from the oaths for the governors and magistrates.[81] Plymouth erased the phrase relating to their "sovereign Lord" and underlined "the State and Government of England as it now stands."[82] When the oaths of allegiance to the crown were accepted as a matter of course after the Restoration, there were still conspicuous irregularities.[83] But the Restoration, nevertheless, marks a return of the colonies to the recognition of the sovereignty of England. In 1661, Plymouth "humbly and Faithfully" submitted themselves "for ever" to their "sovereign Lord King Charles the second."[84] The dedication to Eliot's Indian Bible acknowledged the sovereignty of the King, and in 1665 the colonies "freely consented, that all administration of justice" should be in the King's name.[85] In the same year Massachusetts was reminded that the "King did not grant away his Soveraigntie."[86] Although its enemies delighted in referring to the later Confederacy in correspondence with the royal government as "the three united Collonies,"[87] the members of the Confederation sought to fit into the royal scheme of things by stating their mission to be for the "satty and preservation of his Majesties dominions heer against foraigne and domesticke enimies."[88] The Confederation, then, by its own admission, if it exerted sovereign powers, would have had to do so before the Restoration. The question of sovereignty, therefore, is best confined to the first phase of the Confederation.

The New England Confederation was formed essentially as an international alliance. The Articles of Confederation was an agreement of the delegates from four independent colonies and was ratified by the individual courts, which for practical purposes were supreme. The colonies, in theory, according to the Articles of Confederation, surrendered to the intercolonial union limited powers, in the realm of war powers and arbitration of disputes, and pledged themselves to cooperate in all matters of general concernment. But as is demonstrated by the history of leagues and confederations, actual power rested ultimately in the contracting members of the Union; namely, in the general courts of the colonies (considering that governmental authority from England at the time was nil). Yet there was an atmosphere of sovereignty in the early Confederation.

Because a governing body was constructed that was to meet annually to deal with problems of common concernment, and because the colonies were bound to accept its decisions according to the strict interpretation of the Articles, an illusion was created that the Confederation exercised sovereign powers. This illusion was strengthened by the founding fathers, all prominent men in their colonies, who expected this union would serve as the voice for all the colonies. The Confederation, also during its first decade, took over the administration of foreign affairs, which created the impression that this was a special jurisdiction of the Confederation, an area in which the sovereign will of a state is expressed. Even the French ambassadors were compelled to treat directly with the Commissioners, and the Dutch regarded them as a sovereign body. But, latently simmering beneath this illusion, there was the fact that the general courts had never surrendered their sovereign powers, as was evident by the instructions of the Massachusetts General Court to its Commissioners in 1643. In reality, then, the Commissioners never exercised sovereign powers. Only because of the close harmony of the colonies and the tremendous activity during its first decade was the Confederation able to pass as a sovereign body. This illusion of sovereignty was finally brought to light by the Constitutional crises of 1653-5, which ended with the explosion of the myth.

Basically, the Confederation was never invested with sovereign authority: (1) the general courts retained the powers and means of enforcement; (2) the general courts never expressly acknowledged the supremacy of the Confederation; (3) no oaths of allegiance or loyalty were taken to the Confederation; (4) no specifications as to treason against the United Colonies were made; and (5) the Commissioners were, first of all, officials of the colonies they represented (unlike the United States Senators, who, though elected by the individual states, become federal officials).

After the dispersion of the illusion of sovereignty, interest in the Confederation faded away, and the Confederation became of value more in special areas rather than as an instrument of national transcendence. Ultimate authority, in the final analysis, rests with the people of a government. In order to exercise sovereign powers, a governing body must have direct jurisdiction over the people. The failing of the Confederation was due to the Commissioners' not being directly responsible to the people. Instead they were the ambassadors of the general courts.

There is yet one more aspect of sovereignty that may have been manifested by the Confederation during the Decade of Optimism. If the theory here set forth is correct, a grandeur is added to the Confederation and the missing link is provided in the evolution of our National Ensign. There would also be grounds for purporting that the New England colonists asserted an independence and national sentiment normally interpreted as belonging solely to the era of the American Revolution. The theory, simply stated, is this: during the first decade of the Confederation, 1643-53, citizens of the Puritan Colonies of New England flew from the masts of their coastal vessels a flag of four red stripes, representing their Union. The theory is originally that of Mr. Lawrence Phelps Tower, based upon his extensive research in tracing the orgins of the American flag through paintings.

During the American Revolution, striped banners began to

appear everywhere in the colonies.[89] At the Stamp Act Congress of 1765, a flag of nine red and white stripes was flown. The "Stripes of Rebellion" became a rallying standard of the Sons of Liberty. In December, 1775, aboard the *Alfred* of John Paul Jones was hoisted the famed "Grand Union Flag," a flag of thirteen red and white stripes with the "Union Jack," and thus is seen the beginning of the "Stars and Stripes." The stars may have originated in the Rhode Island starred flag or the flag of East Friesland, where many of the early settlers of New England had lived, or it may have originated overnight when the colonists hastily sought to shear their flag of any English semblances. However, the starred flag apparently has had no recurring significance in American history before the American Revolution. Such is not the case of the striped flag, which appeared many times in colonial history, and when linked to Dutch origins, via the New England Confederation, it takes on added significance.

Of the several theories of the origins of the American striped flag, two may be immediately dismissed: Washington's coat of arms—at least as far as stripes are concerned—and the invention of Betsy Ross. Two plausible theories, however, are: Dutch origins and the use of striped banners on commercial vessels such as those of the East India Company. These two theories are in no way contradictory and may even complement each other.

Since the time of the Tudors, English trading vessels often flew striped flags, and as early as 1701 the East India Company flag consisted of thirteen red and white stripes; but the number of stripes and the color of the stripes varied. It is from the trading company flags then, we shall concede, that the colonists over a long stretch of time had become familiar with the striped flag. However, there is one essential characteristic of the American flag and the flags of the Revolutionary period not explained by the British striped ensigns on the trading vessels: that each stripe symbolizes a political unit. This feature has a counterpart in the seven red-striped flag of the United Provinces of the Netherlands, each stripe representing a member of the Union. It is possible that this flag was carried to England, as Mr. Tower believes, by Dutch refugees, or it may have been flown as a symbol of trade alliance between Dutch and English trading companies banding together to ward off Spanish privateers. This use of the striped flag to symbolize a trade "confederacy" be-

tween England and the United Provinces is attested to by an
early writer, who says that in 1619

> there was a Solemn League and Agreement by King *James*,
> and the States of the United Provinces, in a strict Alliance,
> and social Confederacy of the English *East India* Company,
> and that of the United Provinces, for the better advancing
> and carrying on of the Trade and Commerce...[90]

Note that the "Alliance" was between the East India Company
(the companies having monopoly grants by the government, in
fact represented the government) and the United Provinces (not
the West India Company, which was established two years later)
—company and government and both had like striped standards
except for the number of stripes. Thus the flags of the East India
Company and the Dutch Union were not so far apart after all.
Both flags may have symbolized amity of trade. A striped flag
may have suggested to the founders of the New England Confederation the kind of flag they were looking for: one that
had been used in the mother country by a trade company
rather than by the crown and at the same time a flag representing equally the members of the League, after the pattern of the
Dutch Union.

It is possible the New England Confederation was actually
represented by a flag of four red stripes. The frontispiece of this
book shows a picture painted in New Amsterdam by a Dutch
painter in 1647 of a scene in New Amsterdam harbor.[91] In the
painting are Dutch flags with a solid red field and the three-
striped red, white, and blue flag of the West India Company.
But there is also a flag on one of the vessels that has four red
stripes. It is important to note that the vessels pictured are
small and, therefore, must have been confined to the coastal
trade, which would apparently eliminate their being owned by
the English East India Company. A four-striped flag could not
have belonged to the Dutch since the standard for their Union
was a flag of seven stripes, symbolizing each province; and the
Orangian and West Indian Company flags in the picture may
have been deemed sufficient by the artist to depict the Dutch
atmosphere. Granted the above assumptions and that the artist
wished to convey a cosmopolitan effect in this view of the

82 THE UNITED COLONIES OF NEW ENGLAND

harbor, it is reasonable to regard the ship flying the four-striped flag as belonging to a merchant vessel of the United Colonies of New England.

The flag of four stripes in New Amsterdam harbor may or may not have been a flag representing the United Colonies, but on the basis of this evidence this is not an unreasonable assumption. Yet, even without this remarkable painting, it may be assumed that individuals took it upon themselves to fly a four-striped flag of the Confederation on their trading vessels. No evidence of official sanction by the Confederation for a flag has been uncovered. But this does not subtract from the possibility—it even lends weight to it—that an unauthorized flag was flown over merchant vessels. Ever since the *cause célèbre* in 1634 when Endicott boldly slashed the Cross of St. George out of the English flag, the colonies had left well-enough alone, feeling that no flag was better than one asserting the royal authority of England. In the first decade of the Confederation, then, there was no official flag—either of the mother country or of the colonial governments. This was a period of optimism, and in some degree a consciousness of unity was beginning to emerge. It is possible, therefore, that some patriotic person ventured to fly a flag after the fashion practiced in Holland—a flag which would represent under one banner the combined strength of four New England colonies.

Since the ship pictured in the New Amsterdam harbor is a coastal vessel—assuming there is a basis in fact for the painter's imagination—it most likely came from the New Haven Colony. The New Haven merchants, a class furnishing quite a number of Confederation Commissioners during this period, were then engaged in a prosperous trade with the Dutch and were busily planning new commercial ventures to operate under the very noses of their Knickerbocker brethren. New Haven settlers were already encroaching upon the Dutch on Long Island Sound. The importance of commerce in New Haven is illustrated by one of the leading Commissioners, Stephen Goodyear of New Haven, who occasionally sailed on one of his trading vessels to New Amsterdam, where he was also a citizen of the Dutch Colony. More will be said of the commercial ventures of New Haven. Suffice to say here that New Haven, small and located on a barren coast, could best prosper by invoking the combined power of the United Colonies.

It might also be added that the date of the New Amsterdam picture is significant—1647, when the Confederation was at its peak, operating under what has already been pointed out, an illusion of sovereignty. There is one other impressive bit of evidence which further attests to Dutch influence on New England's notions for a flag. This evidence is found by comparing the famous "Three County Troop Flag," the militia standard of the Massachusetts counties of Suffolk, Essex, and Middlesex with an earlier Dutch battle flag of the late sixteenth century. In this flag an armed fist reaches out of the heavens clutching a sword, signifying that the fight against the Spaniards has the blessing of God. The two flags are practically alike. A similar flag, known as the Bedford Flag, was also probably of Dutch origin since it was found in the southern counties of England, which were overrun by Dutch refugees. Here may be the link between the original Dutch standard and the "Three County Troop Flag" of the counties by the same name in the New World.

To the chosen settlers of New Canaan, a striped flag must have had a peculiar fascination. It is probable that the origin of the Dutch striped flag was rooted in religious symbolism of the time. The flag of the little principality of Monaco today has its origins in the legend of her patron saint, whose body after having been murdered by the Corsicans was set adrift, wrapped in striped linen of red and white. Another religious theme was the flag of Poland, which was symbolic of the body of Christ. An interesting painting has been found by Mr. Tower at Hampton Court Palace of the Christ child wrapped in striped cloth—painted by an Italian painter during the time of the Dutch struggle for independence. The stripes in this early painting and those of the flags of Monaco and Poland symbolize either the patron saints or the Saviour, whose shedding of blood (represented by the red stripes) would redeem Mankind—a role in which the little Dutch provinces may have seen themselves, sacrificiously, though victoriously, throwing off the fetters of foreign domination. Perhaps the Dutch had in mind the passage from Isaiah (53:5) which has been interpreted by Christendom as foretelling the coming of the Messiah:

he *was* wounded for our transgressions, *he was* bruised for our iniquities: the chastisement of our peace *was* upon him; and with his stripes we are healed.

That the origins of our Striped Flag may have had religious
significance is, of course, hypothetical, and any future evidence
may continue to be too speculative to be conclusive, but nevertheless it will remain an intriguing subject. This phase of Mr.
Tower's research is mentioned for its possible connection with
the creation of a four-red-striped flag for the Confederation..
It may have been that such a flag was the only one which would
not smack of Roman or Anglican symbolism and yet show the
Puritans endowed with a mission, like the Dutch, to preserve the
True Way, and in Confederation save mankind from the arms
of tyranny.

The conclusions of this brief inquiry into the seventeenth
century origins of the American flag are several. There seems
sufficient evidence to indicate that the forerunners of the American flag came from the Dutch Republic[92] and the early trading
company ensigns. From the Dutch came the idea that each red
stripe represented a component part of federation. Although
no New England flag was flown during the first decade of the
Confederation, there are grounds for believing that certain merchants on their own initiative flew a four-striped flag on their
coastal trading vessels—it may have been a general practice in
order to awe the French and the Dutch. It is also possible,
though at present extremely tentative, that a flag of the Confederation may at the same time have symbolized the religious
mission of the Puritans, the red stripes not arousing the Puritan
distaste for symbolism.

That a four-striped flag might have been flown by the
United Colonies of New England has far greater significance
than establishing a vital link between the Dutch flag and the
"Stars and Stripes" in the evolution of the American flag. If it can
be established without a doubt that such a flag existed, then on
the American continent among the early English colonies there
was an experience in Union and an assertion of sovereignty that
was never erased from the colonial mind.

A flag of New England, however, did appear when the Confederation was fading away and the British government was
turning to the consolidation of the New England colonies. The
flag of 1686, though never officially authorized,[93] acknowledged
the supremacy of the mother country by providing inside a
white canton on a red field, the cross of St. George—but, so as
not to leave the idea that New England could not fend for her-

self, a pine-tree,[94] which for over thirty years had been used as a symbol for sturdy manhood and self-reliance, was included in the canton. The revival of the Confederation was attempted in 1689, and had the Union again been achieved at this time, this banner might have become the official flag of the United Colonies of New England. There might even have been some lofty-inspired poet about, who in the time of crisis would soar on high with gusts mixed with a spirit of New England patriotism and only a slight deference to England. He might have been moved to write:

> Oh, thus be it ever when freemen shall stand
> Between their loved home and the war's desolation;
> Blest with vict'ry and peace, may the heav'n-rescued land
> Praise the Power that has made and preserved us our
> union.
> Then conquer we must, when our cause it is just,
> And this be our motto: "In God is our trust";
> And the pine-tree and the cross in triumph shall wave
> O'er the land of the free and the home of the brave.

---

[1] *PCR*, IX, 27.

[2] MA, II, 355 and 358A, 10Oct67.

[3] *PCR*, IX, 271.

[4] The Commissioners first assumed responsibility for this work as agents for the Society for Promoting the Gospel (see below) in London. Soon the Massachusetts General Court was asking the Commissioners to apportion an allowance "for and towards the chardg of the Indian business." (MA, XXX, 74a, 8Jun58).

[5] *MCR*, II, 245.

[6] *PCR*, IX, 119-20.

[7] *Ibid.*, p. 127.

[8] See Chapter 12. The Massachusetts committee appointed in 1648, headed by the Governor and Deputy Governor, was to "publish the articles of confederation" and the acts of the Commissioners "which may serve either to confound the power of our general Courts or to interfere with it, as may in a short time prove not only prejudicial, but exceedingly uncomfortable." They should propose "remedies of what they "found amisse, that our posterity may have no cause to Blame us, for uniting ourselves in such a way as is feared . . ." (MA, II, 302, May48). Often the Secretary of the Mass. Court would send the report of the Commissioners to the other colonies with "emendations" of the General Court. (MA, III, 435.)

[9] Joseph B. Felt, *History of Ipswich* (Cambridge: 1834), p. 139.

[10] *PCR*, XI, 157.

[11] *Ibid.*, p. 62.

[12] *PCR*, X, 323.

[13] *Ibid.*, V, 90.

[14] Thomas Hutchinson, *The History of the Colony and Province of Massachusetts Bay*, ed. by Lawrence S. Mayo (Cambridge, Mass.: Harvard University Press, 1936), I, 145.

[15] *CCR*, I, 256. This manner of choosing Commissioners became frequent after 1660.

[16] *Ibid.*, p. 156. Commissioner Whiting was later reported lost at sea.

[17] *CCR*, II, 182.

[18] *Ibid.*, III, 194.

[19] The attempt to revive the Confederation and the meeting of 1689 will be discussed in Chapter 15.

[20] Gov. George Willis to George Willis, 28Oct44, Willys Papers, CHS.

[21] Deposition of John Marshal, MA, VIII, 4, 2Oct77.

[22] *The Boston Society Publications*, VI, 129-30.

[23] This was accomplished by the passage of the "Body of Liberties," which fixed penalties rather than leave them to the discretion of the General Court.

[24] J. D. Phillips, *Salem in the Seventeenth Century* (Boston: 1937), p. 162.

[25] *PCR*, IX, 13.

[26] Transcribed in the *Pilgrim Society Notes*, No. 5, 1Dec1955. Commissions are scattered throughout the colonial records and the papers of several of the individual Commissioners.

[27] *MCR*, II, 71.

[28] *Ibid.*, IV, Pt. 1, 41.

[29] *PCR*, IV, 72.

[30] *Ibid.*, VI, 219.

[31] *CCR*, I, 105.

[32] *MCR*, II, 69.

[33] MA, II, 353, 11Jun58.

[34] Inventory of the Estate of James Richards (d. 11Jun80), CA, Misc. MSS, II, pt. 1, 16.

[35] *MCR*, II, 69.

[36] *CCR*, I, 241.

[37] *MCR*, II, 151.

[38] E.g., *MCR*, IV, 354.

[39] When the Acts were not signed, they were not considered binding. (E.g., *PCR*, X, 419-20.)

[40] The longest series of meetings was held from Sep75 to Apr76.

[41] See Josiah H. Benton, *The Story of the Old Boston Town House, 1658-1711* (Boston: 1908), *passim*.

[42] *PCR*, IX, 140.

[43] *Ibid.*, p. 119.

[44] *PCR*, IX, 84-5.

[45] From Sep43 to Sep64, approximately one-half of the meetings were held in Boston. A further word on the Town House may here be added. At eleven each morning a bell was rung, summoning the merchants of the town to meet in a room on the ground floor (Bridenbaugh, *op. cit.*, p. 38). Though the taking of any "tobacco" or using "fire" in the Town House was prohibited (*Boston Town Records, 1660-1701*, p. 9), the structure perished in flames in 1711.

[46] MA, II, 303-26.

[47] The Massachusetts Council had written Plymouth that the Commissioners had agreed "that we should againe . . . make offer of the place . . . to your Government." (4Mar50, MA, XXX, 16a).

[48] *PCR*, X, 324-9.

[49] *Ibid.*, p. 352.

[50] PCR, X, 386-9.

[51] *MCR*, III, 289-90.

[52] *PCR*, X, 374.

[53] *Ibid.*, pp. 34-5.

[54] *Ibid.*, p. 456.

[55] *PCR*, III, 67.

[56] *Ibid.*, X, 253.

[57] E.g., a letter from Conn. to Gov. Endicott of Mass. requesting an opinion "whether nothing be fitt to be considered before the usuall meeting of the commissioners." (*MHSC*:5:VIII:55, 27Mar59).

[58] *PCR*, X, 391.

[59] E.g., *ibid.*, p. 374

[60] E.g., *ibid.*, p. 111.

[61] *Ibid.*, pp. 322-380.

[62] Trumbull, *Connecticut*, I, 144.

[63] *PCR*, IX, xi.

[64] *Ibid.*, p. xii. In the general courts the Acts were to "lye open to the view of all men." (*Ibid.*, X, 243.)

[65] *MCR*, IV, pt. 1, 146.

[66] See Hutchinson's *History* (Mayo, ed.), I, 154-5, 165; *PCR*, IX, 137.

[67] MA, XXXVIII, 241, Order of the Mass. Gen. Ct., 1645; *MCR*, II, 109. Mass. claimants in the land controversy at Southertown (New London) were to write: "wee have layed before the Court and Counsell and Commissioners of the united Collonys . . ." (MA, II, 43.)

[68] PCR, X, 106, 190, 131, 145, 199.

[69] *Ibid.*, IX, 191.

[70] *Ibid.*, X, 187. More will be said of this Corporation for Promoting the Gospel in later chapters.

[71] *Ibid.*, IX, 190-1.

[72] *PCR*, IX, 206.

[73] *Ibid.*, X, 194.

[74] *Ibid.*, p. 52.

[75] *Ibid.*, IX, 37.

[76] *Ibid.*, X, 359.

[77] John Quincy Adams, "The New England Confederacy of 1643," *MHSC* (1843), 3, IX, 199.

[78] Herbert L. Osgood, *The American Colonies in the Seventeenth Century* (New York: The Macmillan Co., 1904), I, 403.

[79] Elisha Coles, *A Practical Discourse of God's Sovereignty* (Newburyport: 1798(1667)), Columbia University Library.

[80] Cotton Mather, *Magnalia Christi Americana, op. cit.*, II, 201.

[81] Winthrop, *Journal*, II, 99.

[82] W. Brigham, "The Colony of Plymouth and its Relation to Massachusetts," *Early History of Massachusetts*, (Boston: MHS, 1869), 173.

[83] E.g., the Plymouth revised oath for freemen in 1671 left out "Charles," and in 1672 Massachusetts acknowledged royal authority only under their charter (C. Evans, "Oaths of Allegiance in Colonial New England," *AASP*, Pt. 2, 407ff.)

[84] E. Hazard, *State Papers* (Philadelphia: 1794), II, 590.

[85] J. R. Brodhead, ed., *London Documents*, Vol. III of *Colonial History of the State of New York* (Albany: Weed & Parsons, 1853), II, 97.

[86] *Ibid.*, King's Commissioners to Gov. of Mass., 16Jul65, p. 99.

[87] Stevens Transcripts, II, 157, Holden and Green to William Blathwayt (Sec. to Comm. for For. Plantations), 20Aug80, John Carter Brown Library.

[88] *PCR*, X, 326.

[89] For reference to Mr. Tower's research, see *Time Magazine*, 20Jun55, pp. 24ff. Also consulted were the following works: Col. W. H. Waldron, *Flags of America* (Huntington, W. Va.: 1935); Bryon McCandless and Gilbert Grosvenor, "Our Flag Number," *Nat. Geographic Magazine*, XXXII (Jul-Dec1917), pp. 281-420; R. C. B. Thurston, *The Origin and Evolution of the U. S. Flag*, (Nat. Soc. of Sons of the Amer. Rev., 1915); Howard M. Chapin, "Colonial Military Flags," *NEQ*, IV (July, 1931), pp. 448-459; Oliver A. Roberts, *History of the Ancient and Honorable Artillery Co. of Massachusetts*, (Boston: 1895), I, 271.

[90] William de Britaine, *The Dutch Usurpation: or, a Brief View of the Behaviour of the States-General of the United Provinces Towards the Kings of Great Britain*, (London: 1672), Columbia University Library, p. 14.

[91] The artist was Augustine Herrman, a literal pictorialist who set down everything he saw. At the date of the painting, he had strong mercantile interests in the New England area, and like several New Haven merchants had dual citizenship in New Haven and New Amsterdam.

[92] Benjamin Franklin and John Adams, while in Holland, were reported as having told the Dutch that America owed much to them, including the basic principle of the American flag. (McCandless, *loc. cit.* p. 297.)

[93] Mrs. Frank L. Vance and J. S. Bletcher, *Our Nation's Flag* (Milwaukee, Wisconsin: 1917), pp. 5-6.

[94] The pine-tree might have remained the only symbol in the flag and the

cross of St. George never inserted, had not the Royal Government renewed pressure on the colonies in the 1680's. A contemporary traveler wrote in July, 1680, that the English flag in New England was as follows: "a red ground with a small white field in the uppermost corner where there is a red cross, they have here dispensed with this cross in their colors, and preserved the rest." (Jaspar Dankers and Peter Sluyter, "Journal of our Voyage from New Netherland," *Memoirs of the Long Island Historical Society* (Brooklyn: 1867), I, 393.

CHAPTER V

Great Expectations

"MUCH HONORED IN OUR BLESSED SAVIOUR, at the returne of our Magistrates," wrote Hooker jubilantly to Governor Winthrop, "when I understood the gratious and desired successe of ther indeavor" for promoting "so good a work" and laying "a foundation of safety and prosperity in succeeding ages"— a "meanes not only to mayntayne peace and truth in your dayes, but to leave both, as Legacy to those that come after, untill the coming of the Sonne of God in the Clouds."[1] Thus is expressed the buoyant feeling of optimism which prevailed at the inception of the United Colonies.

It was fortunate that the hopes in the Confederation were high, for from the very beginning the Commissioners were faced with matters of gravest importance. The years of 1643-52 nevertheless were a period of success; and during this time the Commissioners, in the areas of their jurisdiction, exercised almost unbridled power—creating the illusion that the Confederation possessed sovereign powers, while in actuality it did not. With a firm hand, the Commissioners commanded allegiance from the Indians and won respect from the French and Dutch, while on the home front they skillfully handled many intercolonial problems. The crowning achievement was the preserving of peace in a time when peace was unlikely, thereby meeting the highest expectations of the founders. Only towards the end of this decade of activity were there rumblings of discontent; but these only quietly foreshadowed the storm that was to follow. The years of 1643-52, when the United Colonies of New England worked in coordinated action and followed the direction of one governing body, mark the first successful experiment in American federalism.

The main order of business throughout the early Confederation dealt with the continual threat of Indian hostilities, friction with the Dutch, and the controversy over lands in the Pequot and Narragansett country—all three of which will be treated separately in the following chapters. The hodge-podge of business of the early Confederation in other fields will be treated in this chapter

One sovereign characteristic of the Confederation during this decade of optimism was the readiness to let the Commissioners of the United Colonies take over the administration of foreign affairs. The Commissioners could best guide the colonies, which were hard pressed on three sides from the Dutch, French, and, most threatening, the Indians, along a common line of defense. It is not surprising then that one of the first acts of the Commissioners was of a military nature—recommending to the general courts that every man keep with him a "good gunn and sword one pound of pouder with four pounds of shott with match or flints suitable," and that the general courts also keep arms close at hand at all times. It was ordered that there be six "trayneings" per year, reports of which were to be submitted to the Commissioners.[2] The power of the Commissioners to regulate matters concerning defense was for the remainder of the decade left undisputed by the colonies.[3]

The United Colonies inherited from the diplomatic bungling of the Bay Colony a most difficult problem in the relations with New France. The strain in the relations with the French in North America came from the meddling of Massachusetts in their internal affairs in Canada. It all started upon the death of the French governor, Isaac de Razilly, in 1635. A bitter contest for the supreme power in New France soon followed between his two principle deputies, Charles d'Aulney and Charles de la Tour. D'Aulney, through his extensive land purchases and by a royal grant from the king, soon became in effect governor of New France. His title to Acadia, however, was contested by La Tour, whose office and tenure to the land antedated that of d'Aulney.[4] Both vied for control of the fur trade. In vain the King tried to intervene between the two parties. As internecine warfare developed, the trading interests of Massachusetts became involved. But d'Aulney was finally confirmed in the governorship by royal decree, thus leaving La Tour in New France in the position of a rebel. La Tour then turned to the Bay Colony for aid.

La Tour visited Boston in April of 1643. He was able to connive with the authorities to permit him to raise an expedition. A filibustering expedition of four ships with nearly a hundred troops was fitted out. With this Massachusetts force, La Tour led an attack against a fortified mill of the d'Aulney forces, which proved unsuccessful, and the Bay contingent lost heart for further battle and returned home in August. This action of Massachusetts in permitting the raising of a volunteer force to participate in the civil strife of a foreign country has been characterized as a "gross violation of neutrality and international law,"[5] and created serious repercussions in the politics of the Bay. Winthrop was accused of inviting attack from the d'Aulney forces, of aiding idolaters, and of promoting a shrewd scheme for capturing trade for Boston at the expense of the Essex County towns.[6] The popular reaction was such that in the following election of 1644 Winthrop lost the governorship and even his post as Commissioner of the United Colonies. It was a clean sweep for the Essex faction. But in 1645, after public reaction had cooled, the Winthrop party was back in power.

When the authorities of the Bay realized how serious the consequences of their indiscretion might be and that again they might be duped by another opportunist such as La Tour, who during his sojourn in Boston had posed as a Huguenot,[7] saner heads were allowed to prevail. A committee headed by Richard Saltonstall found that the "grounds of warre ought to be just," and for "the justice of this Warre by la Tore agaynst Daulnay, we conceive that all the light and information, New England hath, or may probably receive, cannot be sufficient for us to determine it positively." Foreign affairs affecting one colony affected all the New England colonies as a whole, and therefore properly belonged to the jurisdiction of the Confederation:

> Warres ought not to be undertaken without the Counsel and command of the supreame Authority whence expeditions issue. It is not hard to say, the present reference betweene the Kingdomes of England and France considered that the subjects of the one, ought not to wage warre against the other without a publike Commission of State, unlesse it be in defence upon a sudden assault.... It is a rule observed amongst Confoederates, that during any league of peace betweene them, one freind may not ayd another against any part of his province til that part be prescribed by the authority of a general assembly whereof it is a member, and the Confoederates, assured thereof in a state way. The breach of this rule is a breach of league. Publike actions of

hostility worke farre and wide haveing their national and confederal influences and consequences. The Daggers we draw here may happily prove swords in Christendome for ought we know.[8]

The matter of the La Tour-d'Aulney rivalry was thus brought before the next meeting of the Commissioners of the United Colonies. Realizing that such filibustering expeditions as Massachusetts had allowed to go forth might in the future provoke war with a foreign power, the Commissioners took upon themselves the responsibility to order that "no Jurisdiction within this Confederation shall permitt voluntaries to goe forth in a warlike way against any people whatsoever," without "order and direction of the Commissioners of the severall Jurisdictions."[9] The Massachusetts authorities were not held responsible for the aid given La Tour; rather the expedition had proceeded without commission or encouragement.[10]

Although cleared of responsibility in the La Tour expedition, Governor Winthrop at the time staunchly defended the right of one Confederate to allow a party to accompany La Tour to his destination—it being not an act of "hostility, but a meere Liberty of commerce." The Puritan Governor, nevertheless, pointed out that the "jesuiticall State have had an evill eye uppon us," and the Bay Colony if need be could well take care of itself from that quarter. It would not be the first time that Massachusetts would take a stand:

> In the treaty about our late Confederation, the doubtful construction of it in England, the danger from a Generall Governour (especially in regard of our brethren of Plimouth) the necessity of being involved in the quarrel with the Dutch, on the behalfe of our brethren of Hartford, were taken notice of by the Generall Court and many of the Elders...yet neither would the court be deterred hereby from entering into that brotherly league, nor were our Elders or people troubled with feare of those dangers.

Those of faint heart and little faith should once again take note of the ends of their coming into this wilderness and should not be afraid of tribulations.

> The Lord hath brought us hither through the swelling seas, through perills of Pyrats, tempests, leakes, fyres, Rocks, sands, diseases, starvings: and hath preserved us those many yeares from the displeasure of Princes, the envy and Rage of Prelats, the malignant Plotts of Jesuits, the mutinous contentions of discontented persons, the open and secret Attempts of barbarous Indians, the seditious and undermineing practises of hereticall false brethren, and is our Confidence and Courage all swallowed up in the fear of one D'aulnay?[11]

Trade intercourse, however, between Massachusetts and La Tour continued, until finally d'Aulney began seizing vessels belonging to the Bay. Thereupon Massachusetts sought terms with the Governor of Acadia at the first opportunity, which was soon forthcoming when an envoy of d'Aulney, M. Marie, journeyed to Boston in the autumn of 1644. Proceeding with the approval of the Confederation,[12] Massachusetts negotiated a preliminary treaty with the French envoy, by which the neutrality of Massachusetts was guaranteed in the French controversy.[13] But there was the stipulation by the Commissioners that if any more Massachusetts vessels were seized by d'Aulney, Massachusetts would have the right to make retaliation.[14] In 1645, Captain Robert Bridges was sent by the Commissioners,[15] via the Massachusetts General Court, to negotiate a treaty with d'Aulney in Acadia concerning the "speciall affaires of the commissioners for the United Colonyes."[16] The articles of a treaty had already been agreed upon by Marie and the Commissioners, who gave their consent only after "serious advice and consideration." By the Articles of Agreement both sides promised the continuance of peace, mutual trade, and that questions concerning injuries in the past be duly heard.[17]

But the French Governor did not take kindly to this treaty. At first he refused to sign the treaty borne by Captain Bridges, suspecting that the Massachusetts authorities were seeking to gain time. Finally when the Bay Colony offered to demonstrate its good faith by sending messengers to Penobscot with plenary powers to conclude a treaty on the spot with d'Aulney, the French Governor of Acadia was satisfied and in turn sent several of his deputies again to Boston. The French commissioners, arriving in Boston in August, 1646, met a grand reception, and after much ceremony a treaty was again concluded, by which both parties agreed to forget the past, provided that in the future Massachusetts should refrain from assisting La Tour. Meanwhile, during La Tour's absence, his fort was brutally subdued by d'Aulney—every prisoner taken was hanged, except one who acted as hangman and Madame La Tour who was forced to watch with a halter around her neck. This macabre finale had yet another peculiar twist: Madame La Tour soon died, and several years later so did d'Aulney, and in 1650 we find La Tour marrying the widow of his arch-enemy. For a number of years following, the relations with Acadia were to remain on the surface cordial with the New England authorities. In 1651 the Massachusetts Council declared only "neighborly" and "loving" friendship existed between themselves and the Acadians,[18] and in the same year Monsieur Belle-Ile of Port Royal paid a friendly visit to Boston.[19] La Tour, having come into possession of Acadia by marrying his rival's widow, was later forced to surrender to Cromwell's forces; but, forever an opportunist, he then changed allegiance to England and died the master of Acadia. In 1667, however, Acadia was returned to the French by the Treaty of Breda. Thus we have seen the course of the d'Aulney-La Tour-Massachusetts controversy. Control of foreign policy was given to the Confederation but was implemented on the Colony level.

One other aspect of the foreign policy of the early Confederation dealt with the French in America. Governor Winthrop and the commercial interests of the Bay Colony were back in power and sought again to further a commercial alliance with New France. Letters flowed from the Governor's office and finally an envoy was dispatched to Quebec; but before much progress could be made on a treaty Governor Winthrop died and negotiations were to lag for several years.[20] Yet conditions remained favorable for a treaty with New France: New England sought free trade, while the French were desirous of assistance in order to halt the increasing perimeter of Iroquois extermination of friendly Indians.

After Winthrop's death, the recently appointed Governor of New France, Louis D'Ailleboust, decided to resume negotiations with New England. Early in 1650 Father Gabriel Druillettes, the French Apostle to the Indians, was ordered to Boston to "treat with the Massachusetts and Plymouth Colonies about a league offensive and defensive."[21] But upon the arrival of the French envoys it was learned that the four English colonies were "confederate and that all treaties and leagues conserning warr or peace with others naighboring Nations or Collonies'" were now referred to the Commissioners of the United Colonies, and the French delegates were forced to return home for further instructions.[22]

After the return of Druillettes and his party, the Council of Quebec met early one morning with the French Governor, and it was decided to send two ambassadors to the Commissioners of the United Colonies: Druillettes again, and Jean Godefroy, a member of the Council—their object being a "Union between the Colonies of New France and New England for mutual trade."[23] It is of interest to note in what respect the authorities of New France viewed the New England Confederation. The instructions to the French envoys called for them to treat with either the Governor and Magistrates of New England or the "general Court of Commissioners and Deputies of the United Colonies."[24] Here is evidence again that the Commissioners were considered as an extension of the colonial councils of magistrates. It is not surprising that the French Governor was confused about who represented the supreme authority in New England. for he was informed by the Massachusetts Council that his propositions were referred to the "Generall Courte for their Consideration and Determination," but that they could not be finally approved until passed upon by the Commissioners of the United Colonies.[25] In a letter to the "commissioners of New England," the Quebec Council proposed that the basis of the treaty should be to "knit trade" and for its own advantage "lighten the expenses" of war against the Iroquois.[26]

During a visit in early 1650 Father Druillettes was met by John Winslow, brother of the agent of the colonies in London and a founder of the Confederation, at Augusta, an outlying English settlement, and was accompanied by Winslow to Boston.[27] During his several months' stay he was most hospitably entertained. Even a Puritan in that day could be broad-minded. The Jesuit priest was lodged in a house of one of the Assistants. He received a few pointers from John Eliot, the New England missionary to the Indians, and even was given a fish dinner by Governor Bradford of Plymouth. Undoubtedly Father Druillettes was also hospitably received on his return visit. Arriving in time for the annual meeting of the Commissioners then convened at New Haven, Father Druillettes and Councillor Godefroy laid their proposals before the Commissioners for what has been called the negotiations for the first reciprocal trade agreement in America.[28]

The proposals of the French called for the English to join them in a "holy war" against the Mohawks, the dominant member of the Iroquois Confederacy, in order to rescue some captured converted Indians. It seems that the primary motivation of the French was to save face with their Indian allies. If the Puritan colonies could not condescend to join, then they should at least permit the raising of volunteers and afford passage to the French forces—in return the French would guarantee free trade.[29] The French delegates did not realize it, but they were offering a proposal directly contrary to the purpose of the New England Confederation, which was to preserve peace. Touching upon the starting of an offensive war was also a sore point. Moreover, the policy of the Puritan colonies called for the neutralization of one Indian tribe while dealing more harshly with another— with the state of Indian affairs in New England as it was the neutrality of the Mohawks was essential.

The Commissioners of the United Colonies saw it was to their advantage to treat the French ambassadors firmly, yet with diplomacy. It was conceded that the French had just grounds for war and that "the English looke upon such Indians as Receive the yoake of Christ with another eye then upon others that Worship the Divell." But the Mohawks had shown respect for the English in the Pequot War and had not been hostile since. If the French wanted a direct route into Iroquois territory, why not take one of the Indian trails which penetrated into Canada? It would be out of the way to go via the New England Colonies. Alluring as a reciprocal trade treaty might be, it was not worth the price of a general Indian uprising. The Commissioners, therefore, refused to assent to any of the French proposals.

Though the English in these Jurisdictions are free to performe all Naighbourly offices of Righteousness and peace towards the French Collonie, yet they foresee they can neither permitt volenteers or Ausiliarye forces to bee taken up against the Mohaukes not that the French or Eastern Indians to pase through the English Jurisdictions to envade them; but they shall expose both the Christian and other Indians and some of the smaler English plantations to danger.[30]

The decision of the Commissioners "against a treaty for trade and defence against the Iroquois," in the words of one author, "is the only instance where the Council of the Confederation took formal action in the affairs of New France and held conference with a delegate from its Governor."[31] Because of their firm policy with the French and their refusal to be taken into alliance with them, the Commissioners showed an air of independence and strength that deterred the French from antagonizing the United Colonies for many decades.

During this "first Combination of the four united Colonies,"[32] the Commissioners showed a good deal of concern in the economic affairs of the colonies, but not to an extent that might have been expected. The medieval theory of a just price and the love of a well-ordered society prevailed among the Puritans, but the matters of regulation and economic policy were left largely to the individual general courts. Nevertheless, the Union was used as a springboard in certain economic fields in an attempt to establish uniform policy among the colonies.

In intercolonial as well as in foreign affairs, trade was an important concern of the Puritan colonies.[33] At the time of the forming of the Confederation, Indian trade was at its height,[34] and the colonies turned to the Confederation for encouragement in this activity. At the second annual meeting of the Commissioners at Boston in 1644, a plan was forwarded to the general courts for consolidating the Indian trade into one corporation of shareholders: the capitalization was to be from £5,000 to £10,000, with the minimum share at £20. Stockholders could buy shares with money or items fit for trade, such as wampum, beaver, English corn, or cattle;[35] and it may have been this lack of a single monetary system that prevented putting this joint-stock company in to effect, since it would be hard to determine the value of each contribution. The accounts of the proposed corporation were to be submitted to the Commissioners for certification.[36] Connecticut consented to go along with this joint-stock company,[37] and it is probable that Massachusetts and New Haven might also have consented, if Plymouth had not unalterably refused,[38] possibly on the grounds that very little capital

John Winthrop, Jr.

John Eliot

would be forthcoming from this, the poorest of the colonies, and she wished to retain what control over Indian trade she still had.

It is interesting to note the paradoxical attitude of the colonists in the seventeenth century towards the regulation of trade. The colonists themselves could regulate trade, require licenses, set standards on quality of goods, or even limit profits. But it was not thought within the power of the mother country to do so.[39]

The lack of a uniform specie in New England was a serious hindrance to the regulation of commerce and to the provision of a stable monetary policy. A tremendous amount of wampum was in existence in the colonies,[40] due to the intercourse with the natives, and until 1661 it was a lawful currency among the United Colonies.[41] Often the English were duped by the Indians with counterfeit wampum, such as dyed stone rather than the shells required, which led the Commissioners to recommend that the general courts take action against counterfeit wampum. Connecticut in 1648, therefore, ordered "that no peage, white or black, bee paid or received, but what is strung suitably"; and Massachusetts followed with similar legislation.[42] The so-called pine-tree shilling of Massachusetts came into use in 1652 to commemorate, during this first decade of the Confederation, the "Era of their Common Wealth, wherein they erected themselves into a free state, enlarged their dominions, subjected the adjacent Colonies under their obedience...."[43] The Confederation itself, however, made no attempts to establish a specific mode of exchange, The various forms of exchange continued, with silver from the West Indies continuing on a "quasi legal foundation" for a long time.[44]

A number of regulatory measures were enacted by the Commissioners, which were left to the individual colonies to implement. No articles of war were permitted to be sold to the Indians, and it was left to each colony to determine, in its trade with the French and Dutch, those articles of war that might fall into Indian hands.[45] By 1646, three of the colonies had followed these recommendations of the Commissioners, and had regulations on articles of war in the Indian trade. The general courts were also requiring that anyone dealing with war implements outside of the colonies should have a license given "under the hands of two magistrates of the Jurisdiction or at least under the hand of one Magistrate and two Deputies." Such licenses were to be recorded in a booke or memoriall in writinge that all the parcells or particulars with the quantities soe licensed, the persons to whome, and the grounds for which, upon occasion may be considered by the generall Courte or Comissioners for the Colonies.[46]

But a year later, when the Commissioners learned that their Indian enemies were being well supplied with English guns and ammunition, it was ordered for the present safety of the colonies that all licenses issued under the above authority be revoked.[47] The real source of supply, however, in arms and ammunition to the Indians came from the outside. To meet this situation the Commissioners in 1649 declared an embargo on French and Dutch goods entering English ports that were destined for the Indians, and it was recommended to the general courts to seize any goods or vessels engaged in such trade.[48]

Selling liquor to the Indians was a cause of much concern in all the Puritan colonies. In the many trading houses it was an easy thing to "give Indians a quart or two of liquors when they come with beaver,"[49] but the colonists were all too aware what the Yankee firewater could stir up among the young hotbloods of the Indians. Although several of the leading Commissioners in performing their magisterial duties on the colony level worked diligently in prohibiting spiritous liquors from coming into the hands of the Indians,[50] the Commissioners thought it best to leave all such legislation to the individual colonies, a lesson also learned from our own Prohibition Era. The only recommendation of the Commissioners was "That some safe provision bee made against selling or giveing strong Liquors to the Indians without particulare expresse Lycence" from an officer of a colony.[51] From time to time the Commissioners undertook to regulate the various aspects of New England economy through recommending a common policy for the members of the Confederation: the fields of their concern included wage fixing;[52] prohibiting mackerel fishing before the fish had spawned, since this was the "most staple comoditie in this Countrey";[53] in the face of the great influx of horses from the West Indies, keeping horses from falling into the hands of the Indians;[54] and establishing a uniform measure of eight gallons to the bushel.[55] Because of the lack of private capital and the early collective experience of the colonists, the colonies' general courts were

prone to aid the start of manufacturing in the colonies.[56] Grants
of land were given to aid new enterprises. Monopolies, such as
that of glass works in the Bay Colony, were permitted.[57] The
regulation of monopolies was left at the colony level. An attempt,
however, was made to divert funds sent over to the Commissioners from the Corporation to Promote the Gospel in order
to provide capital for the iron works at Lynn.[58]

The Commissioners during the early Confederation were much
concerned with the procedure for returning fugitives from justice.
Their most significant order provided that verdicts of one General Court should be honored in the General Courts of the other
colonies. If sufficient evidence should turn up after a conviction,
then the sentence of a fugitive from another colony might be
invalidated.[59] Interpreters were frequently sent out by the Confederation in search of Indian fugitives. Upon refusal of a tribe
to give up a fugitive, hostages were to be seized from the chief's
household.[60] The Commissioners tried to secure some form of
agreement with Rhode Island for the return of fugitives from the
United Colonies, but no agreement was reached.[61]

Several attempts were made by Rhode Island and the Gorges
province to come into the Confederation. In 1644, such an
attempt by Rhode Island failed because Rhode Island needed
a "better frame of government" and would have to submit
"absolutely and without reservation" either to Massachusetts or
Plymouth.[62] In 1648 a similar request from the Ishmael colony
was turned down for the same reasons and because Rhode Island
offered no security from the Indians. If Rhode Island, however,
would correct these deficiencies, then the Commissioners would
consider how they might come into the Union and thereby receive
"the same advise, protection And helpe which other Plantations
within the united Colonies Injoye."[63] When the Gorges province
expressed the desire to join the "consociation of the United
Colonies" in 1644, Winthrop advised the petitioners that there
was an "order not to receive any but such as were in a church
way."[64]

If an inhabitant from Rhode Island sought redress from
wrongs committed by the Indians by petitioning the Commissioners of the United Colonies, he would receive the reply that
the Commissioners pitied his condition, but since he belonged
to a jurisdiction outside of the United Colonies they could do
nothing about it. In 1649, a similar request came from the

town of Warwick and was turned down on the grounds that help could not "Rationally bee Expected" in the condition they were in.[65] By 1651, the Warwick community had a number of complaints against the Confederation which they were prepared to submit to Parliament, but first showed to the Commissioners. Chief among the grievances were the commercial restrictions imposed by Massachusetts and the attempt of Massachusetts to have them vacate their lands, in spite of an "order of Parliament" to the contrary.

> these Barbarius Indians about us with evill minded English Mixed amongst us under pretence of some former personall Subjection to the Government of the Massachusetts ...kill our Cattle, offer violence to our families, villifye Authoritie of Parliament vochsafed to us ....[66]

More will be said of the strife between the Warwick settlers and the United Colonies in Chapter Seven. The Commissioners were to give the Bay Colony the right of proceeding with a lone hand against the Warwick settlers, "according to what they should find Just engaging the Rest of the Jurisdictions to approve of and concure in the same as if theire Comissioners had been present."[67] But the summoning of Gorton before the Massachusetts Court was declared by the Commissioners to be "directly contrary to the order of the honorable committe of the parliament of England" and "Contrary to the articles of confederation With the Rest of the Collonies."[68]

Even during this early period of the Confederation the services of Roger Williams were acknowledged. In 1649, the Commissioners in recognition of the assistance of Williams in providing intelligence of Indian intentions, ordered that Providence was free from the authority of Massachusetts.[69] Williams's services continued, and, in 1651, he wrote that he was a "professed and known servant" to "all the Colonies of the English in peace and war," so that hardly a "weeke hath passed but some way or other I have bene used as instrumental to the peace and spreading of the English plantings in this Countrey."[70] Thus were the relations of the United Colonies to the New England colonies outside of the Confederation: where aid was given it was duly acknowledged, but as for those settlements on the fringe of the United Colonies, they were expected to be absorbed into one of the confederated colonies—as the settlements on Long Island Sound were coming under the jurisdiction of Connecticut or New Haven.

In the field of religion the Commissioners lent their weight to promote Puritan orthodoxy in the churches and colonies. A unified policy in ecclesiastical matters was deemed necessary because of the fear that if Presbyterianism triumphed in England, the churches of New England, which were running an Independent course themselves, might be brought under the tight control of the English Presbyterians.[71] Unity among the Congregational churches was, therefore, necessary as a means of self-defense, especially with the movement among the Puritan colonies for a broader base of toleration.[72] Ever since the first synod was convened in the 1630's to combat the Antinomian heresy, roots of dissension were everywhere spreading, whether in the form of the celebrated "Remonstrance and Humble Petition" of Robert Child et al., or the outright defiance of the colonial authorities by the Quakers.[73] To check the spread of error, it was time for another general meeting on consociation of representatives from the New England churches. Upon request from Massachusetts, the Commissioners of the United Colonies propounded to all the general courts the possibility of getting the elders together "to consider of some confession of doctrine and discipline with solid grounds to be approved by the Churches" for the "confirmeing the weake among our selves, and stoping the mouths of adversaries abroad."[74]

With the go-ahead signal given by the Commissioners a bill was passed in the Massachusetts General Court calling upon all those plantations "in the same Civill Combination and confederacie" as Massachusetts to send their "Elders and messengers" to a general assembly to be held at Cambridge.[75] A copy of this order was sent to all the governors and Commissioners of the "Confederate Jurisdictions."[76] The result of the ensuing Synod and the Platform of Church discipline adopted in 1648 further enhanced Puritan orthodoxy by making heresy punishable by the "coercive power of the Magistrate."[77] To keep heresy out of the colonies, however, would be a difficult task, as we shall see later. The narrow course of the confederated colonies was set. One of the pillars of the conservative party in the Bay Colony and Commissioner of the United Colonies, Thomas Dudley, wrote in his own epitaph the orthodox views

Let men of God in Courts and Churches watch
O'er such as do a toleration hatch,
Lest that ill egg bring forth a cockatrice,
To poison all with heresie and vice.
If men be left and otherwise combine,
My Epitaph's, I dy'd no libertine.[78]

The first decade of the Confederation saw the groundwork
laid for the "Indian Worke": the spreading of the Gospel among
the New England savages. Because of the threatened hostility
of the Indians throughout the decade and their preoccupation
with other things, the Commissioners were slow in establishing
a policy for converting the Indians. Noting the good work of
John Eliot in his labors among the conquered Pequots, however, the Commissioners were to recommend to the colonies that
an annual allotment of guns and ammunition be issued to the
converted Indians. In 1646 Edward Winslow of Plymouth was
sent to England by the Commissioners "as their agent about
some public affairs" which boiled down chiefly to securing a
charter for the Colony of Massachusetts. While he was there,
Winslow solicited Parliament to "constitute some worthy and
known persons of piety and integrity, to be a corporation to
receive and improve the free contributions of all persons for the
encouragement of this design, in propagating the christian religion among the Indian natives of New England in America."[79]
Such an act was passed by Parliament in 1649. The Commissioners at the Hartford meeting in 1650, assuming the Corporation would work through them, requested that £200 be advanced immediately by the Corporation so that there would be no
delay in the missionary work.[80] Edward Rawson was appointed
as agent to receive and distribute whatever the Corporation
would send over.[81] The Commissioners began the practice of
certifying the requests for provisions by those in the Indian
work and then forwarding these requisitions to the Corporation.[82]
Thus the powers of the Commissioners, by accepting responsibility of the Indian missionary work, were greatly enlarged, at
least in the sense that this field became the special jurisdiction
of the Commissioners. But little was it realized then that in
later years—indeed for the majority of the years of the Confederation—this would in actuality be their sole area of jurisdiction. After the nullification crisis of 1653-5, when the Confed-

eration was permitted to run down, to the time of its revival under a new set of Articles, the "Indian Worke" provided the cement of the Union.

The beginnings of federal aid for internal improvements[00] and for education can be found in this early period of the Confederation. In the field of education, the Commissioners were particularly active. The Puritan colonies at the time of the founding of the Confederation were becoming intensely aware of the need for general education. Harvard College, established in order to give to New England a well-trained clergy and civil leaders, sought to draw talents from all the confederated colonies. Because of the intercolonial interest in the college, the Commissioners of the United Colonies took it upon themselves to establish a means for the raising of funds, and until the incorporation of the college in 1650 functioned in many respects as a super board of trustees.

Although the college was the recipient of gifts, such as its library,[84] or received revenues from the Boston-Charlestown ferry,[85] or was even alloted large land grants,[86] there was need to provide for the support of "poor scholars" at Harvard. The Commissioners, therefore, appealed to all the colonies, asking that the freeborn of each family give annually the "fourth part of a bushel of corn" or its equivalent for this purpose.[87] In the ways that this revenue was to be put to use, President Dunster in 1647 asked that the Commissioners clear up certain questions: should students be taken from those jurisdictions which did not contribute; should all scholars benefit; would absence have any effect upon receiving aid; should grammar schools benefit from the collections; and what amounts should be applied to the president's salary, repairs, and books?[88] In their reply to these queries, the Commissioners recommended that those colonies and places which contributed the most should receive the first consideration in the selecting of students, but those jurisdictions that did not contribute, however, should not be neglected. None of the contributions should be applied to the grammar schools—their administration belonged to the individual colonies; it was the college that was the general concern of the United Colonies. Supplies obtained from the collections should be employed first for the use of the poor students and then for the common "advantage" of the college. Students receiving the benefits of the contributions were obligated to "attend the service" of their "country," and if not, to repay what they had received.[89]

The Commissioners, in perhaps the first instance in our history when the federal government through self-restraint sought to preserve the demarcation of powers between the central government and the state governments, stated that it was not their intention to encroach upon the right of the individual colonies in education. They would

> promote the contributions accordinge to the former propositions, but doe not judge it meete to put it into any other frame. The other particulars mentioned belonge properly to this Jurisdiction wherein the Commissioners will not intermeddle, but refer the consideration therof to the wisedome and piety of the general Courte for this colony.[90]

The efforts of the Commissioners to "stir up" a "yearly contribution," so observed a contemporary, was observed by some, but "by the most very much neglected."[91] Indeed, the "Corne" contributions, which were to amount to a peck of wheat or a pine-tree shilling or the same in wampum from each family, was a disappointment.[92] Nevertheless, three of the United Colonies wholeheartedly backed this scheme of the Commissioners, and in the first year it was put to test New Haven reported that forty bushels were contributed for the college.[93] A campaign was conducted throughout the colonies to encourage raising of these funds. All officials were requested to use their influence in whatever capacity they served—whether in church or civil affairs.[94] In Massachusetts a circular was put out by the "Committee on Contributions to Harvard College" entreating the inhabitants to "contribute freely as the Lord should enlarge there Spirits."[95] Even the bachelor theses at Harvard appealed to the union sentiment of the colonies, bearing a dedication not only to the governor but also to the governors and magistrates of all the United Colonies.[96] Certain towns were more enthused than others: for instance Haverhill went on record for an annual contribution at £4 7s,[97] while Newbury after a very hard winter came up with a donation of £15.[98] Collectors were annually appointed by the towns to receive the "Colledg corne," and in the town of New Haven a former Secretary of the Colony, James

Bishop, was appointed to do what he could to compel "those which are behinde in paying the colledg corne."[99]

Nevertheless, the collection of the "Colledg corne" asked for by the Commissioners went a long way in the support of Harvard.[100] Although complaints about the "yearly decay" of the buildings were voiced until the original buildings became uninhabitable in 1677,[101] these contributions for at least seven years supported two or three teaching fellows, eight or ten scholars and exhibitioners, and two undergraduate stewards. "In other words, the farmers of New England, with voluntary contributions amounting to 6,000 pecks of wheat, or their equivalent at a shilling a peck, supported the entire teaching staff of Harvard College, excepting the President, for a space of eight years; as well as assisting ten or twelve poor scholars."[102] One of the reasons that the gifts declined was due to many of the graduates migrating to England where they hoped to take advantage of opportunities opened by the Civil War there[103]—thus many New Englanders felt their contributions to Harvard for educating leaders for service to the "Countrie" were being wasted.

The role of the Commissioners as a board of arbitration in land disputes during this decade was particularly useful to the United Colonies. Chapter Seven will deal with controversies in this field; it will suffice here to point out only several of the decisions of the Commissioners in order to illustrate the independent course they were capable of taking.

In 1644, the plantation of Seaconck was awarded to Plymouth, thereby invalidating the Massachusetts claim. The Commissioners again decided against Massachusetts in 1646, when they awarded the plantation of John Winthrop, Jr., in the Pequot country to Connecticut.[104] In 1647 a claim of Winthrop, Jr., who was to become the man of greatest prestige in New England, to a "greate quantity of land at Nyanticott" was invalidated by the Commissioners because the certificate of purchase bore no date, the boundaries were not defined, and the Indian who deeded the lands to Winthrop did not possess the lands to give the grant being a verbal "transient airy passage." It was also ruled that Winthrop was an agent of Saybrook at the time and was not acting individually, and that the lands had been justly conquered by Connecticut before Winthrop's claim.[105]

In 1649, the question arose concerning the division of certain

Indian lands between Massachusetts and Plymouth. The Bay Colony denied the right of arbitration by the other Commissioners to "resigne or pase over any tracte of londe within theiro patteni to another jurisdiction without Concent and expresse lycence from the Generall Court Intressed."[106] The Commissioners from the two colonies then got together, and with the spirit of magnanimity prevailing, each side offered to give the territory to the other. But in the settlement Massachusetts won the dispute.[107]

Related to the impost controversy between Massachusetts and Connecticut was the question of the boundary at Springfield. Both the River and the Bay colonies were adamant in their claims on Springfield. Massachusetts would not submit the question to arbitration by the Commissioners,[108] and the question, therefore, was settled only by the voluntary decision of Springfield to come under the Massachusetts jurisdiction.[109] Many disputes such as this one which came before the Confederation were not settled; but the Commissioners were useful at least in airing the controversies and defining the issues.

The most bitter controversy among the United Colonies and one which severely taxed the ingenuity of the Confederation during this first decade was the tariff war between Massachusetts and Connecticut. When Connecticut bargained for the Saybrook Fort at the mouth of the Connecticut River, it was agreed that the Colony would take over the duties of 2d. per bushel upon exported grain, 6d. upon biscuits at the Fort and an annual tax upon hogs and cattle.[110] Springfield, up the river, was doing a flourishing trade with Boston, and when Connecticut started collecting duties at the Fort, it was expected that Springfield would be forced to depend more upon the River Colony than upon the Bay. But Massachusetts would have none of it. The right of Connecticut to levy a custom at Saybrook was challenged because it affected the shipping from Springfield, which was counted in the Bay fold.

The question was brought up at the New Haven meeting in 1646, but because William Pynchon of Springfield could not be represented, full debate on the subject was postponed until the next meeting. The next meeting proved strategic. Massachusetts did not wait until the regular session of the Commissioners convened in September, but rather took advantage of an extraordinary session called for dealing with the Indian menace, which was meeting in Boston under the eyes of the General Court. William Pynchon was there this time, and, with Massachusetts backing, bluntly refused to pay the 2d. per bushel on grain.[111] The Massachusetts argument stated that there was no legal power to force other jurisdictions to pay for the maintenance of a fort at Saybrook to which the custom was applied, that this fort was injurious to those who were having to pay for it, and that the territory occupied by the fort originally belonged to Massachusetts. It was also noted that while members of the Confederation had to pay the impost, foreign shipping, such as that of the Dutch, was exempt. It was declared that if this impost were continued the Bay Colony would take retaliatory measures.[112] The Commissioners from Connecticut defended the impost: it was based upon equity and righteousness; the fort had been useful to all the colonies since the time of the Pequot War and would continue to be useful; the Massachusetts claim of original jurisdiction over the river towns was merely a false pretense; a trade as profitable as the beaver traffic ought to contribute to the maintenance of the fort; and it was conceded that the other confederated colonies had the right to levy an impost in parallel cases.[113]

For settling this dispute, the New Haven and Plymouth Commissioners were selected as arbitrators. As might have been expected these small colonies decided against the haughty Bay. The decision was entirely favorable to Connecticut, stating that trade from Springfield should be subject to a custom upon passing Saybrook at the rate of 2d. per bushel of corn and 20s. per hogshead of beaver; while in the future no impost could be levied upon any inhabitant of Springfield unless allowed by the United Colonies. At the session of the Commissioners in 1648, however, the Massachusetts Commissioners refused to accept this decision, claiming that the New Haven Commissioners were not impartial in their findings. The Connecticut Colony was accused of not having a patent for Saybrook, and had no right to exercise authority there without the consent of the Bay. To the Massachusetts Commissioners, the whole affair was a "boane Cast in by Sathan to interupt our happy peace and brotherly union, and to raise discord amongst us."[114]

During the course of this long debate, the Commissioners from the three smaller colonies held firm that Connecticut had the right to levy an impost on the Springfield shipping: Springfield was receiving greater benefit from Fort Saybrook than New Haven, and to make a comparison with a town away from the river was not actually fair; the Connecticut patent, which the Commissioners had seen, had been upheld by Parliament; the impost was used for erecting and maintaining the Saybrook fort and not to purchase land or for any other purpose; the fort provided for the safety of all the river towns; and it would be difficult to force foreigners to pay the impost, especially the Dutch, who claimed all the lands from Cape Cod to Hartford. The maxim in law should hold, that if one possesses something in the way of another, he has a right to levy a charge for passage.[115] The Massachusetts General Court attempted to nullify the Commissioners' decision,[116] but the impost remained in effect despite this effort. Six of the eight Commissioners, according to the Articles of Confederation, thus had acted independently and contrary to the will of Massachusetts, thereby demonstrating they would and could repudiate on occasion the dominance of the Bay. If in the Union a quorum of seven was required for determining questions, as was the case of the Massachusetts Council,[117] a rending of the Union may have been avoided.

That Massachusetts was ready at this point to pursue a course of nullification, may be explained by the pressure put upon the Bay from the inhabitants of Springfield, whose support was needed to make good Massachusetts' jurisdiction over Springfield. A committee of the leading men of Springfield had drawn up a petition, pointing out that the Commissioners from New Haven and Plymouth in their findings against Massachusetts had not proceeded as "Judges of Record ought to do." These Commissioners should have first judged the record rather than pursued arbitration at once, assuming the record to be straight —that is, they should have begun with asking Connecticut to produce an order establishing the impost, which it was assumed she could not do. After going into other equally fine points, the Committee asked the General Courts and Commissioners of the colonies for the "utter nullifying of all former proceedings against Springfield as God hath put into theyre hands by the Articles of Confederation."[118]

At the meeting of the Commissioners in 1649, the Massachusetts General Court was put on record holding that the fort at Saybrook was not worth paying for, that the Bay Colony had its own forts to support. Furthermore, goods from all three of

the other confederated colonies, imported or exported from any
fort in the Bay, should pay a custom duty upon penalty of
forfeiture.[119] This was viewed by the Commissioners from the
other colonies as a "Returne or Retalliation uppon the three
colonies for sebrook and the law Requires it of no other English
nor of any stranger of what nation soever." The Commissioners
now had their fill of the controversy and realizing they could
do nothing to get the Bay to mend her ways, declared that they
henceforth be "spared in all further agitations Concerning sprink-
field."[120] Nevertheless, an extraordinary session was arranged
to treat with the question again, but the Massachusetts General Court and Commissioners ignored the invitation.[121] There
the matter rested until 1650, when upon hearing the "Rumore
that Connecticut was requiring no more custom," the Massachusetts Court immediately suspended its retaliatory impost
until word would be received that Connecticut was again charg-
ing a custom fee at Saybrook.[122] Meanwhile the fort had burned
down and it seems, declares one author, "to have been so providential an event that the fire might have been set by some
adherent of either party."[123]

Thus the Springfield impost controversy was finally settled
outside of arbitration or negotiations, but not until the Commissioners, in a duly constituted quorum, had stood firm against the
demands of the Bay. The division in the Confederacy between
the largest member of the Union and the three smaller members,
however, was shaping up, and was portentous of things to come.

In spite of the fact that certain constitutional questions
were raised during this period,[124] the Confederation for the most
part functioned smoothly and efficiently. The activities of the
Confederation covered a tremendous scope of problems, a number of which were successfully settled. Three major areas of the
work of the early Confederation, that of policies concerning the
Indians, lands, and the Dutch, will be treated in subsequent
chapters. The Confederation during this first decade had provided leadership in both internal and external affairs, creating
a solidarity in action essential to the existence of the infant New
England colonies. The diplomatic skill of the Commissioners in
foreign policy and Indian affairs could well be studied with
profit today. The singular outstanding contribution of the period,
of which it cannot be denied that the Confederation was largely
responsible, was the preserving of peace. The New England Con-

federacy was indeed meeting the expectations of its founders. The United Colonies of New England, for all practical purposes, was functioning as a sovereign body. Except for a few instances from tumbling with the general courts in matters such as the impost controversy, the decisions of the Commissioners were unanimous, and there was no need to question their authority. The Confederacy was dealing exclusively in foreign affairs on the policy level, and was acknowledged as the sovereign body of New England by both the French and Dutch. The Indians would be forced to acknowledge the supremacy of the United Colonies. Though mistrusted in the realm of intercolony affairs, the Commissioners acted in many instances as a final court of arbitration.

The view of those who may have considered the Confederation invested with sovereign powers would soon be proven illusory. By the very construction of the Confederacy it could not be otherwise. The idea that the Confederation was sovereign was to be exploded during the constitutional crises of 1653-5.

The year 1652 marks the end of this decade of optimism of the Confederation, although the three following chapters will carry the work of the Confederation to the breaking off point: Indian affairs until the appearance of the factors leading to King Philip's War; the Dutch relations to the end of the first Anglo-Dutch War; and the intricate land disputes until the revival of the Confederation under the new Articles. Because of the procedural questions involved in the meeting at Plymouth in 1652, this meeting was held "frustrate," and the Commissioners relaxed, giving advice only on several Indian problems. But the energy conserved was not wasted, for it was to be consumed in the heated controversies of the following year.

---

[1] Hooker to Winthrop, 15Jul43, *Winthrop Papers*, IV, 401-2.

[2] PCR, IX, 12.

[3] Cf. *MCR*, III, 151.

[4] Francis D. Davenport, ed., *European Treaties Bearing on the History of the United States and its Dependencies to 1648*, (Washington, D. C.: Carnegie Inst., 1917), Pub. No. 254, pp. 247-52.

[5] Howard M. Chapin, *The First Century of American Colonial Privateering, 1625-1725* (Toulon, France: 1926), p. 24.

[6] Joseph H. Twichell, *John Winthrop* (New York: 1892), p. 208.

[7] Augustine Jones, *The Life and Work of Thomas Dudley* (Boston: 1899), pp. 350-1.

[8] Richard Saltonstall, et. al. to the Gov., Dep. Gov., Assistants and Elders, 14July43, *Winthrop Papers*, IV, 397-399.

[9] *PCR*, IX, 22.

[10] *Ibid.*, pp. 50-9.

[11] *Winthrop Papers*, IV, 406-10.

[12] *PCR*, IX, 25.

[13] Count Julius de Menou, "Notice of the Sieur D'Aulnay of Acadie," trans. by W. Jenks, *MHSC*, 4:IV:463-8.

[14] *PCR*, IX, 59.

[15] Winthrop, *Journal*, II (Savage), 259.

[16] *MCR*, III, 44.

[17] *PCR*, IX, 59.

[18] Endicott with consent of all the magistrates to Madame De Aulnay, 12Jun51, Council Records, I, MA.

[19] "Papers Relative to the Rival Chiefs, D'Aulnay and La Tour," *MHSC*:3:-VII:117. D'Aulnay's father, after his son's death, in behalf of his daughter-in-law also sought a "good and powerful alliance friendshipp and Confederation" with New England. (To Governor and Magistrate of Mass., 2Mar51, Council Records, I, MA.)

[20] S. Roy Weaver, "The First Negotiations for Reciprocity in North America," *Journal of Political Economy*, XIX (1911), 411-2.

[21] Palfrey, *op. cit.*, II, 306.

[22] *PCR*, IX, 200.

[23] Extract from the Registers of the Ancient Council., 20Jun51, *Colonial History of New York*, Paris Docs., IX, 6; James P. Baxter, ed., *Documentary History of Maine*, Baxter MSS (Portland: 1889), 2nd Series, IV, 22. The French envoys were empowered "pour traitter avec les commissaires de les Nouvelle Angleterre."

[24] Commission to the Rev. Father Druillettes and M. Jean Godefroy as Ambassadors to N. E., *Colonial History of New York*, Paris Docs., IX, 6-7.

[25] Meeting of the Mass. Council, 3Dec50, Council Recs., I, MA.

[26] Council of Quebec to commissioners of New England, 20Jun51, *Colonial History of New York*, Paris Doc., IX, 5.

[27] Weaver, *loc. cit.*, pp. 413-4.

[28] Weaver, *loc. cit.*

[29] *PCR*, IX, 200.

[30] *PCR*, IX, 202-3.

[31] James Douglas, *New France and New England*, (New York: G. P. Putnam's Sons, 1913), p. 495.

[32] In the words of a contemporary. John Josselyn, *An Account of Two Voyages to New-England, 1638 and 1663* (Boston: 1865), p. 198.

[33] A. H. Buffington in "New England and the Western Fur Trade, 1629-75," *PCSM*, XVIII, pp. 169-73 and in "External Relations" A. B. Hart, ed., *Commonwealth History of Massachusetts, I*, 492-521, presents the thesis that trade was the sole cause of the Confederation and the chief problem after it was

formed. This of course is an oversimplification, but trade was nevertheless a most important factor.

[34] William B. Weeden, *Economic and Social Hist. of N. E., 1620-1789,* (Boston: 1890), I, 42.

[35] *Ibid.,* p. 179.

[36] *PCR,* IX, 22-3.

[37] *CCR,* I, 113.

[38] *PCR,* II, 82; Massachusetts had already formed a "free company of adventurers" for trade, and probably originated this plan. (*MCR,* II, 60-1.)

[39] E. A. J. Johnson, *American Economic Thought in the Seventeenth Century,* (London: 1932), pp. 142-3.

[40] Frank G. Speck, "The Functions of Wampum Among the Eastern Algonquins," *Memoirs of the American Anthropological Association,* VI (1919), p. 57.

[41] Weeden, *op. cit.,* p. 44.

[42] Henry Bronson, "A Historical Account of Connecticut Currency," *Papers of the NHCHS,* I, (1865), 4-6, takes the view that the period of commercial intercourse with the natives corresponded with the attempts of the colonies for their religious conversion. William B. Weeden, *Indian Money as a Factor in New England Civilization, JHUS,* 2:VIII-IX:49.)

[43] Stevens Transcripts, II, John Carter Brown Lib. These are the words of that arch-enemy of Puritan Orthodoxy, E. Randolph, 12Oct76.

[44] Weeden, *Economic History, op. cit.,* p. 44.

[45] *PCR,* IX, 21.

[46] *PCR,* IX, 65-6.

[47] *Ibid.,* p. 105.

[48] *Ibid.,* p. 149.

[49] "Return of those . . . appointed to make search for stronge liquors and powder and shott" (Mass.), Peck Coll., MSS, I,4, RIHS, 13Nov55.

[50] E.g., on the part of William Hathorne in refusing to allow liquor to be sold to Indians unless properly licensed (Hathorne to the Court, 26Oct70, Essex Institute, Hathorne Papers), or one of the first orders under Thomas Danforth's administration of the Province of Maine was the prohibition of the sale of liquor to the Indians (Folsom, George, *History of Saco and Biddeford, Maine,* (Saco: 1830), p. 189). In 1654 Massachusetts began clamping down on the "sinfull and offensive abuse" of selling liquor to the Indians. (Order of the Gen. Ct., 4Nov54, MA, XXX, 35.)

[51] *PCR,* X, 158.

[52] R. B. Morris and J. Grossman, "The Regulation of Wages in Early Massachusetts," *NEQ,* XI (Sep, 1938), 480.

[53] *PCR,* X, 251.

[54] *Ibid.,* p. 156.

[55] C. M. Green, *loc. cit.,* p. 237.

[56] Victor Clark, *History of Manufactures in the United States,* (1607-1860), (Washington, D. C.: Carnegie Institute, 1929), I, 42.

[57] Andrew McF. Davis, "Corporations in the Days of the Colony," *PCSM*, I (Trans., 1895), 195.

[58] Petition . . ., 22July53, MA, LIX, 46.

[59] *CCR*, I, 113n.; *PCR*, IX, 25.

[60] E.g., *PCR*, IX, 142.

[61] *Ibid.*, pp. 215-6. Many "notorious delinquents" had been escaping to Portsmouth.

[62] *PCR*, IX, 23. "The worst disavowal of his own principles was when Coddington applied . . . to be admitted to the Confederation." (Weeden, Paper on "William Coddington," *MHSP*, XLIV, 587.)

[63] *PCR*, IX, 110.

[64] Winthrop,

[65] *PCR*, IX, 150.

[66] *Ibid.*, pp. 217-8.

[67] PCR, IX, 218-9. The Massachusetts claim was based upon purchase from the Indians and that Plymouth, the original settlers, had relinquished their claim in favor of Massachusetts.

[68] *Ibid.*, p. 222.

[69] Williams to Winthrop, Jr., 14Sep49, *MHSC*:2:III:256-7.

[70] Petition of Roger Williams, *MHSC*:4:IV:471-2.

[71] Palfrey, *op. cit.*, II, 165-6.

[72] *Ibid.*, p. 170.

[73] The Puritans and Quakers, it has been pointed out, differed on but two points. The Puritans felt that the church was necessary and that "the Holy Spirit paid his official visit of notification to the justified heart, and then left him to his own self-management . . . with a new ideal of manhood, and a new moral ability to fulfill that ideal"; while the Quakers held that the church was superfluous and that the Holy Spirit "came in to stay and keep complete control of that life." (Charles E. Park, "Puritans and Quakers," *NEQ*, XXVII (May-Dec., 1954), 73.

[74] *PCR*, IX, 28.

[75] A Bill for a General Assembly of Churches . . ., 15 May46, MA, X, 189.

[76] *Ibid.*

[77] David B. Ford, *New England's Struggles for Religious Liberty*, (Philadelphia: 1896), p. 56.

[78] *Ibid.* The advantages of united action was set forth in the Preface to the Cambridge Platform of 1648, picturesquely: "Bees may bring more hony, and wax into the hive, when they are not limited to one garden of flowers, but may fly abroad to many." Williston Walker, *The Creeds and Platforms of Congregationalism*, (New York: 1893), p. 201.

[79] Daniel Gookin, "Historical Collections for the Indians in New England," *MHSC*:1:I:212.

[80] *PCR*, IX, 166.

[81] *Ibid.*, p. 206. Among the goods sent over the first year were hoes and other

iron ware, linen, wooden shoes, and stockings (192-6). The Commissioners, taking a precaution against backsliders, ordered that if any fall off after receipt of such help a mark should be put on them so that they wouldn't deceive the second time. (201)

[82] *PCR*, IX, 195.

[83] In 1644 the Commissioners, acting upon a petition "desireing the mending of some places in the way from the Bay to Connectacutt," ordered the President of the Confederation, Edward Hopkins, to employ someone or persons to "lay out the best way to the Bay, and the charge to be borne by the whole." (*PCR*, IX, 25.)

[84] Samuel E. Morison, *The Founding of Harvard College*, (Cambridge: Harvard University Press, 1935), p. 269. The total cash receipts up to 1654 amounted to £928 14 4. (Josiah Quincy, *The History of Harvard Unversity* (Boston: 1860), p. 459.

[85] Morison, *op. cit.*, p. 299.

[86] E.g., the 500 acres granted by the Massachusetts General Court in the Pequot Country. (Decl. of John Richards, 21Jun70, CA, Boundary (R.I.), I, 68.)

[87] *PCR*, IX, 20-1. To collect this revenue in Connecticut, it was ordered "that 2 men shalbe appoynted in every Towne within this Jurisdiction, who shall demaund what every family will give, and the same to be gathered and brought into some roome, in March; and this to continue yearely as that shalbe considered by the Commissioners." (*CCR*, I, 112.) The Rev. Thomas Shepard of Cambridge was credited with suggesting this voluntary method of taxation. (Andrew McF. Davis, *Hints of Contemporary Life in the Writings of Thomas Shepard*, (Cambridge: 1908), pp. 138-9.)

[88] *PCR*, IX, 94-5. Dunster in 1651 also requested Winslow to secure the consent of the Corporation in England to divert some of their funds to Harvard College, since it would aid the Indians indirectly. (216-7) Dunster had also made three previous drives to secure funds on his own. ("Harvard College Collections," *PCSM*, XXXI, 304.)

[89] *PCR*, IX, 95-6.

[90] *Ibid.*

[91] Jameson, ed., Johnson's *Wonder-Working Providence, op. cit.*, p. 201.

[92] Samuel E. Morison, *Harvard College in the Seventeenth Century*, (Cambridge: Harvard University Press, 1936), p. 26.

[93] Morison, *Founding of Harvard College, op. cit.*, p. 315-6.

[94] Felt, *Ipswich, op. cit.*, p. 92; Frederick Freeman, *Annals of Barnstable County*, (Boston: 1860-2), II, 258.

[95] MA, LVIII, 24, 31Oct53.

[96] Morison, *Founding of Harvard College, op. cit.*, p. 315.

[97] George W. Chase, *The History of Haverhill, Mass.* (Haverhill: 1861), p. 78.

[98] Joshua Coffin, *The History of Newbury*, (Boston: 1845), p. 58.

[99] Franklin B. Dexter, ed., *New Haven Town Records, 1649-62*, (New Haven: 1917), p. 131.

[100] Morison, *Founding of Harvard, op. cit.*, p. 318.

[101] Andrew McF. Davis, "The Early College Buildings at Cambridge," *AASP*, New Series, VI, 343-4.

[102] Morison, *op. cit.*

[103] *Ibid.*, p. 319.

[104] *PCR*, IX, 79.

[105] *Ibid.*, pp. 103-4.

[106] *Ibid.*, pp. 158-9.

[107] *Ibid.*, p. 170.

[108] *Ibid.*, pp. 150-1.

[109] S. E. Baldwin, "The Secession of Springfield from Connecticut," *PCMS*, XII, 82. In May, 1649, the first deputy from Springfield took his seat in the Massachusetts General Court. In 1650 the Commissioners washed their hands of the Springfield controversy, and from that time on the incorporation of Springfield in Massachusetts was never seriously contested. (S. E. Morison, "William Pynchon," *MHSP*, LXIV, 89.)

[110] Mason A. Green, *Springfield, 1636-1886*, (Springfield: 1888), p. 83.

[111] *Ibid.*, p. 87.

[112] *PCR*, IX, 89-90.

[113] *Ibid.*, pp. 90-2.

[114] *PCR*, IX, 124-5.

[115] *Ibid.*, p. 135.

[116] *Ibid.*, p. 133. ". . . wee concaive the Commissioners have Noe power to macke ane order to Injoyne Custom or Impost to bee payed by any perticuler towne to its owne or any other Jurisdiction . . . that being an act of Government . . . preserved Intire," by the third and sixth Articles of Confederation to each colony.

[117] Narrative by Edward Randolph, 12Oct76, Stevens Transcripts, II, 104, John Carter Brown Library. The Tory historian, Thomas Hutchinson, wrote of this period: "The union or confederacy had rendered the colonies formidable to French and Dutch as well as to the natives, and a breach at this time would have given great advantage to the enemies of New-England." (re Springfield controversy. Hutchinson, *op. cit.*, I, 156.)

[118] Committee of Springfield . . ., 9 Apr49, Misc. MSS, I, MHS.

[119] *PCR*, IX, 155.

[120] *PCR*, IX, 158; *MCR*, II, 268-9.

[121] *PCR, ibid.*

[122] *MCR*, III, 191.

[123] W. DeL. Love, "The Navigation of the Connecticut River," *AASP*, XV, 391.

[124] Besides the Springfield impost controversy, the debates on the amending process. See Chapter IV.

CHAPTER VI

Quest for Indian Policy

Inimical clouds of war loomed on the horizon of the infant Confederacy. The Union of 1643 had been conceived in a decade of Indian unrest, during which time the colonists experienced the terrors of the Pequot uprising. The civilizations of the white man and the red man were not destined to live side by side. As settlers swarmed over the New England hills—making themselves at home in the hunting grounds of proud Indian tribes—the friction between the two races mounted until the inevitable flames of war engulfed the countryside. Massachusetts was confronted by potentially hostile tribes in several quarters: the Nipmucks and remnants of various tribes within her midst, the deadly Iroquois League on the west, and the Abenakis spurred on by the French from the northeast. Plymouth was ill at ease with the Pokanokets (Wampanoags), who later produced King Philip; near New Haven were the Quinnipiacs; and on the upper Connecticut were the Pocomtucks. The great Narragansett alliance of tribes in southern New England was a concern for all the United Colonies. The Mohegans of the lower Connecticut River constantly vied for the support of the English against their Narragansett enemies. Everywhere it appeared there were legions of the Devil, whom in time Jehovah would lead into the hands of a faithful People.

The year 1643 saw a fresh outbreak of Indian wrath. Anne Hutchinson of Antinomian fame, who after her exile from the Bay had found a haven on Long Island, was massacred with her family. The Dutch Governor at New Amsterdam was having his hands full with Indian vengeance against his indiscreet policy; and within the confines of New England a great war was shaping up between the Mohegans and the Narragansetts. Once the powder keg of local Indian warfare was touched off, it was feared a conflagration throughout the countryside would bring all of the Algonquian tribes in one grand alliance against the snug English settlements. Every tree was suspected to conceal

118

the eyes and ears of a lurking savage. The Indian situation had hastened the calling of the Confederation. The task of keeping the Indian malcontents of New England in line demanded urgency, and it now belonged to the Commissioners of the United Colonies to direct the course of Indian affairs for all the four United Colonies.

What policy would the Puritan colonies adopt? They were committed to the spreading of the Gospel throughout the new Cannan, including the poor ignorant savages who had never heard of the True Word and Saving Grace. Only a few savages could be reached: those whose will had been broken by the English conquest (the premise for the converting of the Indians in New England was not essentially different from the necessity of the Spanish conquistadors preceding the Catholic missionaries in their far-flung American empire); those savages who would tolerate the New England missionaries as a curiosity; or in the case of the Mohegans, those seeking to court the favor of the English. But since most of the natives of New England could not be reached with the soothing hand of the Gospel, the various Indian tribes had to be treated much as if they were foreign nations. Fortunately for the New England settlers, the American Indians had a natural inclination to fight among themselves. Thus, taking advantage of this propensity by making friends with some of the Indians while dealing sternly with others, the colonists sought to establish a balance of power, which they could use in a divide-and-conquer fashion to bring one tribe after another into submission. The remarkable thing about the early Indian policy of New England was the consistency with which the Puritan fathers went to great lengths to pacify certain tribes, while, equally as consistent, antagonizing other tribes. In Indian affairs, the dominant note was expediency rather than principle.

At the beginning of the Confederation, the Narragansetts did not "sit down quiet" as was expected because of the Treaty of 1638.[1] These natives in alliance with a brother tribe, the Niantics, occupied the coveted lands on the rim of Narragansett Bay, east of the present-day site of New London. There were rumors in the air that the Narragansetts were setting about to incite the other Indians against the English, even to the extent of having sent an "incredible" amount of wampum to "procure" the Mohawks to harassment of the western flank of the English settlements.[2] Already there had been several murders committed by the Narragansetts on the Mohegans, one of the victims being the squaw of a sachem.[3] The Narragansetts were not friendly to the English, having long resented the protection by the English of tributary tribes which had deserted;[4] the Mohegans, however, were considered allies of the English and had even afforded valuable aid during the Pequot War. There was no doubt in the Commissioners' minds that it was better to retain the friendship of the Mohegans, who had demonstrated their military value, than to follow a middle-of-the-road course, seeking justice for all, which would run the risk of alienating both tribes. As war clouds threatened from the two opposing camps of the Narragansetts and the Mohegans, the great Narragansett sachem, Miantinomo, asked leave of the United Colonies, in keeping with his obligation to do so by the Tripartite Treaty of 1638,[5] to permit the two tribes to fight it out alone, without English intervention. Since the Mohegans had been as guilty as the Narragansetts in the committing of murders and hostilities which were leading to warfare, the Governor of Connecticut, to whom Miantinomo took his appeal, stated that a conflict between the two tribes would be considered strictly Indian business, "that the English had no hand in it, nor would encourage them.[6]

This guarantee, however, of nonintervention is called by an able observer as the "sheerest hypocricy" on the part of the Puritan fathers, for once the Narragansetts were on the warpath, the English looked upon war as an opportunity to deal a blow to this unfriendly tribe. The same authority of Rhode Island sees even a deeper motive on the part of the Puritan colonies than the attrition of their Indian enemies; if the war went against the Narragansetts, the United Colonies, which were "driving ahead impetuously on a course of imperial expansion," could assert their jurisdiction over Rhode Island,[7] whose lands were based upon deeds from the Narragansetts. A full-scale battle was soon joined by the two rival Indian tribes, and the Narragansetts were decisively defeated. Miantinomo, wearing a heavy coat of armor, was unable to flee, and was captured by his arch-enemy, Uncas, the Mohegan sachem.[8]

With his enemy delivered into his hands Uncas sought to make the most of the opportunity. To kill his rival outright would have been too easy, and might bring down the fury of all the Narragansett people, who were far from being crushed, and in such an event the aid of the English might not be forthcoming. Moreover, the settlers at Warwick were demanding that Uncas release his enemy.[9] If Uncas, however, could secure the permission of the Confederation to execute his enemy, then he would have committed the United Colonies to his side, and an attack on him in the future by the Narragansetts would, in view of Puritan consistency and the idea of covenant, be looked upon as an attack upon the Puritan colonies. Uncas thus turned the fate of his prisoner over to the Commissioners of the United Colonies.

Miantinomo was held prisoner at Hartford, while the Commissioners at their first meeting at Boston, in the form of a high court, judiciously debated the fate of the unfortunate sachem. It was concluded that "it would not be safe to set him at liberty, neither had we sufficient ground for us to put him to death." Thus the authorities had already decided upon death, but a justification for execution had to be found—by obtaining the consent of "five of the most judicious elders." The decision unanimously was death. But the Puritans did not want blood on their hands, and much in the fashion of a Pontius Pilate, stipulated that the death sentence must not be carried out in English territory. For fear of a Narragansett uprising, the Commissioners ordered that their decision be kept secret until after the execution. The Connecticut Commissioners, therefore, on their return home were to deliver the captive sachem over to Uncas to be put to death with "all mercy and moderation." The Mohegan chieftain thus was authorized to "justly put such a false and bloud-thirstie enimie to death," one who conspired to bring about a "general conspiracy among the Indians to cut off all the English." An English witness was required to be present. Thus on the road back to Mohegan country, near present-day Windsor, a brother of Uncas crept behind the Narragansett captive and "clave his head with an hatchet, some English being present." In order to let the Mohegans know that the action had approval of the United Colonies, a dozen or so troopers were sent "home with Onkus to abide a time with him for his defence, if need should be."[10]

The Commissioners defended their act by citing the Treaty of 1638. In their prejudiced view, Miantinomo had been a disturber of the "Comon peace," and had committed treachery against Uncas, one of the parties to that treaty, by attacking him outright.[11] It is interesting to note that the Commissioners, in passing sentence upon Miantinomo, had sat as judges in a criminal proceeding, which resembled a case of treason in that the accused was working against the established order. Miantinomo had been a powerful leader of his people and his death was not taken lightly by the Narragansetts, who began biding their time for an opportunity to attack the Mohegans. The Commissioners, fearing an outbreak of hostilities, sent messengers to the various tribes to appraise the situation and to secure explanations for violations of the Hartford treaty of 1638. The tribes consented to refrain from making war on each other before the planting of corn, and that once deciding upon war a thirty-day warning be given.[12] The Commissioners also devised a plan whereby peaceful Indians be issued certificates of allegiance to the English.[13]

The Narragansett sachems, headed by the younger brother of Miantinomo, at the time only twenty years of age, were soon crying for vengeance of the "judicial murder"[14] of their chief. Thus the "sons of old Canonicus having not inherited theire fathers prudence" fell into "hot contention with their own neighbours and native inhabitants."[15] A letter from Roger Williams stated that soon the "whole country would be all of a flame."[16] Many a Mohegan were waylaid and tomahawked by their enemies, and one pitched battle, involving a reported one-thousand Narragansetts, was fought near the Mohegan fort.[17] The colonies fearing involvement in the war began military preparations.[18] On the intercolonial level, the United Colonies saw an opportunity, by combining forces with the Mohegans, to reduce the power of the Narragansetts. The Commissioners in their first meeting as a council of war called in the magistrates and elders of Massachusetts along with some of their military commanders. The decision reached by this mixed council was that the Mohegans be defended and aided, that this aid should be speedy, and that three hundred troops be raised proportionately from the colonies.[19] The Commissioners, partly in deference to Massachusetts, chose Major Gibbons of that colony as commander in chief of the expedition to be raised.[20] Major Gibbons, as commander in chief, was charged with preserving military law among his troops, upholding the worship of God in his army,[21] exercising command over any barques or vessels used, presiding over his council of war,[22] and agreeing upon any articles of peace, which would be subject to approval by the Commissioners.[23] Major Gibbons must have had military experience in England, otherwise such veterans as Standish, Atherton, Leverett, and Mason would probably never haven been placed in subordinate positions.[24] Thus at the first emergency session of the Commissioners in July, 1645, the Commissioners of the United Colonies, much as a council of war, had made military preparations to bring the Narragansetts into line.

Twice during their meeting in the summer of 1645, the Commissioners dispatched messengers to the Narragansetts requiring their sachems to send deputies to Boston to sue for peace, but twice the offer was turned down.

> Thus while the commissioners in care of the public peace, fought to quench the fire kindled amongst the Indians, these children of strife breath out threatenings, provocations and warr against the English themselves, so that unless they should dishonour and provoak God, by violating a just ingagement, and expose the Colonies to contempt and danger from the Barbarians, they cannot but exercise force, when no other meanes will prevail, to reduce the Narrowgansets and their confederates to a more just and sober temper.[25]

As the situation deteriorated, the frontier towns began to expect an invasion from the Narragansetts. Watches were provided for on the outskirts of these towns,[26] and in Plymouth the house of Edward Winslow, Commissioner of the United Colonies, was deemed a place for "fit refuge" against any attack.[27] Plymouth and Massachusetts seemed the most willing of the four United Colonies to bring the war to the Narragansetts. This was undoubtedly due to their proximity to these Indians, and also the desire to demonstrate to Connecticut and New Haven, who without sanction from the United Colonies had dispatched aid to the Dutch in their war against the Indians,[2] that they could also take forceful measures to clear the Indians from the frontier.

In August, Captain Standish led the Plymouth contingent into Rhode Island to search out the Narragansetts, and found that not only had Roger Williams negotiated a neutrality treaty with the Narragansetts, but that even some of the Providence settlers took the Indians into their houses "familiarly." This so enraged the fiery captain that he warned that any Rhode Island settler aiding the Indians would be taken captive. Thus, writes Williams' able biographer, "to members of the Puritan confederation the question of lawful jurisdiction was secondary and the Rhode Island charter of no consequence."[28] Meanwhile, Roger Williams took over for the messengers of the United Colonies, who were afraid of their lives if they again ventured into Indian territory. The envoys from the Confederation gave Williams their instructions, and this outcast from the Bay used his influence to persuade the leading Indian sachems to come to Boston to settle their differences with the English. Though the Commissioners of the United Colonies owed Williams their gratitude for his efforts in preserving peace, he received no thanks; instead, the messengers were rebuked on their return for having exceeded their instructions in letting Williams act for them.[29] Thus the man who had been kicked out of the United Colonies, in true Christian spirit, actually worked for them in the preventing of bloodshed.

The combined expedition against the Narragansetts therefore never got under way; but before the troops were disbanded the colonies were put to a substantial expense.[30] The Indians, "hearing of this preparation against them," sent representatives to the Commissioners sitting at Boston, whereupon they sued for peace, speaking "no more English, but peace, peace."[31] The leading sachems of the Narragansetts and Niantics came, including Pessacus, who was regarded as the head man after the murder of his brother, Miantinomo. The Indians were somewhat disillusioned over the intense disposition of the Commissioners, who told them that Williams probably did not make clear the "waighty passages" of the terms proposed for peace.[32] These "waighty passages" declared that the Narragansetts must pay back tribute, as agreed upon by the Treaty of Hartford (1638), and that fugitives from the English be restored. The Narragansett sachem was to supply four sons as hostages,[33] whom were to be returned in two years. Selling of land by the Indians would in the future require the consent of the Commissioners, and if differences arose between the

Narragansetts and the Mohegans, they were first to acquaint
the English with them, and start war only when permitted by
the Commissioners.[34] This was a stern exactment upon a proud
tribe such as the Narragansetts, and it is not surprising, therefore, to find that the next year after this agreement that the
right hostages had not been sent to the English, nor had the
captives and fugitives been restored, and as evidenced from the
type of wampum the Narragansetts had been using they were
again "practicing" with the Mohawks.[35]

The Bay Colony took upon itself the task to exact the required tribute from the Narragansett Indians. In 1646, Pessacus
was summoned again to Boston by the Massachusetts authorities. However, he sent his delegates instead. The two Massachusetts Commissioners before the regular meeting received
partial payment of the wampum due from the Narragansetts,[36]
and at the regular meeting of the Confederation the Indians
were ordered to complete their payments.[37] A committee of the
two leading military men of the Colony, Edward Gibbons and
Captain Keayne, was appointed to consider measures to be
taken in securing the back wampum from the Narragansetts
"agreed on by our Commissioners with the Indians.[38] It was
not until two years later that the whole amount was received,
when Captain Atherton was dispatched by the Bay with twenty
troopers to demand of the chief sachem in person the wampum
due, which after a little hesitancy was paid.[39]

The Commissioners recognized that much of the hostile attitude of the Narragansetts had been provoked by the miscon-
duct of Uncas of the Mohegans. If he did not behave, the
English would reverse their policy, leaving him and his brother
sachem to "shifte for yourselves and then (we knowe) the
Naragansetts wilbe well pleased, and doe what we will require
of them."[40] Thus the Indian policy of the Confederation would
continue to be the playing of the balance of power of one tribe
against another. Yet the Commissioners hoped for some degree
of impartiality in their treatment of the Indians. Uncas, to show
that he was not regarded as a privileged character, was several
times summoned to account for his actions before a meeting of
the Commissioners, wherein he was reminded of his responsibility to the English.[41] Uncas soon came to be more cooperative,
and an opportunity to demonstrate his good faith was soon
forthcoming. In 1646, Sequasson, a disgruntled Narragansett

sachem on the Connecticut River, sought to increase his power
by detaching the Mohegans from the English. An ingenious
plot was conceived to hire one of his followers to murder one
of the two Connecticut Commissioners of the United Colonies,
Haynes or Hopkins, or the reserve Commissioner, William Whiting, and on his way from the murder, fleeing to the Mohawks,
to spread the word that Uncas had performed the deed.[42]

But this murderous plot backfired. Instead of carrying out
his part of the bargain, the hired assassin laid bare the plot
before the English authorities, and, needless to say, the mere
relation of such a bold conspiracy sent a cold shiver down
the spines of the Saints. The Commissioners immediately ordered the arrest of Sequasson when he refused to face his
accusers at a session of the Confederation.[43] Uncas only too
gladly took upon himself the responsibility of apprehending
the fleeing Narragansett sachem, and when he was taken he
was turned over to the English authorities for trial.[44] But the
Commissioners were more cautious than in their examination
of Miantinomo, realizing that the condemnation of a second
Indian chief within three years would certainly signal the
beginning of hostilities. The testimony of the hired assassin was
not deemed sufficient proof, and Sequasson was allowed to
go free, but not permitted to return from exile until 1650.[45]

The Commissioners in order to meet the general tendency
of the Indians to harbor fugitives, ordered that if such practices continued, then the magistrates of any one of the colonies
"might at the plantifs chardge send some convenient strength
of English, and according to the nature and value of the offence,
and damadge" seize all those Indians who had protected or
rescued the offender regardless of the colony in which he should
be found. If the culprit could not be found, then other Indians
might be seized. But because of the expense to keep an Indian
in jail, they could be shipped out and traded for Negroes.[46]
This order was significant, for an offender could now be pursued across the colonial "line"; and also shows again the willingness of the Puritan colonies to sell Indian prisoners as slaves.[47]

Signs of Indian unrest continued to persist during this early
period. Swarms of warriors were reported arming in the Connecticut valley,[48] and Thomas Stanton in the summer of 1647
was sent by the Commissioners to sound out any war sentiment among the Narragansetts.[49] His findings did not relieve

the concern of the colonists, and as a result of the continuing
Indian tension, the colonies kept part of their troops in readiness to march at as little as a half-hour's notice.[50] As the settlers
came more and more into contact with the red man, incidence
of violence continued to mount.[51] One proposal to neutralize the
power of the Indians was to remove the remnant Pequots at a
distance from the English so that they could not be used as tools
of the Mohegans and Narragansetts, to whose care they had
been entrusted by the Treaty of 1638.[52]

In 1648, it was again rumored that the Narragansetts and
Niantics had hired a number of outside Indians to "about one
thousand Indians armed, three hundred or more having guns,
powder, and bullets," and were preparing for war. The Commissioners sent out messengers, warning these Indians that if
they attacked the Mohegans, the English would defend the
Mohegans.[53] It was ordered that if war broke out before the
next meeting of the Commissioners, the Connecticut and New
Haven Commissioners could order whatever aid was necessary
to help Uncas. But again the Narragansetts and their allies
were hesitant. The messengers were informed that the Indians
knew the English to be a wise and warlike people, and they
intended not to fall out with them, therefore for the present
they would desist, and consider further of the matter.[54] Again
the prompt action of the Commissioners had averted a war
among the Indians which would have eventually involved the
colonists. Roger Williams continued to work for peace among
the colonies, sending from to time to time what intelligence
he received to the Commissioners of the United Colonies,[55] and
hardly "a weeke hath passed but some way or other I have
bene used as instrumental to their peace and spreading of the
English planting in this Countrey." The precarious position of
the Providence Plantation also made it necessary for Williams
to work for peace between the United Colonies and the Naragansetts, but his "Labouring . . . to work a League between the
English and the Narigansetts"[56] was, except for preserving the
peace, working at cross-purposes for the Confederation, which
counted upon their friendship with the Mohegans to hold the
Narragansetts in check and even had open designs on Narragansett territory.

Uncas, in 1649, again complained to the Commissioners
that the Narragansetts and Niantics were "still underminding

his peace and seeking Ruine," not only in attempting to bring the Mohawks upon him but also attempting to murder him.[57] Further dark suspicions were raised when it was rumored that a rebellion was afoot among the conquered Pequots, possibly in alliance with the Narragansetts, which, if this alliance were accomplished, would throw the Mohegan-Narragansett balance of power out of kilter. At the core of the conspiracy was thought to be a daughter of Ninigret[58] and a brother of

> Sassaquas[59] the mallignant furius Pequot wherby probably theire aimes are to gather together and Reunite the scattered Conquered Pequates into one body and sett them upp againe as a distinct nation which hath alwayes been witnessed against by the English and may hassard the peace of the Colonies.[60]

Though this first decade of the Confederation was a period of peace, there was nevertheless continual tension over the possibility of the outbreak of Indian hostilities. The Puritan Commissioners favored a policy of absolute justice, but for their own self-preservation whether divine Providence liked it or not, they were forced to follow one of expediency.

By 1650, the strain in Indian relations had reached its peak. The Long Island Indians attacked the friends of the English, the Mohegans. The Commissioners, not dispatching a force themselves but hoping to encourage the Mohegans, gave the Connecticut authorities the right of way to bring the offending Long Island tribe to account.[61] The Narragansett situation, however, continued to give alarm, and in the same year the Commissioners ordered that twenty well-armed troopers be sent out of Massachusetts to demand of Pessacus 308 fathom of wampum, so that the wampum might not be used to employ other Indians against the English and the colonies might not fall into contempt with the Indians. If the wampum was refused or delayed, its value was to be made up from the most suitable goods found. If this plan should meet opposition, however, then the Commissioners at their next meeting would order preparations for war.[62] This plan met approval in the Bay, but it was held up for awhile over a question of procedure—the order of the Commissioners had not been signed—and the Massachusetts Council, which could act only in the most clear-cut cases, felt that the order unsigned by the Commissioners "will not satisfy the generall Courte, or Country." Nevertheless, when any four of the Council should see the signatures of the Commissioners affixed to the regular "return" of the meeting of the Commissioners, then the Colony would impress the twenty men for the mission to the Narragansetts.[63]

In the "vacancy of the Generall Courte," four members of the Council implemented the instructions of the Commissioners, and ordered the Major General of the Colony, Edward Gibbons, to raise twenty "able and sufficient souldiers" to be sent to the Narragansett country under the command of Captain Humphrey Atherton.[64] The town constables were directed by the Council to take any provisions or munitions needed for the expedition from any person, giving in exchange "ticketts under your hand," which would be redeemed at the next town "levye."[65] Atherton was given the instructions "agreed upon by the Commissioners for the United Collonies" by this "Counsell of this Commonwealth" with wide discretion to use whatever tactics he might see fit in "defending or offending" the English position against the Indians.[66] Considering the possibility of a general war with the Narragansetts, the Council of the Bay also ordered that the watches at the towns be tightened and every soldier be provided with adequate arms; moreover, all "neighbour Indians" were forbidden to enter any town after sunset, and if any should be found in the towns at night, they should be arrested and held for trial.[67] These stern measures under the direction of the Commissioners brought the colonies into preparedness and warned off for a while longer the likelihood of Indian hostilities.

The Commissioners slightly shifted their Indian policy and began the task of alienating the Pequots from the influence of the Narragansetts. If the remaining Pequots could be weaned away from the Narragansetts, even though the Narragansetts had once been authorized by the English to absorb part of the Pequots—and the Mohegans, the other part—the balance of power would become even more favorable to the English. An intensive plan was put into effect to convert the Pequots and the Mohegans into "Praying Indians," more of which will be related later. Also the Commissioners put the Narragansett sachems on notice that the Pequots were not to be oppressed "in huntings" or in any other way.[68]

In the early 50's the Indian alarm continued to spread, and by 1653 "there was a great *commotion* and *agony* raised in the spirits of people throughout the country, upon the apprehension of a horrid conspiracy among the Indians throughout the country to cut off all the English."[69] There was even coming intelligence of a plot "between Dutch and Indians" to drive out the English;[70] and on the northern frontier, the alarm was sounded.[71] Ninigret, the sachem of the Niantics, was making war on the friendly Long Island Indians and was even seen paying a visit to the Dutch.[72] The Niantics were also beginning to take out thier wrath on the virtually helpless Pequots. Since the meeting of 1652 became bogged down over the question of procedure, individual Commissioners wrote to one another about what actions should be taken against Ninigret.[73] It was doubted, however, if Ninigret would "respect the advice of a single Commissioner,"[74] and though grievances and discontent were ignored by the Commissioners in 1652, they were to mount to such a pitch in 1653 that they were to bring on a crisis in the Confederation.

What policy did the Puritan Commissioners of the United Colonies attempt to pursue? First of all they sought justice. This they can be credited with, as can the officials of our National Government in the 1780-90's; but well-meaning intentions do not always measure up to the facts. The Puritans of the central government, like Henry Knox and his associates at the later time, could proclaim broad platitudes of justice and respect of the rights of the red man, but they could not restrain the frontier passions. The basic driving forces of the colonists were economic, and the ways of the red and white men were so different that they were destined only to clash. Where the white man bought land of the Indians to become his absolute property, the savage sold only the right to share in his hunting grounds. Thus the mores of both societies were so unlike that each could act in good faith and yet be wrong in the eyes of the other. As one author has pointed out, the question in the relations with the Indians should not have been whether justice was done or not, but whether the Indians *thought* that justice was done.[75] The Indians, who were not steeped in Biblical or English law, had only a rudimentary concept of justice, and, therefore, quite naturally resented the self-righteousness of the Puritans in making demands upon them. That the English had a right to compel

Ninigret

Simon Willard

them along certain lines was in itself resented; compulsion the Indians understood, but did not like. The requiring of tribute from the tribes may not have been a wise policy, serving to deepen the hatred against the English, but it had the advantage of seeing where the English stood in the eyes of the savages— whenever payment of tribute was not forthcoming, then they knew something was wrong.

In their quest for an Indian policy, the Commissioners of the United Colonies were the first American governmental agency to put into effect what now, since 1953, has been the official policy of our Federal Government: the policy of "termination." This policy has been defined as "one of terminating and curtailing Federal responsibilities and services to Indians while preparing them for full citizenship."[76] The New England colonists attempted to establish the English form of government among the conquered Pequots, making use of native leaders; in religious affairs Indian teachers were used to a large degree. A number of Indians entered Harvard under the auspices of the United Colonies, though only one lived to graduate. But was this policy of termination wise? It was based on the assumption that the English way was better, and it was only done in the spirit of making the Puritan Saints feel that they were performing their worldly obligation to a people they had seen fit to crush. The epic of America has seen the demands for equalization and sameness—this desire for homogeneity may be a worthy standard when not carried too far, but to bring a savage race, on both feet, into a society it is not accustomed nor fitted to compete in does in the long run an injustice to the group affected.

The best policy for the Confederation in so far as fair treatment of the New England natives was desired—viewed in the perspective of three centuries of the miserable plight of the red man—would have been to permit only those Indians willing to enter the white man's society and adequately prepared to do so. The heavy death toll of the Indian scholars at Harvard during the time of the Confederation points to the consequences of too rapid amalgamation. To compete in the white man's society, the Indian needed help economically; but to raise a subjected race to the level of its competitors was not to the liking of the New England Puritans. A savage, in Puritan days, who became "very inquisitive after knowledge both in things divine and also human" learned very little from his curiosity. The first principles of the English way of life he would learn were, in the order of their importance salt (to preserve fish), iron (to fell trees) and ships (for trade). Without being given the means and the know-how no wonder the inquiring savage soon became resigned to a defeatist attitude:

> Alas! (saith the Indian) then I fear, we shall never be a commonwealth, for we can neither make salt, nor iron, nor ships.[77]

The Commissioners of the Confederation were at least pretentiously if not honestly concerned with the welfare of the savages; but good intentions were lost in the attempt to establish unconditionally a strong arm over the Indians. But whether a policy of conciliation would have been possible with the two conflicting civilizations and the lust of the settlers, and whether such a policy would have headed off the bloody struggles of King Philip's War can only be a matter of speculation. Basically, it was the survival of the fittest.

The Commissioners learned that consistency paid off in the long run. The Mohegans may not have been always right just because they sought English support, but it was wise to cultivate a friendship with them, and thereby count them as allies. Supported consistently by one Indian tribe, the Puritans could make exactments to their liking on other tribes, such as the Narragansetts, since the balance of power was on the side of the United Colonies. Also a stern policy with the Narragansetts might put pressure on the allies of these Indians, the Rhode Island inhabitants, which might lead to opening lands of the Narragansetts to settlement and to bringing the Ishmael republic under the jurisdiction of the United Colonies.

The Commissioners hoped in the future to keep this balance of power on the course that it had developed. They wanted to consolidate their influence on the Mohegans and the Pequots into a firm friendship, dependent upon the English and not upon the Narragansetts. Missionary work among the friendly Indians would be intensified. The colonists were also learning the value of military expediency. At all costs they would survive—now, in the Promised Land, they would be a Nation.

[1] John Haynes to John Winthrop, 17Feb44, *MHSC*:3:I:230-1.

[2] John Mason to John Winthrop, 10Mar43, *Winthrop Papers*, IV, 419.

[3] Haynes to Winthrop, 17Feb44, *loc. cit.*

[4] Samuel H. Brockunier, *The Irrepressible Democrat. Roger Williams,* (New York: Ronald Press Co., 1940), p. 154.

[5] See Chapter II; participants in the treaty were Connecticut, the Narragansetts, and the Mohegans.

[6] Winthrop, *Journal*, (S), II, 155.

[7] Brockunier, *op. cit.*, p. 154.

[8] Winthrop, *Journal*, (S), II, 157.

[9] Winthrop, *Journal*, (S), II, 158.

[10] Winthrop, *Journal*, (S), II, 157-61; *PCR*, IX, 10-12.

[11] *PCR*, IX, 15.

[12] *Ibid.*, p. 29; Bradford, *op. cit.*, p. 511.

[13] *PCR*, IX, 18-9.

[14] Brockunier, *op. cit.*, p. 155.

[15] Johnson's "Wonder Working Providence of Sion's Saviour," *MHSC*:2:VII:-2-3.

[16] Bradford, *op. cit.*, pp. 432-3. The Narragansetts had already concluded neutrality with the Rhode Island towns. (*PCR*, IX, 33.) From the Rhode Island viewpoint the submission of the Narragansetts to the United Colonies was never accomplished because they owed their allegiance, through the Rhode Island settlements, to "the government and protection of that honourable state of old England." (Stevens Transcripts, I, 16, 19Apr44.)

[17] Thomas Peters to John Winthrop, May45, *Winthrop Papers*, V, 19.

[18] In Plymouth every township was to provide a barrel of ammunition to be kept in a central place, and "the cheefe military commanders of every Towne" were authorized to call into service troops of the towns in order to meet an emergency. A Council of War in Plymouth, consisting of men who served as Commissioners of the United Colonies and other officials, was convened with "full power to order all things concerning the gen'all warrs for the government." (Pierce, *Civil Lists, op. cit.*, pp. 41-2, 87).

[19] *PCR, IX*, 33-4; Bradford, op. cit., p. 431. The three hundred broken down was: Mass., 190; Ply., 40; Conn., 40; N. H., 30.

[20] Massachusetts took the liberty to appoint Leverett as assistant commander in chief. (*MCR*, II, 122-3.)

[21] *PCR*, IX, 37-9. ". . . the reverend Mr. Tomson, on the Elders . . . at Braintree was to accompany them." (Johnson, *op. cit.*, pp. 2-3.)

[22] Viz., Captains Standish, Mason, Leverett, and several lieutenants.

[23] *PCR*, IX, 37-9. The full military equipment of the time included 1) a musket, firelock or matchlock; 2) a pair of bandoleers; 3) a powder pouch, plus bullets, sword, belt, and a knapsack. (Justin Winsor, *A History of Duxbury, Mass.* (Boston: 1849), p. 92.)

[24] Roberts, *Honorable Artillery Company, op. cit.*, p. 40.

[25] Declaration of Former Passages and Proceedings Betwixt the English and

the Narrowgansets, with their confederates, *Ten Facsimile Reproductions*, (Boston: 1902) ; also *PCR,* IX, 55.

[26] Order of the Mass. Gen. Ct., 1645, MA, XXX, 4a.

[27] Lysander R. Richardo, *History of Marshfield*, (Plymouth. 1901), p. 26.

[28] For the Underhill expedition to the aid of New Netherlands, the two "northerly confederates refused to bear any part of the cost." (See Calder, *op. cit.,* pp. 178-9.)

[29] *PCR,* IX, 42-3.

[30] For Plymouth the cost was over £66 (Pierce, *op. cit.,* p. 89). At least one military career was aided by this call for troops—Captain Standish was soon to become the commander of all the Plymouth forces and the Commissary General (Winsor, *Duxbury, op. cit.,* p. 92).

[31] Johnson's "Wonder Working Providence," *MHSC*:2:VII:2-3.

[32] *PCR,* IX, 43.

[33] Johnson, *loc. cit.*

[34] *PCR,* IX, 45-8.

[35] *Ibid.,* p. 75.

[36] Winthrop, *Journal,* (S), II, 321. "But the commissioners . . . refused to accept so small a sum, and rebuking them sharply . . . told them that if they were forced to fetch the rest, they could as well fetch this." (Indians, therefore, sold the kettles which they had brought the wampum in, and left the proceeds with the Commissioners.)

[37] If not, then an emergency session would be held in the spring at Plymouth to consider further coercive measures. (*PCR,* IX, 82.)

[38] MA, XXX, 7.

[39] William L. Stone, *Uncas and Miantonomu,* (New York: 1842), pp. 125-6.

[40] John Winthrop to Uncas, 20Jun46, *Winthrop Papers,* V, 82.

[41] *PCR,* I, 71-3. Uncas's men had also committed offenses against the English, viz., when a band of Mohegans roamed down to Winthrop, Jr.'s plantation, dividing themselves into "squadrons" and committing general pillage. (Petition of the Inhabitants of New London to the Commissioners of the United Colonies, 15Sep46, *Winthrop Papers,* V, 111.)

[42] See Sheldon, *History of Deerfield,* (Deerfield: 1895), I, 56-8.

[43] *PCR,* IX, 66-8.

[44] Winthrop, *Journal,* II, 349.

[45] *PCR,* IX, 169-70.

[46] *Ibid.,* pp. 69-71.

[47] Cf., Mason's Commission from the Commissioners, 1645, *PCR,* IX, 35; also Almon W. Lauber, *Indian Slavery in Colonial Times within the Present Limits of the U. S.,* (New York: Columbia University Press, 1913), pp. 138-9. Indian slaves were usually freed at the age of 25. One Indian slave proved of much value to the Mass. Commissioners and in aiding John Eliot in learning the Indian language. William W. Tooker, *John Eliot's First Indian Teacher and Interpreter, Cockenoe-De-Long Island* (New York: 1896), pp. 11-2.) The

Puritan justification for Indian slavery was not only scriptural but it also brought civilization to them.

[48] Sheldon, op. cit.

[49] Instrs. to Thos. Stanton, 27Jul47, MA, XXX, 12a.

[50] The first "minute men" in the colonies. (Spencer P. Mead, "The First American Soldiers," *Journal of American History,* I 1907), 120-8.

[51] E.g., see O. P. Fuller, *The History of Warwick,* (Providence: 1875), p. 42.

[52] John Winthrop, Jr., to the Commissioners, 18Jul49, MA, XXX, 13.

[53] Winthrop, *Journal,* II, 348.

[54] Winthrop, *Journal,* II, 349.

[55] Roger Williams to John Winthrop, Jr., 11Sep48, *MHSC*:3:I:178.

[56] Roger Williams to Gen. Ct. of Mass., Oct51. Facsimiles of Letters and Papers of Roger Williams from the Mass. Archives, NYPL.

[57] *PCR,* IX, 143-4.

[58] Ninigret was the sachem of the Niantics, a Narragansett tribe.

[59] Sassacus, the Pequot chief who had fled to the Mohawks after his tribe was crushed by the English, and was beheaded by these Indians.

[60] *PCR,* IX, 145.

[61] *Ibid.,* pp. 167-8.

[62] *PCR,* IX, 167-8.

[63] At a meeting of the Council at Boston, 25Sep50, Council Records, I, MA.

[64] Warrant to Edward Gibbons, Sep50, Council Records, I, MA.

[65] To the Counstables of Boston, Sep50, *ibid.*

[66] Meeting of the Council, 26Sep50, *ibid.*

[67] General Order of Mass. Council, Council Records, I, MA.

[68] 13Sep51, *MHSC,* 4:VI.

[69] Mather, *Magnalia op. cit.,* II, 558.

[70] John Hull, *Diary,* printed in *AASTransactions,* III(1857), 174. Because of the fear that the Dutch had hired the Indians to attack the English settlements on L. I., Indians coming into the towns there if they didn't heed warning of the watch were to be shot on sight. (*Easthampton, L.I., Records,* I, 31, 26Apr53.)

[71] Edward Rawson (Sec. of Mass.) to Military Officers of Dover, 23Mar52, Council Records, I, MA; Joseph Dow, ed., *History of the Town of Hampton, N. H.,* (Salem: 1893), I, 47-8.

[72] Joseph Willard, *Life and Times of Major Simon Willard,* (Boston: 1858), pp. 195-6.

[73] Haynes to Winthrop, Jr., 1652(n.d.), *MHSC* 4:VII:457; Eaton to Winthrop, Jr., 5Aug52, *MHSC,* 4:VII.

[75] Douglas E. Leach, "The Causes and Effects of King Philip's War," Unpublished Ph.D. thesis, Harvard University (1950), p. 39.

[76] *New York Times,* 5Jun56 "Quakers Propose Plan for Indians."

[77] Winthrop, *Journal,* (S), II, 371.

CHAPTER VII

Naboth's Vineyard

"Dost thou now govern the Kingdom of Israel?" asked the wicked wife of Ahab. If so, then let not this stubborn subject of yours rest in content with this coveted possession, for which you have offered a just price. Remember that you are King. "Let thine heart be merry: I will give thee the vineyard of Naboth the Jezreelite." Soon it was decided "in the presence of the people" that "Naboth did blaspheme God and the king. Then they carried him forth out of the city, and stoned him with stones, that he died. . . . And it came to pass, when Ahab heard that Naboth was dead, that Ahab rose up to go down to the vineyard of Naboth the Jezreelite, to take possession of it."

In the Israel of the New World, the united Puritan colonies, under the shadow of the Bay, were supreme. Having found themselves at home in the new Canaan, it was time to tighten up loose corners and govern all the kingdom of Israel. Expansion of the Puritan colonies were on all sides widening the walls of the Confederacy.[1] But on the south, along the eastern coast of Connecticut up through the present boundary line of Rhode Island and the Bay State, were lands that the settlers of the United Colonies coveted. These lands, as those of Naboth of ancient times, belonged for generations to the Indian tribes of the region or to those settlers who had received deeds from these Indians. They were not for sale to the Puritan colonies. The Puritan longed to be master of New England, and he could not sit idly by while valuable lands so near lay fallow or were used as a place of refuge for malcontents, who in this haven became thorns in the flesh. This chapter depicts the rivalry over the Narragansett-Pequot country and the attempt to settle the jurisdiction of this territory by the United Colonies, Rhode Island, and the King.

Roger Williams journeyed to England in 1643 to secure a charter for Rhode Island in order to contain the pressure of the United Colonies and the Gortonists. Twelve followers of

Samuel Gorton, fresh from their ejection from Pawtuxet, which
had submitted to Massachusetts jurisdiction, purchased of the
Narraganeott sachem Miantinomo a large tract of land a dozen
miles south of Providence on the west side of Narragansett
Bay.[2] A warrant had been served on the Gortonists by the Bay
Colony expelling them from Pawtuxet, a place which Winthrop
wished to use as an outpost to attack the Narragansetts if need
be.[3] As the Gortonists cleared away their new lands at Shawomet, they made it plain to the Massachusetts authorities that
they would stand by their new property, recognizing no power
of the Bay to enlarge its bounds, except by consent of the King.[4]

Meanwhile, the Commissioners of the United Colonies de-
creed death for Miantinomo[5] and the Gortonists thus lost the
chief witness to their purchase in the Narragansett territory.
Moreover, two of the sachems who, with Miantinomo, had been
party to the sale to the Gortonists retracted their deed and
were persuaded to come under the jurisdiction of the Bay
Colony. Massachusetts now sought to extend its jurisdiction
over Shawomet (Warwick) as it had already done over the
settlement north of the Pawtuxet River. Thus a second warrant against the Gortonist settlers was issued by the Massachusetts Court, summoning them to appear in Boston to answer
the complaints of the two Narragansett chiefs, Pomham and
Sacononoco. Not only did this small group of settlers refuse to
come into the Bay with guarantees of "safe conduct," but they
flaunted in the faces of the Saints "two letters full of blasphemy
against the churches and magistracy, and other provoking terms,
slighting all we could do against them."[6] Resolved that such defiance of authority in new Canaan should not go unpunished,
the Massachusetts authorities, in their determined Puritan way,
"took testimonies against them both of English and Indians,"
and decided "to proceed with them by force."[7]

In October, a force of forty soldiers under Captain George
Cook was sent from the Bay to overawe the settlers at Shawomet.[8] According to the Gortonists, as soon as they had received a "Writing immediately from the Court, to informe us,
that they were resolved to come downe amongst us, to exercise
Justice there" a company of soldiers and Indians appeared
bearing a commission "either to bring us away by force of
Armes, or else to put us to the sword."[9] The handful of settlers
was determined to resist this show of force, and when the

Massachusetts troops appeared the Gortonists were found huddled up in a "musket-proof" house. A Providence delegation appeared on the scene, which offered to refer the dispute to arbitration, claiming that Massachusetts as a party in the dispute could, therefore, not serve as a judge.[10] This proposal was sent back to the General Court for its advice while the uninvited guests lived off the fat of the land. A minister had accompanied the armed band "to see if they could convert us to be their minds," and if not then the Gortonists would be treated as "men fitted for the slaughter."[11] During the brief truce, there was an interchange of letters between the Massachusetts and the Providence authorities. The Bay called together a number of its elders. It was found that the Gortonists had no right whatever to settle on lands belonging to the two chiefs, who had given their allegiance to the Massachusetts Colony.[12]

While the elders of the Bay were considering the proposals for arbitration of the dispute, the controversy was brought before the Commissioners of the United Colonies, then meeting for the first time in Boston. It was found that if the Gortonists refused to come to Boston, as ordered by the Massachusetts Court, then the magistrates of the Colony would have leeway to "proceed against them according to what they shall fynd just," and "the rest of the Jurisdictions will approve and concurr in what shalbe so warrantably donn, as if their Comissioners had beene present at the Conclusions."[13]

The Gortonists, now only ten in number,[14] had no choice but to yield to the demands of this armed party, but not until the English colors had been fired upon.[15] The settlers of Shawomet, in order "to prevent the spilling of blood," consented to go into the Bay if they were treated as free men, but, according to Gorton, this was not done, for they were taken to Massachusetts as prisoners to stand trial. The proceedings of the Court were quite arbitrary, and the Court even took a vote on whether the death penalty should be meted out, but the prisoners were saved by only two votes. The victims of this purge, nevertheless, were put in chains and forced to work for their board and keep in the Charlestown prison.[16] An order was issued by the General Court, applying particularly to these prisoners, that anyone who

shall reproach, or reprove the Churches of our Lord Jesus Christ in these united Colonies, or the civill government,

or the publicke Ordinances of God therein (unless answer
to questions by proper authority) . . . upon accusation of
any such writing or speech . . . be committed to prison, till
the next Court of Assistants, then and there to be tryed
by a jury . . . and upon his conviction be condemned to
death, and executed.[17]

Thus, sedition in the United Colonies was no joking matter. As
usual, when the orthodox colonies went overboard with repres-
sive action, popular opinion soon counteracted it. Within a few
months then, these settlers who had been snarled in the web
of the Bay were released, but they were forbidden not only
to reside in Massachusetts and Plymouth but also could not
return to Shawomet nor even Providence, except upon pain of
death.[18] Moreover, they were forced to pay for the expenses incurred by the Massachusetts expedition.[19] Upon their release,
the refugees went to Aquidneck, and from there began to lay
the "legal case against unlawful dominion" by Massachusetts.[20]
First, the Bay's jurisdiction over Shawomet was denied by the
new charter obtained by Roger Williams and second, the
Narragansett head sachem was induced to declare allegiance
to the British crown.[21] The Bay Colony was determined to
annex this area; and if they could not establish their claim in
law then they would do so by actual possession. Thus the Massachusetts Court granted permission to some twenty families to
re-settle the Shawomet plantation.[22] Unexpected opposition,
however, developed from the Plymouth quarter, when the Commissioner of the United Colonies from Plymouth, John Brown,
who sought to protect his trading interests, issued an order prohibiting settlement of this area, claiming jurisdiction for Plymouth. Nevertheless, the Commissioners again decided for
Massachusetts,[23] and the only recourse for the Gortonists was
to appeal to the royal government. The controversy was now to
be taken to England by both sides; "Messengers and Agents,"
in the view of the Rhode Island settlements, would be sent
"unto the head of fountaine."[24] As representative of the United
Colonies, Edward Winslow of Plymouth was sent.

Before discussing the new turn in the land controversy between the United Colonies and the settlements on Narragansett
Bay, it is well to look at the efforts of Massachusetts to extend
her jurisdiction over the Pequot Country, which bordered the

Narragansett territory on the west. Connecticut and Massachusetts both claimed these lands: the Bay by her contribution in the conquest of the Pequots; the River Colony by considering itself the successor by purchase of the Warwick patent, which the colony had come into possession of when Fenwick sold out to Connecticut. At that time the patent was declared to include all lands on the Connecticut River; the patent was also stretched to take in the territory between the Saybrook fort and the Narragansett River.[25] Without a charter government at this time nor with the Warwick patent formally turned over to Connecticut,[26] the claims of the River Colony to the Pequot country were extremely tentative.

Settlers from Connecticut nevertheless continued to stake out lands in the Pequot country. The first large grant was given to Captain John Mason, who was to see many years of service as Commissioner of the United Colonies from Connecticut; in January, 1642, for his services in the Pequot War he received five hundred acres for himself and a like amount to divide among the veterans of that war.[27] In 1646, John Winthrop, Jr., was given the right by the Massachusetts General Court, to govern his Pequot plantation though it was suspected that Connecticut might be able to make good its claim to this jurisdiction. It "mattered not much," however, "to which jurisdiction it did belong, seeing the confederation made all as one; but it was of great concernment to have it planted, to be a curb to the Indians."[28] The Bay Colony soon increased its grant to Winthrop, Jr., to 3,000 acres, provided he would set up "a considerable salt worke" within three years of the grant.[29] Winthrop, Jr., lost no time in laying the question of jurisdiction before the Commissioners of the United Colonies. The year after his removal from Boston to his Pequot lands, he attended the emergency session of the Commissioners in Boston, wherein he petitioned the Commissioners to confirm his lands and "cleare it from any clayme of English and Indians according to the equity of the case." Because he lacked deeds for his lands, Winthrop secured testimony from a number of Indians that the sachem of the Niantic tribe had granted him these lands. The Commissioners from Connecticut successfully challenged Winthrop on maintaining a separate jurisdiction there. A variety of reasons were presented, perhaps the most telling, that the Winthrop lands were part of the territory acquired by the Colony in its conquest

of the Pequots. The Massachusetts Commissioners seem not to
have contested the Connecticut claim at this meeting. The decision of the Commissioners, however, stated that "they see no
grounde for themselves to intermeddle or determine any thinge
concerninge the clayme and title in question." In effect, then,
the Pequot lands of John Winthrop, Jr., (present site of New
London) were allowed to come under the jurisdiction of Connecticut, and Winthrop, Jr., was destined for the next twenty-six
years to carve out a most distinguished career as a magistrate
from that Colony.[30]

Though lengthy debate resulted in the Confederation concerning the northern boundary of Connecticut with Massachusetts,[31] the question of jurisdiction over the Pequot country was
to remain relatively quiet for a decade. In 1657, the inhabitants
of Stonington (New London) petitioned to come under the Bay
government as a township, but they could not obtain the consent
of Connecticut to this proposition. A second petition from
Stonington was referred by the Bay General Court to the Commissioners at their September meeting in 1658.[32] Meanwhile,
Massachusetts asked that the River Colony refrain from exercising authority on the east side of the Mystic River until the
Commissioners could decide on the question.[33] At the September
meeting, the Commissioners of New Haven and Plymouth,[34]
the colonies not involved in the dispute, were asked to sit in
arbitration.[35] Two days later this committee returned a compromise decision. Finding "that the Pequot Countrey which ex-
tendeth from Nianticke to a place called Wecopaug about ten
miles eastward from Mistick River may conveniently accomo-
date two plantations or townships," it was therefore decided
that the Mystic River be the dividing line between the two
colonies. Lands on the west side came under the jurisdiction of
Connecticut; those on the east side, under Massachusetts.[36] The
decision was to the advantage of Connecticut, bringing into its
bounds actual settlements; whereas the Bay reaped a wilderness of discontented Niantic and Narragansett Indians, not to
mention the conflicting claims of Rhode Island and later of the
Connecticut Charter to these Narragansett lands. But the Confederation was useful in resolving the uncertainty over the
jurisdiction of the Pequot Country.

The Narragansett country was to remain a sore spot in New
England affairs. The Puritan colonies of Connecticut, Plymouth,
and Massachusetts each had a claim on it. But their designs were

meeting frustration: Williams had secured a patent for Providence Plantations from the royal government; and Gorton was soon reinstated by the Commissioners for Foreign Plantations, To combat the influence of the Gortonists in England and to seek reversal of the award of Shawomet back to these malcontents, Massachusetts ordered its agents in England to negotiate with the Earl of Warwick, the Commissioners for Foreign Plantations, or Parliament.[37] The return of the Gortonists armed with the order for their reinstatement caused grave concern in the Bay. The General Court thought it was time to decide "in what relation we stood to the state of England; whether our government was founded upon our charter, or not; if so, then what subjection we owed to that state." In the course of the debate it was unanimously agreed that the Colony was founded upon the Charter, but there was serious disagreement as to the degree of sovereignty of the home government. Many thought that "by our character we had absolute power of government." Such power of government, to illustrate the federal thinking of the time, implies "a perfection of parts"—governmental organization at all levels, and a "self-sufficiency"—which "should not need the help of any superior power," either of a governor general or otherwise. In this discussion is the first mention of the colonies considering themselves federally related to the imperial government—"independent in respect of government," but yet owing "homage" to the home government.[38] This remarkable debate in the Bay General Court serves again to illustrate that at this early time the Puritan colonies thought of themselves virtually independent of the mother country.

The order borne by the Gortonists[39] on their return indeed gave alarm to the United Colonies. Not only were they given immunity from arrest while passing through the colonies and permitted to resettle their lands, but the order also generally stated that "we shall expect a conformity, not only from yourselves, but from all other governours and plantations in New England."[40] The General Court in reply to the home government questioned the right to give lands to the Earl of Warwick or any others without subjecting them to the existing colonial governments.[41]

From all directions, New England found itself attacked by its enemies. The United Colonies were accused of arbitrary rule and disregard for the government of England. Moreover, there was heard among these colonies a "great boasting" that they

> are *growing into a Nation;* high conceits of a Nation breeds
> high thoughts of themselves, which makes them usually
> term themselves a *State,* cal the people there *Subjects,* unite
> four Governments together without any authority from the
> King and Parliament, and then term themselves the United
> Colonies, are publikely prayed for by that title; not giving
> forth their Warrants in his Majesties name, no not in time
> of his most peaceable government, neither taking the Oath
> of Allegiance before they take upon them their Govern-
> ment. . . . Now (Reader) observe their policie, they take
> the advantage of promoting this designe, by beginning to
> write against *Gorton,* a man whom they know is notorious
> for heresie, that so behind him they may creep and get a
> shot at a better game, may beget a good opinion in the
> Honorable Commissioners by writing against such a evill
> man; as also that they may wash away the opinion that
> good men heretofore have had of them, that they are
> Separatists and Schismaticks. . . .[42]

The celebrated *Defense* of Samuel Gorton sought to expose the
United Colonies as a theocracy running

> not onely against some of the Natives and Subjects, but
> against the Authority also of the Kingdome of *England,*
> with their execution of Laws, in the name and Authority
> of the servant, (or of themselves) and not in the Name and
> authority of the Lord, or fountain of the Government.[43]

Gorton believed the primary aim of "New England Policy"
was to "suppresse Hereticks, and to confirm that to be the
truth which the Unity of the most Colonies hold"; in the case
of Massachusetts they had bathed "themselves in blood and
feed themselves fat, by devouring the good name, estates, and
lives of their brethren."[44]

Edward Winslow of Plymouth, formerly a Commissioner of
the United Colonies, was immediately dispatched to England as
an agent of the United Colonies, though in the pay of the
Massachusetts Colony,[45] to refute the charges which had been
raised against the government in the colonies. Besides his regu-

lar instructions, Winslow was given secret directions to assert
that the government of the Bay was derived from "a free donation of absolute government," and that the powers exercised
under the charter were broad, including the right to "defend ourselves and offend our enemies, as well by sea as by land."[46]
Winslow made a vigorous defense of the colonies while in England. He claimed that since the Gortonists claimed to come
under no jurisdiction, the Bay had no means of redress, and the
only way Massachusetts could assert its position was through
force of arms; the Gortonists even refused to put the matter
before the Court of the Commissioners of the United Colonies.[47]
The sinister motives assigned to Massachusetts in Gorton's *Defence* were vehemently denied by Winslow. As for the New
England Confederation:

> 'Tis true that the *Massachusets new Plimouth, Conectacut,*
> and *Newhaven,* I meane the severall Colonies there en-
> tered into a civill combination, and are called by the name
> of the *United Colonies,* and this was occasioned by the
> generall conspiracy of the Indians against the body of the
> English there feated, together with the distracted condi-
> tion of *England,* from whom we could expect no helpe at
> that time.[48]

The Gortonists, according to Winslow, sought to bribe the
Indians for their lands and delighted in deriding the Massachusetts authorities. Thus did the agent state the case for the
Puritan colonies. The Committee for Foreign Plantations, however, declared that they would decide for the United Colonies
only if it could be demonstrated that Shawomet, now named
Warwick in honor of the Earl, came within the patents of
Massachusetts and Plymouth; in the meantime the Shawomet
settlers should be allowed to go their own way.[49] The settlers
went home, but the controversy over their land would continue
to rage, and soon become embroiled in the question of jurisdiction over all the Narragansett country.

In 1649, the Commissioners of the United Colonies were
asked by the Warwick plantation whether they had not "received
an Injunction from the Parlement" to provide for the defense
of this settlement. This the Commissioners denied, and pointed
out that no help could be expected "in the state wherin you

now stand"; but whenever it would be decided that they came under the jurisdiction of one of the United Colonies then they would be given aid.[50] In June, 1650, Warwick and Pawtuxet were placed in Suffolk County of Massachusetts, although it was not long before the Bay General Court, acting upon the recommendation of the Commissioners, reassigned the territory to Plymouth Colony.[51] The Warwick settlers, however, did not appreciate being transferred from one colony to another; yet they demanded protection of their settlement by the United Colonies, and would again petition the government in England to enforce this guaranty which they had been given.[52] The rivalry over the Narragansett country became even more enmeshed when William Coddington returned with a commission from the Council of State to govern Rhode Island and the "island of Conanicut" for life, thus vying with Williams for the control of the colony.

The designs of the United Colonies to expand their boundaries during the first decade of the Confederation kept Rhode Island in a constant state of fear of being absorbed by them, and led to the adoption of compulsory militia service in Rhode Island.[53] Whether the United Colonies wished to infringe upon the charter of Rhode Island is open to question, but there is no doubt that they intended to assert their dominion over every inch of territory to the very door of the Colony, and if possible to retain Warwick, which denied Plymouth or Massachusetts jurisdiction and had been making its way since 1647 as a town of the corporation of Rhode Island.[54] The attempt of Coddington to bring Rhode Island and "Conanicut" into the Confederation was thwarted by certain Anabaptists who journeyed into the Bay, waving the "red flag of the anabaptistical fanaticism" in the "face of the Bay Bull," seeking to show by the harsh treatment they received that the Puritan State would not be inclined to toleration if the Rhode Island Baptists were annexed to Massachusetts.[55]

Elsewhere the United Colonies continued to expand. The authority of the Bay was established over the New Hampshire towns, and the Province of Maine was created under a President named by the Massachusetts Court.[56] The Commissioners permitted Massachusetts to receive Martha's Vineyard into the Colony;[57] and New Haven and Connecticut extended their arm on Long Island, with permission also being given by the Confederation.[58] The Treaty of Hartford with the Dutch[59] in 1650

confirmed within the United Colonies the English settlements
reaching towards the Hudson River. But the attempts to extend
the rule of the United Colonies over the Narragansett country
repeatedly met frustration. To seize these coveted lands by force
was a venture the Confederation hesitated to pursue for fear
of inciting further disfavor in the homeland. But high-handed
policy could always be resorted to.

The Rhode Island Assembly in 1659 appointed a committee
of eight (two from each town) to handle all correspondence
with the United Colonies concerning the Narragansett lands.[60]
With this unity among the Rhode Island towns the Ishmael
colony could afford to take a more firm stand in its dealings
with the Puritan colonies. The relation between Rhode Island
and the United Colonies could now resemble that of independent nations. Rhode Island, therefore, notified the Puritan
colonies that it had appointed commissioners to meet with any
plenipotentiaries to settle the dispute over the Narragansett
territory.[61] But Massachusetts declined to meet with the commissioners from Rhode Island.[62]

Meanwhile the United Colonies were reluctant to surrender
any claims to the Narragansett lands. Indeed, to the contrary,
they resorted to several schemes. Previously, in 1648, Captain
Atherton had been dispatched with troops to collect back tribute from the Narragansetts, which had been levied to pay for
the expedition in 1645; and like the earlier expulsion of the
Gortonists, the present inhabitants of Warwick accused the
Atherton force of breaking into their houses and driving off
their cattle.[63] The Bay was determined to make good its claim
in this region.[64] Since the Narragansett tribes continued to delay
in the payment of tribute, the Commissioners of the United
Colonies worked out a scheme whereby they declared the lands
of these tribes—"all our whole Countrie with al our Rights and
tightels"[65]—to be in mortgage to the Commissioners.[66] When
the Indians again defaulted in their payments, a land company
was formed from the leading men of the United Colonies, many
of them having served as Commissioners, thus giving the Commissioners of the Confederation a vested interest in their land
policy.[67] The Atherton Company, as the new company was
called, was given lands in the names of the various sachems in
the Narragansett, "Neanticot," and "Cowesset Countrie," providing

they ... shall clearly and Absolutely Aquit and discharge
us [the sachems], from an Ingagement made by us, to the
Commissioners of the united Colonies, for six hundred
fathom of marchantable Wampum, given Capt. George
Denison and Thomas Stanton in behalfe of the said Commissioners for that ende.[68]

The lands involved were two large tracts overlapping the Gorton purchases, extending southward on Narragansett Bay—some
of the richest land in New England. Thus was begun a land
speculation which has been characterized as "one of the most
brazen pieces of land jobbery in early New England history."[69]

But all was not quiet as expected in the Pequot country. For
several years the decision of the Commissioners in 1658 was
allowed to stand. Soon, however, inhabitants from Rhode Island
were settling those lands that had been awarded Massachusetts
by the Commissioners. A letter from the President of the United
Colonies to Rhode Island asked that their people desist "soe
peace and Good agreement maye be performed Betwixt your
selves and the united Collonies."[70] The Connecticut Charter of
1662, which extended the claims of the River Colony in the Pequot country, ordered Mystic and Stonington to refuse allegiance
to Massachusetts or Rhode Island, thus contradicting the 1658
decision of the Commissioners of the United Colonies.[71] Because Rhode Island and Connecticut claimed the lands which
the Bay Colony had taken under its jurisdiction, a heated controversy was inevitable. The brunt of the rivalry among these
colonies for control of the Pequot and Narragansett country
fell to the town of Southertown, later called Stonington. Southertown, on the Massachusetts side of the Mystic River, as determined in 1658, had been incorporated under the Massachusetts
government.[72] The Southertown controversy pushed a new
splinter into the side of spirited cooperative action, and was a
factor in bringing the colonies of the Confederation to a falling
out in the decade of the 60's.

Rather than worry about the extension of the Connecticut
boundary by the Charter of 1662, the Bay instead vigorously
assailed the Rhode Island authorities for allowing settlers to
come down to Southertown, which was causing disturbances
with settlers from the United Colonies.[73] Massachusetts based
its claim of jurisdiction over Southertown upon several grounds:

conquest by themselves and their "confederates" during the
Pequot War; actual settlement under the auspices of the Massachusetts General Court; and the recognition of the Bay's jurisdiction by the Commissioners of the United Colonies.[74] The
Rhode Island settlers in Southertown were given notice by the
Massachusetts Court to evacuate the area on pain of expulsion
and assessment of the charges for legal proceedings.[75] The Connecticut authorities also entered the fray. Seeking to extend to
the very limit the boundaries set forth by the Charter, they
ordered the inhabitants of the Pequot country in "His Majesties
Name to forbear to exercise any power by vertue of former
Commission from any other Colony" and refer all questions
to the Deputy Governor of Connecticut.[76]

The government of Rhode Island protested as vehemently
against the Connecticut claims as they did against those of Massachusetts; but they suspected some "underhand dealing" between the two Puritan Colonies—"for as much as now you or the
Commissioners pretend Authority by vertue of a Patent, (newly
Come over from England granted to some Gentlemen of Quon-
neticott to clayme the Narragansett Countrey . . . you suppose
it is taken for granted" that Rhode Island jurisdiction is excluded.[77]

It was not long before Massachusetts turned its wrath on its
confederate for attempting to take Southertown, Mystic, and
Pawcatuck away from Massachusetts authority. Connecticut
was accused of tempting these settlements into "disobedience
unto the Authority" of Massachusetts, and the towns in question had "long since orderly settled there upon the determination
of the Commissioners of the united Colonies." This was not only
"unneighborly," but also tended to "violate the articles of Confederation."[78] The Commissioners from New Haven, Plymouth,
and Massachusetts, at their regular session in 1663,[79] asked that
"all things Remaine as they have bine agreed by the Commissioners formerly."[80] In the meantime, the colonies of Massachusetts and Connecticut were to "comply with all means that are
Judged suitable to atteine the perpetuateing of correspondency"
between the two colonies.[81] The Connecticut authorities, however, were obstinate—they were now wooing the support of the
royal government, which the Bay was less inclined to do. Connecticut without delay proceeded to establish jurisdiction over
the contested territory.[82]

By the agreement of John Clarke and John Winthrop, Jr., in London, the Atherton Company could choose to which colony it cared to belong, and permission was given by the King in a letter to each of the United Colonies for the Atherton Company to "improve their colony and plantation in New England."[83] This land company, consisting mostly of Massachusetts men, probably would have favored Massachusetts. But, at about the same time the Bay and River colonies were thus strengthening their claims on the Narragansett country, Rhode Island, in 1663, received a charter taking in virtually the same lands in the Narragansett country as did the Connecticut Charter of 1662. Because two of the colonies now had charter rights to this area and there being small chance of the Massachusetts claims being confirmed in a like grant, the Atherton Company, using its prerogative under the Clarke-Winthrop agreement, elected to come under the jurisdiction of Connecticut.[84] The Rhode Island Assembly, however, ordered that all persons coming into the disputed territory should first obtain clearance from their colony.[85] In 1664, the wrangling over the Narragansett country was partially eclipsed by the Dutch War and the absorption of New Haven into Connecticut Colony. A committee appointed by Connecticut to treat with Massachusetts and Rhode Island, consisting of men experienced as Commissioners of the United Colonies,[86] was appointed;[87] and Rhode Island selected commissioners to treat with Massachusetts, but before a conference of the colonies could be held over these lands, the King's commissioners appeared on the scene. Both Rhode Island and Connecticut were adamant, refusing compromise.[88] Even the efforts of the Commissioners of the United Colonies were of no avail, because they completely ignored the rights of Rhode Islanders to settlement in the Narragansett country.[89]

After investigating conditions in the colonies for a few months, the King's commissioners in March, 1665, declared the Narragansett territory to be of open jurisdiction until the dispute could be settled in the future. In the meantime, the western limits of this no-man's land were drawn at the Pawcatuck River. All subjects, until final determination of the dispute, were to be "tennants" of the King,[90] and the Narragansett country was to be known as the King's Province. In their recommendations to the King, the royal commissioners favored the claims of Rhode Island over those of Connecticut. Rhode Island had a patent from the King in the 1640's; yet the Puritan colonies admitted New Haven and Connecticut (with lesser right to legal existence) into "their great combination," but excluded Rhode Island. The royal commissioners proceeded to indict the Indian and land policies of the Confederation. The United Colonies were accused of playing one Indian tribe against another. Furthermore

> The Commissioners of the united Colonies disposed of a great part of his country (R. I.), pretending they had conquered it from the Pequid Indians, but evidence being made that the Nanhygansett, had conquered it before the English began their warre, and that the right was in him who sold it to the Road Islanders, and his Majesties Commissioners not thinking it justifyable for any Colony to dispose of land without their own limitts, determined it for the Roade Islanders.[91]

Thus the royal commissioners showed that they favored the claims of Rhode Island to those of the Confederation, and, therefore, officers of the King's Province were to come from Rhode Island.[92] Elsewhere the royal commissioners declared lands of the United Colonies in abeyance until His Majesty's will should be known.[93] The Atherton Company was found not to have been formed within the proper authority of the King, and its purchasers were ordered to vacate their lands in the Pequot country.[94] But the harshest blows were saved for the Bay Colony, whose claims to Warwick and lands east of the Pawcatuck River under "that usurped authority called the United Colonies" were unequivocally voided.[95]

Although Connecticut and Massachusetts did not wish to antagonize the royal commissioners, they were reluctant to give up their claims, as was ordered by the royal commissioners. In protesting the encroachments of Rhode Island settlers west of the Pawcatuck River (boundary of the King's Province) the River Colony was on sure ground,[96] but in continuing to assert its jurisdiction over Wickford, one of the Atherton grants, it was obviously intermeddling in the King's Province.[97] The Bay Colony again sought jurisdiction over the Narragansett lands by obtaining allegiance from tribes which had fallen out with the Narragansetts.[98] Letters of protest continued between the Connecticut and Rhode Island authorities, and, in 1668-9, an attempt was made by Connecticut to bring commissioners of the two colonies together at New London to arrive at some compromise, but the letter from Connecticut reached the Rhode Island Assembly only after its adjournment.[99] Rhode Island, however, proceeded to appoint the officials of the King's Province, and lost no time in defining its boundaries, which, when later confirmed to the Colony, would form the limits of the present state of Rhode Island.[100] The Confederation, in the meantime, had been rent asunder, and the meetings of the Commissioners had been reduced to triennial sessions. The Commissioners, therefore, were able to lend little weight to the Connecticut claims on the Narragansett country at this time. Commissioners from Massachusetts and Connecticut, however, did meet in 1669—though their meeting was not considered a regular session of the Confederation; and they again spoke out with little avail against the spreading of Rhode Island settlers throughout the Pequot and Narragansett country.[101]

The New England Confederation was dedicated to the expansion of the Puritan way throughout New England in matters ranging from the governing of conscience to actual extension of territory. As for the coveted lands in the Narragansett-Pequot country the Confederation sought to extend its jurisdiction in this area, and might have succeeded had not the Stuart banner once again been raised in the homeland. The colonies of New England now had to reckon with imperial oversight. The venomous shafts against Puritan independency would be aimed at the Puritan state on the Bay. Massachusetts was slow to understand the gravity of the situation and sought to meet rebuff after rebuff from the home government. It would have been better, instead of following the paths of obstinacy, to have courted royal favor, as her sister colonies of Plymouth and Connecticut were learning to do. But the Bay bull remained recalcitrant until the revocation of its charter in 1684 brought it to its senses. In land policy, the Bay sought to confirm its claims by force or conniving with disgruntled Indian sachems, the episode with the Warwick settlers an example. Instead of turning to the home government, they sought official sanction from the Commissioners of the United Colonies. But this was not enough. The Confederation, started on the road of strict construction and narrow policy, was becoming obsolete in the face of a growing liberalism and expansion in all walks of New England life.

Though at one time they possessed the means to force dominion over the Naboth's Vineyard of New England, which was coveted as the final piece in the Puritan Commonwealth, the United Colonies found that it no longer commanded the moral force of the country; rather, it was on the defensive. The New England Confederacy in the 1660's, therefore, was allowed to fall apart—its mission for consolidating New England orthodoxy was obsolete. When the Confederation was revived in 1670-2, it was dedicated solely to one principle, that of military defense of the colonies. Though the early Confederacy did not meet success in the Narragansett land controversies, one area of success during the first Confederation remains to be told: that of the conduct of New England's relations with the Dutch.

---

[1] Massachusetts early annexed the New Hampshire settlements, wits its inhabitants becoming "freemen of the Countrie." By 1653 the Bay had extended her jurisdiction as far as Kittery, Maine, and not long after as far as Casco Bay. This was easily accomplished because of the death of Ferdinando Gorges and the turmoil of civil war in England; also there was need for protection against the Indians, and the granting of freemanship to these settlements. Bradstreet, while a Commissioner of the United Colonies, in 1652 represented Massachusetts in settling the "Eastern affairs." (See M. W. Jernegan, *The American Colonies, 1492-1750*, (N. Y.: 1930), I, 148; H. S. Burrage, *The Beginnings of Colonial Maine*, (Portland: 1914), 360, 374-5; C. E. Banks, *History of York, Maine*, (Boston: 1931), I, 177-194; M. F. Farnham, *The Farnham Papers*, (Portland: 1901). VII, Jul49, 265-6). Southold on Long Island in 1643-4 and Southampton at the same time came under the jurisdiction of New Haven and Connecticut, respectively. Southold, "almost from the settlement of the Town, possessed the advantages of this larger and more comprehensive and powerful Union, as well as the fostering care of the government of the colony of New Haven." (J. W. Case, ed., *Southold Town Records*, (New York: 1882), vii.) The New England Confederation represented actually smaller confederations (even in the case of Mass.—with town deputies in the General Court)—thus, Southampton, in voting to join with Connecticut, stated they should "enter into combination with the Jurisdiction of Connecticote." (G. R. Howell, *The Early History of Southampton, L. I.*, (Albany: 1887), p. 5.) In the case of Southampton, final ratification was given by the Commissioners of the United Colonies in Sep44.

[2] Brockunier, *op. cit.*, p. 136.

[3] Winthrop, *Journal*, (S), II, 102.

[4] Brockunier, *op. cit.*, p. 137.

[5] For contrary interpretations of this episode see Palfrey and Brockunier.

[6] Winthrop, *Journal*, (S), II, 165.

[7] *Ibid.*

[8] *Ibid.*, pp. 166-7.

[9] Samuel Gorton, *Simplicities Defence against Seven-Headed Policy*, Vol. IV of *Force Tracts*, (New York: 1947), No. 6, 46-8.

[10] Winthrop, *Journal*, (S), II, 168.

[11] Gorton, *op. cit.*, pp. 50-1.

[12] Winthrop, *Journal*, *ibid*; Kenneth W. Porter, "Samuel Gorton," *NEQ*, VII (Sept., 1934), 423-34.

[13] *PCR*, IX, 12.

[14] Palfrey, *op. cit.*, II, 133.

[15] Gorton, *op. cit.*, p. 53. Winthrop writes: "It was a special providence of God that neither any of them nor of ours were slain or hurt, though many shot passed between them." (*Journal*, (S), II, 169.)

[16] Jarvis M. Morse, *American Beginnings* (Wash., D.C.: 1952), pp. 136-7; Gorton, *ibid.*, pp. 59-60, 72.

[17] Gorton, *ibid.*, pp. 73-4.

[18] *Ibid.*, p. 83.

[19] The cattle of these settlers were confiscated to the amount of £160. (Winthrop, *Journal*, (S), II, 179.)

[20] Brockunier, *op. cit.*, p. 156.

[21] *Ibid.*

[22] Winthrop, *Journal*, (S), II, 308.

[23] *Ibid.*, p. 309.

[24] Ltr of Henry Watson of Providence Plantations, 9Aug45, Council Records, II, R. I., MA.

[25] Hollister, *op. cit.*, p. 135.

[26] Charles J. Hoadly, "The Warwick Patent," *Acorn Publications*, (Hartford: 1902), VII, 9, 46.

[27] *CCR*, I, 70.

[28] Winthrop, *Journal*, (S), II, 325; ". . . Reserveing To the Commissioners of the United Colonies, what properly belongs to them coming by Disposeing the sayd Pequots . . ." Eva Butler, "Beginnings of Pequot Plantation," with New London Town Recs., typewritten, CHS, VI, 289.)

[29] *MCR*, III, 126.

[30] Hollister, *op. cit.*, p. 151; Thomas F. Waters, *John Winthrop, Jr., Publications of the Ipwich Hist. Soc.*, VII (1899), 38, 43-4; Clarence W. Mowen, *The Boundary Disputes of Connecticut*, (Boston: 1882), pp. 16-7; *PCR*, IX, 103. Most historians have held, since Connecticut could not produce a copy of the Warwick patent upon request of the United Colonies, that there was no such copy in the colonies. But among the papers of Edward Hopkins, Commissioner of the United Colonies, has been found a copy. (See Coleman, *The Old Patent of Connecticut*, (Westport, Conn.: 1936), p. 48.

[31] *PCR*, IX, 150-4.

154   THE UNITED COLONIES OF NEW ENGLAND

[82] William Haynes, *Stonington Chronology*, (Stonington, Conn.: 1949), pp. 13-4.

[83] 21Oct57, Towns and Lands, CA, I, 40.

[84] Plymouth: Winslow and Prence; New Haven: Newman and Leete.

[85] 16Sep58, MA, II, 354.

[86] *PCR*, X, 209. Connecticut sought to revive the controversy in 1659. (MA, II, 175; CCR, I, 335.)

[87] *MCR*, III, 48. The agents at this time were Saltonstall, Cooke, and Pocock. For Plymouth and Connecticut to assert claims on the Narragansett lands was difficult because these colonies were without a charter and could not assert their claims through legal proceedings in the homeland. (See Thomas Aspinwall, *Remarks on the Narragansett Patent)* (Providence: 1865), p. 24.

[88] Winthrop, *Journal*, (S), II, 340-1.

[89] Viz., Samuel Gorton, Randall Holden, and John Green.

[40] Winthrop, *Journal*, (S), II, 344.

[41] *Ibid.*, p. 345.

[42] John Childe, *New-Englands Jonas Cast Up at London*, printed in *Force Tracts*, IV (No. 3, 1947), pp. 14, 21.

[43] Title page, *op. cit.* Pub. Aug46.

[44] Gorton, *op. cit.*, p. 17.

[45] Winthrop, *Journal*, (S), II, 359.

[46] *Ibid.*, pp. 365-6.

[47] Edward Winslow, *Hypocrisie Unmasked* (1646) (Providence: The Club for Colonial Reprints, 1916), pp. 5-6.

[48] *Ibid.*, p. 65. In his dedication of this work to the Earl of Warwick, Winslow wrote: "Were not your Wisdome and experience . . . so well known . . . I might be discouraged to appeare in the righteous cause of the *United Colonies of New England*, and more especially in the behalf of the *Governour and Company of the Massachusets.*"

[49] Samuel G. Arnold, *History of Rhode Island*, (New York: 1859), I, 193-4.

[50] *PCR*, IX, 150.

[51] Felt, *op. cit.*, II, 31-2; *PCR*, IX, 170-1.

[52] Arnold *op. cit.*, pp. 238-9.

[53] Brockunier, *op. cit.*, p. 225. Prof. Brockunier consistently derides the United Colonies for its "imperial arrogance."

[54] Arnold, *op. cit.*, p. 216.

[55] Henry M. Dexter, *As to Roger Williams* . . . (Boston: 1876), pp. 119-22. This is a painstaking effort to debunk Roger Williams, and is quite prejudicial.

[56] The Mass. jurisdiction over these towns did not affect the property rights of the proprietors. (Otis G. Hammond, "The Mason Title and Its Relation to New Hampshire and Massachusetts," *AASP* (1916), XXVI, 245-263. Exeter was the only hesitant town to come under Massachusetts jurisdiction of the New Hampshire towns. (C. H. Bell, *History of Exeter*, (Exeter: 1888), pp. 44-6.)

[57] *PCR*, IX, 21; F. B. Hough, *Papers re Nantucket*, (Albany: 1856), p. x.

[58] *PCR*, X, 195. (e.g., Oyster Bay and Huntington under N. H. Colony.)

[59] See Chapter VIII.

[60] *RICR*, I, 421, 426; 23Aug59, *Trumbull Papers, MHSC*, 5:IX:10-2.

[61] Benj. Arnold to John Winthrop, Jr., 20Oct59, Winthrop Papers, MHS, X, 83; Same to Thos. Prence, 26Oct59, Winslow Papers, MHS, I, 12.

[62] 31Oct60, States (R. I.), CHS.

[63] 22Aug61, letter to Mass. General Court, MA, II, 20.

[64] Bradstreet *et al.*, to the Gov. and Council of Conn. (n.d., 1662?), *Trumbull Papers, MHSC* 5:IX: 31-2.

[65] James Arnold, ed., *The Fones Record* (Providence: 1894), I, p. 14. 16Nov60.

[66] *Ibid.*; MA, XXX, 83. In 1659, in Dedham, there was also a movement to acquire lands by revoking Indian deeds. The Gen. Ct. of the Colony, however, intervened by granting the affected Indians, many of them "Praying Indians," lands elsewhere. *(Dedham Town Records.*, IV, 9.) Often Indian deeds to the white man carried the stipulation they could retain "full liberty to hunt fowls and fish." (Ind. Deeds, 14May61, CHS.)

[67] Among the Commissioners in the Company were John Winthrop, Jr., Bradstreet, Denison, Josiah Winslow, and John Brown.

[68] *Fones Record, op. cit.*, pp. 10-12, 13Oct60.

[69] Brockunier, *op. cit.*, p. 253.

[70] Thomas Prence to the Gov. of R. I., 13Sep61, *PCR*, X, 266-7; MA, II, 355; *RICR*, I, 452-3.

[71] In the Pequot Country, for thirty years, Connecticut had granted to its leaders 13,000 acres. Forrest Morgan, *Connecticut as a Colony and as a State* (Hartford: 1904), p. 183. The Connecticut claims by the Charter also violated the settlement in London between Winthrop of Conn. and Clarke of R. I., that the Pawcatuck River was to be the boundary between the two colonies and land controversies were to be submitted to arbitration. (Stevens Transcripts, I, 27.)

[72] Palfrey, *op. cit.*, II, 383.

[73] William Haynes, *op. cit.*, p. 15; Misc. Corres., MA, II, 24-5, 25A.

[74] The Confederation had given leeway to Massachusetts to grant lands in the Pequot Country to the conquered Pequots—which helped to stake out these lands for Massachusetts. (Declaration of the Gen. Ct. of Mass., 7May62, MA, XXX, 108.) The Commissioners continued to receive lands deeded from Narragansett sachems. *(MHSC,* 5:IX:34-5.)

[75] Mass. General Court to General Court of R. I., 10May62, MA, II, 29.

[76] MA, II, 176. The Deputy Governor was John Mason, who, having lands in the area claimed by Massachusetts, had protested the decision of the Confederation in 1658.

[77] MA, II, 33; *RICR*, I, 492-5.

[78] Mass. Council to General Assembly of Conn., 31Oct62, Trumbull (Early MSS), CHS; MA, II, 176a.

[79] The possibility of bringing the controversy before an extraordinary session of the Confederation was explored. (MA, II, 38.)

[80] *PCR*, X, 299; MA, II, 40.

[81] MA, II, 182; Conn. Misc. MSS, NYHS (Allyn, 13Oct63). The Confederation also appointed a committee to investigate the claims of the Mohegans in the Narr. Country. (R. C. Winthrop Coll., II, 125, Conn. Lib.).

[82] *Ibid.*

[83] Palfrey, *op. cit.*, II, 564.

[84] *Ibid.*, p. 571. *RICR*, II, 30.

[86] E.g., John Mason, Mathew Allyn, Samuel Wyllys, John Talcott; but they "shall not give away any parte of the bounds of our charter."

[87] *CCR*, I, 435; CA, Col. Boundaries, I, 25.

[88] Conn. found it necessary to assert complete loyalty to the royal government in regard to the provisions of the charter, though the "advise of the united Colonies" would constantly be sought. (Winthrop-Davenport MSS, NYPL, Jul64,4, #47.) The Confederation continued to grant lands in this territory to the Pequot Indians. (MA, XXX, 125; R. C. Winthrop Coll., II, 140). Rhode Island settlers were assessed a bushel of corn an acre from Pequot Indians attempting to plant east of the Pawcatuck River under authority of the Commissioners of the United Colonies. (Stanton to Winthrop, 14Nov64, Winthrop Papers, MHS, XVIII, 135.

[89] *PCR*, X, 320-1.

[90] Instrs. to the King's Commissioners, 23Apr64, Stevens Transcripts, John Carter Brown Lib., 1, 38.

[91] *RICR*, II, 128.

[92] *Ibid.*, p. 127.

[93] A tentative boundary between Plymouth and Rhode Island had been set by the Royal Commissioners, in such a way as not to "hinder or forbid Either Colony to go in all sorts of boats . . ." etc. Plymouth displayed a much more amiable spirit than the two other united colonies, and pledged cooperation with "soe near neighbour" as Rhode Island. (R. I. Archives, R. I. and Mass. Boundary Settlements, I, 2, 3; *MHSC* 1:VI:203-5.) Mass. stubbornly defended its taking of jurisdiction in Maine, even though the royal commissioners proclaimed this a royal province. (Answer of Mass. General Court, (1665, James Baxter, ed., *Sir Ferdinando Gorges and his Prov. of Maine, PPS* (1890), II, 207ff.) Also, M. F. Farnham, ed., *The Farnham Papers*, Vol. VII of *Documentary History of Maine*, (Portland: 1901), 317-9.

[94] Arnold, *op. cit.*, p. 316.

[95] *RICR*, II, 95.

[96] *CCR*, II, 180.

[97] Arnold, *op. cit.*, p .335.

[98] Viz., the Nipmucks. The Narragansetts were "ingaged to the United Colonies . . . not to doe any wrong or enter into any hostility with our neighbor Indians." *(MCR*, IV, p. 2, 357-9.)

[99] *RICR*, II, 225-235, 247-9; *CCR*, II, 526-33.

[100] Arnold, *op. cit.*, p. 338.

[101] MHS, II, 130; *MHSC* 3:III:209-10.

CHAPTER VIII

The Eagle and the "Beetle Fly"

New Haven Colony and the Dutch at New Amsterdam were the chief commercial rivals in the New World at the time of the forming of the Confederation. For a few triumphal years during the early Confederacy, the New Haven adventurers sought to establish a trading empire in the New World and to touch the mainsprings of English commerce. The glory that was New Haven's, however, was brief: disaster soon put an end to the far-flung trading ambitions of its founders. Their great ship, laden down with rich goods for the homeland, was lost at sea; the Dutch expelled them from settlements on their southern flank; and eventually the Colony was overshadowed by its mightier neighbor on the river. But before disaster struck, the prospects of New Haven's future indeed looked bright. New Haven had been hewn from a string of seaport towns along the Sound; even more, it was elevated to equal membership in the great Confederation of the Puritan colonies. With the protection of this mighty league, the New Haven traders could afford to be daring with their Dutch neighbors.

The story of the early relations of New England and New Netherlands, with the Dutch always on the defensive, is a rich and amusing tale—though, from the Knickerbocker point of view, there were tragic overtones. The foreign policy of the Confederation in relation to the Dutch during the first decade of the Confederacy was set by the bouncy Colony on the Sound. Indeed New Haven, secure in the arms of the Confederacy, was likened by the Dutch Governor to an eagle swooping down to enrage the "Beetle Fly" (the Dutch), after which the eagle would return to its secluded nest.[2]

The concern of the New England colonies for their Dutch neighbors was a primary force in the forming of the Confederation. As early as 1634, the Plymouth traders saw, when they sought passage up the 'Fresh River', Dutch guns from the Fort of Good Hope at Hartford turned on them.[3] Though the Puritan

157

colonies lost little time through legislation to display their fear of infiltration by transients from other colonies,[4] their interests in regard to the Dutch were of an offensive nature, even encroaching upon the outlying Dutch settlements. Yet the Dutch fort at Hartford gave grounds for the English to fear the Dutch, and the flourishing beaver trade in Connecticut[5] was competing with New Netherland in trade with the West Indies. Thus the colonies of Connecticut and Massachusetts, even before the establishing of the Confederacy, found it necessary to present a united front against their Dutch neighbors. A compromise was offered to the Dutch at Hartford in the form of additional land grants. But the Dutch refused to accept this offer, and in 1641 they would have sent an armed band to Hartford to prevent English encroachment had not an Indian uprising at Fort Orange prevented such a maneuver. In the same year the Reverend Hugh Peter was sent by the Puritan colonies ot England and, should it become necessary, to the Netherlands to work out a "neighbourhood" of trade in the New World and the West Indies. But this mission also was unsuccessful.[6] The presence of so near a neighbor with a strange language and strange customs—one who professedly sought the Golden Calf which might lure away New England settlers — certainly gave cause for uneasiness to the Puritan colonies bent on establishing a consolidated Puritan commonwealth in the New World.

In 1641, the menace of the New England colonies to Dutch settlement in the New World became quite clear when Captain Nathaniel Turner of New Haven purchased a large tract of land on both sides of the upper Delaware River, to which New Haven settlers moved the following spring. Under the leadership of George Lamberton, who had already been trading with Virginia and the Barbados, a blockhouse was built at the new settlement, and the enterprising New Englanders busily engaged in the beaver trade of the region. This action was actually a direct challenge to the Dutch and Swedes, who had staked out the trade in these parts for themselves. It looked as if the English settlers had come to plant a colony at the back door of the Dutch, and the New Haven town (two years before the seacoast towns were united in the Colony) lost no time in voting itself authority over this region. Not long afterwards, the Dutch sent two sloops to oust the English from the Varkens Kill region,[7] and with the cooperation of the Swedes on the lower Delaware this was accomplished.[8]

But the crushing of the infant New Haven settlement on the Delaware had far-reaching consequences, of which the Dutch were not aware at the time. The ousting of these settlers only whetted the appetite of New Haven to settle further within the bounds of the Dutch, and this "doleful experience" also hastened the forming of the New England Confederation. If the Dutch had permitted the venture to continue unmolested, it is possible that the settlement, lacking sufficient capital, which soon became scarce in New Haven, might have turned its allegiance to the Dutch in order to secure their aid; in any event, Dutch policy at this time would not have alienated the United Colonies.

Even the Bay Colony was now interested in the prospects of opening up the beaver trade on the Delaware to the English, and in 1644 sent a vessel up the Delaware under the pretense of making an exploratory cruise. Though the vessel returned unscathed, it had aroused the heated protests of the Dutch and Swedes, not to mention the volleys of their cannon fire.[9] Nor could the New Haven adventurers be prevented from spying out the Delaware country. Under the auspices of the Delaware Company, whose most prominent members were also Commissioners of the United Colonies,[10] George Lamberton and his associates continued to try to nose in on the beaver trade; but again these efforts were thwarted. Lamberton was arrested by Governor Printz of New Sweden, subsequently tried, and heavily fined.[11] The Dutch at the Fort of Good Hope at Hartford continued to be a source of irritation in their relations with the English. Though Governor Kieft of New Amsterdam consented to lease the lands about the fort to the English, he intrusted the command of this small garrison to a headstrong Dutch officer, who was determined to hold his own against any abuse from the English.[12] Thus were the uncompromising and hostile attitudes of these rivals in the New World at the time of the forming of the Confederation in 1643.

Fortunately for the United Colonies in 1643, the Dutch were engaged in putting down a general Indian uprising on all flanks of the Dutch settlement. The policies of the Governor at New Amsterdam were blamed for inciting the Indians to warfare,[13] and this greatly weakened his prestige. But it was an opportune time for conciliatory dealings with New England; possibly, the Dutch could even secure aid in putting down the savage revolt, the flames of which might spread to New England.

When the news of the forming of the United Colonies reached Fort Amsterdam, the Director-General and Council felt this event provided a fitting opportunity for obtaining a redress of grievances and establishing a better understanding with the English.[14] A sloop was then sent to Boston with letters in Latin addressed to the "governour and senate" of the "United Provinces of New England."[15] These letters protested against English encroachments in territory claimed by the Dutch in Connecticut and New Haven. Because the "chief council" (Winthrop's designation of the General Court) was "far dispersed," and the first meeting of the Commissioners of the United Colonies had not yet been held, a general letter from the Governor, which deferred to the advice of several elders, was sent in reply. The Bay Colony made clear its intention to promote the interests of the four Puritan colonies through "our confederation," and suggested that the territorial disputes be referred to the home countries for arbitration.[16] The Dutch letters were passed around from colony to colony and Winslow skeptically observed that "many of the passages" agreed "too well with common Fame and I fear our breathren of Hartford will be found faulty in them whosoever shall have the hearing of it."[17] The time, however, was not yet ripe for arbitration; the claims of both parties were vague, and any referral of the dispute to the home governments would have to wait until the clouds of civil war cleared in England.

In this first year of the New England Confederacy, the Dutch of New Netherland were having their hands full in waging war against the Indians. In the words of Irving, "Every day or two some broad-bottomed express-rider, covered with mud and mire, would come floundering to the gate of New Amsterdam, freighted with some new tale of aggression from the frontier."[18] The Dutch finally became emboldened enough to swallow their pride and ask the New England colonies for an auxiliary force of a hundred men to send against the Indians. The New Haven General Court seriously considered this proposition, for they were on the New England perimeter nearest the Indian hostilities and the Indians did not always discriminate between an Englishman and a Dutchman. But New Haven refused to send aid because, as a member of the newly formed Confederation, she would have to defer to the decisions of the Commission of the United Colonies. Nevertheless, New Haven promised to present the matter at the annual meeting of the Commissioners, and in the meantime help would be given, if need be, in the form of supplies.[19] The Bay Colony, however, was reluctant to send an expedition to aid the Dutch for fear that Director Kieft was attempting for his own advantage to draw the English into a quarrel with the Indians.[20] But Massachusetts did provide the machinery for war within its own colony, which included organizing the militia of the four counties[21] under the command of a Major General appointed by the General Court and ordering that a "standing Councel for peace or war" be comprised of the Governor and Magistrates.[22]

When the Commissioners of the United Colonies met for the first time in September, 1643, the New Haven Commissioners, Gregson and Eaton, reviewed the grievances against the Dutch, especially the ouster of the New Haven settlers from the Delaware region. The Commissioners immediately decided that John Winthrop, as President of the Confederation, should send a letter to Governor Printz of New Sweden stating the English position and protesting against the trial of Lamberton and his associates.[23] A member of the Delaware Company, Nathaniel Turner, delivered this letter to the Swedish Governor. It was asserted in the letter that the New England colonies, by *"vero confaederatos nostros,"* were entitled to lawful trade with the Indians on the Delaware.[24] Correspondence, which was begun by the Commissioners, via Winthrop, with the Dutch, denied the right of the Dutch to lands at Hartford. The profuse correspondence, conducted in Latin, accomplished little, except to issue such broad platitudes as wishing that *"omnia inter vos et confaederatos nostros Neuhauenes, summa pace et concordia, transignatur negotia."*[25]

The New England Puritans, as obstinate as usual, continued to intermeddle in the Delaware region. In 1644, the Bay dispatched William Aspinwall to examine "the western bounds of our colony" by sailing up the Delaware River, but he was prevented from going very far by the Dutch at Fort Nassau.[26] In the same year, a bark with seven men from the Bay, trading at the site of the original English settlement at Varkens Kill, was seized by the Indians and all but two of the traders were mur dered. Although the English at Boston liked to think of Governor Printz as being void of Christian and "moral conscience" and a man "very furious and passionate, cursing and swearing," they appreciated his efforts in bringing the murderers to justice.[27] Separate English settlements on the Delaware were thus prevented by the stern policies of the Dutch and the Swedes. But the expansion of the English colonies could not be held in check, and already English settlers were setting up trading posts in the Hudson Valley.[28]

Tension between the Dutch and the English continued to mount despite New Haven's and Connecticut's authorization of an expedition under Captain John Underhill to be sent from the English colonies to aid the Dutch. The Commissioners, however, refused to apportion the charge of this expedition upon all the United Colonies because an "Actual Assault" had not been committed upon the colonies,[29] which if such had been the case would have required the colonies to act together for their defense. The calendar of business for the Confederation during 1644-5 was filled with the controversy with the French in Acadia and the domestic Indian situation. The only significant development with the Dutch during these two years was the proposal of the New England colonies that commissioners from New Netherland meet with the Commissioners of the United Colonies at Hartford to settle their differences,[30] which was actually accomplished six years later.

In 1646, the Commissioners turned their full attention to the grievances between the United Colonies and the Dutch. Director Kieft and the "Senate of new Netherland" sent their uncompromising views to the "most noble and worthy Commissioners of the federated English met togeither at the Red Mounte, or New Haven," which Kieft claimed was within the bounds of New Netherland. The Dutch Governor accused the Colony on the Sound, with its long-reaching arms penetrating everywhere in Dutch territory, of an "unsatiable desire of possessing that which is ours." Counterassertions were made, with New Haven stating she would make good her claims, and the Dutch replying that they would "manfully" recover any further encroachments made by English settlers.[31] Connecticut Colony also had its complaint to register against the Dutch. The watch at Hartford had been highly insulted when it was refused admittance to the

Dutch Fort of Good Hope to capture an Indian servant who had fled from her English master; but to top it all, the Dutch commander boldly met the English guard, and after breaking his rapier over one of the Englishmen, turned his heels to the startled guard and returned to the confines of the fort. When the Dutch authorities were asked to explain this brazen affront to the Connecticut guard, the reply was given that "we seeme to heare Esops wolfe complayninge of the lamb." With the worsening of Dutch-English relations, insult after insult was hurled at the Yankee pride. The Hartford incident served to prove, the Dutch asserted, "that such mischeifes happen" because of committing such a trust to "ignorant boyes who when they once finde themselves loaden with armes, thincke they may alsoe lawfull cry out."[32]

For the next several years, the Commissioners made plain to the Dutch, their grievances, pointing out that they were of a most serious nature. The Dutch, in the meantime, had received a new Governor, the wry Peter Stuyvesant. Stuyvesant in his relations with New England did not live up to his reputation for stubbornness, but instead chose a course of compromise and magnanimity, which was the only way that English aggression could be deterred. One of the first acts of Stuyvesant in the New World was to send his secretary to Boston to discuss a settlement of their differences.[33] But the light-headedness and evasiveness of the Dutch envoy pulled no wool over the eyes of the haughty Puritans. The humiliating Hartford incident in itself demanded full explanation.

By 1649, the Commissioners had compiled an impressive list of complaints against the Dutch, bringing their previous grievances up to date, for all of which the Commissioners demanded satisfaction. First of all, the Dutch were accused of harboring escaped English servants and criminals. The beating up of the watch at Hartford by the Dutch commander there and the subsequent jibes of Governor Kieft had not been accounted for, nor had the confiscating of a ship belonging to a Dutch merchant living in New Haven.[34] Furthermore, the Commissioners of the Confederation protested against the selling of "Instruments of warr" to the Indians, whether in their own or in English territory,[35] and against the levying of an impost on foreign shipping at Manhattan.[36] The Commissioners then warned that if the same discriminatory trade measures were continued by the Dutch, they would be forced to take reciprocal action, and, forthwith, if ammunition or guns appearing to be destined for the Indians were found on Dutch trading vessels in English ports, the vessels would be detained until "satisfaction" was made. Amends were also demanded by the Commissioners for the seizure of Mr. Westerhouse's vessel at New Haven and for the interference with English trade on the Delaware. The Commissioners in their representations to the Dutch were taking over in full stride the conduct of foreign affairs of the four quasi-independent Puritan states that formed the United Colonies.

Although the Dutch director and council at New Amsterdam continued to insist that commissioners from the two governments get together, preferably letting the two confederates of the New England colonies not directly concerned in the controversies with the Dutch, and in particular the governors of Plymouth and Massachusetts, arbitrate the disputes,[37] a reply was sent to the Commissioners at their extraordinary meeting in 1649 stating that all of the charges against the Dutch were "defective." Stuyvesant was playing a cool hand in insisting upon jurisdiction over much of Connecticut and New Haven territory, thereby undoubtedly hoping that in the eventual compromise the bounds of New Netherland would not be too contracted. Already the New Englanders, from the Dutch point of view, had "seized nearly the half of New Netherland."[38] The New Haven colonists, after their great loss in 1646,[39] were looking about in desperation for profitable trading ventures, never giving up hope of establishing themselves in the beaver trade on the Delaware.[40] Pressure was therefore put to bear on the Commissioners to set the Dutch straight in their extravagant claim to "all that land betwixt that river called Conneticut and that by the English named Deleware."[41] The Commissioners firmly refuted all Dutch territorial claims to New England:

> Wee Cannot but assert the English Title and Just Right both to New Haven Lands and Harbor and to all the English plantations and theire apurtenances from Cap Cod or point Judeth both on the mayne and the Ilands . . . as anciently graunted by the Kings of England . . . sence duly

Purchased from the Indians and peaceably planted and
Imployed by the Inhabitants of the United Colonies.[42]

If the Anglo-Dutch relations were not to deteriorate to the
point of war, an event which the English Navigation Acts of
1651 would hasten, some means of settling the dispute had to
be found. It suited the New England and the Dutch temper-
ments to work out the details of a treaty among themselves,
rather than submit the whole affair to the home governments—
especially with the dislike of the United Colonies at this time
for interference from without.[43]

By 1650, the Anglo-Dutch rivalry in the New World was at
full blast. The Commissioners spurned on by their confederates
at New Haven and Connecticut, were working overtime in their
correspondence with the Dutch in an attempt to bring them
to terms. New charges were hurled by the Dutch. Besides the
usual territorial claims the Dutch complained the English
harbored fugitives at New Haven, that the English trade with
the Indians was undervalued, and that a Dutch ship had been
stripped of its cargo at Rhode Island. These were largely coun-
tercharges to those which the Commissioners had already made,
the first sign that the Dutch were on the defensive.[44] The Commissioners dismissed the Dutch charges as lacking proof, and
said any matter involving Rhode Island did not concern the
United Colonies.[45] But at last the oft-renewed Dutch invitation
to refer the differences to arbitration was accepted by the Commissioners.[46]

It was agreed that two of the Commissioners, one each from
Plymouth and Massachusetts—instead of the governors of these
colonies as Stuyvesant had requested—and two delegates named
by Stuyvesant should negotiate articles of agreement that would
be binding on both the English and the Dutch. Simon Bradstreet
and Thomas Prence were thereby chosen to "Consider and
Compose all differences."[47] For the meeting to be held during
the session of the Commissioners at Hartford, the Commissioners from the Bay, in their instructions from the General Court
which depict the gravity of the occasion, were given wide discretionary power to avoid measures that might provide cause for
war.[48]

The meeting in Hartford proved to be a gala occasion. As a

demonstration of good will, the Dutch Governor came in person to Hartford. Everywhere he was "entertained with great pomp," and treated "like a Prince."[49] In return for this fine reception, the wry old Dutchman selected as his delegates two Englishmen, George Baxter, his English secretary, and Thomas Willett, a merchant of both Plymouth and New Amsterdam.[50] President Edward Hopkins, Commissioner from Connecticut, presided over this conference during the session of the Confederation, this service being regarded by his biographer as one of the most distinguished of Hopkins's varied career.[51]. The debates were heated, and Hopkins was even personally accused of having engaged in selling ammunition to the Indians,[52] which was outlawed by the Dutch as well as by the English. Finally, articles for a treaty were agreed upon by the four plenipotentiaries. First of all, most of the grievances caused by the Kieft administration would not have to be answered by Stuyvesant. An important concession made to New Haven, though it proved to be only a paper agreement, was that English trading on the Delaware should be allowed to continue in "love and peace," while the matter would be further considered by the home governments. The seizing of Mr. Westerhouse's ship in New Haven harbor was permissible, because he was trading without a license. The extradition of fugitives, which had been a sore point with both governments, would be in accord with the eighth article of the New England Articles of Confederation.[53]

The most important provision of the Treaty of Hartford was the definition of boundaries between the English and Dutch. The dividing line was run on the west side of Oyster Bay on Long Island, and on the mainland from Greenwich Bay, four miles from Stamford, to twenty miles north.[54] Thus the boundaries followed largely the status quo, confirming to the English their setlements on the Sound. In every matter of consequence, the treaty was a triumph for New England, and the permission for the Dutch to keep their lands at Hartford and the awarding of Mr. Westerhouse's ship to the Dutch were only of minor importance. The treaty was to be "kept Inviolate both by the English of the united Collonies and all the Nation" until a "final determination" was reached in Europe.[55]

But did the United Colonies by the Hartford Treaty receive such a bargain after all? The treaty did little more than confirm the status quo. The English had little to lose, for they could maintain by force the settlements they had planted, and the Dutch, far inferior in resources and number of men, could not do much more than protest. Yet, if the boundaries of the Dutch and English colonies could be defined, then the English expansion might be stabilized as it was, rather than continue to spread throughout the countryside. At worst, the Dutch would have grounds in the future for asserting jurisdiction over any future English settlements within the limits prescribed to them by the Treaty of Hartford. Perhaps this is the reason that Stuyvesant went out of his way to placate the English. His part in the treaty has been characterized as unrealistic by historians, who have considered Stuyvesant somewhat foolish for thinking that he could stay English expansion. But such was not the case; no one could have been more realistic under the circumstances. If the Dutch could have continued to treat with the United Colonies of New England as a sovereign state, the Puritans would have been inclined to honor the agreement, and without further meddling from the home governments the Dutch colony might have been preserved. But, of course, such was not the course of history.

In helping the English to think they got something for nothing, Stuyvesant put on a good show. When the decision of the

> arbitrators was brought to the ears of the Governor, he made a great complaint against his two chosen agents, crying out: I've been betrayed! I've been betrayed! Which hearing, some of the English who were waiting outside, supposed that he had run mad, and were disposed to go and fetch people to tie him. It seems he never imagined that such hard pills would be given him to digest. New England is thoroughly united with the Dutch Governor to her satisfaction and is well content with him; speaks of him in terms of great praise, especially because he is so liberal and hath allowed himself to be entrapped by courtesy. . . .[56]

Although the treaty may have been best for New Netherland, the Director-General on his return home faced severe criticism from his Vice-Director and the Council. Having learned of the transaction in New England only indirectly, they demanded of the Dutch Governor a report, but instead, in typical Stuyvesant autocratic fashion, received for an answer "that nothing special was transacted" and they would learn in due time the nature of the proceedings when the matter would be referred to Amstor dam and London.[57]

The relations between New England and New Netherland after the Treaty of Hartford, however, did not settle down quietly as expected. New Haven interpreted the treaty as a blank check for planting again a settlement on the Delaware, and in a town meeting in December, 1650, it was voted to remove part of the town to the Delaware region. But when the expedition was under way, Stuyvesant intercepted their ship at New Amsterdam, and imprisoned the leaders, releasing them only upon promise to abandon their intentions to settle upon the Delaware.[58] Stuyvesant, in defending his actions to the Commissioners of the United Colonies, was even brazen enough to ask the support of the Confederation to check the Long Island settlers from whittling away at his domain.[59] When the Commissioners of the United Colonies met at New Haven in 1651,[60] they took heed of the indignation of the town. In their letter to the agent for the colonies in England, Edward Winslow, the Commissioners of the Confederation asked that he secure clearance from Parliament for the New England colonists to settle on the Delaware according to several old English patents, and also find out what was the opinion of Parliament as to the ousting of the New Haven settlers from settling on the Delaware.[61] The United Colonies were now thinking of war, and for the first time were seeking the backing of the mother country. The policy of the Dutch at New Amsterdam was geared only to the New England colonies' handling their own affairs. Combined policy and possible cooperative action of the colonies and the home government would be much too formidable for the Dutch.

Most of the time of the Commissioners at the New Haven meeting, however, was taken up with negotiations with the French ambassadors.[62] Nevertheless, this year marks the beginning of a feverish preparation for war. A month after the adjournment of this session of the Confederation, the famous Navigation Act of 1651 was passed,[63] aimed at ejecting the Dutch from the carrying trade in English harbors. Repercussions were immediately felt in the New World, and mixed with a general restlessness of the Indians, the New England colonies began to fear an attack from the Dutch and the Indians. The Dutch, too, saw on the horizon the clouds of war, and lost no time in fortifying their towns.[64] It was unfortunate that the Confederation did not convene in 1652 because of a procedural difficulty,[65] but the English colonies, nevertheless, went all out in preparations for war until they would receive further direction from their Federal Commissioners.

"The Time Is a Time of Danger" was the watchword of the United Colonies in 1651.[66] The Boston watch was reinforced in order to better scan the first signs of a Dutch fleet;[67] and the Secretary of the Colony was ordered to withhold the dispensing of arms and ammunition to the Indians sent over by the Corporation for Promoting the Gospel in England, and instead to sell them to Englishmen.[68] Seeing that war was inevitable in Europe, Stuyvesant, consistent with his policy of dealing with the American colonies independently of the home governments, proposed that New England conclude with him a commercial treaty of reciprocity.[69] But when war broke out in Europe during the summer,[70] the United Colonies were too panicky to begin negotiations without guidance from the Confederation, and a year was to pass before ambassadors from the United Colonies could be sent by the Commissioners to New Amsterdam.

The most exposed wing of the Confederacy were the towns of Stamford and Fairfield on the mainland and the Connecticut and New Haven settlements on Long Island. Fear in these frontier towns knew no bounds. All kinds of rumors prevailed, the most terrifying one being that Stuyvesant had directions from home to "make use of the Indians." It is not surprising, therefore, that the colonists in these parts took matters into their own hands without waiting for action from the United Colonies. Fairfield prepared for an invasion and appointed the Commissioner of the United Colonies from Connecticut, Roger Ludlow, commander in chief of the frontier forces; and on the Island that venerable Indian fighter, John Underhill, at the head of a frontier band, demolished a stronghold of the Indians on Long Island.[71] The Council at Boston alerted the militia of the Colony to be in readiness, and declared that if war should break out with the Dutch at New Amsterdam, the Commissioners of the Confederation should immediately convene at New Haven for the purpose of ordering the military movements of the English troops.[72] In April, however, the Massachusetts Council, probably feeling that Boston offered a place of more restraint than New Haven, where the war party was in control, issued a call to the other colonies to meet in an emergency session of the Confederation.[73] The ensuing sessions of the Confederation burst forth with all the accumulated disaffections of the colonies, and not only was there a bitter rift over whether to join in a war against the Dutch and Indians, but in the course of the feud the Constitution of the United Colonies was split asunder.

The course of the Anglo-Dutch War of 1652-4 need not concern us here, for the events of that struggle for ascendancy of the two great maritime powers largely by-passed the American colonies. Nevertheless it did have its effect on colonial affairs. The British fleet, anchoring in Boston harbor, served to remind the colonists of their dependence upon England. A union of six English towns[74] on Long Island west of the demarcation line of 1650 was also the result. The issuing of privateering commissions by Rhode Island[75] brought firm protests from the United Colonies that admiralty jurisdiction belonged to the home government, and not to the colonies.[76] This was a far-reaching concession, for the course of colonial history was to prove that England, in time, would use unsparingly the courts of admiralty and her naval arm in the attempt to bring the American colonies into line with British imperial and commercial policy.

When news came of the arrival of the British fleet[77] in Boston in June, 1654, the two colonies most disposed for war, Connecticut and New Haven, sent commissioners to Charlestown to confer with the British commander concerning an expedition to be raised against New Amsterdam. New Haven and Connecticut[78] had requested military aid from England because their war measures were bogged down in the Confederation. At this meeting, William Leete and Thomas Jordan represented New Haven, and John Mason and John Cullick, Connecticut. This meeting was held in haste and the Commissioners to the meeting received their commission only at the last minute. Plymouth sent two observers, and since they had no power "for a treaty" soon returned home. The only representatives from Massachusetts (who opposed the efforts for war) were military officers of the Bay, Robert Sedgwick and John Leverett. These officers, however, did not officially represent the Bay Colony, but instead, bore a commission from Cromwell to take the English squadron, "as providence shall order the wind," into any port of the United Colonies, and there to cooperate with the Confederation in an expedition against the Dutch.[79]

Although Frothingham, in a chapter on the Confederacy in his *Rise of the Republic,* treats this meeting at Charlestown as a meeting of the Confederation, it was not properly a meeting of the United Colonies. It was strictly a military council, meeting with Cromwell's commissioners. It had a single purpose, that of raising the expedition against the Dutch; it had not been former-ly convened as an emergency session as had been done the preceding year; nor were the proper Commissioners in attend-ance, and in the case of Massachusetts, none represented the Colony. The subject of extraordinary government (e.g., the early colonial councils, the rise of central government during the Revolution, the Committee of States of 1784) is a fascinat-ing study because it brings into focus the existing government, and the success or ill success of the alternate form, and charts the course of the government for the future. Such was this war coun-cil of 1654. It was convened for one particular purpose, to meet an emergency, when it was felt that a regular meeting of the Confederation would be fruitless, as it had been the preceding year. This council left its imprint on the New England Confed-eration, demonstrating that the chief purpose of the colonies in confederation was of a military nature, to provide for the com-mon defense.

Although Massachusetts had refused to go along with the demands of the other colonies for war, she could not ignore the pressure brought to bear by the other confederated colonies act-ing jointly with the mother country. It was, therefore, agreed in the Bay that as many as five hundred volunteers be raised with-in the Colony to go against the Dutch. In all, the Council at Charlestown counted on nine hundred foot troops and a troop of horse, but before they could be put in the field, news of the peace signed by England and the Netherlands arrived, and the New Haven and Connecticut Commissioners of the Council vot-ed to give up the expedition. Thus the design for "extirpate-ing the Dutch" at New Amsterdam collapsed.[80] But the war factions in the colonies on the River and the Sound were not so easily appeased as we shall see in the next chapter.

Soon after the crises years in the Confederation, New Haven again prepared to send settlers to the Delaware region. Letters were sent to New Sweden with the endorsement of the New England Confederation, claiming the right of New Haven to plant a settlement on the Delaware. The Swedes immediately refuted the New Haven claims by sending copies of their Indian deeds to the New Haven authorities. But an unforeseen event took place in late summer, 1655, when the Dutch conquered New Sweden. Thus, with one power well entrenched on the South River opposed to the settling of the English in that area, and with the colonies of Massachusetts and Plymouth not interested in the project, the New Haven adventurers soon gave up their hopes for extending their seafaring colony into this region.[81] As sea power became the primary force in the international equilibrium,[82] England grew more concerned with the Dutch at New Amsterdam, and the responsibility for bringing the Dutch to terms passed out of the hands of the New England colonists. By the time of the Restoration, the English imperial designs on New Netherland were becoming evident.

In the course of the first decade of the Confederation, 1643-53, the Commissioners thus dealt effectively in three areas of foreign affairs: the French, Indians, and the Dutch. The Confederation straightened out the bungling Massachusetts-French negotiations pertaining to the northern border and offered a unified policy of good will, yet refrained from entangling alliances with the French. Their treatment of the Indians foreshadowed later American policy of considering Indian tribes of the original thirteen states as domestic nations, and playing rival tribes against each other. The success of the foreign policy of the Commissioners with the Dutch at New Amsterdam avoided a conflict in the New World—yet war raged in Europe. The New England Confederation during its first decade was a force for peace—actually a combined New England force would have had little difficulty in gaining the capitulation of New Netherland. The Director-General at New Amsterdam honored the Confederation with a visit. The Treaty of Hartford in 1650 was the high water mark of the Confederacy, with the ambassadors of the United Colonies negotiating a pact with the Dutch without leave from the governments in Europe. The relations with the Dutch best demonstrate the illusion of sovereignty hanging over the New England Confederation during its first decade.

The Anglo-Dutch War and the discontent of the Indians with their English yoke precipitated crises in the Confederation. Within the walls of the Confederacy itself, fears and suspicions made tempers flare and wrought a radicalism and intolerance incompatible with a Confederation founded on good will and cooperation among the colonies. The constitutional crises of 1653-5 would crush forever the hopes of New England to establish a quasi-sovereign Puritan commonwealth in the New World.

---

[1] For an enlivened, well-written account of New Amsterdam, and the Dutch point of view during the heyday of the New England Confederation, see the recent study of Henry H. Kessler and Eugene Rachlis, *Peter Stuyvesant and his New York*, (N. Y.: Random House, 1959).

[2] Ltr. of Gov. Kieft, 1646 q. in W. Andrews. "The Trading-House on the Paugasset," *Papers of the NHCHS*, III, 379.

[3] Hollister, *op. cit.*, I, pp. 18-9. The "Fresh River" was the Dutch name for the Connecticut River.

[4] Governor and Assistant (Plymouth) to same (Mass.), 6Feb32, Winthrop Papers, III, 164-5.

[5] See Roland M. Hooker, "The Colonial Trade of Connecticut," *Tercentenary Committee of Conn., Pub. no. 50* (New Haven: Yale University Press, 1936).

[6] *Holl. Docs.*, I, 150; Winthrop, *Journal*, (S), II, 38-9 Because of the "standoffishness of the United Colonies" Rhode Island was forced to promote its trading interests with the Dutch. (See Emily Williams, *William Coddington*, (Newport, R. I.: 1941), p. 52.) The colonies in this period, relatively free from English control, were nevertheless regarded as "adjuncts of the European economic system rather than as separate centres of western civilization." G. N. Clark, *The Seventeenth Century* (Oxford: 1950), p. 207. This is also Prof. Andrews, basic premise in his treatment of the American colonies.

[7] Today, the lower part of Philadelphia.

[8] Frederic Kidder, *The Swedes on the Delaware and Their Intercourse with New England*, (Boston: 1874), p. 4; Amandus Johnson, *The Swedish Settlements on the Delaware, 1638-1644*, (New York: 1911), I, 208-14; Charles H. Levermore, *The Republic of New Haven*, (Baltimore: 1886), pp. 90-5; *The Clarendon Papers, NYHSC*, II,(1869), 4-5.

[9] Winthrop, *Journal*, (S), II, 193-4, 229.

[10] Viz., Theophilus Eaton, Stephen Goodyear, and Thomas Gregson. One authority, however, A. Johnson, questions whether the Delaware Company actually existed. In any event, the New Haven merchants as a group had a hand in these commercial ventures of the colony.

[11] See Thomas Trowbridge, "History of the Ancient Maritime Interests of New Haven," *Papers of the NHCHS*, III(1882) ; Johnson, *op. cit.*, I, 384-7.

[12] See E. Bacon, *op. cit.*, p. 61.

[13] Winthrop, *Journal*, (S), II, 117.

[14] E. B. O'Callaghan, *History of New Netherland* (N. Y.: 1846), 279ff.

[15] Winthrop, *Journal*, (S), II, 155.

[16] *Ibid.*, pp. 156-7. The use of the phrase "United Colonies of New England"— even recorded in Winthrop's *Journal* is significant in that it again points to the Dutch influence on the Confederation. An author, a generation removed

174 THE UNITED COLONIES OF NEW ENGLAND

from the Confederation, speaks of the Confederation as after the "Manner of the Provinces of Holland." Daniel Neal, *The History of New-England to 1700,* (London: 1720), Columbia University Library, I, 203.

[17] Winslow to Winthrop, 2Aug44, *Winthrop Papers,* IV, 453.

[18] Washington Irving, *Knickerbocker's History of New York,* (Philadelphia: 1891), p. 228.

[19] *NHCR,* I, 116-7.

[20] Winthrop, *Journal,* II, 161.

[21] Suffolk, Essex, Middlesex, and Norfolk.

[22] Jameson, ed., Johnson's *Wonder-Working Providence, op. cit.,* pp. 228-9. The first Major General of the colony was Thomas Dudley, who was one of the first two Commissioners from the colony. Practically all of the Commissioners of the United Colonies had some military experience, if not in the field, at least on the town or colony councils of war. Indeed, matters of war touched all citizens, but it is still nonetheless significant that the essential character of the Confederation was military (this became more apparent in the later Confederation) and bears out the thesis that the beginnings of American federalism are found in the military cooperation of the colonies.

[23] *PCR,* IX, 13; A. Johnson, *op. cit.,* pp. 387-97; See A. Johnson, ed., and trans., *"The Instruction for Johan Printz"* (Philadelphia: 1930) for the ensuing correspondence.

[24] Johnson, *ibid.,* p. 211.

[25] *Ibid.,* p 220. In the words of Irving, there came "letter after letter, protest after protest, bad Latin, worse English, and hideous Low Dutch . . ." (Irving, *op. cit.,* p. 228.) Irving depicts the forming of the Confederation as arousing great fear among the Dutch at New Amsterdam. When "the Great Amphictyonic Council of the Pilgrims" was formed, the "tidings of this great Yankee league struck William Kieft with dismay, and for once in his life he forgot to bounce on receiving a disagreeable piece of intelligence. In fact, on turning over in his mind all that he had read at The Hague about leagues and combinations, he found that this was a counterpart of the Amphictyonic League, by which the states of Greece obtained such power and supremacy; and the very idea made his heart quake . . . The rise of this potent confederacy was a death blow to the glory of William the Testy . . . the league rolling onward, gathered about the red hills of New Haven, threatening to overwhelm the Nieuw Nederlandts . . ." (pp. 229-30).

[26] Winthrop to Printz, 20Apr44, and Printz to Winthrop, 20June44. Johnson, ed. *Instructions, op. cit.,* pp. 222-3; Winthrop, *Journal,* (S), II, 194. Earlier, Printz had asked of Winthrop, "How far do the mainland and islands of New England extend?" (Johnson, *ibid.,* p. 213).

[27] Winthrop, *Journal,* (S), I I,170, 250, 289.

[28] W. C. Andrews, *loc. cit.,* pp. 384, 390.

[29] *PCR,* IX, 26-7; Winthrop, *Journal,* (S), II, 190.

[30] Winthrop, *Journal,* (S), II, 212.

[31] *NHCR,* I, 265-6; IX, 76.

[32] *PCR*, IX, 64, 76-7.

[33] Winthrop, *Journal*, (S), II, 382. The Dutch proposed that they join with New England in a league because of their similarities in religion and the need for a common front against the Spanish and the Indians. (Felt, *op. cit.*, II, 2-5.)

[34] That of Mr. Westerhouse, who had dual citizenship in New Haven and New Amsterdam. The ship had been snatched out of the New Haven harbor by the Dutch. *(NHCR*, 1, 355; *PCR*, IX, 113-5.)* Mr. Westerhouse appealed directly to the Commissioners. (MA, LX, 145.)

[35] "The United Colonies having made strict orders to restrain all trade of powder and guns to the Indians, by occasion whereof the greatest part of the beaver trade was drawn to the French and Dutch." (Winthrop, *Journal*, (S), II, 380.)

[36] *PCR*, IX, 113.

[37] Winthrop, *Journal*, (S), II, 384, 401-2.

[38] Adrian van der Donck, *Remonstrance* . . . (O'Callaghan, ed.), u. 21.

[39] The so-called phantom ship, as before mentioned. Thomas Gregson, a Commissioner of the United Colonies, was aboard. New Haven authorities urged the holding of the special session in 1647, ostensibly to meet the Indian situation, but more likely to secure a forum for their grievances against the Dutch. (*Winthrop Papers*, V, 167, 27May47.)

[40] Johnson, *Swedish Settlements, op. cit.*, I, 400.

[41] Stuyvesant to Winthrop, 25June47, *Winthrop Papers*, V, 171.

[42] *PCR*, IX, 147-8.

[43] ". . . wherein we finding ourselves comprehended as wrapped up in one bundle with all the other colonies; our case being different from all the other English colonies in America . . ." (Petition to Parliament from Mass. Gen. Ct., 1651, Mayo, ed. *Hutchinson's Hist.*, I, 516-9)

[44] Stuyvesant also denied responsibility for Kieft's actions, thus implying that the Dutch had wronged the English.

[45] *PCR*, IX, 175-6.

[46] *Ibid.*, pp. 177-8.

[47] *Ibid.*, pp. 189-90.

[48] MA, II, 327.

[49] *Holl. Docs.*, I, 459.

[50] Calder, *op. cit.*, p. 190; *PCR*, IX, 186-7.

[51] Thomas B. Davis, *Chronicles of Hopkins Grammar School, with Life of Edward Hopkins*, (New Haven: 1938), p. 40.

[52] *Ibid.*, p. 42. According to Davis, the Commissioners had expected oral negotiations and did not take too well to the "clumsy written" documents of Stuyvesant. Hopkins was addressed by the Dutch Governor as "Govert Lockmans." Also, *PCR*, IX, 178.

[53] *PCR*, IX, 189-90.

[54] *Ibid.* On Long Island, the present boundary between Queens and Suffolk counties. Connecticut and New Haven continued to incorporate the towns of

Long Island into their colonies, and after the Charter of 1662, Connecticut asserted jurisdiction over all L. I., but soon was forced to yield to the Duke of York.

[55] *PCR,* IX, 190.

[56] *Holl. Docs.,* I, 460-1.

[57] *Ibid.,* p. 459.

[58] See Calder, *op. cit.,* 191-2; Alexander Johnston, *Connecticut: A Study of a Commonwealth Democracy,* (Boston: 1887), p. 149ff.; *The Clarendon Papers, NYHSC,* II, 7.

[59] Calder, *ibid.*

[60] New Haven Town looked forward to this meeting of the Commissioners and expected the expense of being host to the Commissioners would be great. *(New Haven Town Records,* I, 78-9, 4Aug51.)

[61] *PCR,* IX, 199.

[62] See Chapter 5.

[63] George Edmundson, *Anglo-Dutch Rivalry* . . . (Oxford: 1911), pp. 154-5.

[64] Maud W. Goodwin, *Dutch and English on the Hudson,* Vol. VII of the Chronicles of America Series, (New Haven: 1921), pp. 77-9.

[65] See Chapter 4.

[66] *New Haven Town Records,* I, 174-5.

[67] MA, Council Recs., I, 5Mar52/3.

[68] *Ibid.,* 22Mar52/3; *PCR,* X ,424.

[69] *Ibid.,* 6Mar52/3; *PCR,* X, 425-6.

[70] The Dutch were hard pressed by French conquests in the southern Netherlands and the loss of a number of ships due to a storm and English attacks. (See George Edmundson, *History of Holland* (Cambridge, England: 1922), pp. 61, 177, 216.)

[71] John M. Taylor, *Roger Ludlow,* (New York: 1900), pp. 129-31; Henry C. Shelley, *John Underhill,* (New York: 1932), pp. 350-6; Martha Flint, *Early Long Island,* (New York: 1896), pp. 48-9.

[72] Order of the Mass. Council, MA, I, 1653 (n.d.) ; Elizabeth Schenk, *The History of Fairfield,* (New York: 1889), p. 74.

[73] The magistrates summoning this eventful meeting, as they were empowered to do by the Articles of Confederation, were Bellingham, Hibbins, Nowell, and Glover. (MA, III, 7, 2Apr53.)

[74] Viz., Hempstead, Gravesend, Flushing, Newton, Oyster Bay, and Jamaica.

[75] Underhill, acting under one of these commissions, took the Dutch Fort of Good Hope for Connecticut. (Shelley, *op. cit.,* pp. 365-6.) This ubiquitous freebooter for the English cause wrote the Commissioners of the United Colonies: "It is true often times Nessesitie hath noe law I ame as Jephthah forced to lay my life in my hands to save English blood from destruction . . . I pray god move youer harts to vindecate the Common cause of England against the Duch." *(PCR,* X, 52.) The United Colonies particularly objected to the seizure of a French ship destined for Boston by a Rhode Island privateer, and also giving a commission to Thomas Baxter who was indiscriminate in his raiding,

and even brought a Dutch fleet chasing him into Fairfield harbor. (MA, Council Recs., *op. cit.*, I, Aug53; H. M. Chapin, *Privateering*, *op. cit.*, pp. 25-37, 46; Palfrey, *op. cit.*, I, 378; M. Appleton, "Rhode Island's First Court of Admiralty," *NEQ*, V (Jan., 1932), 148-50.)

[76] MA, Council Recs., I, Aug53.

[77] A squadron of four ships and 200 men.

[78] Anne L. de Forest, *Captain John Underhill* (New York: 1934), pp. 74-5; Calder, *op. cit.*, pp. 198-9.

[79] *Ibid.*, MA, I, 174; Thurloe, *State Papers*, II, 419-20. Mason wrote to Winthrop, Jr. skeptically that "the end of sending these ships is to settle Government amongst the Colonyes, as alsoe make warre upon Manhatos." But he confided that he "may please to conceale the last a little" because of the influence it might have on the Commissioners of the United Colonies. (11June54, *Winthrop Papers, MHSC* 4: VII:417-8.)

[80] Thurloe, *State Papers*, II, 418-9, 425-6; Mass. General Court to Cromwell, Mayo, ed. *Hutchinson's History*, I, 434-5; Mason to Winthrop, n.d., *MHSC* 4:VII:418. The best summary of this episode is in Calder, *op. cit.*, 199-203. Plymouth had a ready contingent of 60 men to draw on from the ten towns of the Colony. (Peirce, *Civil Lists, op. cit.*, p. 92). The Mass. forces were to rendezvous at Charlestown, 22June, and from there meet the other confederate troops at Black Point. (James P. Baxter, ed., *Documentary History of Maine*, (Portland: 1900), VI, 172.) The Commissioner of the United Colonies from Connecticut, Roger Ludlow, was soon to move to Virginia, tradition having it, because of his disgust in the failure of the United Colonies to prosecute the war against the Dutch. (R. V. Coleman, *Mr. Ludlow Goes for Old England*, (Westport, Conn.: 1935), p. 15.)

[81] *PCR*, X, 127-8; *New Haven Town Records*, I, 223; *The Clarendon Papers*, *NYHSC*, II, 11-3; Calder, *op. cit.*, pp. 203-5; A. Johnson, *The Swedes on the Delaware*, (Phila.: 1915), pp. 287-8; Bernard Bailyn, *The New England Merchants in the Seventeenth Century*, (Cambridge, Mass.: Harvard University Press, 1955), pp. 56-8. Cromwell, probably having in mind to sparse the realm with Puritans, offered to send New England settlers to Jamaica, but there were few subscribers, and the "godly" seemed little interested. (Thurloe, *State Papers*, V, 509-10.)

[82] The second half of the seventeenth century in Anglo-Dutch relations revolved around the attempt of the Dutch to win the English to a policy of freedom on the high seas and in commerce. (See Ralph C. H. Catterall, "Anglo-Dutch Relations, 1654-60," *Annual Report of the American History Association*. (1910), p. 103.)

CHAPTER IX

The Constitutional Crises of 1653-5

New England awoke with mixed reactions to the news that a state of war existed between the United Provinces and Great Britain. To the Colony on the Sound, here was the opportunity to extend its trading empire, which in the past had been repeatedly frustrated by their Knickerbocker brethren. Connecticut and Plymouth, sharing in varying degrees the trading and territorial interests of New Haven and out of sheer desire to antagonize the Bay, acquiesced in the necessity of war; but Massachusetts, the most remote from the danger of war and upon whom the burden would be the greatest, stubbornly refused. The smaller colonies then, by invoking the Articles of Confederation, attempted to coerce the mighty Bay into joining them in an offensive war against the Dutch at New Amsterdam. The violent controversy which followed, with New Haven, representing the small colonies, pitted against Massachusetts, raised for the first time in American history the question whether the central authority or the individual states were supreme.

Because of the disappointment and distrust sown among the contracting parties during this first great constitutional debate in America, the Confederation was nearly ripped apart. Indeed, these debates formed the back-drop for the actual event that brought virtual collapse to the Confederacy. But, contrary to the analyses of historians in the past, who never delved deep into the Confederation, the debates of 1653-5 were *not* the event which brought down the Confederacy. The United Colonies, under the Articles of 1643, was on the road to survival from the scars of these debates, and even was emerging strengthened. But, alas! with its guard down, it was to falter unsuspectingly upon an incident of apparent triviality, but an incident which struck at the very heart of the Confederation, and by which the Confederation lost its ascendancy in colonial affairs.

In every year since the beginning of the Confederation the fear of an Indian uprising had been present, but in 1653 this

178

fear loomed even larger when it was rumored that a Dutch-Indian conspiracy, involving particularly the Niantics of southern New England, was being formed to drive out the English. New Haven Colony, in its intent upon war with the Dutch, hoped to play up this rumor in order to influence the United Colonies into adopting a war policy. Intelligence of the alleged conspiracy reached the Puritan colonies daily.[1] Moreover, contributing to the war scare were many grievances against the Dutch held over from the previous years. Chief among these were the denial by the Dutch of the right of New England to trade on the Delaware, the refusal to alleviate the discriminatory impost against English shipping at Manhattan and to surrender Greenwich, as Stuyvesant had promised in the Treaty of 1650, and giving ammunition to the Indians. With the clouds of war continually hovering over them, the United Colonies were becoming impatient for some kind of action. Because of their "extreordinary watchings and wardings" they were "hindered in theire plowing sowing preparation for planting and occations to theire exceeding great damage." The rumors of an attack from the enemy and the mounting grievances thus put the New England colonies extremely on edge and gave rise to such reports as that "some of the Duch att or about the Monhatoes tell the English they shall shortly have an East India breakfast."[2]

As the alarm of pending war, largely based upon information collected by the New Haven Colony,[3] continued to spread, the Boston magistrates deemed it wise to call an emergency session of the Confederation. Thus, acting upon this call of the Massachusetts Council of the second of April, 1653 (O.S.), the Commissioners of the United Colonies, seventeen days later, met in special session—a session that would last for a month and a half.[4]

The Commissioners immediately adopted a two-pronged course of action: one to please the overwhelming war sentiment in the smaller colonies; the other to please the conservative, anti-war faction in the Bay. It was agreed that the United Colonies should raise a force of five hundred soldiers, duly proportioned according to the Articles of Confederation.[5] For those who wanted all the facts before embarking upon war, the Commissioners decided to send three messengers to the frontier English towns on the coast and on Long Island to investigate the charges that the Dutch and Indians were preparing to attack the English. But this was not to be the end of their mission; they were to proceed on to New Amsterdam as ambassadors of the Confederation in order to get the Dutch point of view. For this level-headed policy, however, the Commissioners were not too fortunate in making their selection of agents to go on this mission. John Leverett and William Davis, both of Boston, and Francis Newman of New Haven were named; but Leverett was soon to be in the pay of Cromwell for raising an expedition in New England to send against the Dutch, and Newman, a leading merchant and afterwards Governor, was naturally disposed to bring the Confederation in on the side of New Haven in that Colony's determination to right the hardships inflicted on them by the Dutch. Thus it is not surprising to find the report of these special agents prejudiced for war. Having paused only long enough to collect testimony, not consenting with Stuyvesant to engage in a conference with Dutch envoys, these special agents for the Confederation returned home while the Commissioners were still in session. Their report helped to confirm the war views of the colonies, but was still ambiguous enough to state the intentions of "friendshipp" and "mutuall Justice" on the part of the Dutch Governor. Thus the report was of little value, and did not change any opinions of either the anti- or pro-war factions.[6]

The General Court of Massachusetts was not satisfied with the way things were going in the Confederation. The overwhelming testimony collected by the ambassadors of the Confederation to New Amsterdam was being used as evidence by the Commissioners from the three small colonies to push through a resolution for war against the Dutch. Although messengers sent to the Indians suspected of intriguing with the Dutch returned to the Commissioners with denials of such a plot, the Commissioners listened with more eager ears to those savage witnesses summoned by the New Haven Commissioners.[7] The Puritan conscience did not deny that war belonged in the course of things, but it did demand that all wars, as in scriptural times, be founded upon just grounds.[8] The Articles of Confederation embodied the Puritan distinction between offensive and defensive wars; and the conservative party in the Bay, represented by the majority of the magistrates and the churchmen did not consider that the colonies to the south, with their special grievances against the Dutch, had as yet mustered ample proof of a

Dutch-Indian conspiracy to justify an offensive war. Of course, it must be remembered it was not all a matter of principle with the Bay, for in any military preparations, the proportion of Massachusetts' contribution would exceed that of all the other colonies put together—an obligation not to be entered upon simply for the self-interest of her lesser confederates.

The Bay was well adept to political maneuvering. When it became apparent that the six Commissioners from the three small colonies would vote for a war resolution, it was found that the commissions for the Massachusetts and Connecticut Commissioners had expired. Thus continuing in session was legally impossible until the commissions had been renewed. Before messengers could return with the proper commissions to resume the meeting, the Bay would have a breathing spell to consider for itself whether the evidence submitted during this emergency session warranted a declaration of war. Taking advantage of this interim, the Massachusetts General Court appointed a committee of four members from the Court to meet with four Commissioners of the United Colonies to "draw up the case respecting the Duch and Indians."[9] The selection of this mixed committee was not a wise one, from the point of view of the Bay, for every member, with perhaps the exception of Major Denison, was known to have war views. The elders of the Colony were soon called in, and the restrained judgment of these church fathers checked the movement in the Bay for war:

> wee humbly conceive it most Agreeable to the Gospel of peace which wee profess, and safest for these Colonies to forbeare the use of the sword, till the Lord by his providence and by the wisedome of his servants set over us, shall farther cleere up his mind, either for our settled peace or more manifest grounds of war.[10]

Even the deputies of the Colony, who in the lower house were prone to take more emboldened steps than the magistrates, added their opinion in this recess with "apprehensions" as to the necessity of a war policy. A fresh declaration of grievances was issued to the Dutch. It was then felt that both sides of the question had been sufficiently aired, and the Massachusetts General Court could safely leave the question to the "honered Commissioners of the United Colonies to determine of as they in thoire

wisdomes shall Judge most meet; using as much care and ten-
derness to avoid warr."[11]

When the Commissiouru resumed their meeting the last
day of May (O.S.), they were entrusted with the executive
task of determining whether cause for war existed and, judicial-
ly, whether under the constitution of the colonies all members
of the Confederation were bound to abide by the decision of six
of the Commissioners as specified in the Articles. There were
thus two fundamental interpretations of the Articles of Confederation now coming to light. The Massachusetts position was
consistent with the stipulation in the Records of the Colony at
the time of the forming of the Confederation that ultimate power resided with the general courts.[12] In the view of the other
three colonies, however, the Commissioners of the United Colonies, as delegates with plenary power and as senators to the
central government from the individual colonies, possessed in
their areas of jurisdiction powers transcending those of the
general courts. The best statement of this later position is found
in a letter of William Pynchon during the first rumblings of
constitutional discontent over the impost controversy and proposed amendments to the Articles in 1647-8. In the words of
the Springfield trader, who was then at odds with the River
Colony:

> Hopkins said it was nothing to them what the Generall
> Court had don in the Bay; for the Court of Commissioners
> was the *supreame Court* and what they did must stand. . .[13]

There was now a basic cleavage in the government of the Puritan colonies. The particular interests of the Bay General Court
was pitted against the nearly unanimous determination of the
Commissioners of the United Colonies for war. Unfortunately
for Massachusetts in her efforts to restrain the colonies from
entering into war, that independent spirit of Essex County, William Hathorne, refused to be bound by the decision of the
Massachusetts General Court, and voted along with the rest
of the Commissioners[14]—leaving the lone dissent of Simon Bradstreet to uphold the non-aggressive policy of the Bay in the
Court of Commissioners.

While the Commissioners of the United Colonies were still
in emergency session, the Massachusetts Court wrote a letter

questioning their power to determine offensive war. If the power
to determine offensive war was left unconditionally in the hands
of the Commissioners, then it would be acknowledged that the
Confederation could exercise sovereign powers. Since Massachusetts had entered the Confederation with the implication
that the ultimate powers rested with the individual general
courts, she could not escape the unrestricted right of the Commissioners in determining war. The debates over the right of
the central government to commit all the member colonies to
an offensive war was essentially the question of sovereignty:
whether the particular or the central government was supreme. The Massachusetts General Court, therefore, drew up a
series of arguments, by which the right of the Commissioners to
determine offensive war was denied. The arguments (here again
we have the "federal thinking" of the Puritans) were divided
into two parts: the particular, which were derived from the interpretation of the Articles of Confederation, and, secondly,
those which were based on "fundamental law."

By the first line of reasoning, it was argued that the third and
sixth articles[15] left the "whole power" of government to each
colony, which could invest the Commissioners with any part of
that power. The ninth and tenth articles applied only to defensive war; while the fourth and fifth articles merely settled
rules for "leagues" in case of war, such as the number of men
participating and the division of spoils, and in no case provided for the "determination of the justice of offensive warr,"
which was reserved "wholely to the determination of the supreame power of the severall confederate jurisdictions." Furthermore, the sixth article implied that because the "supreame powers of the severall jurisdictions could not assemble," they were
forced to substitute delegates "to order such thinges" of "urgent
necessitie, or meerly prudentiall and politicall, or of inferior
nature." The "highest acts of authoritie" (i.e., offensive war),
by nature a "morall consideration," the "contrivers of the confederacy did not judge meete to referr to the commissioners,"
and therefore did not provide rules as they did in "all cases of
inferior nature."[16]

According to the second series of arguments, Massachusetts
contended that governments could not act contrary either to
fundamental law or those rights reserved to the people. The
people exercise "Imediate choise" of their own governors be-

cause the "Supream Governors are betrusted with theire lives
and estates in whom under God they doe acquics." If strangers
(i.e., the Commissioners) were so impowered, they then could
make the people enter into an offensive war, an "acte of power
in the highest nature," which might prove destructive to the
Commonwealth.[17] In the peroration of the Bay's arguments, it
was stated that this could not be the meaning of the colonies,
"whoe are so tender of theire power in Governing theire owne"
that they "should put theire power out of theire own hands in
the most waighty point." Granting such an assumption, this would
constitute a "bondage hardly to bee borne by the most Subjec-
tive people; And cannot bee conceived soe free a people as the
united Collonies should submite unto."[18]

In these arguments, Massachusetts was now insisting not that
the general courts had the right to determine offensive war,
but that they had the power to review such a decision made by
the Commissioners, the right of judicial review. This was the
reverse of the position of the smaller colonies, who thought of
the Commissioners of the Confederation as the Supreme Court
for the colonies.[19] According to the interpretation of Massachusetts, the Commissioners reserved only the right to levy war,
but the issuing of war was subject to review by the general
courts, which reserved the right to void the act if the grounds
for it were deemed unjustifiable. Before this argument, however,
could be fully developed, Massachusetts blandly stated that,
in regard to offensive war, the Articles of Confederation could
be interpreted only in two ways: either the Commissioners had
the discretionary power to determine the beginning of war or
they had power solely to direct it after it had begun; the first
was contrary to "fundamental law," while only the second
course was safe.[20] This proposition of alternatives, not allowing
that the Commissioners could have a hand in both determining and directing the course of a war, was but a temporary gen-
eralization by Massachusetts, which proved to be but a stage
in reaching the final synthesis, to come only after much careful
thought.

This choice of alternatives, nevertheless, was immediately
taken at face value by the other members of the Confederation.
After the Commissioners adjourned in early June, the smaller
colonies, intent on war, vigorously sought to get all of New
England to make war on the Dutch. Mention has already been

made of the attempt to by-pass the Confederation by meeting
in Council with Cromwell's commissioners the following year,
but in 1653 special delegates from New Haven and Connecticut,
during the interim between sessions of the Commissioners and
the Massachusetts General Court, spent the summer trying to
work out a compromise with the Massachusetts Council. The
Council was reluctant to speak for the General Court, where it
was felt that such questions of a constitutional nature could
only be decided by the court.[21] The convening of the Massachusetts General Court, which would be meeting simultaneously
with the regular session of the Commissioners in the fall, was
eagerly looked forward to for answering the question whether
Massachusetts would abide by the decisions of the Commissioners of the United Colonies. It was common knowledge that
an affirmative finding on the part of the Court would bring the
United Colonies into the Anglo-Dutch war. For the renewal of
the debates in the fall, the smaller colonies began to prepare
their arguments. They would seek to refute the Massachusetts
position that the full determination of war belonged solely to
the general courts and not to the Commissioners of the Confederation.

The smaller colonies considered that the fundamental principle of the Confederation was that a decision by the proper
majority of the Commissioners was binding upon all the member colonies. To them the Confederation exercised sovereign
powers in the determining of war, offensive as well as defensive.
New Haven formulated the arguments for the smaller colonies,
attacking directly the position of the Bay. It was argued that
the Articles and their interpretation were not separate and
therefore must be considered as one, and that the Confederation
was "no rash and sudden ingagement," since it had been several
years under consideration, and Massachusetts, after a large and
serious debate" of the committee sitting at Boston, had accepted
the Articles. Articles Three and Six "till now" were "never understood to cross or abate the power of the commissioners in
things proper to the confederation." As for offensive and defensive war, the distinctions between the two were difficult to
define.[22]

New Haven pointed out that the colonies could well profit
from the examples in history of other leagues and confederations, which were continued among "other people and provinces,"

some in "subordination" and others in "consociation," in all of
which the central authority was invested with specific powers,
while at the same time "customs, priviledges and parts of government" were reserved for the "safety of the whole and conveniency of the parts."[23] It was further argued that the Articles
of Confederation did not violate fundamental law because they
were duly entered upon and had for ten years worked properly.
The role of the Commissioners was similar to that of the general courts, especially in cases of emergency when a delay pending the decision of the courts might be injurious. There was
also a rule in law that all "expressions and sentences, though of
a doubtful construction," be rationally understood—this being
especially the case in confederations and covenants.

The Colony on the Sound was arguing strict construction, in
that Puritans would never have agreed to the particulars of a
treaty if the obligations of that treaty were vague. If the Bay
Colony could not be held to account according to the Articles,
in the New Haven view, it would have been better never to have
combined at all, because "while that interpretation stands in
force at the Massachusetts," they would be more "exposed to
enemies and dangers" than they were before the Confederation.[24] New Haven, strictly adhering to the literal sense of the
Articles and defending the theory that the Commissioners were
invested with sovereign powers in determining war, had thus
met the Massachusetts argument for the ultimate authority of
the general courts head on. New Haven was insistent that the
Massachusetts interpretation of the Articles, if it were allowed to
stand, violated the covenant which the four Puritan colonies
entered upon by agreeing to the Articles of Confederation. Thus
we have presented the two contradictory interpretations of the
fundamental nature of the Confederation, which if not soon resolved would disrupt the Confederacy. Lines of cleavage had
developed between the small colonies and the mighty Bay—between the Massachusetts Court and the Commissioners of the
central government. Here the debates rested. The two opposing
views were considered by both factions irreconcilable. Something had to give. New Haven, however, had hit a vulnerable
spot in the Puritan conscience in accusing Massachusetts of
covenant breaking, and this charge would lead eventually to a
reconsideration by Massachusetts of its original position.

The question whether the Commissioners had the power to

determine offensive war was thus debated during the emergency session of the Confederation of April-June, 1653, and during the interim by the leading men of the colonies until the regular session of the Commissioners and the Massachusetts court convened in the fall. But in the meantime, with the Massachusetts dissent, the war could not be carried to the Dutch. New Haven and Connecticut tried once again to raise forces for a war, sending a joint committee to the Bay Colony to request a reconsideration by Massachusetts.[25] The request was refused; and New Haven, still desirous of war, proposed that a council of war be held at New Haven without the participation of Massachusetts, and in the meantime the whole issue be referred to England. With the small colonies showing that they intended to remain firm and bring pressure to bear from England if necessary, Massachusetts took the initiative to conciliate the two opposing views, and thereby to preserve the Confederation.

At last the long-awaited meetings of the Commissioners and the Massachusetts General Court convened at Boston in September. Seeing that the other colonies would not give in to the Massachusetts position, the Commissioners from the Bay took on a more compromising attitude, pledging

> to keep ourselves free from haveing any share in the breach of Soleme and perpetuall Confeaderation or that which manifestly tendeth thereunto and the sadd consequences therof that may ensue.[26]

But the Bay, however, was not yet ready to redefine its position, and this session was to be filled with more strife than the one which had adjourned three months before. The Massachusetts Commissioners had orders not to decide on any war whatsoever.[27] In view of this, it is surprising that a meeting was held at all. Only the spirit of compromise prevailed; to treat the issue realistically at this time was out of the question. New Haven, having found "such ill fruit from the Massachusetts of the two former meetings," sent Commissioners only in order to show "themselves followers of peace, and that they earnestly desire to continew their confederation upon the termes it first began and for sundrie yeares hath bine carried on."[28]

During this session of the Confederation, the Massachusetts General Court presented to the Commissioners in writing their

considered views of the constitutional question involved. It was
pointed out that the Commissioners might determine the justice
of an offensive war, but they did not have the power to bind the
colonies. Thus the Massachusetts position was essentially the
same as it had been during the emergency session: the Commissioners were sort of a moral force to guide the colonies, to
help establish uniform policy among the colonies, but not a
superstructure with powers for enforcing its decisions. The General Court "cannot grant that the several jurisdictions are subordinate or subject to the Authoritie of the Comissioners" and
therefore "not bound in *toto civili* to Execute these determina-
tions nor act according to their judgment in making offensive
warr."[29]

Before this annual meeting of the Confederation closed its
doors in frustration, the Commissioners from the three small
colonies seized upon a shrewd maneuver, sure to cause a showdown with the Bay. Ninigret, the sachem of the Niantics whose
loyalty to the English since the treaty with his tribe in 1645
had long been dubious, continued to stir up resentment in the
smaller colonies, especially in his raids upon Long Island Indians under the jurisdiction of Connecticut and New Haven.[30]
If Massachusetts could be made to participate in an expedition
against this wayward tribe, then, as a matter of principle, she
could also be committed to a war upon the Dutch. In the last
days of the session, therefore, a resolution calling for an armed
band of two hundred and fifty men[31] was pushed through by the
war party with the requisite majority of six of the eight Commissioners. The Massachusetts Commissioners, Bradstreet and
Hathorne, were forced to abstain because of their instructions
to that effect from the General Court. Nevertheless, an expedition against a small Indian tribe by a force raised by the Confederation was in itself not contrary to the views of Massachusetts; but the Bay was wise enough to read the handwriting
on the wall and see the implications it would have at this time on
raising a larger force to send against the Dutch. Bradstreet entered a formal dissent against the resolution, and the Bay in a
special Council meeting officially nullified this act of the central
government,[32] the first nullification proceeding in American federal government. The failure of Massachusetts to sustain the
Commissioners in the raising of this expedition brought from the
Commissioners of the other three colonies the denunciation that

the Bay had "Actually broken theire covenant." The pro-war colonies were somewhat set back at the Massachusetts decision, and did not know what course of action should follow. Although it was hinted that this use of the Bay's prestige and power to nullify an act of the United Colonies would be viewed as secession from the Confederacy, it was decided to let the general courts decide the seriousness of the rift.

The real purpose of New Haven and the other small colonies was soon revealed, for they were again talking outright of an invasion of New Amsterdam. The Bay had thus closed all courses for war until more sufficient grounds for war should be forthcoming. It had exercised a veto when no veto was provided for by the Articles. Had veto powers been invested in the Confederation from the start, the Confederation would have had more strength, and the rashness of the three small colonies might have been prevented. The small colonies remained nonetheless determined upon war, although they did not condone the "mutinous way" of Fairfield and Stamford in taking the matter into their own hands and electing their own commander in chief.[33] The colonies clamorous for war, however, still demanded some general authority. For this reason they now turned away from the Confederation to secure English backing, though even outside of the Confederation they would feel the Bay dragging its feet.[34]

In October, after the meeting of the Commissioners, New Haven received a letter from the Massachusetts General Court requesting a committee be appointed to "consider the Articles of Confederation," because "something in them wants explanation, and some alteration."[35] The New Haven Court, however, replied that the "articles of confederation in their judgment wants neither alteration nor explanation, and they are fully satisfyed in them as they are."[36]

Still exploring for a compromise, the Massachusetts Court then sent out a questionnaire to the other colonies asking such questions as: (1) whether the Commissioners could speak for the general courts; (2) whether in "cases of greater Concernments" should not the courts be first satisfied with the correctness of the Commissioners' actions before acting upon their advice; (3) whether the entire power for determining peace or war should be in the hands of six Commissioners "whoe as such are not members of any Court and may probably bee noe members

of a desenting Jurisdiction"; and (4) whether the Commissioners, as Commissioners, should be subject to the general courts
of their respective jurisdictions or the general courts subject to
the Commissioners. Massachusetts also asked that a committee
be appointed from the colonies for the purpose of amending the
Articles.

But the result of this letter was not what Massachusetts expected. In March of 1654, the Plymouth Court answered, "how
sadly wee Resent and how deeply wee are affected with that
sadd breach of the Confederation." Plymouth still held to the
theory, as did the other two small colonies, that in the determining of war, offensive or defensive, the powers of the Commissioners were sovereign. In the Plymouth view, whatever the
Commissioners did was the same as if the general courts had
taken a similar action, and in the "proper Spheare" the general
courts should be subject to the Commissioners; yet the Commissioners should be held answerable for any "Male-adminestra-
tions of theire trusts and power in things proved to be unjust,"
wherein there was a higher law and it would be better to "obey
god then man."[37] The Plymouth interpretation implied mixed
responsibility on the part of the general courts and the Commissioners to see that the acts of the Commissioners were in
accord wth fundamental law. But the primary responsibility in
determining war belonged to the Commissioners of the colonies;
only when they violated their trust could their decisions be
impeached. This answer of the Plymouth General Court anticipated the next stage in the Massachusetts argument, which
in 1654 would seemingly heal the breach in the Confederacy.

Before the Commissioners convened at their annual session
at Hartford in 1654, and while the war council of the colonies
was meeting with the Cromwellian naval commander to raise
an expedition against the Dutch, news of peace between Holland and England was received in New England. Now Massachusetts had no reason to fear involvement in a war with the
Dutch. At the Hartford meeting in 1654, the Massachusetts
Commissioners repudiated their proposition of alternatives of
the preceding year (that the Commissioners' power in regard
to offensive war was subject to only two interpretations: either
they had the sovereign power of wholly determining the war or
simply the direction of it after it had commenced). With the
Dutch threat thus removed, they now offered their more mature

and definitive conception of the right to determine offensive war.

> To the Intent all former differences and offences may bee Issued determined and forgotten betwixt the Massachusets and the Rest of Confeaderate Collonies; wee doe heerby professe it to be our Judgment and doe beleive it to bee the Judgment of our generall court that the Comissioners or six of them have power according to the articles to determine the Justice of all warrs. . . . That our generall court hath and doth Recall that Interpretation of the Articles which they sent to the Commissioners att Boston . . . and doe acknowledge themselves bound to execute the determination of the Commissioners according to the litterall sence and true meaning of the articles of Confeaderation soe far as the said determinations are in themselves Just and according to God.[38]

Massachusetts had now come up with the theory that the Commissioners and the general courts shared powers in the determination of offensive war. The Commissioners could commit the general courts to an offensive war, but it was left to the general courts to decide whether the war was in accord with the "fundamental law." Though we shall soon see that this position was basically unrealistic, it was not a reversal of the Massachusetts position of the year before, but rather a clarification of a policy which she had held since the beginning of the Confederation. When Massachusetts entered the Confederation, it was with the reservation that the general courts retained the right to decide upon the justification of offensive war.[39] The Massachusetts participation in the raising of an expedition to send against the Narragansetts in 1645[40] was also consistent with this policy since the justification of such an offensive maneuver was recognized. By 1653, because Massachusetts had participated in this maneuver of 1645 and the Confederation had been running smoothly during the first decade, the smaller colonies had assumed that Massachusetts would participate in *any* offensive war according to the strict interpretation of the Articles. This, of course, was never the intention of Massachusetts, and hence the constitutional crisis of 1653.

Massachusetts, in its puritanical way, had sought to assume

moral responsibility to prevent war with the Dutch and their
Indian allies. Actually, practical considerations were foremost:
the brunt for carrying on a war would rest with Massachusetts,
the largest member of the Confederation, and the Bay Colony
would have the least to gain. The smaller colonies had taken
Massachusetts' refusal to join the war as a breach of the Articles, and in the strict interpretation it was, but a breach in
covenant or the Confederation was not the intention of Massachusetts. The Bay, then, was faced with the problem of reconciling her seemingly contradictory positions, and this she managed to do successfully by invoking a higher law than the
Articles, of which the general courts were to be the judges.
With the clarification of this issue, the powers and the areas
of jurisdiction of the Commissioners were now more precisely
defined, and in theory, therefore, the Confederation was more
firmly established. In this sense the Confederation emerged
strengthened from the nullification controversy of 1653.

But the Commissioners and the general courts could not
share ultimate powers over the same jurisdiction. In the determination of war, whether beginning it or deciding upon its
justification—both of which were aspects of the same sovereign
power—either the general courts or the Commissioners were supreme, but both could not be at the same time. That the Commissioners could be sovereign along with the general courts
was still an illusion which hung over from the Decade of Optimism. The nullification controversy[41] had almost exposed the
weakness of the Confederation, but Massachusetts by redefining
offensive war had removed the source of dissension, and thereby postponed the showdown.

To demonstrate her good faith in the now definitive conception of determining offensive war, by which the Commissioners
retained the right to declare such a war, Massachusetts consented (during the debates of the preceding year they had refused) to join the smaller colonies in an expedition against the
Niantic Indians, the purpose of which was to coerce them into
compliance with the English demands.[42] Such an occasion
would not be nearly as demanding as an expedition against the
Dutch would have been, and by going along with the other
colonies in this maneuver, the war party would be satisfied and
the Confederation preserved. The eagerness of the smaller colonies to send a punitive force against Ninigret now committed

them to the Massachusetts view of offensive war. The Commissioners, therefore, "finding by experience that the forbearance and lenity of the Collonies doth but enoroase" the "insolency" of the Niantic sachem, decided to send a force of sixty men, forty troopers and twenty horse, to root out Ninigret and bring him to terms. This was a paltry force compared to that of two hundred and fifty men that was to be raised the year before. Nevertheless, it is significant that it was to be a military expedition under the auspices of the United Colonies, and it was treated as such.

For the commander in chief, the Commissioners ordered that the Massachusetts General Court should chose any one of her three leading military men: Major Edward Gibbons, Major Daniel Denison, or Captain Humphrey Atherton. The commission to the commander in chief stated in specific terms that he should demand from Ninigret that the Pequots under his jurisdiction be required the collection of tribute which had long been overdue, as well as to charge the Indians with the expenses of the expedition, and secure a promise that there would be no further hostility against the Long Island Indians.[43]

This is the only instance in the history of the Confederation that the Commissioners put into effect an "offensive" engagement, wherein one of the confederates, Massachusetts, reluctantly participated. All other military expeditions had the full and whole-hearted cooperation of the United Colonies. In the light of the subsequent development of American federalism, it is most significant. If the Confederation could effectively make the expedition succeed in its purpose, without approval from its most powerful member, then the Confederation could exercise a supreme authority over the colonies, to the extent that a colony dissenting against an act of the Commissioners could be morally coerced into line. That the raising of this expedition occurred after the nullification controversy is significant. The Confederation, therefore, had not faltered over the debates of whether it was within its jurisdiction to commit the colonies to an act involving offensive war, for here was a specific example. It was now acting under what was thought a more clear conception of offensive war. But the belief that the Confederation retained a mixed sovereignty with the general courts still had to be dispelled. This maneuver of 1654, however, would bring to the confederated colonies the realization that the Confederation in itself lacked the powers of coercion, the very basis of sovereignty.

The expedition agreed upon by the Commissioners did not prove popular in the Bay. All three of the Massachusetts men nominated by the Commissioners for the post of commander in chief proved unavailable.[44] The General Court of Massachusetts, then, took it upon itself, without consulting the Commissioners, to name another for commander in chief. Even then, Simon Willard, the man finally chosen, did not receive the unanimous consent of the Massachusetts Court and Council. Nevertheless, all the colonies lost no time in raising the troops for the preliminary expedition of sixty men and for the reserve of two hundred and seventy to be held in readiness at Thomas Stanton's house in the Pequot country.[45] But in order to make the rendezvous, there was only time to raise the troops for the preliminary expedition,[46] and even then the troops from New Haven and Connecticut with their supplies were late in coming because of a storm.[47] When the small bands from the colonies were finally assembled, Major Willard, as their commander, marched at the head of this joint force into Niantic country. Upon arrival, Willard found the Niantics taking refuge in a swamp, and decided to station his troops at a safe distance so as not to make a "sturr amongst the Indians."

The whole affair was a fiasco. Willard proceeded, undoubtedly to the satisfaction of the Bay, as if he had no forces under him. Negotiations were held with Ninigret, with the Englishmen offering him hostages "for the cecuritie of his person." The only accomplishment was the securing of the release of the Pequot Indians; other than this, Ninigret was merely informed that if he molested the Long Island Indians "or any other of the frinds of the English" his head would be "sett up upon an English pole."[48] Although failing in their primary mission to bring the Niantics into complete subjection, through force if necessary, the small army after this haphazard effort returned home and disbanded.[49] To the war party of the Confederation the expedition had hardly been more than a visit; the assertion of English authority over the Niantics had not progressed any farther than when Massachusetts utterly declined to be part of an expedition the preceding year. The punitive expedition was thus a failure. Had military reasons been the grounds for not attacking, Willard could have awaited the arrival of reinforcements which were then being raised in the colonies and at least the troops after his return would not have been immediately discharged from service. The expedition proved two things: the Commissioners of the United Colonies were unable to control the expedition as such, and they were unable to hold Major Willard responsible for the violation of his commission. The Commissioners from the three small colonies, nevertheless, pushed through a resolution in the Confederation rebuking Willard's conduct, stating that Willard could have wrung almost any concession from Ninigret, had he but made an effort to do so. The issue was referred to the general courts, but there the matter rested.[50]

It was now demonstrated that the Confederation could not coerce the individual colonies to act in measures of substantive nature. The Commissioners could not enforce their directives; they lacked power to do so. Having no means of enforcement of their own, the Commissioners had to rely entirely upon the discretion of the individual general courts. During the Constitutional crises, the Confederation had successfully passed the theoretical hurdle by clarifying the conception of offensive war, but only to find itself wholly incapable of meeting the practical test. Here is an interesting paradox. The Puritans, through their hair-splitting, had explored and solved one of the most difficult questions which could possibly confront a confederation, that of determining offensive war, but had failed to work out the really basic question, which should have been more obvious, that of giving to the central authority the powers of enforcement. The colonies, however, hardly past the throes of settlement and too appreciative of their guarded liberties, were not yet ready to transcend their particular interests to the extent of establishing a national government; nor could they in the face of the rise of imperial policy of the next decade. The problems of the central government without a coercive agency would again have to be faced by another confederation in American history before the problem would be solved.

In summary, a Confederation exercising sovereign powers had never been more than an illusion created by the Decade of Optimism, 1643-53. The Confederacy was never more than a treaty, endowed with a permanent board of Commissioners. By 1653, it had become so completely out of step that a crisis was fomented. The nullification controversy almost dissipated the illusion of sovereignty. But the *coup de grâce* was postponed when Massachusetts removed the source of contention. The assumption that the Commissioners and the general courts shared powers in determining offensive war, however, was soon tested. The inevitable result was the affirmation of the indivisibility of sovereignty. Thus, with the weakness of the Confederation once exposed, the Confederation never again exerted a dominant influence in colonial affairs.

The growth of the federal principle in America since this initial episode has shown that for a governing body to possess sovereign powers it must survive practical tests. Thus the United States Federal Government, from the Whiskey Insurrection of 1794 down to such recent episodes as the school-integration crisis of 1957, has time after time been called upon to demonstrate that, in the areas of its jurisdiction, it possesses ample authority for enforcing the national will.

---

[1] Among the reports that the English had received was that Ninigret, the sachem of the Niantics, had made a visit to the Dutch at Manhattan, under the pretense of seeking a cure for a disease, but while there he and several sagamores were observed to be two days in a closed room with the Dutch governor, and emerged afterwards with presents. *(PCR, X, 22, 44-5).* Ninigret, it was reported, was then brought home in a Dutch sloop, accompanied by strangers, one of whom turned out to be a poisoner, being hired to "poison the waters" of the English. *(PCR, X, 11-2, 48-9).* The Dutch also had supposedly shown the Indians trenches they were digging which were rumored to be able to hold off ten thousand English. *(Ibid., pp. 48-9).*

It was thought that a conspiracy was in the making for attacking the English on the day "of election of Majestrates in the severall collonies because then it is apprehended the plantations will be left naked and unable to defend themselves . . ." *(Ibid., p. 12.)* According to this rumored plot, Ninigret was to attack Stamford and the surrounding area, while the Dutch attacked the English plantations near Manhattan. *(Ibid., p. 43.)* It was also heard that a Dutch fleet was expected any day in Manhattan. *(Ibid., p. 22; also MA, Council Records, ltrs dtd 28Mar, 2Apr, 18Apr53.)* The indefatigable Captain John Underhill, who wished to throw off Dutch authority over Hempstead and other Long Island towns, was very active in spreading these rumors. (See deForest, *op. cit.,* p. 65.)

[2] *PCR,* X, 23. On Long Island the fears of an Indian uprising were so great that the watches of the towns were ordered to shoot to kill any Indian trying to pass into town at night. (James T. Adams, *History of the Town of Southampton, L. I.* (Bridgehampton, L. I.: 1918), p. 79.

[3] Shelley, *op. cit.,* p. 355.

[4] There was a break in this session, with the first part from April 19 to May 18 (O.S.) and the second part from May 21 to June 2 or 3, but the Commissioners remained in Boston during the interim. (*PCR*, X, *passim*.; MA, II, 331-350.)

[5] The four colonies were to furnish 500 soldiers; viz., Massachusetts, 333; Plymouth, 60; Connecticut, 65; and New Haven, 42. Also, ammunition recently sent over from the Corporation was to be divided among the colonies, to be paid for by supplies "as the Commissioners from time to time may direct." Cf. (for different implementations of this order) *CCR*, I, 239; and *NHCR*, II, 14. (*PCR*, X, 33-4.)

[6] *PCR*, X, 35-52; deForest, *op. cit.*, pp. 66-9. Stuyvesant had recommended the appointing of such a commission from the United Colonies. (Ltr to Endicott, via Winthrop, Jr., 6Mar53/4; see above notes, also NYC Misc. Mss. NYHS.)

[7] "A brief Narration of the proceedings of the united Colonies since their Confederation and more perticularly respecting A warr with the Dutch and Narraganset Indians," MA, XXX, 36.

[8] That both offensive and defensive wars could be lawful, as stated in the Articles, was a traditional view inherited from the scholastics. Waging war was justified when for defense, recovering of property, or punishment of wrongs. (See Arthur H. Buffington, "The Puritan View of War," *PCSM*, XXVIII, 67-85.)

[9] The Massachusetts members of this committee were Captains Atherton and Leverett, Major Denison, and Mr. Simons; the Commissioners appointed were Hathorne, Bradford, Ludlow, and Eaton. (*PCR*, X, 52; MCR, III, 311.)

[10] "A brief Narration . . .," *loc. cit.*

[11] *PCR*, X, 56-7.

[12] *MCR*, II, 31, *re* offensive war.

[13] To Winthrop, 9Mar46/7, *Winthrop Papers*, V, 136.

[14] An actual vote on a war resolution, however, never took place. If such had been the case it would have passed, seven to one, but would have invited the secession of the strongest member of the Confederacy, which, of course, would have made Massachusetts aid even less forthcoming.

[15] Article Three deals with the preserving of the integrity of the individual colonies; Article Six concerns the selecting of the Commissioners and their powers.

[16] *MCR*, III, 311-2; *PCR*, X, 74-6.

[17] *PCR*, X, 77.

[18] *Ibid.*, pp. 74-6. These arguments were now superficial, for it was accepted practice by this time for all the confederated colonies to choose their Commissioners from the magistrates. In most cases the Commissioners were elected at the annual court of elections or at least they were selected from the general officers of the Colonies. Thus, in effect, they were general officers, contrary to the Massachusetts argument, standing next in rank to the Governor and Deputy Governor and above the military commander of the colony. (Adam Winthrop to J. Winthrop, 3May49, *Winthrop Papers*, V, 340.)

[19] As for the origins of the U. S. Supreme Court, the Commissioners of the United Colonies afford undoubtedly one of the most important colonial precedents. Certainly the arguments before the Commissioners in this constitutional debate form the beginning of constitutional law in America.

[20] PCR, X, 77.

[21] MA, II, 171, 351-2; III, 10; XXX, 27; New Haven Town Recs., I, 181, 185. The Massachusetts Council thought the other colonies had "not so charitably conceived the Declaration of the Gennerall Court." It was not their intention "to breake the Confederation or infringe the power of the commissioners," rather "wee are all desirous to Continew our Confederation."

[22] To support this last contention, it is interesting to note that New Haven drew an analogy to the Israelites securing the land of Canaan. The question was asked whether these battles were offensive or defensive. It was pointed out, therefore, that if this question were raised, then the question might also be raised whether there was a right to enter into a confederation at all. Even "Jehosophat the king of Judah sinned and was rebuked by two prophets, Jehu and Eliezer, for joyning with an helping Ahab and Ahaziah, kings of Israel." (NHCR, II, 7.)

[23] ". . . as may appeare in the different agreements and settlements of the Netherland Provinces, and the confederation of the cantons of the Switzers . . ." (NHCR, II, 8.)

[24] NHCR, II, 7-15. In pleading for a "loose construction" of the Articles, Massachusetts argued that the whole picture must be considered rather than merely the "grammattical course." (MA, II, 351-2.)

[25] NHCR, II, 7-15.

[26] PCR, X, 86-7.

[27] At this meeting, the Mass. Court tried to block the sitting of the New Haven Commissioners, which was permitted after ten days debate. Note this early attempt to be judge of their own elections. (MCR, III, 324).

[28] NHCR, II, 111.

[29] "A Brief Narration . . ." loc. cit.

[30] Messengers were sent unsuccessfully to demand explanation by the Niantic sachem. (PCR, X, 88-98.) It is thought the Niantics were in the pay of the Pocomtucks of the Connecticut Valley. George Sheldon, History of Deerfield, (Deerfield: 1895), p. 59.)

[31] To show the heavy demands that would be made upon Massachusetts, that colony was to furnish 166 of the 250 men for the expedition.

[32] MA, XXX, 29; MA, Council Recs., I, 24Sep53; PCR, X, 99, 101-2. When the "justice" of a war with the Dutch (not an actual declaration) was voted upon again in this session twice and carried by six of the Commissioners, the final time as an answer to the negative decision of the Massachusetts Council. (PCR, X, 102.)

[33] A formal declaration was sent to Cromwell by the New Haven General Court, and the agents for New Haven and Connecticut in England worked

for an invasion against the Dutch. *(New Haven Town Records,* I, 188, 192; Coleman, *op. cit.,* pp. 16-20; E. Huntington, *op. cit.,* pp. 74-5.)

[34] Which culminated in the war council of 1654. (See Chapter 8.)

[35] *NHCR,* II, 7-15.

[36] *Ibid.,* pp. 38ff.

[37] *PCR,* X, 109-112.

[38] *PCR,* X, 114.

[39] *MCR,* II, 31. This has received emphasis in this chapter because the historians of New England, whether favorable or unfavorable to the Puritans, have treated the Bay's position in the debates of 1653 as on the spare of the moment, when actually their reservation existed from the time of the forming of the Confederation.

[40] See Chapter 6.

[41] Undoubtedly the New England settlers had learned from a precedent of their nullification controversy during the sojourn of the Pilgrims in Holland. For the "Sharp Resolve, which stated the doctrine of State sovereignty in its plainest form" on the part of the legislature of Holland in 1617 and that it must have been "lively talk" for the Pilgrims, see William E. Griffis, *The Pilgrims in Their Three Homes,* (Boston: 1898), pp. 142-3. Perhaps there was never any intention of the Confederation to engage in war with the Dutch, for as Irving humorously puts it: "The grand council was composed of men too cool and practical to be put readily in a heat or to indulge in knight-errantry . . . They knew the advantage, however, to have always a snug, justifiable cause of war in reserve with a neighbor who had territories worth invading . . ." (Irving, *op. cit.,* p. 260.)

[42] Surely, here is no clearer example of consenting to engage in an offensive war—yet historians, in stating that the debates of 1653 and the refusal of Massachusetts at that time to engage in offensive war was the point on which the Confederation fell, have overlooked the importance of this event. (Hutchinson and Palfrey discuss it, but fail to realize its significance.)

[43] *PCR,* X, 125-134. As a safety measure in case a general Indian uprising broke out, a much larger force of two hundred and seventy was ordered by the Commissioners to be in readiness. The decision of the Commissioners to make these preparations for war was the cold reception of messengers from the Confederation by Ninigret, his refusal to attend the Hartford meeting, as he was summoned to do, and his intention to attack the Long Island Indians again to avenge the loss of a number of his braves. *(PCR,* X, 115-6, 125.) Also MA, XXX, 52, 54.

[44] Gibbons and Denison refused, and Atherton was absent at the time. Massachusetts had little heart for the expedition itself, but was primarily interested in order to "sodder and unite the Collonies in the very way of theire former Combination. . . ." (MA, II, 352a.)

[45] *CCR,* I, 261-2; *PCR,* III, 67-8; *NHCR,* II, 219-20. The actual expense to the colonies was small, the total being £44 3s., of which Massachusetts con-

tributed its proportion. (MA, XXX, 47; Peirce, *op. cit.* (*civil lists*), p. 93.) On the town level, e.g., Windsor contributed eight soldiers and a sergeant, plus two barrels of meat, one of peas, and a little. (Henry Stiles, *The History of Ancient Windsor* (New York: 1859), p. 145.) The Mass. Council, unlike a similar situation the year before, upheld the resolution of the Commissioners raising this expedition. (MA, Council Recs., 4Oct54.)

[46] Hull, *Diary*, p. 176.

[47] *PCR*, X, 145.

[48] *Ibid.*, pp. 145-7.

[49] *MCR*, III, 359. The army disbanded on October 27, 1654, two weeks from the time of the appointed rendezvous. In Massachusetts the reserve forces raised to back up the Willard expedition in case general hostilities were to break out were likewise disbanded. (MA, XXX, 44.) The decision not to fight was not Willard's alone, in the opinion of his biographer, but must have had the concurrence of his council of war. (See Joseph Willard, *Life and Times of Major Simon Willard*, (Boston: 1858), pp. 221-8.) In any event the influence of Massachusetts was deciding.

During this period, while the Commissioners were deciding upon war against the Niantics, the Massachusetts authorities kept up a running commentary on the proceedings in relation to the Articles of Confederation. Here was proof that the Bay did not approve the expedition, but rather was going along with it to preserve the Confederation. Only "vindicative and defensive warrs" were approved; and if the Commissioners had power to determine offensive war without "commission" from the general courts, then they had a power "beside and Above that power which they derived from their General Courts and above the fundamentals of Government." (MA, XXX, 48-50.)

[50] *PCR*, X, 149; *NHCR*, II, 153. The Commissioners in their rebuke to Willard pointed out that Indian hostility had become even more threatening. ". . . som bloud is alreddy shead how much more may be shortly shead is not yett knowne and how farr out chardge and danger may bee Increased by his [Ninigret's] pride and Threachery in Ingaging forraigne Indians against us and what further Inconveniences may arise from youer non attendence to youer Commission is yett uncertaine. . ." (*PCR*, X, 149.) In the Bay, however, Willard's popularity continued, and he commanded the Middlesex troops until his death. (Willard, *op. cit.*, p. 227.)

CHAPTER X

A Time for Falling Out

As a result of the failure of the Union to bind its confederates to coercive action, the utility of the Confederation was greatly impaired. The Confederation which survived the crisis years found itself no longer leading the Puritan colonies in united policy; rather the Commissioners now merely gave expression to the particular wills of the general courts. Whereas the Commissioners on occasion had sought to exercise executive powers, such functions now rested indisputably with the individual councils of the magistrates of the colonies. The only real jurisdiction retained by the Commissioners was the "Indian Worke," the administrative policy of which will be discussed in the following chapter. With the coming of Charles II to the throne in 1660, it was soon apparent that the Confederation of 1643 was an anomaly in the royal scheme of things. Its right to exist was denied by royal authority; Connecticut's absorption of New Haven by royal charter, which left only three members, completely violated the Articles of Confederation; and the remaining confederates, on the defensive for fear of royal intervention, acted in many ways contrary to the Articles.

By 1667, the Confederation under the old Articles had for all practical purposes ended. If the Confederation were to be revived, a new covenant was obviously necessary. Except for the need to administer the funds of the Corporation for the converting of the Indians, the Confederation might have ended in that year. The period from 1655 to 1667 is of importance because of the denouement to the Confederacy resulting from the jarring experience of the New England colonies; coming face to face for the first time with imperial policy. Moreover, this period is of interest because during this time the lack of guidance by the Commissioners in Indian affairs, which was a vital concern of the early Confederacy, contributed to the great uprising of the New England Indians in 1675.

Indian problems were essentially the same; but it seemed

that as the periphery of contact with the natives widened, the influence of the Commissioners diminished. The Narragansetts and the Mohegans were still at each other's throats, and with the Pocomtucks and other Connecticut Valley Indians favoring the Narragansetts, the old alignment of power began to shift against the friendly Mohegans. The Commissioners, however, instead of placing demands on the hostile Indians or making a show of force, chose now to function only sa an advisory council in Indian affairs. When Uncas in 1656 was accused of violating the past treaties by allowing the murder of a Narragansett and other violations, the Commissioners merely decided to let him know "what wee hear and how offencive such speeches and carriages are to the Commissioners."[1] Messengers were sent out as usual, such as Thomas Stanton, to remind all of the Indians of their previous agreements with the English, and insist always that the tribes should not engage in war until "first theire hath been a full hearing of all such Differences and upon Satisfying proofe a determination by the Commissioners with damages ordered to such as have been wronged."[2] In 1657, however, Massachusetts was tiring of this procedure, and would not consent to have the messengers sent out as usual. There had been too "many messengers to this purpose" sent by the Commissioners," and their advice was "seldom observed" by the Indians. To the Bay, continually dispatching messengers without armed force to back them up would

> Render us lo and Contemptable in the eyes of the Indians or engage us to vindecate our honor in a dangerouse and unesessarie war upon Indian quarrells the grounds wherof wee can hardly ever satisfactorily understand.[3]

The Pocomtucks were becoming the tribe to reckon with. In 1657 they attacked the Mohegans, inflicting heavy casualties and besieging them in their fort. A Connecticut force was sent to relieve the hard-pressed Mohegan garrison. This action of the River Colony, however, was disowned by the Commissioners at their meeting in the fall, but this dual policy of Connecticut, in sending aid to the friendly Mohegans and at the same time reprimanding Uncas, helped to avert war, since both tribes experienced the English favor and their rebuke.[4] The policy of neutrality of the colonies in Indian disputes would have proved a fatal policy, and only encouraged hostilities. The very next year, the Pocomtucks were again on the warpath, attacking Uncas, and one lawless element boldly raided an English plantation. The owner of the plantation brought the case before the Commissioners of the Confederation and was awarded forty fathom of wampum by that body, to be paid by the offending Indians. But the messengers of the Confederation to the Indians continued to be treated coldly, and the Commissioners were put on notice that in the future "if any Messengers bee sent to us from the English they may bee such as are not lyares and tale carryers, but sober men; and such as wee can understand."[5]

That the diplomacy of the messengers representing the Commissioners was not always level-headed in dealing with the Indians is attested to by an account of a visit to Thomas Stanton by Cassasinamon, who had been appointed "governor" of a group of the conquered Pequots. This well-intentioned savage, in an appeal to the Connecticut General Assembly, resented the headstrong intrusions of the Puritan envoys. On this occasion

> a great many other Indians mett together in the place where we dwell to make A daunce after the Indian fashion Intending noe hurt at all to the English and when we were about to daunce Mr. Stanton cam with some souldiers to carry Away Ninicraft[6] Mr. Stanton said he would dye in that place but he would have him and chargd the pequott Indians to Assist the English . . . I was much afraid that some men would be keild because I then saw Ninicrafts men Almost one hundred of them have clubs in their hands and the english men layd their hands upon their swords Redy to draw then I cryed out to them and Asked them what would satisfy them . . .

The English messenger replied that he must have "a great deal of wampum," and that "wampum was like the grass when it was gon it would com againe but if men be once kild they will live noe more." Thus the terrified Pequot governor agreed to buy off Stanton and his men for £20, because he was afraid that Ninigret's men would fire English houses and the Pequots would be blamed. But after receiving the wampum, Stanton was not satisfied with the quality of it and demanded as much again. The bewildered Indian thus turned to the Connecticut authorities.

He had paid the money simply to buy off the Englishmen, who in their rude intrusion on a festive occasion of the savages would have brought the spilling of blood; therefore, "I hope you will consider my great love I have for lives of Englishmen."[7] This is but one example of the indiscriminate handling of Indian affairs during this period, and, needless to say, hastened the coming of King Philip's War.

The New England colonists were ever on their guard against Indian attack. During this period, with no intercolonial expeditions sent out against the emboldened savage tribes, the individual colonies kept their military organizations intact on the local level.[8] Although, on a number of occasions, Commissioners from the colonies wrote one another advising that emergency sessions might be necessary to treat with the Indian problem,[9] it is interesting to note that during this period no emergency session of the Confederation was called. The chief act of the Commissioners in regular session was to send Captain John Youngs of Southold to cruise up and down Long Island Sound as a sort of blockade to prevent an invasion of the Long Island Indians by the Niantics.[10] But the Commissioners would not forbear the "righteous use of the civil sword" if the occasion presented itself, and Roger Williams, scanning the horizon, felt that "God calls us to a just war" with either the Mohawks or Narragansetts, but woe to the English if they had neither one on their side.[11]

Most significant of the acts of the Commissioners concerning Indian affairs during this period was the specification of emergency action to be taken by the English in the event that war should break out among the Indians. In such an event, no armed Indians were to be allowed within a one mile radius of any English settlement, except for Indians residing in these areas. It would be lawful, however, to harbor fleeing Indians if this action were reported to the sachems concerned.[12] This was not a new regulation, for many of the towns already had such a provision in force, especially on Long Island where an attack by the Niantics or other Narragansett tribes was constantly feared. In 1659, it was ordered that for any damage done to the English by any of the Pequots,[13] satisfaction should be made by delivering the guilty party to the party injured "soe hee may Recover his Right from him or them in an orderly way."[14] The general courts were urged to make laws or provisions for dealing with specific offenses committed by the Indians.[15]

The Commissioners took a small hand in prosecuting criminal offenses by the Pequots. When some Pequots tried to pass off bad wampum, two of them were committed to jail until the whole amount was paid by their brethren; on another occasion a Pequot, having aided Uncas against the Pocumtucks, was jailed "during the pleasure of the Commissioners." In the case of the "counterfeit" wampum, the Commissioners ordered the remaining culprits, whom they were unable to seize, to attend a meeting of the Commissioners, but this call went unheeded because of the "sicknes and stubbornes of some Indians and that they were ashamed to appear before the Commissioners with such slight excuses."[16] Nothing further could be done since the Commissioners had no means of enforcement, and, moreover, criminal proceedings, except in rare instances such as the hearing before the Commissioners which condemned Miantinomo during the early Confederation, were not within the jurisdiction of the central government.

The Indian picture was darkest in 1660. In that year the Commissioners issued several orders to the Narragansett and Niantic sachems to deliver to the governor of Connecticut the culprits who had been firing English houses and to pay back tribute also to the Connecticut authorities.[17] The Commissioners also "desired" the General Court of Connecticut to "send a convenient company of men under some discreet leader to force satisfaction" from the recalcitrant Indians, and any culprits they should find should be sent to Barbados.[18] The hands-off policy of the Commissioners in coercive measures may again be noted. In the same year Josiah Winslow wrote to Winthrop, Jr., that because the Indians were plotting against the English it would be wise to "hasten the meeting of Commissioners, that soe, if the case require, we may enterprise something agaynst them before winter."[19] Because of the weak state of the Confederation during these post-crisis years, however, the only action the Commissioners would have taken, if such a meeting were called, probably would have been merely to confirm the directives of the general courts and to supervise whatever they deemed necessary. The Indian situation only continued to worsen. The powerful Mohawks of the Iroquois Confederacy were making depredations among the New England Indians, and sometimes indiscriminately attacking Indians friendly to the English. Moreover, in the face of war between England against the states of France and Holland, the Mohawks were making peace with their French rivals in the New World; and, in the very midst of the Puritan plantations, Philip, succeeding his brother Alexander, on the latter's death, as chief of the Wampanoags, was rightly suspected, in his negotiations with other tribes, of intending to live up to the reputation of his namesake, the Greek conquer.[20] But the Commissioners of the United Colonies, with the Articles of 1643 in disrepute, could not now lead the Puritan colonies in united policy. New Articles were needed. Lion Gardiner, the chronicler of the Pequot War, writing in 1660, best depicts the lack of ascendancy of the Commissioners in effecting Indian policy during this period. The Indians

> say to our faces that our Comissioners meeting once a year, and speak a great deal, or write a letter, and there's all, for they dare not fight.[21]

The Commissioners had only a small part in settling land disputes during this period. In 1657, liberty was given to New Haven to incorporate Oyster Bay and Huntington under its jurisdiction "according to the Articles of Confederation,"[22] but in view of the waning fortunes of the Colony on the Sound, Huntington soon chose to come under Connecticut, and Oyster Bay remained independent. When the Duke of York took over in 1665, however, all the towns on Long Island belonging to the colonies of the Confederation were severed from New England.[23] The most notable judgment of the Commissioners concerning lands was that of 1658, dividing the Pequot country between Massachusetts and Connecticut, which has been treated in Chapter VII. The impotency of this decision was soon evident when the River Colony still contested the right of the Bay to jurisdiction in this territory. The claims of Massachusetts, it will be remembered, were based on her participation in the conquest of the Pequot lands, whereas the River Colony based its rights on a patent which it never actually produced, although in the records of the Commissioners in 1648 there is testimony that such a patent existed. Since the Connecticut authorities never did produce the patent, the records of 1648 were in themselves being cited a decade later in support of the Connecticut claims. When the Bay called this maneuver a bluff, the Connecticut authorities replied that "we are not able to see any Reason why our Confederation should breed any Scruple about the Right and Title which never would have bin questioned had not that Confeaderation bin."[24] Thus the Confederacy now was even too weak to serve as an effective board of arbitration for land disputes. In the same area the encroachments of the Rhode Island settlers continued, and all the Commissioners could do was to keep on referring the cases to the general courts.[25] While the Confederation was falling apart and the individual colonies beginning to go their own way, the New England colonists awoke to find themselves included in an imperial picture drawn by the home government.

The Restoration of the Stuart monarchy in 1660 gave rise to a new depth in British colonial policy. Hitherto, the mercantile and commercial views on the importance of colonies, reinforced by the struggle for power, which lessened governmental interference, had looked upon the colonies as economic ventures to increase the wealth and trade of the home country. But with the Restoration came the longing for empire, the desire to extend British control throughout the world. Colonies were now looked upon with a strategic eye. Colonial possessions were no longer merely sources of trade, but their very position could also be used as bases to harass the commerce or possessions of enemy nations; in peacetime they would be necessary for the mastery of the seas; and they could influence the continual manipulating of the balance of power in Europe. In the words of one colonial writer: "Whoever holds possession of our colonies in America will keep the sovereignty of the Atlantic ocean."[26] Although the New England colonies in many ways duplicated the economy of England and offered competition in sending provisions to the West Indies, they could be valuable in the fisheries and in the carrying trade.[27] By establishing a uniform system of administration under the revived Privy Council and later under a select council from that body, the Council for Foreign Plantations, the mother country sought to bring the colonies into closer union with each other and into greater dependence upon the home government.[28]

When Charles II came to the throne there was no doubt that the New England Confederacy was on its last legs. Samuel Mayerick, later one of the royal commissioners to the colonies, summed up in 1660 his impressions of the Confederation: "Each of the 4 Governments annually choose two commissioners to meet and Conoult as occasion may serve; their power lasting for one yeare. These meetings prove chargeable, and it is conceived of many of no great use."[29]

The Commissioners, whenever the opportunity prevailed, acknowledged the sovereignty of the king. The dedication in Eliot's Indian Bible, penned by Commissioners Bradstreet and Danforth,[30] was the best example of the many expressions the Commissioners used to show their recognition of the royal prerogative. But in spite of the decrepit condition of the Confederation and its expressed subordination to the royal government, it was yet to receive several lethal blows from the royal authority.

The colonies lost no time in sending agents to England to defend their course of action, such as forming the New England Confederation without consent of the home government. Petitions were especially mounting against the arbitrary course of the Massachusetts government, and it was therefore feared that its charter was in peril.[31] The immediate result of Winthrop's negotiations in London was the securing of the Connecticut Charter in 1662. Thus, like Rhode Island, the River Colony had definite legal existence, and might well be won over to an attempt of the royal government to bring the other New England colonies into line. As a matter of fact, the granting of this charter was a most devastating blow to the Confederation, for it brought New Haven, which had no prior legal existence to the English government, into the bounds of Connecticut.[32] The charter violated the political integrity of each colony guaranteed by the Articles of Confederation, and the New Haven Colony caught off guard by this surprise grant made a last ditch stand by calling upon her confederates to keep Connecticut from enforcing the extension of authority according to the charter. The first reaction of the Commissioners from the other colonies when they received the news of the Connecticut charter was favorable. It was expected that there would be no further intrusions from Rhode Island. The Ishmael colony was thus more emphatically warned that if such "Injuriouse dealing" should continue, then the "united Collonies are Inocent of the sad consequences and disturbances" which may result.[33]

The stalwarts of the theocratic-commercial party of the New Haven Colony decided to resist union with Connecticut, or at least to delay it until they should elect to come within its jurisdiction. Union in any event would have been a natural course, for the two colonies had been one in facing practically the same frontier problems and had sided together in more than one controversy against the Bay. Moreover, the star of New Haven had faded; the dreams of establishing a great maritime republic were gone forever; and control of the Colony passed to the small farmers and traders who remained to eke out a living on the rocky soil.[34] No longer were there the great names of such men as Eaton and Newman,[35] who since the founding of the Colony, as chief magistrates or as Commissioners of the United Colonies, had sought to forge a Phoenicia in the New World. A new generation had arisen, more liberal and willing to learn from the frustrations of the past. For them, union with the River Colony was progress.

But the diehards of the Colony were determined at this time to delay the union, despite strong sentiment on the town level favoring coming under Connecticut. The Connecticut authorities took advantage of this situation, and wherever possible recognized town officials appointed by the Connecticut party, even when like officials were named by New Haven. In this manner Connecticut soon claimed Southold, Guilford, Stamford, and Greenwich. In New Haven, Milford, and Branford, however, there were no large groups of disaffected inhabitants.[36] A package deal was proposed to New Haven: the citizens of that colony would enjoy the privileges of freemanship under Connecticut; deputies would be sent from the New Haven towns to the Connecticut legislature; and the towns of New Haven Colony would be united into a county under the Connecticut jurisdiction.[37] The Long Island towns readily accepted Connecticut jurisdiction.[38] From London, however, the great statesman from the River, the younger John Winthrop, urged moderation in bringing the New Haven towns into Connecticut so that nothing "prejudicial" would be done to their confederate on the Sound.[39] The anti-union forces organized in their opposition to coming under the Connecticut jurisdiction. In the spring of 1664, William Jones, who with William Leete was the last Commissioner of the United Colonies from New Haven, proposed that "we have abundant cause to refuse union" with Connecticut, and cited the authority of the Articles of Confederation.[40] New Haven rested its case upon the Puritan covenant of 1643, by which the four United Colonies agreed to respect the political integrity of each confederate colony.

In May, 1663 a "remonstrance" was drawn up by the New Haven General Court and sent to the Connecticut authorities as a protest against subverting its government. The River Colony was accused of violating the Articles of Confederation, which, having been entered upon in "Consociation," was to be "perpetuall," and therefore "we Conceive ourselves bound to adheare, untill with satisfaction to our Judgements and Consciences, we see our duty with like unanimous Consent of the Confederates orderly to Recede Leaveing the issue unto the most wise and righteous god."[41] During the summer, special committees from Connecticut and New Haven, comprised of the men who at one time or another served as Commissioners from the two colonies,[42] tried to work out a compromise, but the negotiations soon became deadlocked.[43] The annual meeting of the Confederation was soon at hand, and once again the flames of constitutional strife were fanned over the charred remains of the Confederacy. Whereas the great issue in 1653-5 was the right of nullification and secession, the debates now centered upon the right to preserve the political integrity of one of the member colonies and to allow for self-determination in that colony.

When the Commissioners convened in September, 1663, the New Haven Commissioners placed formal charges against the political subversion of the River Colony because of the attempt to incorporate New Haven within its jurisdiction. It was charged that Connecticut had already transferred the freemanship of some New Haven inhabitants to that of Connecticut, and that others were openly encouraged to disown New Haven authority. The result was that the New Haven citizens refused to perform their civic duties, such as attending courts or meetings. Constables and other officials were "appointed and sett up" by Connecticut. The New Haven Commissioners asked that some effectual course be found so that "such actings may bee Recalled" and the Articles of Confederation "duely observed towards us as a distinct Colloney."[44] The Commissioners from Massachusetts and Plymouth reviewed the argument of New Haven and upheld its validity, finding that New Haven, accord-

ing to the Articles of Confederation, should continue to be regarded as a distinct colony. Undoubtedly their decision was influenced by the fact that their governments in the future could
be as easily abolished by the royal government as that of New
Haven: the Bay had only a commercial company charter, while
Plymouth had no charter at all, only questionable patent rights.
By act of the Commissioners of the United Colonies, therefore,
the Colony on the Sound

> may not by any act of violence have there liberty of juris-
> diction infringed by any other of the United Collonyes with-
> out breach of the articles of confederation, and that where
> any act of power hath bin excerted against there authority,
> that the same ought to be recalled and there power reserved
> to them intire, untill such time as in an orderly way it shall
> be otherwise disposed....[45]

Because of this united front of three colonies, the Connecticut Commissioners were forced to disregard the Articles of
Confederation completely. They denied that the Commissioners
had any right whatever to question their jurisdiction over New
Haven, because such proceedings were "directly opposite to the
tennor of the Charter lately granted" by which the New Haven
"plantations" were included within Connecticut.[46] Thus again
the Commissioners adjourned split over a grave constitutional
issue. But neither side was to be deterred. Connecticut continued
to negotiate with various groups of individuals in New Haven
who had no authority from the General Court to represent New
Haven.[47] The General Court of New Haven, or what was left
of it, increased its opposition to union with Connecticut.

However, the New Haven Colony now was inclined to consider
the wishes of the apparent majority of the Colony to come under
the government of Connecticut, provided its original jurisdiction were restored and all the methods of subversion were re-
linguished by the River Colony. The high-handed methods of
the River Colony would have to cease. To the Bible Commonwealth on the Sound it was not that the liberalism on the River
was so much to be feared or that union was economically un-
desirable, it was a matter of principle—they would come only
upon their own free choosing.[48]

New Haven, as it had done during previous crises, vigorously wielded the moral force of the Confederacy. An emergency session of the Confederation was sought, but the proposal was turned down by Plymouth.[49] The Massachusetts Court, considering our "duty in relation to you our confederates," asked that the River Colony make "an orderly issue" with New Haven, that the Confederation would be "more precious" to them if they worked out a solution in that agency rather than outside of its walls.[50] Meanwhile, the New Haven Court elected Commissioners for the regular session in September, 1664, on which all hopes were pinned.[51] The Connecticut Council, however, viewed the sending of the New Haven Commissioners to the Confederation as an act contrary to "regall authority" and because it "doth not appeare that they are a colony." Because of the inclination of New Haven to continue the Confederation, the River Colony was willing to preserve the union with three members instead of four.[52]

The odds against New Haven's maintaining a separate jurisdiction became even greater after the Commissioners had adjourned. The royal commissioners sent to investigate New England affairs and to secure aid against the Dutch soon appeared on the scene. It was therefore thought advantageous to the Bible Commonwealth to submit to Connecticut, rather than take chances on being set aside by the royal commissioners and ending up as a province of the king. In November, the town of Milford, second largest in the New Haven Colony, unanimously voted to come under Connecticut.[53] Less than a month later, the General Court convened, and there was little choice except to follow suit and bring the entire colony officially within Connecticut authority. The last general court was held December 23, 1664, and on August 24, 1665 the laws of Connecticut were read at a public meeting in New Haven.[54] Protests were still heard from the small group of diehards, consisting mostly of churchmen such as Davenport, who feared corruption of what had been the most purely theocratic state of the New England colonies. These protests, however, went unheard. In May, the freemen of New Haven met with those of Connecticut in a Court of Election and united together in voting for the magistrates and general officers of the new colony. At the General Assembly, deputies from all the towns of the two colonies were represented.[55]

With the union of these two confederates, the Articles of Confederation of 1643, "that ancient wall of New Englands safety,"⁵⁶ became even more inadequate. The royal commissioners were also breathing down the back of the Confederacy, condemning it in every respect. It is not surprising, therefore, to find in a contemporary journal that "the Commissioners for the United Colonies kept not their wonted yearly meeting this year. The Lord grant it be not protentous."[57]

One of the reasons that the royal government was so willing to approve the incorporation of New Haven under Connecticut was the belief that New Haven was harboring two of the judges who had condemned Charles I, Edward Whalley and William Goffe, and possibly a third, John Dixwell. All were on the king's list of proscription, and were wanted for trial at home. The three escaped capture, which event would have meant their subsequent execution, by fleeing to the New World. A £100 reward was placed on each, dead or alive. Governor Endicott, bowing to the pressure of His Majesty's commissioners, issued a warrant for the arrest of these regicides, but this haughty Puritan was shrewd enough to delay the warrant because of the Sabbath, which gave time for the friends of the regicides to hide them. The two young men entrusted with the duty of apprehending the regicides, a merchant and a shipmaster from Boston, traced the whereabouts of the regicides to New Haven. But there the trail ended.[58] What exactly happened to the regicides has been the subject of much folklore and even found its way into an epic by Sir Walter Scott. It has been generally supposed that they were hidden, with the help of John Davenport and others, at the so-called Judges' Cave on the outskirts of New Haven. The Commissioners of the United Colonies had recommended that the general courts order a diligent search for those who "stand Convicted of high Treason for the horred Murder of his highnes father," and it was further ordered that anyone giving refuge to the regicides would be "accounted publicke enimies of the peace and welfare of the united Collonies and may expect to be proceeded with accordingly."[59] Although the royal investigators were unable to locate the regicides, in their report to the home government they were strongly convinced that New Haven had played a considerable part in their hiding.[60]

The Commissioners of the United Colonies, at their annual meeting in September, 1664, with his Majesty's commissioners in the colonies, dared not raise their voice as they had done the preceding year in protest of Connecticut's absorption of New Haven. As a matter of fact, they wore in a sort of dilemma whether to continue with the Confederation or not. And they had good reason for concern. Within a year the invective heaped upon the Confederacy by malcontents, and even the royal commissioners themselves, gave cause to question the expediency of salvaging the union. From Rhode Island, the king learned of the "envious and subtle contrivances of our neighbour Colonies round about us," and was beseeched to stretch "forth your Princely and Patent hand, for our speedy releife, and to pluck us as a spoil out of their teeth."[61] This "Combination of all the Colonies" was the very cause of forcing refugees from them into "seeking out new Places of the Willderness," and once evicted from the United Colonies they were denied help in their greatest sufferings.[62]

The four commissioners appointed by the king to investigate New England affairs were an unfortunate choice, and therefore hindered the effectiveness of the mission. Colonel Nicolls was a good choice, but was preoccupied by the conquest of New Amsterdam, and afterwards as the deputy governor of New York. Carr and Cartwright had served as officers in the royal army, while Samuel Maverick had long been a leading critic of the Puritans in New England, himself wishing to establish the Anglican Church there.[63] Cartwright was outspoken in his criticism of the Confederation:

They had made a combination amongst themselves (but left out Rode-island) in immitation of the States of the United provinces,[64] and styled themselves, the United Colonies, by this they took more power than was ever given, or entended them, as by the copy if not lost, might have been seen. That there should be an agreement amongst all the severall colonies, for assisting of each other, and for keeping a good correspondence betwixt each other, as that servants, debtors, and murtherers, or thieves might not be defended against their just prosecutors, is absolutely necessary. But then it ought to be under a head, so long as there is a king, nether ther are they to exercise the Kings prerogative without his leave and consent.[65]

Moreover, the United Colonies

> did usurp authority is certainly plain in that, that the authority of disposing of lands, without the limitts of their respective limitts, which they exercised, was not given them by the King; if that act be justified, they may dispose of all new England both when, and as they please.[66]

The Commissioners of the United Colonies, taking heed of the hostility raised against them and realizing that the Articles were obsolete, ordered at their meeting in September, 1664, that if the royal commissioners approved,[67] the remaining three colonies should reconstruct the Confedcrccy. It was proposed to the three confederates that they invest their Commissioners will full power to act in

> any case that may be of Comon Concernment to the whole that soe as much as in us lyes wee may approve our selves faithfull and Loyall to his Majesties Just Interest and the best good and welfare of these Plantations ... that the Confederation may be Continued in love and Amity which seems to be the desire of all.[68]

In order to let the Confederation cool off a bit, it was decided that the next meeting should not be until 1667, and thereafter, perhaps in imitation of the Triennial Act of Parliament of the same year,[69] the meetings were to be held once every three years. Then the chief concern of the Confederacy would be the "disposall of the Indian Stocke."[70] This was a wise maneuver, for surely by 1667 the royal investigation of the New England governments would be completed, and it would be safe then to proceed again in their experiment with federal government. The sharp rebuke meted out to the Bay by the royal commissioners indicated that this was a wise policy.

The brunt of the royal investigation was to be borne by Massachusetts. That colony had long displayed an air of independence and was becoming a powerful state in the New World. The policy of the commissioners, therefore, was to visit all other of His Majesty's subjects first, as far north as the New Hampshire settlements, where Massachusetts was still collecting cus-

toms and "Coine money," and lining them up in allegiance to
the king.[71] The reception of the royal commissioners in all the
New England settlements, except that of Massachusetts, met with
"great satisfaction" to the commissioners.[72] The Massachusetts
authorities had the gall to frustrate completely the efforts of the
king's commissioners, but because they openly proclaimed allegiance to the king,[73] professed to observe the English Acts of
Trade,[74] and because the conduct of the royal commissioners
was not always too commendable,[75] the Bay in this brush with
royal authority would emerge with its charter still intact.

The royal commissioners timed their visit to Massachusetts
with the convening of the Court of Elections in May, 1665.[76]
Undoubtedly it was their intention to make an appeal to the
freemen of the Colony, to encourage them to make a determined
effort against the theocracy.[77] Upon complaint to the commissioners of one Thomas Deane, the commissioners demanded to
see the laws of the Colony.[78] A committee was immediately appointed by the Generall Court to meet with His Majesty's commissioners, and the Massachusetts government was accused outright of arbitrarily using its charter to establish a virtual independent government. In defense, the Massachusetts committee
placed the responsibility for its high-handed policy with the
Narragansett Indians and the Rhode Island settlers on the
Commissioners of the United Colonies.[79] But the Bay could not
convince the royal commissioners that the other colonies had
an equal hand in the various harsh policies of the Confederation. Moreover, there was not even the power to confederate.
Among the necessary "alterations" and "additions" that should
be made to the General Laws and Liberties of Massachusetts,
the royal commissioners found that:

> There is no power in the charter to incorporate with other
> colonies, nor to exercise any power by that association:
> both belongs to the kings prerogative. If there by any other
> undecent expressions and repetitions of the word "common-
> wealth," "state," and the like, in other pages, wee desire they
> may be changed.[80]

This statement and an earlier order to Governor Prence of Plymouth from the royal commissioners, wherein it was stated

that they believed the New England Confederation was a "war combination made by the four colonies, when they had a design to throw off their dependence on England,"[81] might have been enough to discourage the continuing of the Confederation, except for several reasons.

First of all, the actual policy of the royal government was one of conciliation. Most of the strong accusations against the Bay and the New England Confederation were uttered by the three prejudiced members of the commission, without the head of the commission, Richard Nicolls, who was the only one with veto powers on the commission. When the Massachusetts Court refused to allow Commissioners Carr, Cartwright, and Maverick to conduct hearings on the colony[82] and sought to refute all their accusations when they met with the committee appointed by the General Court in May, 1665, they were forced to give up in exasperation.[83] But Nicolls was not moved when the venerable Connecticut Governor informed him that four members of the Confederation would meet that year for the sole business of administering the funds of the Corporation in England.[84] Indeed, when the commissioners had arrived the preceding year in Boston, the restrained temperment of Nicolls could be seen in their declaration: "It being as much in our desier to preserve and improove a good intelligence and correspondence betweene all our good subjects" in order to "unite them all in a joint dependence and firme loyalty to ourselfe."[85] A league for purposes relating to the home government or for mutual defense, of course, could not be considered contrary to the home government, unless it ventured independently into areas requiring supervision for implementing royal policy. As for Massachusetts, the Puritan utopia, or the Puritan Confederation, it was not wise for a Stuart, newly come to the throne, to be too hostile until he had time to muster support and sure grounds for action. The Bay could afford to bide its time; perhaps it could "easily spin out seven years by writing and before that time a change may come."[86]

Besides the actual conciliatory attitude of the royal government, which was not apparent in the accusations of three of the royal commissioners, another reason for not taking any action to prevent the renewal of the Confederation was its vigorous defense by Massachusetts. The United Colonies were severall colonies under one king, and came from their native country for one and the same end, and were here scattered at a great distance amongst tho wild salvages in a vast wilderness, had no walled tounes or garrisons of soulduers for their defence, they apprehended the least they could doe was to enter into a league of amity and union one with another, ingaging, in case of any unjust and fresh assault made upon any part by the natives, jointly to asist each other as the matter should require, this being the end of their then confoederating....[87]

Secretary Rawson, for the Massachusetts Court, wrote a number of letters to the royal commissioners, defending the past acts of Massachusetts and the United Colonies. Rawson called attention to the fact that all "differences relating to the Indians for more than 20 years" had been transacted and issued by the joint consent and agreement of the United Colonies."[88] Perhaps another reason the home government did not take any action at this time to prevent the colonies from reconfederating was that the recommendations of the three commissioners, drawn up during the absence of Colonel Nicolls, were not considered valid without his approbation.[89]

Drawing the colonies into due subordination to His Majesty and settling "any differences in the Colonies" were not the only tasks of the royal commissioners; they were also to secure cooperation from the New England colonies in sending an expedition to take New Netherland.[90] But time permitted only the raising of a group of volunteers in Massachusetts. In less than a month after the appearance of the four British frigates in Boston harbor, August, 1664, the British force, including two hundred volunteers from the Bay, overawed New Amsterdam without a struggle.[91] The conquest of New Netherland, an action which the Puritan elders had greatly feared and which was the subject of so much debate in the Confederation, was now accomplished with hardly the blinking of an eye. The protective arm of the mother country was now reaching to the American colonies, and therefore made the need for confederation to resist foreign enemies only of value for supplementing a force of the home government. The Anglo-Dutch rivalry for the supremacy of the seas and control of the carrying trade was again the basis of this second conflict, and with England getting the better of her rival, she was determined to insure her naval supremacy by an extensive colonial system throughout the world. The final years of the first Confederation saw this inevitable struggle for possession of New Amsterdam, but unlike the decade before, it was not able to deter the attack or influence English designs on New Netherland in any way.

The Confederacy sat idly by while controversies waged over privateering in American waters—it was now accepted that admiralty jurisdiction belonged to the Council of State in England, although the Massachusetts authorities did not always act as if they were aware of this.[92]

Until the capitulation of New Amsterdam the Dutch continued to protest that encroachments of New Englanders violated the demarcation line set by the Treaty of Hartford, when that solemn treaty was entered upon between the governments of New Netherland and the United Colonies of New England. The Connecticut Charter was interpreted in New England as taking in territory west of the former colony of New Haven all the way to the Hudson River, far past the boundary line of 1650 at Greenwich. Even the Massachusetts boundary was declared to run "from sea to sea," which in Stuyvesant's opinion "would run below the high mountains or your upper pastures straight through the colony." Aware that the King of England, in effect, was claiming all of New Netherland, the Dutch Governor resorted to the same tactics that had resulted in the Hartford Treaty. He paid a personal visit to the annual meeting of the Commissioners of the United Colonies in September, 1663. Unlike the previous visit in 1654, however, he found a different Confederation; no longer could the Commissioners speak as the supreme council for New England. With the Connecticut Charter including New Haven within the bounds of the River Colony and the king's letter of 1662 requiring unswerving allegiance to His Royal Majesty—not to mention the destructive effects of the constitutional crises of the decade before—the Confederacy could be of very little help to the Dutch Governor. It was Stuyvesant's purpose to commit the United Colonies to a boundary settlement, as it had done before, thereby affording him a wedge to use against the aggressive designs of the English king. But the New England colonies, with their union rent asunder, were in no position to act in such an independent way. A month after Stuyvesant returned home, he sent special commissioners to New England again to seek a boundary settlement, but this too failed to produce results.[93]

The flow of English settlers into Dutch territory along the Hudson was only one of the annoyances resulting from English encroachments that faced Stuyvesant. In his own backyard on Long Island, the English settlements rose in revolt against Dutch authority; the "trumpet" call, however, did not confine itself to the Dutch, for the movement soon spread among all the English towns on Long Island. The towns sought to detach themselves from Connecticut as well as from the Dutch and to give their allegiance to the English king. At first, John Scott, the leader of the rebellion in Hempstead and surrounding towns, when he was summoned by the New Haven Colony to account for his part in detaching the Long Island towns from that Colony, replied that he would "stand to the determination of any Court of Judicature, of the United Colonies in New England." When the movement for independence progressed further, Scott declared all the Island towns free from New England authority. Scott was soon arrested by the Connecticut authorities for inciting open rebellion. The rebellion on Long Island challenged expansionism in the New England Colonies, which had been one of the primary forces behind the Confederation.

The Long Island firebrand was sent to Hartford for trial. It was recommended that he be tried before the Commissioners of the United Colonies, but it was finally agreed the other two colonies, which as members of the Confederation were gravely concerned over rebellion against their authority, should send their representatives to the trial.[94] In May, 1664, Scott was convicted of ten charges of usurping the king's authority, forgery, and perjury, and was sentenced to prison. The walls of prison, however, could not contain this early revolutionist. Back in Long Island he proceeded to organize the towns against New England authority, and, with the coming of James, Duke of York, he was able to present him in one package the Long Island towns— hitherto two-thirds of Connecticut Colony. As an epilogue to this little rebellion, it is interesting to note that Scott, through the conniving of Connecticut for his lands and unsympathetic treatment by Nicolls, did not materially gain from the conquest of

New Netherland, and adventurer that he was, soon found it necessary to flee to the Barbados. All the Dutch could do with the Long Island rebellion was to appeal to the Puritan conscience of the inhabitants, that they had forgotten their "oath and Duty" under the "Provisional Limits" of the Hartford Treaty, previously entered into with the Commissioners of the United Colonies.[95]

The surrender of the Dutch at New Amsterdam marked the end of an era in the foreign relations of New England. The "troublesome neighbors of New England," in the words of the vanquished Dutch Governor, "who number full fifty to our one,"[96] in their continual encroachments made the elimination of Dutch sovereignty in America inevitable. The defense perimeter of New England was now enlarged. The American colonies now could expect protection of His Majesty's Fleet up and down their coasts, but they would be required themselves to help fight England's battles in the New World, particularly in the contest shaping up with the French to the north.[97]

The Confederation of the United Colonies was not all lost because of the ascendancy of Britain in colonial affairs. The home government was successful in driving a wedge into the union of the four "generall governments of New England,"[98] and had greatly restricted the territorial limits of the United Colonies.[99] A chorus of all the New England settlements voiced their allegiance to the newly restored Stuart monarch, though it was obvious the Bay was none too sincere.[100] But on the domestic scene, for the settlement of intercolonial controversies, such as the many jurisdictional disputes or the threatened revival of the impost fracas,[101] or administering the funds of the "Indian Worke," or in the event the home government would not provide adequately for the colonial defense, the Confederation could still be of value. And there was still a remote possibility, should the royal government fall again or fail to pursue a rigorous imperial policy, the New England Union might provide the foundation for a great Puritan commonwealth in the New World. It is not surprising then that shortly after the royal commissioners returned home the governors of the New England colonies were writing one another that "in refference to what concernes the Colonies mutually, our articles of confederation directing and concluding us therein, wee know not how to propound any beter expedient, then a regular observance thereof."[102]

According to their determination at the Hartford meeting in 1664, the Commissioners held their first triennial meeting again at Hartford three years later. Thus, in 1667, the royal commissioners having gone home, the way was clear to revive the Confederacy. It was found, however, that the Articles of 1643 were so badly shattered that more than a revision was necessary. If the three remaining United Colonies wished to envigorate their Confederacy once again, a new Constitution would have to be drawn up to replace the Articles of 1643 which had been fundamentally violated. After the meeting of 1667, the following three years became a sort of vacuum in the work of the Confederation, during which time the possibility of re-establishing the Confederation under a different set of Articles was explored. It was not until June 10, 1670, that a committee was appointed in the Bay to iron out, with the other two colonies, the difficulties which stood in the way of renewing their Confederation. By 1672, the Union was re-established.

It is amazing that during this period of falling out the threads of union remained. In almost every way the Commissioners of the United Colonies had refused to accept responsibility—most evident in the abandonment of their early policies in Indian and foreign affairs. They had cowered before the presence of the royal commissioners; the Bay alone maintained any degree of firmness. The Commissioners of the Confederation had acted strictly in an advisory capacity, leaving the general courts to follow their own lines of policy. Without the means of coercion, the will of the majority of the confederates could not prevail. Thus Plymouth and Massachusetts, siding with New Haven, could not prevent the absorption of the Colony on the Sound into the charter bounds of the River Colony. The decisions of the Commissioners tended to follow the *fait accompli;* perhaps this was wise, for by readily recognizing royal authority and by doing as little as possible the Confederacy did not attract much attention from the home government, undoubtedly a factor in its preservation. The domination of Massachusetts can be seen in all the activities of the Confederacy during this period. It was largely due to the efforts of Massachusetts—in a similar role to that of Holland as the leading state in the Dutch Union—that the spark was preserved.

Though the experience in confederation of 1655-67 was a frustrating one, the very fact that union had become a habit was evidence of an emerging national consciousness.

---

[1] *PCR*, X, 158-9. The Dutch were again having their hands full putting down an Indian uprising. (Hull, *Diary*, 178, 181; A. J. F. van Laer, *Corres. of J. van Rensselaer, 1651-74* (Albany: 1932), pp. 21-2.)

[2] *PCR*, X, 171-2.

[3] *PCR*, X, 192.

[4] *Ibid.*, pp. 178-9; Sheldon, *op. cit.*, pp. 60ff; F. M. Thompson, *History of Greenfield*, (Greenfield, Mass.: 1904), I, 15; Francis Caulkins, *History of New London*, (New London: 1852), pp. 127-30; Sylvester Judd, *History of Hadley*, (Northampton: 1863), pp. 123-4.

[5] *PCR*, X, 214-237; R. C. Winthrop Coll., II, 123-4, Connecticut State Library; CA, Indians, Ser. 1, I, 3; Newman to Winthrop, 17Mar58/9, Winthrop Papers, MHS, XV, 113; Sheldon, *op. cit.*, pp. 60-67.

[6] Ninigret.

[7] 5May69, R. C. Winthrop Coll., II, 141, Conn. St. Lib.

[8] Watching and warding, an "adjunct of the police force" in time of peace, "became in time of danger, an important part of the military organization." In peace-time the watch would be on guard for vagrants coming into town, who, with the Puritan dislike for idleness, would soon be run out of town. (See Nelson P. Mead, *Connecticut as a Corporate Colony*, (Lancaster: 1906), p. 90; Marcus W. Jernegan, *Laboring and Dependent Classes in Colonial America*, (Chicago: 1931), pp. 193-4.). The military proportion of troops to come from Mass. for the first thirty years of the Confederation averaged 66.5% of the total. (See R. L. Bowen, *Early Rehoboth*, (Rehoboth: 1945), I, 23.) Besides the drills held, there was more activity in the inspection of arms, sending out scouts, and constructing garrison houses on the frontier. (R. C. Winthrop Coll., II, 153; Winthrop Papers, MHS, XIV, 135; George Wadleigh, *Notable Events in the Hist. of N. Hampshire*, (Dover: 1913), p. 70.)

[9] E.g., letters of Newman, Leete, and Josiah Winslow to John Winthrop, Jr. (Winthrop Papers, MHS, XV, 115; *MHSC* 4:VII:545-6; and *MHSC* 5:I:387-9, resp.)

[10] *PCR*, X, 151, 154. That this blockade by Captain Youngs was successful is pointed out by L. Bradner in "Ninigret's Naval Campaign against the Montauks," *RIHSC*, XVIII (Jan, 1925), 18.

[11] This is a rare bellicose statement on the part of Williams, who labored long for peace and good will among the Indians and the colonies. Though he had written that "all Indians are extremely treacherous," he asks, "how should we expect that the streames of bloud should stop among the dregs of mankind, wher the bloudie issues flow so fresh and fearfully among the finest and most refined sons of men and sons of God." (*RICR*, I, 291-8; *MHSC* 3:X:27.)

[12] *PCR*, X, 196.

[13] Daniel Gookin, appointed the superintendent of all the Pequots under the jurisdiction of Massachusetts, may be regarded as the first superintendent of Indian affairs in America. (DI'L, Misc. MSS, 343.)

[14] *PCR*, X, 225.

[15] *Ibid.* The killing of horses seems to be the crime the English were most concerned about.

[16] *PCR*, X, 226.

[17] Lands of the Narragansett sachems were considered in mortgage by the Commissioners until they would pay the 595 fathom of wampum levied upon them for damages to English and Mohegan property (viz., the Brewster farm.) *Trumbull Papers, MHSC* 5:IX:12,25-6; Winthrop Papers. *MHS*, V, 16Nov60.

[18] *PCR*, X, 248-9.

[19] *MHSC* 5:I:389.

[20] Misc. corres. with Gov. Winthrop, Winthrop Papers, MHS, XIV, 71, 74; CA, Indians, Ser. 1, I, 8; *Winthrop Papers*, V, 49, 64, 208; *MHSC* 3:X:63-4; MA, XXX, 137; Thompson, *op.cit.*, pp. 15-23; George W. Ellis, and John E. Morris, *King Philip's War*, (New York: 1906), pp. 38-9; Charles Hudson, *History of the Town of Marlborough*, (Boston: 1862), p. 82.

[21] "Pequot Warres," *MHSC* 3:III:151.

[22] *PCR*, X, 195.

[23] See Calder, *op. cit.*, p. 170-1; *Huntington Recs.*, I, 23.

[24] *PCR*, X, 199, 223, 229, 234.

[25] "Declaration of the Injustice of the Rhode Islanders in Narragansett Affairs," *MHSC* 3:III:209-10.

[26] Quoted in Klaus E. Knorr, *British Colonial Theories, 1570-1850*, (Toronto: 1944), p. 64.

[27] George L. Beer, *The Old Colonial System, 1660-1754*, (New York: 1912), II, Pt. I, p. 232.

[28] See Percy L. Kaye, "English Colonial Administration under Lord Clarendon, 1660-75," *JHUS*, Ser. 23, Nos. 5-6 (1905), pp. 9-19; also in Ser. 25, Nos. 1-3, *JHUS* (1908), Charles M. Andrews, "British Committees, Commissions, and Councils of Trade and Plantations, 1622-75." For economic regulation, such as the Navigation Acts, in shaping imperial policy, see O. M. Dickerson, *The Navigation Acts and the American Revolution*, (Phila.: 1951).

[29] Samuel Maverick, "A Briefe Description of New England," *MHSP*, 2nd Ser., I, 246.

[30] Felt, *op. cit.*, II, 308.

[31] Bradstreet and Norton were named by the Bay to go to England to "indeavor to take off all scandall and objections . . . against us." (*MCR*, IV, Pt. 2, 37.) The Puritan Bay naturally had favored Cromwell and had hoped for the continuing of that "happy government that under your shadow not only ourselves, but all the churches may find rest and peace." (Mayo, ed., Hutchinson's *History*, I, 523.)

[32] The east-west limits of Connecticut specified by the charter was "that

parte of our Dominions in Newe England in America bounded on the East by Norrogancett River, commonly called Norrogancett Bay . . . to the South Sea on the West parts." (*CCR*, II, 10.)

[33] *PCR*, X, 287-8.

[34] An estimate of the population of New Haven at the time of the forming of New England, 2,500, compares favorably with that of Connecticut, but by 1665 the New Haven Colony had grown little in population, whereas Connecticut's population had more than doubled. (See Franklin B. Dexter, "Estimates of Population in the American Colonies," *Miscellaneous History Papers of Fifty Years* (New Haven: 1918), pp. 162-3.)

[35] Rev. John Davenport, pastor at New Haven and a founder of the Colony, wrote on the death of Commissioner Newman: "He honored God in his personal conversation, and in his administrations of chief magistry in this colony; and God hath given him honor in the hearts of his people." (Ltr to John Winthrop, in Leonard Bacon, *Historical Discourses*, (New Haven: 1839), p. 385.)

[36] Edward E. Atwater, *History of the Colony of New Haven* (Meriden: 1902), p. 465. This book is the best account of the absorption of New Haven into the colony of Connecticut. For the strife over jurisdiction in one of the New Haven towns see Herbert F. Sherwood, *The Story of Stamford*, (New York: 1930).

[37] Some proposals to New Haven, 26Aug62, CA, Misc., I, 69.

[38] Allyn to Winthrop, 12Dec62, Winthrop Papers, MHS, X, 18.

[39] Ltrs of Winthrop to Conn., Mar62/3, *Winthrop Papers, MHSC* 5:VIII:78; Trumbull, *op. cit.*, I, 520-1.

[40] *Winthrop Papers, MHSC* 4:VII, 525-6.

[41] 6May63, Isabel M. Calder, ed., *Letters of John Davenport*, (London: 1937), pp. 212-15. This document is printed in a number of secondary works.

[42] Talcott's name does not appear on the reports of the Connecticut committee, probably because he was still suffering from the effects of a long illness contracted while Commissioner in the Bay. (Allyn to Winthrop, 1Dec62, Winthrop Papers, MHS, X, 17.)

[43] See Atwater, *op. cit.*, pp. 477-491.

[44] *PCR*, X, 308; *NHCR*, II, 495.

[45] *NHCR*, II, 496; *PCR*, X, 309-10.

[46] *NHCR*, II, 497. The full arguments of Connecticut are found in *NHCR*, II, 517, 518-30; those of New Haven, pp. 530-7.

[47] E.g., Order of Conn. Council, 28Dec63, CA, Misc., I, 73.

[48] Willys Papers, CHS, I, 11; R. C. Winthrop Coll., 11, 251, Agreement between New Haven and Plymouth; CA, Misc., I, 78; Bacon, *Discourses*, 358-65; in the words of a contemporary: "sundry agitations and troublesome motions have been this last winter and spring between the United Colonies . . . danger of ruin to all for want of union . . ." (Hull, *Diary*, 211.)

[49] Prence to Sec. Rawson, 28Apr64, *Hutchinson Papers*, II, 109.

[50] 28May64, CA, Misc., I, 85.

[51] *New Haven Town Recs.*, II, 97; Willys Papers, CHS, I, 17.

[52] Ltr of Council of Conn. to N. H., 2Sep64, CA, I (Misc.), 86. The best study of the three factions within New Haven during this time is Bernard C. Steiner, "Governor William Leete and the Absorption of New Haven Colony by Conn.," *Annual Report of the AHA* (1891). The moderates, such as Leete, won out against the other two extremes. For the economic causes of New Haven's downfall, see Charles M. Andrews, "The Rise and Fall of New Haven Colony," *Tercentary Comm. of the State of Connecticut*, Pub. No. XLVIII.

[53] 17Nov64, CA, Misc., I, 87.

[54] *NHCR*, II, 557.

[55] Felt, *op. cit.*, II, 410.

[56] Committee of New Haven to Conn., 6Oct63, *Davenport Letters*, 221-2.

[57] 8Sep65, Hull, *Diary*, 219.

[58] Papers relating to "Whalley and Goffe," *MHSC* 3:VII:123-8; *NHCR*, II, 387-9. Reproductions of the Proscription list may be found in the New Haven Col. Hist. Soc. in New Haven. F. B. Dexter has gone into detail on the mystery of these regicides. See *History Papers of Fifty Years* (New York: 1918), and *Papers of the New Haven Colonial Historical Society*, II, 117-146.

[59] *PCR*, X, 269-70.

[60] Hutchinson *Papers*, II, 53ff. According to an early historian, the regicides were well entertained by the colonial authorities before they were whisked away into secrecy to avoid arrest. See Ezra Stiles, *A History of Three of the Judges of King Charles I* (Hartford: 1794).

[61] Petition of R. I. to Charles II, *The Clarendon Papers*, NYHSC, II (1869), 154.

[62] Brenton, *et al.*, to Earl of Clarendon, *ibid.*, p. 145.

[63] Kaye, *loc. cit.*, pp. 81-3.

[64] Note here an actual contemporary reference to the Dutch United Provinces as the prototype of the Confederation.

[65] Cartwright's Answer to the Mass. Narrative, 5Jan65/6, *The Clarendon Papers*, NYHSC, II(1869), 92.

[66] *Ibid.*, p. 104.

[67] Upon recommendation of the Commissioners of the United Colonies, the royal commissioners and the governors of the colonies were to meet in 1664 to discuss intercolonial government. (*MCR*, IV, Pt. 2, 136: Stevens Transcripts, I, 41, John Carter Brown Library.)

[68] *PCR*, X, 319.

[69] See D. Oswald Dykes, *Source Book of Constitutional History from 1660* (New York: 1930), pp. 180-1. If the Puritans were influenced by this Act, rather than being a coincidence, then it is most significant that they should compare the Commissioners of the United Colonies to Parliament.

[70] *PCR*, X, 319; *MCR*, IV, Pt. 2, 156.

[71] John S. Jenness, ed., *Transcripts of Original Documents in the English Archives . . . Early History of New Hampshire* (New York: 1876), pp. 58-60. The commission of the royal commissioners is printed in a number of places,

e.g., in R. R. Hinman, *Letters from the English Kings and Queens to the Governors of Connecticut* (Hartford: 1836), pp. 50-1.

⁷²King Charles II to Mass. Colony, 10Apr66, Mayo, ed., Hutchinson's *History*, I, 452.

⁷³*MCR*, IV, Pt. 2, 201: Charles II had been proclaimed king before a large crowd in Boston amidst the booming of cannon and musket fire, with four companies of troops and the magistrates mounted on horseback, plus an appropriate contingent of ministers. (Hull, *Diary*, 203-4.) In Connecticut, Governor Winthrop delayed attending the royal commissioners as long as he could, feigning illness. (Winthrop Papers, MHS, V, 46.) (The Connecticut authorities professed their allegiance to the King, "humbly imploreing the continuation of the shines of your royall favour upon our meane beginnings." (*CHSC*, XXIV, 11-2.)

⁷⁴*MCR*, IV, Pt. 2, 202.

⁷⁵The role of the Commissioners was supposed to be that of gathering information and to make recommendations to the king for the settlement of disputes. (Henry Bennet to Winthrop, John Talcott Memorandum Book, Connecticut State Library, 23Apr64.) But Sir Robert Carr "usurped the functions of government in Maine, detaching it from Mass. authority. (See *Magazine of American History* (1882), 623-26.)

⁷⁶*MCR*, IV, Pt. 2, 174

⁷⁷This effort to raise a clamor against the established order met little success. (See Albert McKinley, *The Suffrage Franchise in the Thirteen English Colonies* (Phil.: 1905), p. 325 and S. I. Cook, "Governmental Crisis," in A. B. Hart, ed. *Commonwealth History of Mass.* (New York: 1927), I, 568.] The non-freemen of the Colony (the status of two-thirds of the soldiers) were believed to be royalists. "The distinction of Freemen and non Freemen Members and non Members, is as famous as Cavaliers and Roundheads." (Capt. Thos. Breedon's Narrative, 11Mar60/1, Stevens Transcripts, I, 25, John Carter Brown Library.)

⁷⁸MCR, IV, Pt. 2, 194; *London Documents*, II, 95.

⁷⁹*MCR*, IV, Pt. 2, 195, 198. As late as 1663, the authority of the United Colonies was cited by Massachusetts as grounds for keeping Southertown within hers and later Conn.'s jurisdiction. (*Ibid.*, p. 75.)

⁸⁰*Ibid.*, p. 213.

⁸¹Misc. MSS, II, MHS; *MHSC*, 1:V:192-3.

⁸²Beer, *op. cit.*, p. 250.

⁸³*London Documents*, III, 96.

⁸⁴Winthrop to Nicolls, 14Aug65, Winthrop Papers, 3:X:55; Ltr of 13Sep65, Winthrop Papers, MHS, V, 52.

⁸⁵*MCR*, IV, Pt. 2, 159. In their meeting of 1664, the Commissioners of the United Colonies stated that a revitalized Confederacy should be "faithful and loyal to his Majesty." (Sainsbury, *Calendar of State Papers*, V, #796.)

⁸⁶From Egerton MSS, quoted in Beer, *op. cit.*, p. 250.

⁸⁷*MCR*, IV, Pt. 2, 231.

[88] Danforth *Papers*, *MHSC*, 2:VIII, Doc. XII.

[89] *PCR*, X, 408-9.

[90] Hull, *Diary*, 212.

[91] *Ibid.*; Pynchon and Clark to Endicott, 15Aug64, BPL, Misc. MSS No. 586; *Recs. of New Amsterdam*, V, 105, 115. After this expedition, the Massachusetts General Court offered in case of future invasion "a naiborly assistance" for the military cooperation of the colonies. (Winthrop-Davenport MSS, NYPL, No. 48.) The English forces which brought about the submission of New Amsterdam were aided by a combined Connecticut and Long Island force which made contact with the main force on Long Island. (Winthrop Papers, MHS, IA, 138.) Also, *MCR*, IV, Pt. 2, 120-3: CHSC, XXIV, 16; MA, LXVII, 148.

[92] See the two works of H. M. Chapin, and J. F. Jameson, on New England privateering. In early Massachusetts there was little distinction between admiralty cases and other criminal cases, on the colony level jurisdiction being that of the Court of Assistants. (See John Noble, "Admiralty Jurisdiction in Massachusetts," PCSM, X (*Transactions*, 1907), 150-186).

[93] Stuyvesant to Conn. authorities, 13Oct62, CA, Boundaries (N.Y.), II, 1; 20Jul63, *MHSC*, 5:I:395-6; 13Oct63 and 5Nov63, CA, Boundaries (N.Y.), II, 6 and 8; Conn. Proposals to Stuyvesant's Agents, Oct63, *ibid.*, f. 3; *PCR*, X, 30-4; Stuyvesant to Jeremias van Rensselaer, 6Jan63, A. J. F. vanLaer, trans. and ed., *Correspondence of J. van Rensselaer*, 1651-74, (Albany: 1932), pp. 344-5; J. F. Jameson, ed., *Journal of Van Ruyven, Van Cortlandt and Lawrence*, (Stuyvesant's Commissioners to N. E.), in Vol. VIII of *Orig. Narratives of Early Amer. Hist.*, (New York: 1909), 430-5; Ltr of Jeremias van Rensselaer, 24Apr64, van Laer, *op. cit.*, pp. 348-50; Charles W. Baird, *History of Rye, 1660-1870.* (New York: 1871), pp. 106-9.

[94] Leverett and Davis from Massachusetts, and Bradford and Southworth from Plymouth.

[95] CA, Towns and Lands, I, 21, 23, 34; Winthrop Papers, MHS, V, 28; CA, Boundaries (N.Y.), II, 12; MA, LXVII, 138b; *CHSC*, XXIV, 8, 10-2; *MHSC*, I:VI:209; Willys Papers, CHS, 152, 154; Felt, *op. cit.*, p. 382; Calder, *op. cit.*, p. 248n.; Thomas Aspinwall, *Remarks on the Narragansett Patent*, (Providence: 1865), pp. 33-4.

[96] "Report on the Surrender of New Netherland," printed in Vol. VIII of *Original Narratives of Early American History*, 459-63. The wording of the Peace of Breda, 21Jul67, is of interest to this study, recalling the idea of union in both states, e.g., "firm, and inviolable peace. . . That the said King of Great Britain, and the said States General remain friends, confederate, united, and allied . . ." (See Farnham, ed., *Documentary History of Maine*, VII, 314-6.)

[97] CA, Foreign Affairs, I, 4; MA, C, 111, brdsde, d. 9Aug67; *CHSC*, XXIV, 12; Hinman, *Letters*, Charles II to Gov. and Council of New England, 28Aug66, p. 67.

[98] Rhode Island was also considered a "generall government" by the Bay when the copies of an act of Parliament was distributed among the "coun-

sells" of the colonies. (*MCR*, IV, Pt. 2, 86-7.) An unprejudiced report to the king in 1662 simply stated that "there are four colonies in New England all joined, viz., Plymouth Massachusetts, New Haven and Connecticut. Those of the Isle of Rhodes desire a charter of incorporation. Corn and fish . . . from New England; they maintain and supply the plantations of Barbadoes and Jamaica." (Sainsbury, *Calendar of State Papers*, V, No. 222.)

[99] Viz., the King's province (Ch. 7), the northern settlements of Maine, and Long Island. For Connecticut losing out on Long Island see Benjamin F. Thompson, *The History of Long Island*, (N. Y.: 1843), II.

[100] "This Colony furnished Cromwell with many Instruments out of their Corporation. . ." (Stevens Transcripts, 1, 63.)

[101] MA, II, 185.

[102] *MHSC* 4:VII:597-8.

CHAPTER XI

Cement of the Union

"A great part of time, if not the greatest, which is spent by our honnored commissioner of the United Colonies at theire annuall meetings," it was observed in 1658, "is about affaires relating to the Indians."[1] Thus the Confederation which survived the crisis years of 1653-5 retained as its chief area of jurisdiction that which the individual general courts did not care to accept. The preoccupation of the Commissioners of the Confederation with the "Indian Worke" during the period of the falling out of the confederates best depicts conversely their lack of influence in the affairs of state. The Puritan colonies during the first decade of their union did not pay sufficient attention to the "main ends" of their confederating: the spreading of the Gospel. They had become so involved with worldly affairs they had forgotten things spiritual. But the constitutional crises in the Confederacy left the Commissioners without effective political influence and turned their full attention to spreading the Gospel among the heathen savages and to preserving their own unity in the Gospel. This dual purpose of Confederation—conversion of the Indians and consolidating the control of the Puritan orthodoxy, a purpose with which the magistrates of New England were in one accord—served to keep alive the consciousness for union emerging from the old Confederation until it could again be revived. The chief role of the Confederacy during 1655-70 was not that of a worldly superstructure of the colonies, but, as in Corinthians, a "house not built with hands."

When the Confederacy was formed in 1643, the first of a series of tracts designed to promote missionary work in the New World appeared in England,[2] but little interest was stimulated on either side of the Atlantic until a young minister of the church at Roxbury began preaching to the Indians of his neighborhood in their own tongue.[3] In the same year, Edward Winslow was sent as an agent of the colonies to England, and he carried with him the news of Eliot's ambitious undertaking for converting the Indians. While he was stationed in the mother country, Edward Winslow (three years later) published a tract called *The Glorious Progress of the Gospel amongst the Indians in New England,* which helped to arouse the hopes of the devout among the newly ascendant Puritan party for establishing in the Wilderness Zion fit "Instruments" for converting the children of the forest.

Through the efforts of Winslow, in the summer of 1649, a few months before *The Glorious Progress of the Gospel* was published, the Long Parliament granted a charter to sixteen persons to be known as The Society for the Propagation of the Gospel in New-England. This corporation officially replaced the previous "begging missions," such as the famous Weld-Peter mission whose purpose had been to solicit contributions from individuals in England interested in aiding the Puritan experiment in the New World.[4] Meetings of the Corporation were held every Saturday morning between 9 and 12 o'clock at Coopers Hall, London, to which the public was invited.[5] The members of the Corporation appear to have served without pay, and all the funds and goods collected by this charitable organization were to be sent to the New World. Winslow, remaining as agent for the colonies in England, directed the administration of the funds for New England to the Commissioners of the United Colonies. Thus in 1653 he wrote to John Eliot and others who were becoming engaged in the missionary work that they were first to consult the Commissioners before requesting goods from the Society.[6]

When the Restoration came in 1660, The Society for the Propagation of the Gospel ceased existence, but it was soon recharted by the king in 1662 as "The Company for Propagation of the Gospel in New England and the parts adjacent in America," which was to become the forerunner of the more famous "S.P.G." of the next century. Sixteen persons constituted the self-perpetuating membership of this corporation.[7] Full power was given to the governor of the Corporation or any thirteen or more of the members to appoint Commissioners in the colonies "to treat, contract, and agree with such ministers, schoolmasters, and others, residing, and to reside in any the parts aforesaid, for such salaries, allowances, and recompences. . . ."[8] By the time of this second Corporation, the Commissioners of the United Colonies had become the approved agents of this Corporation to handle their business in America. Thus there developed a dual administration: the receiving end in London, the prominent merchants and men of state who made up the Corporation; and in the colonies those charged with the oversight of the spending, the Commissioners of the United Colonies.[9] Undoubtedly the reason the Confederation during the Restoration period was spared further attacks from the royal government was due to their seemingly innocuous preoccupation of administering the work of the Corporation in America. Thus, the propensity toward American union was kept alive.

The Corporation in London lost little time in forwarding supplies to the colonies. Eliot put the Indians to work with the tools sent over, embarking on such projects as "planting Orchards and Gardens" of their own and helping on the English plantations "in Hay time, and Harvest."[10] Because of complaints from the Commissioners about the articles sent over, the risk of piratical seas,[11] and the want of a fit person to discharge the goods, the Corporation ordered that the colonists should supply the goods for the Indian work themselves, for which the Corporation would be the debtor. It was specified that the "Instruments" be paid by goods in the colonies according to the price they cost in England.[12] This means proved acceptable to the Commissioners, and was adopted. Hezekiah Usher, a Boston merchant, accepted the bills of exchange from the Corporation and supplied the goods for the Indian work. It was thought that Usher gave the best satisfaction "both for prise and choise of goods," which did much to advance the "quantitie of the sallaries."[13] The Corporation once proposed that gold bars be sent to New England to defray the cost of the Indian work, but the Commissioners advised that the mint master considered the coining of the gold too expensive.[14]

The actual administration of this missionary work was in the hands of the Commissioners since they had a free hand to apply the funds of the Corporation and to determine which of the ministers and Indian teachers deserved financial support. The Commissioners supervised a number of teachers and interpreters engaged in the "Indian Worke," chief of whom were John Eliot among the remnant Pequots, the Narragansetts, and the Mohegans, the Mayhews on Martha's Vineyard, William Leveridge on Long Island, and at New Haven, Abraham Pierson and Richard Blinman. But the Commissioners yielded to the dominance of the Bay and the efforts of John Eliot, and most of the funds from the Corporation were spent for the missions about Boston.

On Martha's Vineyard, a province of the Day and later of New York during the Confederation period, Thomas Mayhew performed the unusual dual role of governor and missionary. Settling at Great Harbor, today called Edgartown, in 1642, Mayhew immediately set about converting the Indians of the Island. Fortunately for his efforts, the powwows which were supposed to bewitch enemies and unbelievers who dared defy ancient Indian customs, were at a low in the esteem of the Island Indians, and Mayhew seized the opportunity to show the red man his faith. His greatest triumph was the conversion of the Gay Head tribe, who for twenty years had resisted the inroads of the white man. Thomas Mayhew, Jr., soon took over the work of his father, but it was not until 1654 that the missionary work on the Vineyard came under the auspices of the Corporation and the New England Confederacy. Up to that time the work of the Mayhews had proceeded without fanfare, and probably would never have attracted attention had not the Rev. Henry Whitfield, the pastor at Guilford, on a voyage stopped at the Island. Thomas Mayhew, Jr., thus became a "salaried worker" in 1654, and Thomas Mayhew, Sr., prepared to take a back seat in the "Indian Worke" and to spend more time with the affairs of his public office. But in the peculiar ways of the Lord when His Work appeared most fruitful, the hand of fate fell. The younger Mayhew was lost at sea, and though handicapped by his administrative duties, the elder Mayhew was prevailed upon by the Commissioners to resume his missionary work. For twenty-five years after the loss of his son, the Island Governor preached to the savages of his domain until his death in 1682 at the age of 89. The Commissioners for a long time tried to get a replacement for Mayhew, Jr., for a while sounding out a son of John Cotton and particularly trying to interest Abraham Pierson of Branford, but they had no success. The elder Mayhew did receive able assistance from his grandson, and, as did Eliot, made use of promising young Indians, who became leaders and teachers of their flock.[15] Always reluctant to attend in person the meetings of the Commissioners,[16] the Mayhews received only niggardly financial support from the Confederation. After the loss of Thomas Mayhew, Jr., however, the Commissioners provided for a pension for his widow and family.[17]

The missionary work of John Eliot caught the imagination of the early colonists, and his undying devotion to the betterment of the outcast savage marked him for all time as one of the most honored men of early New England. The early records are filled with his efforts to protect the rights of the red man. Many a petition for preserving the Indians in their lands previously awarded by the General Court bears Eliot's signature.[18] Mention may be made of his demands for strict enforcement of licensed persons only to engage in the selling of "strong drink" to the Indians.[19] But, for all his great work in helping the downtrodden savage of New England, Eliot, unlike the liberality of his counterpart in the Narragansett country, Roger Williams, was first and last a Puritan, whose orthodoxy condoned the extreme penalty for Quakers returning from banishment.[20] Eliot, nevertheless, had an organizational ability and stern discipline that was unmatched among the Puritan divines. The network of Indian towns and reservations that dotted the Massachusetts landscape, which for many years proved stumbling-blocks to the land hunger of neighboring English settlers, attests to Eliot's ability and dedication.

When Eliot first preached to the Indians in a wigwam near the mouth of the Neponset River in September, 1646, he hit upon the idea of settling all converted Indians on one plantation. For several years he preached to an Indian congregation at Nonantum, a village on the south bank of the Charles River. But finding that he could not consolidate the praying Indians into one community, Eliot decided to establish a string of Indian communities not too far from his home in Roxbury, which he could periodically visit. Accordingly, an Indian town was set up in the south part of Middlesex County called Natick, a "place of hills." A second town soon followed, in 1650, called Ponkapoag; other towns sprang up in the Dedham area and one even in the neighborhood of Marlborough, a town of Plymouth Colony. When the praying Indians were gradually pushed out of these towns because of their decrease in population and the encroachments of the English, which in the time of King Philip's War resulted in the Indian towns bordering the zone of friction to be completely evacuated, they were re-established in new communities.[21] Eliot made a habit of visiting two of the congregations once every fortnight, giving a lecture at each place.[22] Although Abraham Pierson among the Quinnipiacks received some recognition from the Commissioners, and like the Mayhews on Martha's Vineyard some financial support,[23] most of the concern of the Commissioners was directed to the closely knit experiments of John Eliot.

The organizational efforts of Eliot among the conquered Pequots fitted into the Indian policy of the early Confederation. Originally the Pequots after their defeat were divided among their Indian rivals who had aided the English, chiefly the Mohegans and the Narragansetts. But with the unfriendly attitude of the Narragansetts and the clouds of war that seemed to hover continually over these two tribes, the Commissioners came to realize that the Pequots, detached into independent communities with an English form of government, could serve as a sort of tiny buffer states against the more hostile Indians. These Christianized communities thus had a worldly value as well as a spiritual one. Roger Williams sensed the value of the "Glorious Worck" among the Indians in preserving the balance of power and thereby deterring war when he protested the sending of a force against the Niantics in 1654: "I beseech you consider how the name of the most holy and jealous God may be preserved betweene the Conversion of the Indians in New England and the Unnecessary Warrs and could Destructions of the Indians in New England."[24] For Eliot these Indian buffer towns should be organized into divisions of tens and thousands, according to the children of Israel who chose their rulers in this fashion, with the "Supreme Council" chosen by all the people.[25] Needless to say the towns at best hardly extended beyond divisions of ten.

In setting up government among the Pequots and other praying Indians, the Commissioners took it upon themselves to delegate limited executive authority. The Commissioners annually appointed Indian governors over the Pequots, the most noted being Robin Cassasinamon of the western Pequots in the Connecticut Colony, but since the same governors were usually named from year to year, this process became automatic. The Indian governors were allowed to appoint inferior officers, provided that the appointees acted in every way honestly and civilly.[26] Among their responsibilities were to see that there be no blaspheming or profaning the Sabbath and to prevent murder, witchcraft, adultery, drunkenness, or stealing. Whoever plotted "Mischeife against the English" should "suffer death or such other punishment as the case may deserve." Making war or joining with other Indians in war was forbidden, except when it was justified as a matter of defense.[27] These officials were also responsible for collecting tribute. As an inducement for the governors to keep in contact with the English, they or a number of Pequots were required to come to the annual meetings of the Commissioners in order to find out whom the English had chosen as governors for the year ensuing.[28] Since the English chose the same governors, it is probable that the Pequots, not feeling much incentive, were not too faithful about coming.

A commission for supervising Pequot affairs was appointed by the Commissioners. The powers of this commission, consisting of Captain Denison, Thomas Stanton, and James Averell, included, for instance, the powers to seize all strong liquors

> that shalbee brought amongst them to bee sold and drunk amongst the Indians and to deliver the same to sume of the English overseers; who shall sell the same to the English and Returne to him that seized it; the one halfe, and to him that disclosed it the other halfe.[29]

Coats from the Corporation stock were given to the governors

> to encurrage them to theire service to the English in Governing the Pequots and perswading them to attend such meanes as shalbee used to gaine them to the knowledge of God.[30]

Major Atherton, who was involved with many of the Commissioners in speculating in Indian lands, received authority from the Bay General Court to name Indian commissioners from among the English to serve as marshals and constables;[31] and thus dealing in the "Indian Worke" of the Confederation,[32] these officials were not unlike the federal marshals in later American territorial history. Among the powers of these commissioners was to hold "Counties Court." When Atherton died, Major Gookin, who had taken an active interest enough in the work and wrote a brief history of this endeavor, was appointed in his place, with like powers to hold county court.[33] Working along with Eliot's organization of the Indian communities, Gookin issued commissions to the Indian rulers of hundreds or fifties or tens.[34] This "pillar in our Indian work"[35] vigorously tried to administer justice among the Pequots[36] and to promote friendly relations between them and the English.

This policy of keeping the Pequots in line by direct administrative control also afforded a way to keep an eye on the Narragansetts, Mohegans, and Niantics to whom the Pequots were originally entrusted. By providing for a patronage system—naming the governors, who in turn named inferior officers—the Commissioners were able to build up a faction of the tribe whose loyalty could be depended upon. This policy did bring results,[37] and therefore stands out along with the blockade of the Niantics as the only success of the Commissioners in Indian affairs during the period of 1665-70. The role of Atherton and Gookin as federal Indian commissioners, though they were appointed by the General Court, anticipated the office of Superintendent of Indian Affairs in the eighteenth century on a much larger scale—an important position in the transition from colonial to national government.

Many problems arose to affect the harmony between the Corporation and the Commissioners, and it was suspected that Massachusetts was trying to gain control of the funds sent over.[38] One of the members of the Corporation told Winslow that "hee heard the worke was but a plaine Cheat and that there was noe such thinge as Gospell conversion amongst the Indians."[39] The main end of "Gods sending so many Saints to New England, was the Conversion of these Indians,"[40] and therefore for the "Gospell worke" there should be "but Gospell spirited men."[41] The average New Englander did not hold in high esteem the natives, whom in the now Canaan they had driven before them, and it is not surprising that there was much resentment against the "roges mayntayned by Corporation."[42] The controversy over the administration of the Corporation's funds continued throughout the fifties. The run of the arguments was always that the Commissioners were not putting to good use the money sent over and that the Corporation was not sending over sufficient funds.[43] Moreover, there was difficulty in England in attracting large donations, and the general solicitations, made according to parishes,[44] were meager.

A wide variety of goods was supplied to the praying Indians, either sent over directly from England during the first years of the Corporation or bought by the Commissioners from Boston merchants with funds from the Corporation. The commodities most urgently needed, as specified by Eliot, were "strong linen cloth, canvas and other good hempen cloth," because "in the hot summers the Indians delight to gon in liuun, and work, it in any garment, only a linnen garment, if they can get it."[45] All kinds of tools and "Ironworke fitt for building and labor" were provided for, plus a number of curious items such as "inckhornes," "spectecles," "white wrighting paper," and "pene knives." The Commissioners of the United Colonies, writes Eliot, "were pleased to let us have 7 cowes and 18 goats which . . . have put us upon mowing, making of hay, building of houses for cowes, goats and such preparations as labours of that kind doe require."[46] The Commissioners were meticulous in keeping accounts of their expenditures, but this still did not stay criticism from the home country concerning their handling of the funds entrusted to them.

The praying Indians were encouraged to put their children as apprentices for a time "proportionable to theire age to any Godly English within the united Collonies with the consent of the Commissioners." The Indians whose children were undergoing apprenticeship were to receive annually one coat from the Corporation stock if they brought in some kind of certificate to the Commissioners stating where they lived. "Meate drinke and clothing" were to be furnished also out of the Corporation stock for the children undergoing apprenticeship or to their masters.[47] Mention has already been made of the Commissioners in their appeals for annual contributions throughout New England of "Colledg Corn" to underwrite the expenses of Indian boys sent to Harvard. In 1658 there were nine such students who were receiving aid from the Corporation.[48] But death from consumption was frequent, and by 1664 there were only three "Indian scholars" left at Harvard.[49] The following year, in a class of seven which included the eminent name of Joseph Dudley, an Indian by the name of Caleb from Martha's Vineyard was awarded a degree,[50] at least one attestation to the sincerity of the Puritan oligarchy to go all the way in bringing the red man into its civilization, even to the extent of affording to certain promising individuals the same level of education without prejudice as their own. The "Indian Worke" at Ponkapoag produced a valuable leader and interpreter, John Sassamon,[51] who, serving a stint as secretary to King Philip, was of great value to the English in exposing this chieftain's plans, and, as is well known, whose murder by Philip's Indians triggered the Great War.

The nature of that august body, the Commissioners of the United Colonies in New England, must have been of some puzzlement to the members of the Corporation in London. Letters to the Commissioners were of various styles, the most notable in the late Confederation being: "To the honorable Cort of Commissioners of his Magisties United Colonies now sitting at Hartford," wherein it was accounted "noe small part of our happiness That wee have such an assembly as yourselves."[52] The Corporation accepted without question that the Commissioners, as representative magistrates from the New England colonies, were the best qualified body to be their agents in dispensing the Gospel in the New World. Indeed they were fortunate to secure the services of the leading men, rather than a committee of lesser prestige that might be appointed from the legislatures of the colonies. During the annual meetings of the Confederation, a regular procedure of correspondence was followed between the Corporation and the New England Confederation. In late spring or early summer the Corporation would send its letters and funds to the Commissioners, and at their fall meetings the Commissioners drafted their replies and accounts to be sent on the long voyage to England. But when the Confederation started to wane after 1664, and with the final adoption of regular triennial sessions, there was a need to fill in the gap between the triennial meetings of the Commissioners.

It was not unusual for Eliot or one of the Commissioners (in case of a single Commissioner he was often acting upon a directive of the Confederation) to write the Corporation direct, rather than go through the channel of the whole Confederation.[53] After 1664, it became the practice for two or three of the Commissioners to meet on their own, during the off years, to transact the business of the "Indian Worke" and the Corporation found it necessary to address its correspondence "to any or either" of the Commissioners.[54] The precedent for not requiring a quorum of the Commissioners to transact the Indian business arose out of the meeting in Boston during September, 1652. It will be remembered that at this time the regular meeting could not be held because of the absence of certain Commissioners. Five of the eight Commissioners, therefore, met at Secretary

Rawson's house in Boston to fulfill their obligations to the Corporation for that year.[55]

The Bay Colony continued to hog the funds sent over. This was easily done since often the only Commissioners transacting the Indian business were from Massachusetts, and, of course, the bookkeeping was performed by Secretary Rawson. Although the Province of Maine was to receive a share of the funds,[56] the governor of that Province, until it became part of Massachusetts, wrote that he had "endeavored to screw into the Great Benevolences that have been so publicly knowne to propagate the Gospel in New England" and discovered in the administration of the funds "a snake in the weeds."[57] The Commissioners seem never to have taken a painstaking effort to equally distribute the funds among the New England settlements. But they cannot be too severely blamed for this shortcoming. The "Indian Worke" under Eliot was the best organized and at least brought forth tangible results, and therefore invited the greater investment. The people of Boston could travel out to visit the villages of the praying Indians without too much effort; on one occasion the Governor and thirty of the leading officials of the Bay spent a Sabbath hearing the preaching of Eliot at one of the Indian towns. Visiting dignitaries, such as the Dutch Jasper Dankers, or the French missionary-envoy, Father Druillettes, found one of the main attractions of New England to be a visit with the Indian Apostle. With the fame and reputation of Eliot it is no wonder that he received priority in the funds for the "Indian Worke." Moreover, living across the way from one of the Bay's Commissioners who figured most prominently in administering the funds of the Corporation, Thomas Danforth, in Roxbury, Eliot may have had another source of influence.

The Corporation considered the possibility of sending over a portion of its capital to the Commissioners.[58] But meeting once a year and having other official duties in their respective colonies, the Commissioners did not encourage the sending over of large sums. When goods were sent over, they were turned over to individuals who agreed to pay money for the salaries of the missionaries, but oftentimes these debts could not be collected. A remedy for this situation, a proposal that the missionaries be paid directly by bills of exchange drawn upon the treasurer of the Corporation, did not materialize because of the fear that the Commissioners, unaccustomed to business, would not always get the highest rate of exchange for these bills.[59] The funds of the Corporation became sparse when contributions started to fall off after 1656,[60] and the Great Fire of London, in 1666, consumed a large part of the "Revenue" of the Corporation.[61] As a result of the fire and the increasing difficulty in obtaining lands for investment in England, the Corporation, in 1669 and on several following occasions, sent a large sum of money to the Commissioners to invest, but because of the high interest rate at which this money was lent in New England, it was not easy to secure the principle when needed.[62] Unfortunately a flexible and adequate credit system among the New England merchants was late in coming in the seventeenth century.[63]

The colonies did little to supplement the funds sent over by the Corporation, and as a result only a few English instructors could be maintained, and those that did serve in the field do not appear to have been of a very high caliber.[64] Yet the "Worke" was attended with a spirit of optimism that always seemed to exaggerate the actual effectiveness of the missionary work. In 1660, the Commissioners boasted to the Corporation that a hundred of Eliot's Indians as well as many at Martha's Vineyard could read in the Bible.[65] But by the time of the triennial meetings of the Confederation, Eliot was to write that "our Indian Work yet liveth in these dark times, though it is still a day of small things."[66] The Corporation was always critical of the Commissioners' handling of their funds, and at the time of the Restoration it was noticed that twenty teachers were underpaid, even though supposedly a sufficient amount had been sent over to cover this expense. The Commissioners seemed little concerned to inspect accounts submitted to them, and thus were reprimanded by the Corporation: "Since our bookes accounts and actions have bine lately Inspected by Sion Colledge as formerly by the Councell of State and are exposed to the view of the Nation you would please to bee more particular in youer next accounts."[67] The lack of auditing or budgeting facilities in the colonial governments, and in particular any system of control or investigation in the Confederation, was a shortcoming of the times. Perhaps such control was not needed—only better scrutiny by the treasurer or the legislative branches (viz., the general courts or the Commissioners). Bureaucracy seems to be the concomitant of complex government. Yet there was sore need during the time of the Confederation for distinct executive powers,[68] a later product in the evolution of federal government in America.

In 1660, the first Corporation came to an end. When the Commissioners in New England learned of this, they lost no time in sending to the king a New Testament printed in the Indian language with a special dedication in English, which sought to flatter His Royal Majesty and acknowledged his sovereignty.[69] Twenty volumes of the Pentateuch and the New Testament were also sent over to be distributed among the high officials of the government.[70] In 1662, the former members of the Corporation conducted a vigorous campaign to get another act passed, pointing out to the king that the income in the past had been too small to carry on "his Majesty's pious intentions," such as perfecting the translation of the Indian Bible, the maintenance of Indian schools, and the "breeding up of the Indian children, not only in the Principles of Christianity, but civilized also and brought to submit to his Majesties gracious government."[71] Thus, by associating the "Indian Worke" with the best interests of the empire, the Corporation won royal favor and was rechartered. Many of the "Nobillitie and other persons of quallitie" of the former membership were continued in service under the new Corporation.[72] The main role of the Confederation during the time of the falling out of the confederates, spreading the Gospel in the Wilderness Zion, was now clearly subordinated to royal authority. The Commissioners, nevertheless, expressed their gratitude for reinstating the Corporation; it was an act done "not onely of a Kingly but alsoe of a truely Godley sperit especially considering the objects of this his bounty."[73] Under the new charter—though with less than ample funds—the Corporation and the Commissioners worked together more cordially than they had before; if they had continued their bickering the Confederation might have been accused of attempting to pursue an independent path from that of the home government.

In the sixties, the "Indian Worke" plodded along much as before, with some evidence of success. Daniel Gookin, the circuit judge and federal marshal of the praying Indians in the Bay Colony,[74] in 1662, felt it his duty to inform the Commissioners of the accomplishments of the praying Indians. According to Captain Gookin, many of the Indians were sober, pious, and

hard workers; the men were cultivating more and more ground
and in the winter were gainfully employed in "sawing of boards,"
while others practiced "usefull trades." Many of the women had
learned to spin and knit.[75] Eliot, in getting the praying Indians to
learn useful trades, has been called "the father of manual training in America."[76] The "ironworke" obtained through the Corporation was put to use in teaching the Indians the use of iron
tools—such implements supposedly bridging the gulf between
the aboriginal savage and civilized man.[77] Thus in this light the
"Indian Worke" was reaping some utilitarian value. Though the
"want of skill and experience" among the New England savages
"maketh them slower in dispatch, then the English," Eliot, in
whatever tasks the Indians undertook—whether in developing
their native skills or serving as laborers to the English—helped
to foster what he thought was the chief purpose of his missionary
work: "to Civilize the wild people, thereby to prepare them for
religion."[78] Indeed, the chief end of the Commissioners' later
Indian policy, recommended by Gookin himself,[79] was the absorption of the Indian into the English way of life. But this policy was made difficult, because, whereas the praying Indians
could be won over to the English way (they had been conquered), the two rival tribes of the Mohegans and the Narragansetts, sensing the early influence of the Commissioners in
maintaining the balance of power between them now fading
away,[80] lost interest in what the English had to say.

The extent of the Commissioners' supervision in the "Indian
Worke" can best be seen in the reports of their annual expenditures of the Corporation stock.[81] It is interesting to note that
these reports differed considerably from year to year, which indicates the rapid turnover of personnel[82] and the absence of any
pattern in the distribution of the commodities.

During the peak of the "Indian Worke" there were fourteen
praying towns, or what have been more properly called "Indian
stations."[83] These towns were classified into two groups by
Gookin, the seven original towns, and seven towns carved out
of the Nipmuck country just before King Philip's War.[84] A high
estimate places the number of Indians Christianized from the
beginning of the work to King Philip's War at between 3,000
and 4,000;[85] and Gookin himself in 1674 estimates eleven hundred "Souls yielding obedience to the gospel."[86] Actually there
seems to have been few Indians converted, and the optimistic

estimates of converted Indians more closely corresponds to the actual Indian population to whom the missionary efforts were directed—infants and "learners" were counted along with the "true believers." The events of King Philip's War greatly destroyed the missionary work Eliot and the others had so laboriously accomplished. The praying Indians on the frontier were suspected of collaborating with the enemy, and on this pretense— their lands were becoming more tempting to the English—the Indians at Natick, for example, on only a few hours notice were evacuated from their homes and sent to Deer Island for the course of the war. Many of the praying Indians were to join with Philip's forces, mainly because they were forced to choose between their divided loyalties, the Indian tie being the stronger, and because of the fear of vengeance from the hostile Indians if they did not. The Commissioners lamented to the Corporation the dire effects of the war on their missionary work among the Indians.[87] Eliot in his last years still labored on despite the fact that the white man was taking over the sites of the praying towns for his own use; yet, although the "work is under great incumberments and discouragements," wrote Eliot to Governor Boyle of the Corporation, "your hungry alumns do still cry" for the "milk of the word."[88]

Five reasons have been given,[89] which seem commonplace enough, for the failure of the missionary work of the Confederation among the Indians. First is the conflict between two cultures: savage and civilized—the one being more capable of self-preservation than the other. The English were also much too busy in settling the wilderness themselves to be bothered with the burden of another race. The methods of these early missionaries were not always the best—with sermons in crowded quarters sometimes as long as three hours. Moreover, there were religious divisions among the teachers; for example, the Quakers competed with Mayhew on Martha's Vineyard, telling the Indians that Mayhew was a priest of Baal. Lastly, there were the seeds of distrust and disruption sown by the great holocaust of war.

But there were some notable accomplishments from the "Indian Worke." The travel of the missionaries to the Indian settlements served to establish better lines of communication with the frontier settlements.[90] Settling the Indians on these reservations and giving them aid from the Corporation, meager though it was, helped the red man to hold his own in the advancement of European civilization. Though these praying Indians were not numerous—most of them were the remnant Pequots—they were for many years used by the Commissioners to sway the balance of power between the Narragansett and Mohegan tribes. The chief contribution, however, was the stimulation given to printing in the colonies, a factor for independence not to be lightly considered in view of the powerful influence of the later colonial press.

Five years before the forming of the Confederation, *The Freeman's Oath* for Massachusetts was printed in Cambridge, the first document printed in the American colonies.[91] Reflecting the religious overtone of the Puritan colonies, the number of publications that followed were of a religious nature. John Eliot early made contributions, such as his setting to meter the Psalms in the famous *Bay Psalm Book*. In 1649, a notable publication by Samuel Green, the third printer, was the *Platform for Church Discipline*. After the Corporation was founded in 1649, the Commissioners of the United Colonies sponsored various publications for the "Indian Worke" with funds supplied by the Corporation in England.

In 1658, Eliot was busily engaged in translating the Bible into the Algonquian tongue, and negotiations were under way between the Commissioners and the Corporation for sending an able printer to the colonies.[92] Abraham Pierson, missionary to the Quiripis of southern New England, about the same time, under the auspices of the Corporation, published in the native tongue a catechism called *Some Helps for the Indians*. Pierson received help for this publication from Thomas Stanton, "Interpreter-General to the United *Colonies* for the *Indian Language*."[93] The Commissioners of the Confederation recognized this accomplishment of Pierson by giving him a salary raise from £20 to £30 in 1661, but when he took up residence in New Jersey it was decreased to £15.[94]

Eliot plodded along with his translation of the Bible, securing help from an Indian boy who could speak both English and the native languages. In 1660, the Corporation sent to America Marmaduke Johnson, a printer of renown in London, to aid Samuel Green in the printing of the Indian Bible. Green had already made a substantial beginning with the Gospels, and although Green harbored a grudge against his young upstart co-

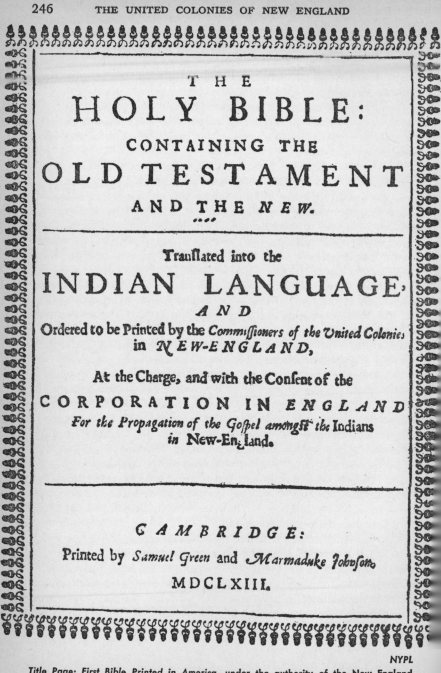

THE

HOLY BIBLE:

CONTAINING THE

OLD TESTAMENT

AND THE *NEW.*

....

Translated into the

INDIAN LANGUAGE,

AND

Ordered to be Printed by the *Commissioners of the United Colonies* in *NEW-ENGLAND,*

At the Charge, and with the Consent of the

CORPORATION IN *ENGLAND*

For the Propagation of the Gospel amongst the Indians *in* New-England.

CAMBRIDGE:

Printed by *Samuel Green* and *Marmaduke Johnson.*

MDCLXIII.

Title Page: First Bible Printed in America, under the authority of the New England Confederation.

worker, the New Testament was completed in 1661. The Commissioners in their September meeting hastily drew up a dedication to the newly restored Stuart king, professing the primary reason for their Confederation was the furtherance of the Gospel.

> The People of these four Colonies (Confederate for Mutual Defence, in the time of the late Distractions of our dear Native Country) Your Majesties natural born Subjects, by the Favour and Grant of Your Royal Father and Grandfather of Famous Memory, put themselves upon this great and hazardous Undertaking, of Planting themselves at their own Charge in these remote ends of the Earth, that without offence or provocation to our dear Brethren and Countrymen, we might enjoy that liberty to Worship God, which informed us, was not onely our Right, but Duty; As also that we might (if it so pleased God) be instrumental to spread the light of the Gospel, the knowledg of the Son of God our Saviour, to the poor barbarous Heathen . . .[95]

A great landmark in the history of printing occurred in 1663 when the entire Bible was completed in the Indian tongue, and was the first Bible printed in America.[96] Approximately 1500 copies were printed in this first edition, at a cost of about £ 1,000. With few books in the New World, it became a "household treasure in hundreds of wilderness cabins," not to mention the fact that it was of value to the younger Indians who were able to read it.[97] In a dedicatory epistle to the king, the Commissioners of the United Colonies again stated that the missionary work among the Indians "we desire ever to keep it in our Eye as our main Design"; and therefore leave was asked "upon this poor Plantation, *The United Colonies of* NEW-ENGLAND, for the Securing and Establishing of our Civil Priviledges and Religious Liberties hitherto Enjoyed."[98]

Other works were undertaken by Eliot under the auspices of the Corporation and the Confederation for the conversion of the Indians. In 1664 appeared Baxter's *Call to the Unconverted;* in 1666 *The Indian Grammar begun; The Indian Primer* in 1669; *Indian Dialogues* in 1671; and *The Logic Primer* in 1672. By the time of King Philip's War the Indian Bibles were scarce, and Eliot sought another grant from the Corporation for another

printing. Permission was granted in 1679: £250 was allowed
for the New Testament and Reading Psalms, and £100 for 500
Bibles.[99] Thomas Danforth of the Confederation seems to have
been the Commissioner responsible for seeing that the books
were properly bound and settling controversies pertaining to
the Cambridge Press, such as the bickering between Green and
Johnson for possession of letter type sent over by the Corporation.[100] In 1685, the Indian Bible, financed by a gift of £400
by the Corporation, underwent a second edition.[101] This monu-
mental effort of John Eliot, Indian Apostle, in translating the
complete Bible into the Indian language is an inspiration for all
time of one man's willingness to lift a people out of the dregs
into a fruitful way of life. Posterity has also been grateful for
this accomplishment for the key it has afforded anthropologists
and philologists in the study of the early American Indian.

The cement of union during the period of falling out was not
solely derived from the Commissioners' preoccupation with the
"Indian Worke." The Commissioners also turned their attention
to other aspects of the Gospel in New England. This greater
concern of the Commissioners for preserving religious orthodoxy
was indicative of the weakness of the Confederation. During the
first decade, when problems of state were all-important, the
Commissioners took little action in religious affairs, except to
recommend a rate to be levied for the support of the clergy and
to offer a few suggestions about checking the spread of error;
it was not, however, until after the constitutional controversy
that the Commissioners found time to be deeply concerned with
the spiritual life of the United Colonies. Contrary to the two
principles of religious freedom being announced by John Milton
in England about the same time,[102] the Commissioners admitted
the right of the colonists to check error and anarchy through
coercion so that an orthodox ministry could be established in
the colonies. Thus it was proposed that a competent maintenance "proportionable to the abillitie of the place and nessesitie of the minnester" be provided by all the members of
the community as well as those of the church. The general
courts were charged with the responsibility of seeing that the
people "professing Christianitie owne and live according to the
rules and ordinances of theire profession and that the despencers
therof bee Incurraged as aforsaid."[103]

A schism in the church at Hartford, resulting in one of the

Connecticut Commissioners, John Cullick, considering it best to emigrate to the Bay Colony,[104] led to an intercolonial correspondence proposing a synod of the churches. Only representatives from the River and Bay colonies got together the following year, and with the absence of the narrow constructionists of New Haven, a more liberal policy for baptism in the form of the Half-Way Covenant was recommended. In 1662 a synod of the churches was held at Boston, ostensibly for defining the nature of a consociation of churches, but this synod was sidetracked due to the earlier question of baptism, adopting the Half-Way Covenant. In 1667, the Commissioners of the Confederation proposed that a synod again be held for arriving at common doctrine and "Matters of faith," that the "Members of such Councell or Synode May consist of the Messengers of the Churches called Indifferently out of all the united Collonies by an orderly agreement of the severall Generall Courts." Though a synod was not convened, the colony courts recognized the need for a "mutuall accord in searching out the mind of God in any matters of publique concernment."[105] But a change was working in the New England churches, a change which shifted the emphasis on conformity to a bill of particulars agreed upon with God to a "more egocentric problem of personal salvation," the Covenant of Grace.[106] Liberal influences were creeping into Puritan Congregationalism, and the magistrates and elders, through their general courts or Confederation, in attempting to preserve their Ideal Commonwealth would soon be forced to give way to a respect for the "civil liberties"[107] and religious beliefs of all the people. It was the people who undermined the Puritan experiment; by too eagerly extending the franchise to frontier setlements, such as the New Hampshire towns, as an exchange for exercising jurisdiction over them, the United Colonies were forced to recognize the liberal elements within these settlements. Moreover, with the rise of Cromwell the Great Migration to the colonies came to an end, and many of the great colonial leaders returned home—thus leaving for the new emigration to the colonies a motley assortment of ne'er-do-wells and those uninspired with the vision of a Puritan State. But before the forces of liberalism were to triumph in the United Colonies, a rearguard movement, fought with all the intensity of the Puritan conscience, was waged against the infiltration of those subverters of New England orthodoxy.

It was the misfortune of the Puritan colonies that there were safety valves in their midst. The settlement of New England io filled with incidents of discontented persons, or whole congregations, leaving their established homes to find peace and fortune in the wilderness. The openly economic venture at New Amsterdam was one allurement; but the real thorn in the flesh was the Ishmael colony on Narragansett Bay, which warily kept off Puritan aggression by securing protection from the home government. Rhode Island, a colony of assorted malcontents, grew in power while the collective government of the Confederation waned. The Puritans had shown the settlers of Rhode Island that in times of distress they would not be spared when the tables turned. One of the best ways to irritate the Puritans was to encourage the immigration of Quakers into their midst—a sure means of undermining Puritan government by the Quaker disdain for oaths and governmental control of conscience driven on by passions for martyrdom. If the United Colonies had been wiser, they would not have erected barriers against the Quakers, thereby destroying the very grounds of negativism that often are necessary for the winning of proselytes.

The Commissioners of the United Colonies, coming as they did from the narrow circle of magistrates and the Puritan oligarchy, decided to establish for the colonies a general policy of keeping out Quakers. At their meeting in 1656 it was ordered that "all quakers Ranters and other notorious heritiques bee prohibited coming into the united Collonies and if any shall heerafter come or arise amonst us that they bee forth with cecured or removed out of all the Jurisdictions."[108] But the Quakers, using Rhode Island as a base of operations, resolutely continued to emigrate to the United Colonies. Thus in the following year when the Commissioners were informed that a group of Quarkers had arrived that summer at Rhode Island, they directed Rhode Island to remove this group of Quakers and in the future to prohibit their moving into that colony.[109] If this were not done, the United Colonies would be forced to such coercive measures, as severing trade with Rhode Island. The General Assembly of Rhode Island, nevertheless, replied negatively,[110] stating that the Quakers were entitled to certain rights; but if Quakers did not perform their civic duties, their agents in England would be notified so "that there may be no damage or infringement of that chief principle in our charter, concerning freedom of consciences." With royal protection in the 1660's Rhode Island could stand on her own; every influence that she had at Hampton Court was used against the Bay, never forgetting that Rhode Island "which now admitts all religions, even Quakers and Generallists" was "begun by such as the Mattachusetts would not suffer to live among them, and is generally hated by the other Colonies, who endeavoured severall wayes to suppresse them."[111]

Knowing that they were not wanted in the United Colonies, the Quakers persisted all the more in going to these colonies, thereby hurling a direct challenge at the ordered government of the Puritans. The Commissioners therefore, in 1658, in view of the rising "insolencies" of this "accursed and perniciouse sectt of heritiques," recommended to the general courts that they seriously consider the weight of the situation and pass laws banishing all Quakers upon pain of death if they returned, unless "they shall plainly and publickly Renounce theire cursed opinnions."[112] This recommendation of the Commissioners was largely secured through the efforts of the Bay, for it turned out that this was the only colony willing to enforce the death penalty. The other colonies of the Confederation were much less harsh in their legislation and treatment of the Quakers.[113]

The Quaker policy of the Confederation called up dissension within its own ranks as well as in the colonies. The most courageous action among the Commissioners was that of James Cudworth of Plymouth. When called upon to sign the letter of protest to Rhode Island, in 1657, Captain Cudworth refused, and the letter was sent to the Providence Assembly without his signature. As a result of this action by Cudworth, Plymouth Colony, firmly controlled by the conservative machine of Hinckley and Prence, stripped Cudworth of all his offices in the Colony, including his captaincy and commissionership in the United Colonies. For this firm stand and his willingness to pay the consequences, James Cudworth deserves a high place in American political history. Nor did the stripping of this early patriot of his high office quiet his tongue, but to the contrary. In a noble discourse to the General Court he hit hard at the very source that was impeding the progress of the Colony: "Our Civil Powers are so exercised in Things appertaining to the Kingdom of Christ, in Matters of Religion and Conscience, that we can

have no time to effect anything that tends to the Promotion of
the Civil Weal or the Prosperity of the Place; but now we must
have a State-Religion, such as the Powers of the World will
allow, and not other: a State-Ministry, and a State way of
Maintenance." Cudworth was so bold during his defense before the Plymouth Court as to ridicule the law pertaining to
Quakers as being the result of the arbitrary control of the governor, "Thomas Hinckley's Law"; at the Court itself he hurled
the indictment that "we are wrapped up in a Labyrinth of Confused Laws."[114] Thus spoke the man who, in emotionally
charged tones during one of the great dramas of our early history, deservedly ranks with Williams, Hooker, or Winthrop, Jr.
in defending the cause of liberty of conscience on the American
continent. Others, to a lesser degree, sacrificed public station to
stand against the harsh Quaker policy of the Puritan oligarchy.
Timothy Hatherly, formerly a Commissioner, was dropped as
an Assistant in Plymouth.[115] John Winthrop, Jr., the great
statesman from the River, was one of the few who could voice
his dissent without fear of reprisal. Thus Winthrop signed the
Act of the Commissioners calling for the death penalty for returning Quakers only upon the condition that it should not be
considered an "Act" but a "Query."[116]

The Bay went the limit to deter the coming of Quakers to
the Colony. The peak year of the persecutions saw the execution
of four Quakers, and though a large group of prominent Bos-
tonians thought there should be even harsher measures, public
opinion was quick to react.[117] Martyrdom always has a way of
awakening a people to sympathize with a cause, especially if
their own liberties are involved. John Davenport, the minister
and one of the founders of New Haven, soon sided with Governor Winthrop, that the "cleare way, and incomparably the
best expedient" for getting rid of Quakers was simply to transport them to some far distant place, such as Acadia.[118] The
persecution of the Quakers in the Bay provided an opportunity
for the Quaker pamphleteers to raise a howl of protest to the
mother country. The New-England's Ensigne accused the governor of Plymouth and former Commissioner, Thomas Prence,
as "not sparing to use his power" against the Quakers;[119] and
one of the most influential of these tracts, New-England
Judged,[120] did not spare the Commissioners of the Confederation, condemning them for having "rolled" themselves "up and

down in Innocent Blood." The harsh laws of the colonies were
brought to the attention of the authorities in London, with special emphasis placed on the recommendation of the death penalty by the Commissioners in 1656.[121]

Massachusetts was soon compelled to take notice of the
mounting public indignation, and as a result, in 1661, replaced
the death penalty with a Vagabond Act, without the penalty of
death.[122] But the most heartwarming aftermath of the Quaker
hysteria was the election of Josiah Winslow to the governorship
in Plymouth. Winslow rode the tide of popular indignation
against the harsh Quaker policy of his predecessor, Governor
Prence, and one of the first acts under the new administration
was to restore the civil rights and public office to James Cudworth. Yet Cudworth had paid a heavy price; for fifteen years
he had been disfranchised. Nevertheless, his vindication was
complete, and in two years he became the commanding general
of the Plymouth forces in King Philip's War.[123]

The Restoration in England was a deciding factor in allay-
ing the persecution of the Quakers in the United Colonies. A
royal mandamus ordered that all Quakers accused of acting
contrary to the laws of New England be sent to England for
trial.[124] Continued persecution of the Quakers would, therefore,
naturally be interpreted by the home government as a recalcitrant attitude. Thus the recommendations of the Commissioners
as well as the laws of the colonies concerning Quakers were in effect superseded by this order. Again the narrow and obstinate
policy of the Puritan oligarchy had played into the hands of
its enemies. A further step toward toleration of dissenters occurred in 1665, when the visiting royal commissioners proclaimed that all Quakers might "peacefuly passe about theire
lawfull occasions."[125]

The Commissioners during the time of falling out in the
Confederation sought to find expression of the general will by
turning to one of the main reasons for their confederating and
their coming into the New World: the spreading of the Gospel
in the wilderness through the dual course of converting the
heathen natives and preserving their own religious unity. The
"Indian Worke" cannot be accounted much of a success as to
the number of Indians converted, but it was valuable in orientat-
ing the savage to English civilization and stimulating the intellectual activity of the colonists—witness the output of the

Cambridge Press. The attempt of the Confederation to keep the colonies in line within a unified orthodoxy, to the extent of religious persecution, was doomed from the start because of the conditions in the colonies—economic, political, and religious— that called for greater freedom.

Thus there was a transition from the emphasis in the early Confederation on practical affairs of state to the now more remote "higher law." In affairs of the world the Commissioners had claimed the right to enact general laws according to the higher law. But now, in the time of weakness, the only relation of the Confederation to higher law was as agent for promoting the "Gospel." The practical result was that the Commissioners, instead of deciding on questions involving a supergovernment for the colonies, or in effect exerting sovereign powers of state, were now concerned only with the "main end" of the Confederation, preserving the religious status quo and promoting the conversion of the Indians.

The colonies, however, were to pay a dreadful price for letting their Confederation slip from the control of colonial policy: that price in the failure to maintain a firm Indian policy was the outbreak of Indian hostilities. Yet for their experiment in intercolonial government that was doomed to fail, they managed to entrench into the conscience of the people the appreciation of united action. Thus, from 1655 to 1670, when by reason the Confederation should have collapsed, there appeared a cement of union—the spreading of the Gospel in the New World.

---

[1] *MCR*, IV, Pt. 1, 324.

[2] Anon., *New England's First Fruits*, (London: 1643), no. vii of *Sabin's Reprints* (New York: 1865).

[3] John Josselyn, *An Account of Two Voyages to New-England, 1638, 1663*, (Boston: 1865), p. 199.

[4] Jeremy Belknap, *American Biography*, III, 110-1; R. P. Stearns, *Hugh Peter, The Strenuous Puritan* (Urbana: 1954), p. 176.

[5] *A Late and Further Manifestation of the Progress of the Gospel*, (London: 1655), p. 23.

[6] *PCR*, X, 104.

[7] For the two corporations of 1649 and 1662, instead of using their lengthy title, they will hereafter be referred to simply as the Corporation.

[8] "Charter of the Corporation . . .," 7Feb61/2, Thomas Birch, ed., *The Works of Robert Boyle*, (London: 1772), I, clvi.

[9] George P. Winship, ed., *The New England Company of 1649 and John Eliot*, (Records and Ledger Book), Vol XXXVI of the *PPS*, xvi-xx.

[10] *The Day-Breaking if not the Sun-Rising of the Gospel* (London: 1647), *passim*; *The Clear Sun-Shine of the Gospel Breaking Forth upon the Indians in New-England*, (London: 1648), p. 28. The latter tract is supposed to have been written by Thomas Shepard.

[11] When one ship laden with goods for the Indian work was lost at sea, Eliot proclaimed a "public humiliation" for the praying Indians. Such, said Eliot, was the "fruit of sin." See Francis Convers, *Life of John Eliot*, in Sparks ed., *Library of American Biography* (New York: 1856), V.

[12] *PCR*, X, 186.

[13] *Ibid.*, p. 244.

[14] *Ibid.*, pp. 239-41.

[15] A well-written and scholarly account of the early missionary work on the Vineyard is Lloyd C. M. Hare, *Thomas Mayhew*, (New York: 1931). For an early account, see, Experience Mayhew, *Indian Converts* (London 1727).

[16] Mayhew to Prence, MHSC 1:VI:197; Mayhew to the Commissioners, 23Aug71, John W. Ford, ed., *Some Correspondence between the Governors and Treasurers of the New England Company and Commissioners . . .*, (London: 1896), pp. 39-41. Transcripts of early records of Great Harbor are in the MHS.

[17] *PCR*, X, 205, 217-8.

[18] The lands granted to the Indians near Dedham were particularly contested by that town, with the Indians being confirmed in those lands they actually possessed, which because the Indians were slow to understand the English land system, soon dwindled. (MCR, IV, Pt. 2, 49, 82-3, 431-2; Dorchester Town Records, 12May54, p. 68; MA, XXX, 21; William Barry, *History of Framingham* (Boston: 1847), p. 31; Charles Hudson, *History of Marlborough* (Boston: 1862), pp. 55-63.

[19] MA, XXX, 12, Petition of John Eliot, 23Oct48.

[20] Eliot to Baxter, 10Jan67/8, F. J. Powicke, ed., "Some Unpublished Correspondence of Richard Baxter and John Eliot, 1656-82," *John Rylands Library Bulletin*, XV, 163-6.

[21] Daniel Gookin, "Historical Collections of the Indians in New England," *MHSC* 1:I:180-96; Convers, *op. cit.*, pp. 162-9; Oliver N. Bacon, *History of Natick* (Boston: 1856), pp. 21-3

[22] John Eliot, *Strength out of Weaknesse* (London: 1652), p. 5.

[23] Pierson to the Commissioners, 29Aug64, Wyllis Papers, CHS, I, 18; Charles H. Townshend, "The Quinnipiack Indians and Their Reservation," *Papers of the New Haven Colonial Historical Society*, VI (1900), 179.

[24] MA, XXX, 58-62.

[25] See John Eliot, "The Christian Commonwealth," *MHSC* 3:IX:127-164. Richard Baxter, a correspondent of Eliot, maintained that in government duty to God was most essential and therefore officials were bound to give "instructions of his Makers will." (*A Holy Commonwealth* (London: 1659).)

[26] *PCR*, X, 285.

[27] *Ibid.*, p. 143.

[28] *Ibid.*

[29] *PCR*, X, 284-5.

[30] *Ibid.*, p. 250.

[31] MA, XXX, 74.

[32] E.g., such as giving bond to those selling goods for use in the "Indian Worke." (MA, XXX, 68a, 22Sep58.)

[33] *MCR*, IV, Pt. 2, 34, 451. In making a report on the progress of the "Indian Worke, Gookin stated that by encouraging them to work he was "infusing into them principles of morality and industry." (CA, Eccles., I, 9.)

[34] Robert B. Caverly, *Life and Labors of John Eliot*, (Lowell, Mass.: 1881), p. 38.

[35] Eliot to Boyle, 15Mar82/3, *MHSC* 1:III:181.

[36] E.g., Warrant issued by Major General Gookin, 21May82, Saltonstall Papers, MHS, XIX, fol. A.

[37] E.g., *PCR*, X, 141.

[38] The Massachusetts Commissioners did most of the supervision and the Secretary of the Colony was in charge of preparing the accounts (which at times proved unacceptable, e.g., *PCR*, X, 129.) In the meeting of 1659 the Massachusetts Commissioners were given complete authority over the accounts for that year. (*Ibid.*, pp. 218-9.) That the Bay dominated this activity is supported by R. G. Stearns, "The Weld-Peters Mission to England," *PCSM*, XXXII, 241-2.

[39] *PCR*, X, 118.

[40] *Tears of Repentence* (London:1653).

[41] Rawlinson MSS, f.24 (Library of Congress Photostats.).

[42] Poem by Deacon Walker: "The first smile of god in this land," printed in Richard L. Bowen, *Early Rehoboth*, (Rehoboth: 1948), III, p. 45.

[43] E.g., *PCR*, X, 160-7.

[44] Baxter's Letters, Dr. Williams Library, 20Jan56/7, III, f.9-10; Rawlinson MSS, 934, Documents f. 16, 34, 42, 52 (Library of Congress Photostats).

[45] Eliot to Hamner, 19Jul52, Wilberforce Eames, ed., *John Eliot and the Indians (Letters to Johnathan Hamner)* (New York: 1915), pp. 8-9.

[46] Rawlinson MSS, 934, f. 13 (Library of Congress Photostats).

[47] *PCR*, X, 251. Before King Philip's War, Indian servitude was much the same as the indentures of the whites during this period. When, at the close of the war, Indian captives were actually sold into slavery, Eliot entered a vigorous protest: "To sell souls for money seemeth to me a dangerous merchandise . . . All men of reading condemn the Spaniard for cruelty upon this point . . . here is land enough for them and us too." (Printed in Caverly, *op. cit.*, pp. 72-3.)

[48] Felt, *op. cit.*, II, 202. There were not enough "Indian Officers" to supply their churches, and therefore it was a "joint Concernment" of all the colonies to train leaders from the Indians themselves. (CA, College and Schools, Ser. 1, I, 4; *A Brief Narration of the Progress of the Gospel*. (London: 1671).

[49] CA, Eccles., I, 8.

[50] Hare, op. cit., p. 135.

[51] See Daniel T. Huntoon, History of the Town of Canton, (Cambridge: 1893). President Dunster while at Harvard had asked that Indian boys placed in his care be removed because "they bring a hindrance to me." (MA, XXX, 9.)

[52] CA, Indians, 1 ser., I, 41.

[53] MA, X, 202-4; Winthrop to Boyle, 25Sep64 and 28Oct70, Winthrop Papers, V, 43 and 95; Winship, ed., op. cit., pp. xxi-iii; J. Ford, ed., op. cit., pp. 27-30.

[54] Winthrop to Nicols, 19Sep66 and 8Sep67, Winthrop Papers, MHS, V, 62 and 68; also various letters with the Corporation or Commissioners: Misc. MSS, MHS, II, 110; MHSC 5:I:491; MHSC 3:X:56-7; MHSC 4:VII:484-6; Misc. MSS, BPL, Ch A2-41; CA, Eccles., I, 7.

[55] Rawlinson MSS, 934, f. 44, Library of Congress Photostats.

[56] Province and Court Records of Maine, I, 204 .

[57] Quoted in Hare, op. cit., p. 131. Only Eliot remained optimistic in his missionary efforts deriving support from the Corporation funds, "the spirit of God thus moving upon these waters." (CA, Eccles., I, 10.)

[58] Winship, ed., op. cit., lv-lviii.

[59] Ibid. Those Boston merchants giving bills of exchange often required prompting from the Corporation. (E.g., MA, XXX, 32.)

[60] Ibid.

[61] Boyle to the Commissioners 4Jun68, J. Ford, ed., op. cit., pp. 15-17. Except in private affairs, the New Englanders were little interested in financial matters, and what financial institutions they set up were those they were familiar with in England. (Charles H. Douglas, The Financial Hist. of Mass. to the Amer. Revol., Vol. I of Columbia Univ. Studies (1892), 16-7.

[62] Winship, ed., op. cit., p. lviii.

[63] In 1681, the Boston merchants organized themselves in a "Fund" for the purposes of adjusting credit. See Colonial Currency Reprints, I (Vol. XXXII of PPS).

[64] The son of Thomas Stanton, Indian interpreter for the Confederation, had his training as an Indian teacher financed by the Commissioners, but was apparently neither bright nor industrious. (PCR, X, 128, 252.)

[65] Ibid., p. 242.

[66] Eliot to Baxter, 22Jan67/8, John Rylands Library Bulletin, (Manchester), F. J. Powicke, "Some Unpublished Correspondence . . . ," XV, 166-7.

[67] PCR, X, 239.

[68] The king's prerogative was not known in the United Colonies during the life of the Confederation until after the Restoration, and then for the most part lightly felt until the Bay Charter was revoked.

[69] PCR, X, 255-9.

[70] Ibid., p. 260. Two well-bound copies of each were to be given to the King and Lord Chancellor; one each to Dr. Reynolds, Mr. Carroll, and Mr. Baxter; two for the Vice Chancellor of the University; etc.

[71] *Orders in Council*, 39 Charles I I(1660). III. "Briefe ordered for England and Wales to be carried out by the Lord Chancellor," *MHSC*, 4:II:284, 12Jul62.

[72] *PCR, X, 270.*

[73] *Ibid.*, p. 274.

[74] Following the circuit of the praying towns Gookin appointed Indian constables and teachers; in his judicial capacity "smaller faults" were left to the ruler-in-chief of the praying towns, while such serious offenses as "idolatry and powowing" were matters for Gookin himself to decide. Whenever the occasion presented itself, Gookin "extorted the people to yield obedience to the gospel of Christ and to those set in order there." (Gookin, *op. cit.*, p. 192.)

[75] *PCR*, X, 280.

[76] Frank Smith, typewritten MS, "John Eliot and the Praying Indian," Excerpts from Dedham Historical Society.

[77] *Ibid.*, viz., seven tools: axe, saw, plane, hammer, square, chisel, and file.

[78] Eliot to Steele, 8Dec52, Rawlinson MSS, 934, f. 13. Library of Congress Photostats.

[79] Gookin, *loc. cit.*, p. 219.

[80] Eliot complained that this rivalry stood in his way. (Eliot to Steele, *loc. cit.*)

[81] One of the most extensive accounts was that submitted at the last meeting of the Confederation under the old Articles. (*PCR*, X, 330-1.)

[82] More were needed of the type of Thomas Mayhew, Sr., who "spares not his body by night nor by day." Mather estimated the number of converted Indians at Martha's Vineyard and Nantucket at 3,000, probably the total Indian population. (Mather, *op. cit.*, II, 428-31.)

The agent of the United Colonies in England, the liaison man between the Confederation ad the Corporation, "Edward Wynslowe one of the Commissioners at Haberdashers Hall," was well paid by the Corporation, which was approved by the Commissioners. (Rawlinson MSS, 934, f. 11, 22, 40, Library of Congress Photostats.)

[83] Caverly, *op. cit.*, p. 61.

[84] For their Indian names, see Gookin, *op. cit.*, pp. 180-95. These towns were located on the site of the present-day communities of Natick, Stoughton, Grafton, Marlboro, Tewksbury, Littleton, Hopkinton; and in the Nipmuck Country: Oxford, Dudley, Woodstock, Worcester, and Uxbridge.

[85] Mary S. Locke, "Indian Missions in the Massachusetts and Plymouth Colonies," DHR (Jan, 1892), III, 61-2. For a biography of Eliot with much of his correspondence, see Willson, *The Life of John Eliot* (Edinburgh: 1828).

[86] Gookin, *op. cit.*, p. 193.

[87] Ltr of 26Dec79, Ford, ed., *op. cit.*, pp. 58-60.

[88] Eliot to Boyle, 21Jun83, *MHSC*, 1:III:182.

[89] See Samuel Eliot, "Early Relations with the Indians," *Early History of Massachusetts*, (Boston: 1869), 305-317.

[90] For our interest in intercolonial cooperative action, the first mail service

between Boston and New York was established in 1673. (Lynn W. Wilson, *History of Fairfield County, Conn.*, (Hartford: 1929).

[91] Robert F. Roden, *The Cambridge Press, 1638-92*, (New York: 1905) contains a list of the books printed during this period.

[92] *A further Accompt of the Progresse of the Gospel*, (London: 1659).

[93] J. H. Trumbull, introd. to Pierson's *Some Help for the Indians*, CHSC, III,6.

[94] Charles H. Townshend, "The Quinnipiack Indians and Their Reservation," *Papers of the New Haven Colonial Historical Society*, VI(1900), 181-2.

[95] PCR, X, 256. Johnson married the daughter of Green, while still having a wife in England, which further complicated their relationship.

[96] Not until the middle of the next century was an English Bible printed in America. See Isaiah Thomas, *The History of Printing in America* (Albany: 1874), *Transactions of the AAS*, I(V).

[97] Ezra H. Byington, *The Puritan in England and New England*, (Boston: 1897), p. 251.

[98] Eliot's *Indian Bible*, (Cambridge: 1663).

[99] Winship, ed., *op. cit.*, pp. lix-lxi.

[100] CA, Misc., I, 91b; Green to Winthrop, *Winthrop Papers*, MHSC 5:I:422-4.

[101] Eliot to Boyle, 22Apr84, MHSC 1:III:182. A second printing of the New Testament had taken place in 1680, also with the approval of the Confederation first obtained. (Eliot to Boyle, 4Nov80, Birch, ed., *op. cit.*, I, ccvii-iii.)

[102] Milton wrote: "Two things there be which have bin ever found working much mischief to the church of God, and the advancement of truth: force on the one side restraining, and hire on the other side corrupting the teachers thereof." (John Milton, *A Treatise on civil power in Ecclesiastical Affairs*, (London: 1659).

[103] PCR, X, 156, and a like resolution in 1667, *ibid.*, p. 328.

[104] MA, XV, 1.

[105] MA, X, 195; CA, Eccles., I, 14; CHSC, II, 66; PCR, X, 328; Felt, *op. cit.*, pp. 149, 168, 293-5, 466; Walker, *Creeds and Platforms, op. cit.*, p. 275.

[106] See Babette M. Levy, *Preaching in the First Half Century of New England History*, (Hartford: 1945).

[107] This phrase is Winthrop's (*Journal*, (3), II, 193.) From 1639 to 1662 in Massachusetts there was "no recognition of a general right of freedom of the press." (Clyde D. Duniway, *The Development of Freedom of the Press in Massachusetts*, (New York), *Hartford History Studies*, XII, 39.

[108] PCR, X, 158.

[109] *Ibid.*, pp. 180-1.

[110] *Rhode Island State Papers*, MHSC, 2:VII:83-4; Letter of the Assembly to the Commissioners, *RHSC*, IV, 234-7.

[111] RICR, II, 126. Benjamin Arnold, President of Providence Plantations, wrote the Commissioners that expelling the Quakers only made them more determined to enter the colonies. If allowed freedom of conscience in the "things and ways of God," they "least desire to come here." (*Ibid.*, I, 376-9.)

[112] *PCR*, X, 212. E.g., declaring themselves immediately sent from God and infallible in matters of conscience; blaspheming; speaking evil of dignitaries; attempting to proselyte; disturbing the peace; and withdrawing the "harts of the people from theire subjection to Government."

[113] Connecticut was the most liberal. If Quakers returned from banishment in Connecticut they were to be shipped out of the colony. Though "hereticall bookes" of the Quakers were to be seized, Quakers were excused from attending public assemblies provided they didn't congregate themselves and disturb the peace. *(CCR*, II, 87, 264; See Henry Bronson, "Early Government of Conn.," *Papers of the NHCHS*, III, 293-403.

Although the recommendations of the Commissioners were written into New Haven law *(NHCR*, II, 217), New Haven had only six trials of Quakers, most of which were neighborhood quarrels. C. H. Levermore, *The Republic of New Haven*, *JHUS*, Ext. Vol. I (1886), 136. Branding the hand with a letter "H" seems to have been the extreme penalty. *(NHCR*, II, 237, 241.)

In Plymouth no "Quaker" or "Rantor" was admitted to the freemanship, and banishment or whipping were the extreme penalties. (E. Hazard, *State Papers* (Philadelphia: 1794), II, 551ff, 556ff.) For groups of Quakers in Plymouth binding together to form new communities, their harsh treatment, etc. see Justin Winsor, *A History of Duxbury*, (Boston: 1849), and Theodate Geoffrey, *Suckannesset* (Falmouth), (Falmouth: 1930).

Though the Court of Assistants were to try Quakers in Massachusetts, it is interesting to note that town officials were appointed to try such cases. (E.g., *Dedham Town Records*, p. 290, 22May61.) The persecution of the Quakers is beyond the scope of this study. For general accounts see Rufus M. Jones, *The Quakers in the American Colonies*, (London: 1911) and Charles Evans, *Friends in the Seventeenth Century*, (Philadelphia: 1875).

[114] *RICR*, I, 374-6; Richard P. Hallowell, *The Quaker Invasion of Massachusetts* (Boston: 1883). Cudworth's message quoted on pp. 168-171.

[115] See Elizabeth C. Jenkins, "The First Church, Interim Years," in *Hist. of Barnstable*, (Hyannis, Mass.: 1939), 35-44.

[116] *PCR*, X, 212.

[117] Lawrence S. Mayo, *John Endecott*, (Cambridge: Harvard University Press, 1936), pp. 241-3; Henry L. Southwick, "The Policy of the Early Colonists of Massachusetts Toward Quakers . . . ," *Old South Prize Essay* (Boston: 1885).

[118] Davenport to Winthrop, 6Dec59, *MHSC* 4:VII:509.

[119] Humphrey Norton, *et al.*, *New-England's Ensigne* (London: 1659), pp. 22-3.

[120] George Bishop, *New-England Judged*, (London: 1661, rep. 1703), p. 227.

[121] Stevens Transcripts, John Carter Brown Library, I, 20, 23.

[122] Frances Robotti, *Chronicles of Old Salem*, (Salem: 1948), p. 26.

[123] Cudworth to Winslow, 16Jan73/4, 20Jul75, *MHSC*, I:VI:80, 84-5; Jacob B. Moore, *Lives of the Governors of New Plymouth and Massachusetts Bay*, (Boston: 1851), pp. 177-8.

[124] Hazard, *State Papers*, II, 595.

[125] *MCR*, IV, Pt. 2, 212-3.

CHAPTER XII

New Wine Into Old Bottles

By the time His Majesty's Commissioners returned home in 1655, the movement for re-establishing the Confederacy was under way. New Haven Colony had been eliminated after an unsuccessful struggle by the diehards of the Colony to invoke the Articles of Confederation as a means of preventing absorption by the River Colony. Three colonies now remained. Though the extremities of empire on Long Island and in Maine had been cut from under them as a result of the restoration of the Stuarts, union could still be of great value. The advantages of union were demonstrated negatively by weaknesses of the Confederation after 1655—witness the failure to maintain a firm Indian policy, the loss of control of foreign affairs, the overawing of the colonies by the demands of the royal government to recognize the sovereignty of the king, and the general distrust sown among the colonies because of their different interpretations of the Articles of Confederation.

Though the walls of the Confederacy had crumbled in 1664 and the Commissioners in that year declared that their annual meetings would thenceforward be triennial, the colonies continued to choose their Commissioners annually. The apparent reason for this anomaly was to enable the Commissioners to get together informally during the interim periods in order to administer the funds for the Indian missionary work. Except for this continuity provided by the "Indian Worke," the Confederation in 1665 for all practical purposes may be said to have been dissolved. Connecticut was blamed by the colonies of Plymouth and Massachusetts for having disrupted the Confederacy,[1] by their refusal to follow the advice of the Commissioners of the United Colonies in the dispute over the jurisdiction of New Haven. It is not surprising then that these two colonies felt it their responsibility, with Connecticut thus unconcerned, to "labor" in the future "to make it our great design to begett and maintayne Union."[2]

Yet lethargy worked against the appearance of plans to revise the Confederacy. Plymouth Colony, faced with the problem of preserving her territorial integrity as was New Haven at an earlier time, realized that her best chance lay in a revival of the Confederation. Something drastic, therefore, had to be done to awaken the other colonies to the need for revitalizing their union. The best way was to propose a clean break, which it was hoped would shock the Bay and the River colonies to their senses. In 1665, the Plymouth Court declared:

> In reference unto the question concerning the continuance of the confederation of the United Collonies, the Court have ordered, that a loveing, curteous letter bee directed to the government of the Massachusetts collonie, therin declaring that wee see not light to persist on therein . . . that if upon further enformation and consideration of any return from them or otherwise, wee shall see cause to send to another meeting in reference unto a more civell and orderly breakeing of that, wee soe doe.[3]

The correspondence between Plymouth and Massachusetts which arose out of this abrupt proposal of the Cape colony stimulated discussion on ways to bring the Confederation into more accord with the views of the royal commissioners who were then present in the colonies. If anything could be found of "fit concernment of all," their Commissioners were to be sent to a meeting and invested with "full power to advise and acte in any case"—with the purpose of removing all "obstructions."[4] But in 1667, in a letter to the Bay General Court, the Plymouth Court wrote that it had not heard anything from the other general courts about continuing the Confederation.[5]

When the first triennial meeting of the Confederation was held in September, 1667, the Commissioners of the three colonies acknowledged that the Articles of Confederation had been so long violated in many particulars that a serious "consultation" was necessary. It is interesting to note that the President of the Confederation for this meeting was William Leete, formerly the Commissioner from New Haven, but now representing the River Colony—thus, visual testimony to the complete elimination of the fourth confederate. The Commissioners considered grounds for re-establishing the Confederacy, which

they declared was "still the meanes of our owne safty and preservation of his Majesties dominions heer against foreigne and
domesticke enimies."⁶ In Massachusetts, the General Court,
acting upon the recommendation of the Commissioners to continue the Confederation, appointed a special committee to consider proposals for union, with their findings to be presented to
the next Court of Elections.⁷ This committee recommended re-
establishing the Confederation, but proposed certain additions to
and clarification of the old Articles. Chief among these were: to
recognize expressly the ultimate authority of the general courts;
the powers of the Commissioners to determine only offensive
war; a clause aimed at Quakers and riffraff to tighten the movement of "vagabonds" among the colonies; and regulations for
the Commissioners concerning the "Indian Worke."⁸

The debates over these changes in the Articles of Confederation proceeded for the next two years, "whereby the confederation seemes to be greatly weakened, and at present useless."
Finally it was agreed to revive the Confederacy, this time with
due expression of royal authority. Committees—actually the
Commissioners for the year, and in the case of Massachusetts
including the alternate Commissioner—were chosen in the fall
of 1669 with plenary power to reestablish the Confederation.⁹
This committee of the colonies was to meet in the spring, during the sessions of the courts of election in the colonies. Renewing their covenant of confederation was a solemn event for the
Puritan fathers; whatever the future would bring they would
stand united in the True Word for their mutual safety and
happiness. Thus, in the following June at the Boston Town
House, the committee of the colonies approved a revised Articles
of Confederation, and on June 12 the delegates affixed their
signatures to the new Articles, returning them to the general
courts for ratification.¹⁰

Two of the general courts, Plymouth and Connecticut, immediately ratified the fifteen Articles, returned from the June
meeting, and prepared to send Commissioners for the triennial
meeting in the fall.¹¹ The procedure of establishing the early
Confederation was to be re-enacted; in the fall session the Articles, after having been ratified by the general courts, would
again be signed by the properly elected Commissioners of the
Confederation. But the Bay General Court questioned the standard for proportioning war contributions, as stated in Articles

Nine and Ten of the proposed Articles. The proportion for each colony in units of men, supplies, or taxes for the support of waging a war were: Massachusetts, 100; Plymouth, 45; and Connecticut, 90. The Bay objected to this proportioning on the basis that the figures did not accurately correspond to the distribution of population. (A recent, scholarly study has taken advantage of this episode to revise the estimates of Palfrey and Dexter of the population in the early colonies.)[12] Massachusetts proposed a higher ratio for herself, which may at first seem contradictory to the attitude of the Bay in the early Confederation, when complaints were heard of the overwhelming burdens she shouldered in relation to the other confederate colonies. Why then, was the Bay now insisting that the quotas of the colonies correspond directly to the ratio of population in the colonies, which would mean that the proportions of the three colonies would be one-hundred-thirty-sixty, instead of the above-mentioned proportions? The answer can be found simply in the experience of the first Confederation; by carrying by far the greater burden, the Bay carried greater weight in the deliberations of the Commissioners, and generally maintained its preeminence.

Although the Connecticut Assembly agreed to minor alterations in Articles Four and Seven, they would not consent at first to the changes proposed by the Bay in the Ninth and Tenth Articles.[13] In the spring of 1672, however, a compromise was worked out, whereby the colonies would agree to the ratio set by Massachusetts for a limited period of fiifteen years, and if before that time the ratio should again be challenged by one colony then it should be considered.[14] After two years of bickering over the two clauses relating to proportionment among the colonies, which had prevented consummating the new union at the logical time, the triennial session of the Confederation in 1670 (called off because of this unexpected controversy) was ready to be resumed. At the annual courts of election in May, 1672, the freemen of Connecticut and Massachusetts elected, as general officers of these colonies, Commissioners to attend the meeting of the Confederation in September.[15] In July, the Plymouth Court likewise followed suit, at which time

> a letter was read in the Court, which was returne of an answare to a letter sent into the Massachusetts, concerning

our collonies acceptance of the proposition made by them for the continuance of the confeaderation, both which letters importeth a joint acceptance and concurrance in the proposition about the continuance thereof.[16]

The second Confederation of the United Colonies was convened at Plymouth on September 15, 1672. The six Commissioners appearing were invested with "full power and authoritie to signe ratify and confeirme" the Articles for the "reestabing of a perpetuall Confeaderation." With the signatures of Winthrop and Richards for Connecticut, Prence and Winslow for Plymouth, Danforth and Hathorne for Massachusetts affixed to the Articles of Confederation, the Union of the Puritan Colonies was again off to a fresh start.

Revived by a new sct of Articles, the Confederation once again came to life. The United Colonies of New England in 1672 was not unlike the Confederation founded forty years before, except that now, having learned from experience, many of the incongruities of the old Confederation had been corrected and the Confederation dealt in more specific and limited areas. A super-government with powers to coerce one of its members to follow united policy was out of the question. The new Confederation was watered down from the start, and was not designed to exercise more than nominal powers. Yet by bringing their Union up to date and along lines more clearly conceived than the earlier Confederacy, the colonists could expect a league of more substance and value than the one that had survived the crisis years.

Chief among the changes wrought by the new Articles of Confederation was that now the general courts had to provide the "comission" and "oppertunitie" for the Commissioners in dealing with any problems: that all powers of the Confederation were to be delegated and there were no inherent powers derived from the freemen, as the earlier Confederation had implied. The Commissioners were subject to the same checks as other general officers of a colony[17] and not members of nor perennial plenipotentiaries to a super-government. Meetings were now officially triennial. Membership was limited to Massachusetts, Connecticut, and Plymouth, although the same provisions of the earlier Confederacy for enlarging or contracting its bounds still applied.[18] A vote of five of the six Commissioners was to be deci-

sive. Two clauses of a particular nature found their way into
the Articles: the disposing of the Indian stock and the regulat-
ing of vagabonds and wandering persons—the latter provision
giving added weight to the existing laws in the towns for the
warning away of strangers not likely to become inhabitants. The
power to determine war was given exclusively to the general courts, and because even "the Justest warr may be of dangerous consequence," no war measures whatsoever would be
binding on any of the colonies unless with the unanimous consent of their general courts. The charges of war, as under the
old Articles, were to be borne proportionately by the individual
colonies.

A year after the re-establishing of the Confederacy, the Commissioners made their only attempt during the second Confederation to amend the Articles. It was proposed that Article
Thirteen dealing with "vagabond and wandering persons removeing from one Collonie to another" should have an insertion
of "or otherwise" between "persons" and "wandering" thus making the definition more precise. The length of stay in one colony
for such vagrants should also be enlarged to nine months instead
of three.[19] The amending process proposed is of interest in view
of the process for amendment in the later American Articles
of Confederation and Constitution: namely, that the Commissioners as a deliberative body would draw up the amendment
and then submit it to the particular colonies for ratification.

The New England Confederation, with a fresh set of Articles,
was now ready for a new trial. This trial, however, would not
be long in coming in the form of a rapidly deteriorating Indian
situation and the most severe Indian uprising in New England.

The "Indian Worke," which a decade before had been the
cement of union for the Confederation, was now beginning to
fade away in importance to the Commissioners. The Corporation
in England was finding funds, especially after the loss of their
buildings by fire, more and more scarce. The Commissioners
under the new Articles once again looked towards their union
as a league for defense, and their interest in the "Indian Worke"
became perfunctory. Writing to the Corporation in 1671 the
Commissioners stated that according to their "usuall Manor"
they had "examined and taken a particular accoumpt of the
progresse of the Gospell amongst the Indian Natives," wherein
it was found that the work was "attended with difficulties and

many discurragements from men and divells." It was also becoming "farr more difficult to obtaine suitable Instruments to
labour therin."[20] Although Eliot noted the increase in number
of churches both on the mainland and on the Vineyard and the
close cooperation of the Indian churches and the English
churches,[21] the missionary work was now carried on more by
church pastors in their spare time, rather than by special instructors as was the case in the earlier period. Governor Winthrop of
Connecticut, saddened by the recent death of his wife and wanting to retire because of his own illnesses,[22] seemed to be the
Commissioner most interested in continuing the administration
of the "corporation for the Indians" during the intervening sessions of the Confederacy.[23]

The greatest obstruction to the missionary work among the
Indians, according to Daniel Gookin, was Uncas of the Mohegans, "an old and wicked wilful man, a drunkard and otherwise
very vitious; who hath always been an opposer and underminer
of praying to God."[24] Thus was voiced the frustrations of the
Commissioners' half-hearted policy of raising up through the
use of the Gospel a buffer community of praying Indians. No
inroads were made among these Mohegans, who were expected,
because of their past friendship with the English, to become
praying Indians. The only success in the "Indian Worke" was
among those remnants of crushed tribes such as the Pequots,
who with the world caving in on them took gladly to the helping
hand of the English. Conversions among this savage race were
more apparent than real; it was no easy task for an aborigine
used to roaming freely about the wilderness to appreciate the
fine points of Puritan doctrine. Disillusionment was thus settling
over the "Indian Worke," and the Commissioners began to
think of the savages in terms of whether they would prove
loyal to the English or not in case of an outbreak of hostilities.
It was not long before some among the "Praying Indians" became
"Preying Indians," when they started to make prey of "much
English Blood."[25]

Although most of the work of the second Confederation was
of a military nature, there were several interesting legal de-
velopments. First of all, some acts and recommendations of
the Commissioners were expressly written into the internal laws
of the colonies. Connecticut, for instance, included the rules for
the Indian Pequot governors under the jurisdiction of the

colony in the laws of the colony, as specified by the Commissioners.[26] On another occasion the Suffolk County Court on November 8, 1672, by invoking the eighth article of the Articles of Confederation, found that one Hannah Bumpus was an inhabitant of Hingham and ordered her to be turned over to the authorities there. But after a few days the court reconsidered the case, and invoking the vagrancy clause, Article Thirteen, reversed its earlier decision.[27] Because the defendant's birthplace was Plymouth, imposing her upon Hingham, a town in the Bay, without warrant, was contrary to the Articles of Confederation. It was then ordered that the constable of Hingham return her to Plymouth.[28] The actual role of the Commissioners in criminal law, however, was only advisory. In 1673, for example, Connecticut was urged to take more active steps in bringing to justice the murderers of a Pequot girl,[29] and in 1676 the Commissioners' advice was sought by Plymouth concerning the number of Indians to be returned to their masters after they had run away.[30] When the Commissioners of the United Colonies from the Bay were sued in a county court, upon appeal of the plaintiff in the Court of Assistants judgment was returned as a nonsuit[31]— thus recognizing the important principle that public officials acting in their official capacity cannot be held to account themselves in a litigious proceeding, but rather the government they represent.

Everywhere war clouds were in the air. The Pequots, tiring of their governors, began deserting to the Narragansetts and the Mohegans.[32] As early as 1669, rumors again began to rise that a general conspiracy was being formed by the Narragansetts, the remnant Pequots, the Montauks on Long Island, and the Mohawks.[33] If the powerful Iroquois Confederacy[34] and the New England Indians should combine forces, then the primitive settlements in the wilderness could be nearly wiped off the map. Fortunately for the United Colonies, however, raiding parties from the Mohawks still made depredations upon New England Indians.[35] Governor Lovelace of New York sensed the danger of a general Indian conspiracy when he sought to establish a "friendly and neighbourly Correspondence" with Rhode Island,[36] thus looking for defensive measures without coming into direct contact with the Confederation. Rhode Island did participate with Plymouth in a conference at Taunton with King Philip, at which the Indians promised to surrender their arms to the English, a promise, however, not kept.[37]

Numerous instances in the early seventies severely strained relations between the white man and the red man. In 1671, Plymouth dispatched a force of one hundred men under Josiah Winslow to seize the arms of the Seconets, but the Indians were able to hide their arms before the arrival of this force.[38] As friction increased between the two races, the Council of Plymouth summoned Philip, sachem of the Pokanokets, better known as Wampanoags, to appear before them in person to answer charges against him.[39] The Commissioners of Massachusetts and Connecticut and "some other gentlemen" were invited to attend this council for a "faire and deliberate hearing of the controversy between our collonies and the said sachem, Philip."[40] But the haughty Wampanoag sachem declined the Plymouth offer, and went instead to Massachusetts, which from Philip's viewpoint was more proper since he had an agreement with the Bay officials for settling difficulties; besides a more objective hearing could be expected from the more remote Bay Colony. The Plymouth authorities, however, considered this action of Philip against their order as "another Outrage,"[41] and accused their northern confederate of unduo interference.[42]

After further negotiations, however, a council was finally held at Plymouth, with the Commissioners and Philip attending.[43] This mixed council of delegates from the three colonies and Indian sachems was handled very unwisely by the English. Instead of being diplomatic and treating with Philip in a respectful way, the Puritan magistrates decided to have their cake and eat it too. Philip was required to swear allegiance to the English king and to his enemy, the Colony of Plymouth. Moreover, he was required to pay every year a tribute of five wolves' heads as a sign of his fealty and to pay the cost of this conference. Thus the impression was given that Philip was not an equal member in this parley, but rather was held for judgment by the Puritan authorities. The conference lasted five days and was conducted as if Philip were on trial, and these articles of agreement were in the nature of a sentence.[44] This type of council meeting, with Commissioners from the colonies sitting as a general council of the colonies for directing the defense and military preparations of the United Colonies, was to become characteristic of the sessions of the Confederation when it was revived the following year. Thus Roger Williams, writing to the Commissioners in face of the mounting Indian threat, requested the Commissioners "as Commanders of a Fleete or Squadron meete in a Councell of war at sea: to meete yourselves in a Councell of peace or war."[45]

For the three years immediately before the outbreak of hostilities in 1675, the Indian situation appeared to have quietened. The usual suspicions that French and Dutch, under the concealment of the fur trade, were engaged in gun-running with the Algonquian Indians, still remained,[46] but there was little stirring on the surface among the New England natives. All was too quiet. The bitter resentment against the oppressive measures of Plymouth against Philip's Indians was giving way to a careful or rather a deliberate plot against the English. John Sassamon, an Indian schoolteacher at Natick, visiting among friends in Philip's tribe, learned of this plot, and lost no time in revealing it to the Plymouth authorities. From then on this Indian missionary was a doomed man. Soon after Philip returned from defending himself before the Plymouth Court—he was dismissed because of lack of evidence of the alleged plot—Sassamon was found murdered. Within a week the supposed murderers were apprehended; three of them a few days later were tried, convicted, and executed for this murder. This was the last blow for the Wampanoag sachem. Hastily he collected his warriors for a surprise attack on Swansea, which would mark the beginning of that life-and-death clash between the red and the white man known in the annals of New England as King Philip's War.

Since the New England Confederacy was now primarily concerned with rallying the colonies for a united defense, intercolonial cooperative action in other fields tended to avoid the Confederacy. The contributions of "colledg corn" for Harvard were still received, but they were the affairs of the individual towns and not of the Confederation.[47] Besides their inter-session conferences concerning the "Indian Worke,"[48] many of the men who served as Commissioners participated in land conferences with delegates from Rhode Island in an effort to settle finally jurisdiction over the King's Province, the Narragansett country.[49] But still no final verdict was reached. Nevertheless, cooperative action was beginning to be recognized as extending beyond the boundaries of the three confederate colonies.

While it appeared that the Indian problem was subsiding, the Commissioners of the United Colonies found themselves for the third time in the midst of an Anglo-Dutch war. The royal government quickly realized the advantages of raising a large military force in the United Colonies to prevent the Dutch from establishing a hold again in the American colonies. A New England force, "though they be factious," combined with troops from the other English settlements in the New World could secure New York and even be used in the "reducing of Cannada." But the New Englanders found that an invasion of Canada at this time was not wise because of the difficulty of marching "over the rocky mounteines and howling desarts about fower hundred mile."[50]

The news of a declaration of war between Holland and England, reaching the New England colonies in the spring of 1672,[51] had hastened the negotiations for union, and because of the need for immediate defense of the colonies, the spirit of compromise prevailed and the union was soon consummated. Because of the fears of a Dutch attack, even Rhode Island was invited to send delegates to the Plymouth meeting of the Commissioners in September, 1672.[52] But there is no evidence to indicate that the Ishmael colony accepted this invitation to participate in "united advice for the publick defence."

The fears of the colonists proved justified. In the summer of 1673 a Dutch fleet appeared in American waters and forced the submission of New York and Albany. When property of one of the citizens of Connecticut was seized by the Dutch, the General Assembly informed the Dutch commander that "we must let you know, that we and our confederates, the united Colonies of New England, are by our Royall Soveraign Charles the Second, made keepers of his Majestyes Colonies in New-England."[53] The Bay, addressing its "very Affectionate friends and Confoederates" of the River Colony declared that for the mutual defense five hundred and sixty foot soldiers and two troop of horse to march at two days warning were being raised— Daniel Denison was chosen commander in chief. It was desired that Connecticut make known its course of action as soon as possible. Connecticut likewise lost little time in making military preparations. A "Grand Committee," consisting of the officers of the colony, all the Assistants, and a group of the Deputies, was named to supervise the raising of a force of five hundred dragoons and to bring the train bands of the colony into readiness.[54] Plymouth because of the Indian threat already had mobilized under the direction of its council of war.

New England shipping suffered in this contest with the Dutch. All intercourse with the Dutch at New York was prohibited, which encouraged smuggling.[55] Trading vessels fell prey to the Dutch "in all parts where we trade or are going to the ports of our traffic"; they "make no difference between New England and Old."[56] There was no question that the Dutch had a powerful fleet in the New World. When the Dutch bombarded New York, guns were heard all day as far away as Stratford, and it was reported that three thousand Dutch troops had landed.[57] Former New Haven magistrates pressed the Hartford Court "to consult what is best to be don for comon safety, both for sea and shore," if necessary to call a special session of the Confederation.[58] The Governor of Connecticut was also requested to send "some fit person" to the Dutch at New York to determine whether "they intend warr on the united Colonyes by land or sea," that the English would not "relinguish any part of our present bounds on Long Island."[59]

Because of the serious threat posed by the recapture of New York by the Dutch fleet, the Governor and Magistrates of Connecticut issued a call for an extraordinary session of the Confederation. It was understood that the Commissioners would let the individual "committees of safety" of the colonies manage their own war preparations. The purpose of summoning the Confederation was to secure a "unanimous resolution" for defending the colonies.[60] Particularly were the Connecticut authorities concerned about the fate of the Long Island towns. These towns had for the most part once been under the jurisdiction of New Haven or Connecticut, and now with "no others of England to take us into protection" they appealed to Connecticut to protect them against Dutch rule.[61] Thus there was ample motive for the River Colony to raise an expedition against the Dutch: by recovering the Long Island towns for England, perhaps a gracious king would restore them to the jurisdiction of Connecticut, severing them from the Duke's rule at New York.

Convening in emergency session on the 31st of August,[62] the Commissioners at Hartford unanimously declared that the colonies would provide for their "comon Safety," giving warning to the Dutch that any damage done to any one of the United

Colonies would be accounted done to the "whole." Furthermore, "we must let you know, that we and our confederates, the united Colonies of New England, are by our Royal Sovereign Charles the 2d, made keepers of his subjects liberties in these parts, and do hope to acquit ourselves in that trust." The general courts of the United Colonies were asked to provide for adequate measures for defense so "that there will be no disappointment of aid to any one of the Colonies which may be first invaded."[63]

Following the recommendations of the Commissioners, military preparations were intensified in the United Colonies. In the Bay, Daniel Denison, Major of the Essex regiment, was "empowered and required to send 'relief and succor' to any port in that county in case of the receipt of tidings of the approach of the enemy."[64] Massachusetts also ordered that a detachment of foot soldiers in addition to the regular number of troopers be kept in readiness in the event of a Dutch attack.[65] The home government was so pleased with the enthusiasm of the United Colonies in its preparations for war, that it was not deemed necessary to dispatch an English army to the New World.[66] The three United Colonies made preparations for a joint expedition to be sent against the Dutch,[67] with the Bay fitting out two of its best ships with a contingent of two hundred troops, "for the deffence of our Navigation; and to Joyne with our Confederates as matters may present and as maybe advised and Agreed on by common Consent of the Colonyes."[68] In Connecticut, the Commissioner of the United Colonies, Major John Talcott, was appointed by the General Court to be "Commander in Cheife of such military forces as shall be raysed in this Colony and sent against N. Yorke."[69]

When it was learned that Southampton was in danger of an attack by a combined force of the Dutch and the Indians, a detachment of Connecticut troops under Fitz-John Winthrop, son of the venerable Governor and Commissioner, was ordered to Southampton. Winthrop's specific mission was to determine the plans of the Dutch, informing the General Court accordingly, and to aid the Long Islanders in case of an attack by the Dutch.[70] Meanwhile the two easterly colonies proceeded more cautiously in their war preparations. Though Plymouth agreed to participate in a joint expedition, the colony would not do so "according to what wee are proportioned by our confeaderates, wherein we are apparently over rated"—but a contingent of a hundred men was authorized.[71] There were other misgivings. A need was felt for more "mature consultations."[72] Governor Leverett of the Bay, an old hand on both sides of the Atlantic in the knowledge of military affairs, pointed out that "in case of proceding to action, there must be Commissioners from the severall Colonys impowered that may bee at some place neere the place for action." Conducting a war through "Long postages" was especially decried by Leverett.[73] In this proposal were envisaged a notion of a unified military command and, with the state of communications as they were in the seventeenth century, the need for flexible authority for battlefield commanders. More important, however, the proposal of Leverett was an early expression of the conception that commissions for intercolonial cooperative action were best suited as councils of war, a theory which hindered the development of American federalism until the time of the Revolutionary War.

The only action between the New England troops and the Dutch came on the 25th of February (O. S.) at Southold, Long Island. There, Winthrop with his motley force of Connecticut militia and Long Island volunteers, in an exchange of volleys with the Dutch ship, the *Snow,* prevented the landing of a Dutch force.[74] After this sortie, Winthrop was ordered by the Connecticut Council to remain on Long Island to repulse any Dutch attack, in which event he would have the assistance of two men of war from the Bay.[75] There was some sentiment in the colonies to go beyond defensive measures and carry the war to the Dutch.[76] News of peace between Holland and England, however, arrived before the United Colonies could take a more aggressive course;[77] in anticipation of the conclusion of the war, the Connecticut Council, already a few weeks before receiving news of the peace, ordered the release of Winthrop's troops on Long Island, expecting them to be transported back to the colonies on the Massachusetts men of war.[78] The Dutch recapture of New York had thus given new life to the Confederation. The war with Holland, beginning in 1672, and the Indian threat hastened the re-forming of the Confederation. The appeal of the Long Island towns for aid from the United Colonies and the very real possibility that the Dutch fleet might make a raid on one of the New England ports, combined with the depredations on English shipping off the American coasts, provided rallying points for all three members of the Confederacy. For the first time, with virtually no guidance from the home country, the three Puritan colonies raised a force on their own to send against the Dutch—in the times of 1654 and 1664, the raising of an expedition in New England was to supplement a force of Cromwell or of Charles II. Once again in intercolonial correspondence were heard such expressions as "in confidence . . . of your complyance with us according to our articles."[78]

The new Confederacy was dedicated to the principle of military expediency. Had it not been for the threats of Indian hostilities and of foreign aggression, the Confederacy would probably have never been revived. The ties of religion were not as great as they had been; nor was there the excuse for uniting because of a disinterested home government. Unlike the great expectations for the first Confederacy, the revived union of 1672 was not required to perform as a superstructure of intercolonial government. The Articles of 1672 dispersed any such ideas; the revised Articles also stated clearly the limited jurisdiction of the Confederation. The United Colonies of New England was now truly a "league of defense." It would seek deterrents to war; in a war emergency it would combine the resources of the colonies; and as a Council of War it would coordinate the efforts of the colonies. There was no longer need for lofty deliberations in the council chambers of the Confederacy, nor need to subject questions of great moment to the hair-splitting of the Puritans. Those times were past. The new Confederacy was an agency to pool the military strength of the colonies for their mutual protection. For this practical purpose it existed—nothing else was required.

---

[1] CA, I, 89, 30Aug62(?).

[2] MA, III, 433, n.d.

[3] PCR, IV, 92.

[4] PCR, X, 319.

[5] Ibid., pp. 324-5.

[6] Ibid., p. 326.

[7] MCR, IV, Pt. 2, 353-4. Members of this committee were Gookin, Hathorne, Stoddard, and Bartholomew.

[8] MA, II, 359.

[9] CCR, II, 122; MCR, IV, Pt. 2, 443; MHSC 3: III:210; Winthrop Papers, MHSC 4:VII:599-600. In the meantime the Governor was substituted for Bradstreet in the Bay; the full committee of the colonies in June consisting of

Bellingham, Danforth, and Leverett for Mass.; Josiah Winslow for Plymouth; and Willys and Talcott for Conn. (MCR, IV, Pt. 2, 461; PCR, X, 345.)

[10] PCR, X, 345; J. H. Benton, op. cit. (Town House), p. 166.

[11] MA, II, 186; CCR, II, 143-4, 154; PCR, X, 451; William Brigham, ed., The Compact with the Charter and Laws of New Plymouth, p. 163.

[12] Bowen, op. cit. (Rehoboth), I, 24. Since the ratio of 100-30-60 was considered the actual ratio of the population of the three colonies, then the percentages of population would be as follows: Massachusetts, 52.7%; Plymouth, 15.8%; and Connecticut, 31.5%.

[13] MCR, IV, Pt. 2, 501-3; also cf. the Articles of 1670 and the final version of 1672. (PCR, X, 334-351.)

[14] A Declaration was drawn up by Connecticut and Massachusetts in May, 1672 (June, N. S.), stating that a compromise was reached and their intent for renewing the Confederation in September. (Winslow Papers, MHS, I, 76.) A large, impressive looking copy of the Articles of 1672 on three folio pages may be found in CA, I, 90.

[15] CCR, II, 169; MCR, IV, Pt. 2, 514. The Commission for the Massachusetts Commissioners for this first meeting under the new Articles is of interest enough to include in full:

"Whereas upon serious Consideration, We have concluded a Confederation with the English Colonies of New-Plimouth and as the Bond of Nature, Reason, Religion and Respect to our Nation doth Require:

We have this Court Chosen our Trustie and well beloved Friends (S. B.) and (T. D.) [Bradstreet and Danforth] for this Colonie; for a full and compleat Year, as any Occassions and Exigents may Require, and particularly for the next meeting at (P) And do Invest them with full Power and Authority, to Treat and Conclude of all things, according to the true Tenour and Meaning of the Articles of Confederation of the United Colonies, Concluded by the General Court held at Boston the fifteenth of May 1672." (Whitmore, Colonial Laws of Massachusetts, (1672), p. 163.)

[16] PCR, V, 99. Because of the Dutch and Indian situation, it was thought possible that an emergency session might have to be called before September. (MA, III, 435a.)

[17] It had become a practice among the colonies to elect three men as Commissioners, the third serving if one of the others was ill-disposed. (For the election of Commissioners by the freemen and not the general courts and the method of proxy voting, see Brigham, op. cit., pp. 97, 123, 259; Massachusetts Colonial Laws, 1647.)

[18] New Haven's union with Connecticut would "alwaies be Interpreted as by theire owne Consession and not otherwise." (Article 15. PCR, X, 351.)

[19] PCR, X, 389.

[20] PCR, X, 354-5.

[21] Eliot to Stiles, 1673, MHSC, 1:X:124.

[22] Winthrop to Lovelace, 9Dec70, W. G. Lane Collections, Yale University Li-

brary; Thomas F. Waters, *John Winthrop, Jr., Publications of Ipswich Hist. Soc.*, VII (1899), 57-9.

[23] CA, Misc., I, 92.

[24] Gookin, *op. cit.*, pp. 207-8.

[25] Samuel Drake, ed., "The Present State of New England," *The Old Indian Chronicle*, (Boston: 1867), p. 168.

[26] *CCR*, III, 574-6.

[27] "County Records of the Suffolk County Court," *PSCM*, III, 193, 219.

[28] "Records of Suffolk County Court," *PSCM*, III, 225.

[29] *PCR*, X, 389.

[30] *Ibid.*, V., 210.

[31] *Records of the Massachusetts Court of Assistants*, I, 95, 208-9. The suits involved the estate of Marmaduke Johnson, deceased, printer for the Corporation, and the guardianship of an Indian sachem's son by the two Massachusetts Commissioners.

[32] DeForest, *History of the Indians of Connecticut*, (Hartford: 1852), p. 259. In Connecticut Thomas Stanton received a good part of the wampum collected from the Pequots in their annual tribute; and Captain Denison of Stonington acted as a superintendent over the two Indian governors, much as Gookin did in the Bay.

[33] *CCR*, II, 548.

[34] This first "Confederacy" in America is interesting for its symbolism. The symbol of the "Great Peace," the ideal of the confederacy, was a tree with roots firmly planted in the earth. "In general the Tree signified the Law, that is, the constitution, which expressed the terms of their union." The "Branches signified shelter, the protection and security that people found in shadow of Law. The Roots, which stretched to the four quarters of the earth, signified the extension of the Law," which could take in all mankind not yet members of the league. As these roots would grow other peoples would follow them to their source and "take shelter with others under the tree." The eagle on the tree in this symbolism of the Iroquois confederacy meant eternal watchfulness and readiness to give alarm to the confederates in time of emergency. (For this picturesque story, see Paul A. Wallace, *The White Roots of Peace* (Phila.: 1946), pp. 6-7.

[35] Allyn to Winthrop, 25Jul70, MHS, Winthrop Papers, X, 19.

[36] John Easton, *A Narrative of the Causes which led to Philip's Indian War*, ed. by F. B. Hough, (Albany: 1858), p. 37, 24Aug69.

[37] *Ibid.*, p. 8; Philip to Gov. Prence, 29May71, Winslow Papers, MHS, I, 59.

[38] Easton, *op. cit.*, Pierce, *op. cit.*, (Civil Lists), p. 93.

[39] Drake, (The Old Indian Chronicle, Introd., p. 78.

[40] *PCR*, V, 77.

[41] Drake, *op. cit.*, p. 79.

[42] Letters from the Bay had been sent to Plymouth accusing it of "being hasty to engage in a quarell" and inciting rebellion among the Indians. (Wins-

low Papers, 13Mar70/1, MHS, I, 51; Gookin to Prence, 12Apr71, *MHSC* 1:VI:198-9.)

[43] From Conn. and Mass., Winthrop, Leverett, Danforth, and Davis were represented (Palfrey, *op. cit.*, III, 119.) There was no meeting of the Confederation this year.

[44] Drake, *op. cit.*, pp. 82-4. For the articles of this treaty see Increase Mather, *Early History of New England*, (Boston: 1864), p. 233.

[45] Williams to the Commissioners, 12Sep72, *MHSP* 2:III:258. In 1678, after the war, Williams proposed to the Commissioners that they join with New York and Rhode Island for a "League defensive against the Barbarians or a foreign Enemy." (25Aug78, *RIHS Tracts*, XIV (1881), 62.)

[46] Douglas E. Leach, "The Causes and Effects of King Philip's War," Unpublished Ph.D. Thesis, Harvard University, 1950, pp. 25, 144.

[47] James R. Trumbull, *History of Northampton*, (1898), I, 224-5.

[48] Sickness and the "tedious" journey often prevented the holding of these informal meetings. (CA, I, 92.) Danforth on at least one occasion substituted for Captain Gookin in holding court. (MA, XXXIX, 387.)

[49] CA, Boundaries (R. I.), I, 33, 79, 80 and III, 2; MA, II, 52, 192; Clarence W. Bowen, *The Boundary Disputes of Connecticut*, (Boston: 1882), p. 37. Massachusetts, still citing the Commissioners' order of 1658, sought jurisdiction in the Pequot Country.

[50] *MCR*, IV, Pt. 2, 316; Sainsbury, *Calendar of State Papers*, VII, #566, 1159.

[51] CA, *Foreign Affairs*, I, 7, 24Apr72. Asked one contemporary in 1671: "What did the United Colonies intend by the publick reading of the King's Declaration? Did they intend to proclaime Warr against the Dutch; or onely to inform theire people that the K. was ingaged in a warr. . . ." *(The Mather Papers*, Ltr of William Goffe, *MHSC* 4:VIII:130-1.)

[52] Winslow Papers, MHS, I, 178; *Winthrop Papers*, *MHSC* 3:X:82-3, 83-4.

[53] CA, Boundaries (N. Y.), II, 14, 16, 20.

[54] *CCR*, II, 204-6.

[55] William B. Weeden, *Economic and Social History of New England*, (Boston: 1890), I, 240-1.

[56] Hull, *Diary*, 237.

[57] Jones to Leete, 31Jul73, Winthrop Papers, MHS, XIV, 81.

[58] Jones, Leete, Nash to Winthrop, 2Aug73, *Winthrop Papers*, *MHSC* 4:VII:570-1.

[59] Jones to Winthrop, Aug73, Winthrop Papers, MHS, XIV, 82.

[60] MA, LXVII, 189.

[61] *Ibid.*; MA, LXVII, 195; R. C. Winthrop Collection, I, 19. Southampton was the town of greatest concern.

[62] 21Aug73 (O. S.).

[63] MA, LXVII, 178; *PCR*, X, 387-8.

[64] MA, LXVII, 195; the quotation is in D. D. Slade, "Daniel Denison," *PCSM*, I, 127.

[65] Slade, *ibid.*

[66] Propositions re N. Y., Sep73, Bancroft Transcripts (N. E.), West Indies, II, 223-7, NYPL.

[67] Winslow Papers, I, 85; MA, LXVII, 185; *CCR*, II, 216, 561-6.

[68] MA, LXVII, 194.

[69] *CCR*, II, 218.

[70] Order of 22Oct73, *CHSC*, XXIV, 17.

[71] Peirce, *op. cit.* (Civil Lists), p. 95, Dec73.

[72] MA, LXVII, 196a.

[73] Leverett to Josiah Winslow, 13Dec73, Winslow Papers, MHS, I, 87.

[74] *CCR*, II, 566-7; George R. Howell, *The Early History of Southampton*, L. I., (Albany: 1887), pp. 63-4.

[75] Conn. Council to Major Winthrop, 2Mar73/4 and Pynchon to Gov. Winthrop, 9Apr74, Winthrop Papers, MHS, X, 21 and XVII, 7, resp.; Mass. Council to Winslow, 14Mar73/4, *MHSC* 1:VI:87-8.

[76] E.g., Mathias Nicolls to Winthrop, *Winthrop Papers*, 16Mar73/4, *MHSC* 3:X:99-100.

[77] MA, LXVII, 199; *CCR*, II, 222.

[78] MA, III, 436; *ibid.*, LXI, 46.

CHAPTER XIII

Triumph of Military Expediency

The darkening skies that hovered over the early days of the second Confederacy now burst forth with the savage fury of Indian warfare. King Philip, wryly smarting under his ill treatment from Plymouth Colony, had chosen the day for vengeance. On a quiet Sabbath in June, 1675, Philip's Indians approached the frontier town of Swansea, bordering on the Mount Hope lands of King Philip, and set fire to several English houses. The savages returned three times in the course of a week, each time more emboldened and more lustful for blood. When they were through with their gruesome mission, the settlement was in ruins and the toll was heavy with the mangled bodies of the unfortunate inhabitants. The burning of Swansea set off the most disastrous Indian war in the history of New England.

A Plymouth force, under two former Commissioners of the United Colonies, Majors Cudworth and William Bradford, was immediately dispatched to the area of hostilities. They were soon joined at Swansea by a Massachusetts force. This prompt action was the result of military preparations that had been under way in both colonies. Upon the arrival of further reinforcements from Boston, the English force pushed on to Philip's quarters at Mount Hope, where all that was found were the heads of eight Englishmen raised on poles. The crafty Wampanoag sachem had fled. While the English forces were thus occupied, parties of Philip's Indians fell upon other Plymouth settlements, massacring the inhabitants.[1] The uprising of the Wampanoags soon proved to be a contagion. By the end of July, Philip's Indians were allied with the powerful Narragansetts, and a second theater of war had opened in the Connecticut Valley. The traditional allies of the English, the Mohegans, anxious to bring their enemy, the Narragansetts, to terms, reaffirmed their loyalty to the English. They pledged that, in the event of war, they would drive the Narragansetts to "their forts and then they will be in a sutable posture for the English to doe their pleasure with them."[2] Virtually all other New England Indians—except the majority of the remnant Pequots—joined in the uprising

What was the nature of this Indian rebellion? Most historians of New England have depicted Philip as a great chieftain, whose exceptional organizing and leadership ability united the diverse tribes of New England for a great, last ditch stand against the encroachments of the English. There is no doubt that Philip was endowed with some military ability, which is evident by his outmaneuvering the English forces on several occasions. There is also no doubt that this second son of Massasoit had long plotted to make a stand against the English—witness Philip's refusal to abide by Indian treaties with the English, even though these were made under duress, the testimony of the trusted Indian servant, John Sassamon, and Sassamon's subsequent murder in January, 1675.[3] But there is a question whether Philip exerted any widespread influence. The Nipmuck uprising and the attack of the English on the Narragansetts were independent of Philip's efforts. Even in Plymouth many of the natives did not give him their allegiance and he was unsuccessful in bringing in the New Hampshire tribes at this time. Although one may not go so far to say that "the King Philip of the annals is certainly a creature of the imagination,"[4] the uprising of the New England Indians was spontaneous rather than resulting from a preconceived plan. The only credit that can be given to Philip was that he had the audacity to attack the English outright, an act which heartened all the red men of the wilderness to throw off the English yoke. If Philip had been a great leader and the inter-tribal rivalry was not what it was, a great Indian confederacy might have been achieved. But as it was, even the powerful Narragansetts were never brought actively into the war, and they were crushed before they could join forces with the other tribes. The power of Philip is more legend than fact; yet his unquenched hatred for the English inspired other savages to deeds they would not otherwise have done—and to the panicky New Englanders he became the Devil incarnate.

The outbreak of King Philip's War, as this general uprising of the New England Indians of 1675-7 has been called, brought the colonists to an even greater awareness of the advantages of cooperative military action. Governor Leverett of the Bay, learning of the Swansea massacres, informed the Plymouth

Governor: "Assure yourself nothing shall be wanting in us to Approve ourselves your loving neighbours and Confederates."[5] Governor Andros at New York immediately responded with aid for his brothers in distress, but in such a way as was not appreciated by the New England colonists. As soon as the Duke's Governor received word of the "Christyan Misfortunes and hard disasters" at Plymouth, he immediately hopped aboard ship with some of his troops and sailed for the Connecticut River. At Saybrook, however, the New York Governor had a surprise in store for him. The authorities of the River did not look upon a visit by Andros as a gesture for aiding the New England colonies in their war against the Indians, but rather that Andros was more interested in asserting the claims of a new patent of the Duke's, which was to take for the Province of New York all lands west of the Connecticut River. A force of a hundred men from Hartford was dispatched to Saybrook to prevent the landing of Andros; the "challeng and attempts to surprize the mayne port of the sayd Colony" was thus firmly met, and Andros, not daring to fire upon the King's colors flown by the Connecticut troops, was forced to return home.[6] For the first time the Stuart regime had thus encountered armed resistance in the New England colonies. Andros continued to manifest his concern for the United Colonies in putting down the Indian uprising, and to demonstrate his good intentions he reinforced Albany, which was of value by showing strength to the Mohawks and deterring the westward movement of Philip's roving Indians.[7]

The Puritan colonies went all out in mobilizing for war. Plymouth Colony already had a firm military organization. In 1658, Plymouth had given local military units regimental organization and combined trainings were held under the generalship of Josiah Winslow. But the most interesting development in the colony was the emergence of the supreme military-civil authority in the form of the Council of War. Similar to the councils of magistrates in the other colonies, which included the Commissioners of the United Colonies for the colony, the Plymouth Council was the only one expressly military. The councils in the other two colonies likewise supervised the conduct of the war in their colonies, but they allowed greater autonomy to the town councils of war, which exercised immediate supervision over the troops in the vicinity of the hostilities.[8] Because the Indians increased their raids on English settlements, attacking

Rehoboth and coming as close as thirty-two miles to Boston,[9] garrison houses, usually the most sturdy houses, where the townspeople could seek refuge and defend themselves as a unit against Indian attack, were designated in the frontier towns.[10] A council, meeting in Boston, declared all trade with the Indians illegal. The emergency plan determined by the Commissioners some years before was now put into effect. By this plan, no Indians were allowed to come within a one mile radius of an English settlement unless accompanied by Englishmen.[11]

Rhode Island, whose backyard with that of Plymouth's was the site for the beginning of hostilities, immediately cooperated with the United Colonies to put down the rebellion. Shortly after the raids on Swansea, several sloops were impressed into service to transport Massachusetts and Plymouth troops and ammunition and arms.[12]

The combined forces of Massachusetts and Plymouth performed mopping up operations in the Pocasset Swamp and searched for the Narragansett sachems who were reportedly allying themselves with Philip. Philip was pent up in the Swamp, which gave rise to the belief that the war would be brought to a swift close. Thus Major Savage and his Massachusetts troops returned to Boston; only a hundred men were left to assist the Plymouth force in rooting out the enemy. The full Massachusetts force had been in the field for twenty-four days, and the main accomplishment during that time, besides cornering Philip in the Pocasset Swamp, was the signing of a treaty of peace with the Narragansett Indians.[13] However, withdrawing the Massachusetts troops at this time was a great tactical error. At no other time during the course of the war would Philip be confronted with so great odds as at this time, estimated at six Englishmen to one Indian.[4] Because the enemy was not destroyed when there was opportunity, Philip escaped with a "flying armie,"[15] and Indians in other parts were encouraged to rise up against the English. It seems, however, that Massachusetts, instead of trying to crush the enemy, was more bent upon accomplishing her ends through diplomacy. The Narragansetts had come to an agreement, not to proceed with the western Indians; if both tribes could be effectively severed from any connection with Philip's Indians, then a general uprising might be averted.

The Massachusetts Council turned to negotiations with the Nipmucks and other Indians of western New England. By the

middle of July seven of the principal Indian towns had made
treaties with the English in this region.[16] But one group of Nipmucks at Quabaug, the present site of Brookfield, remained
defiant. To change this recalcitrant attitude, the Bay Council
dispatched Captains Edward Hutchinson and Thomas Wheeler
with some twenty troopers to bring the defiant Indians to terms.
But after making arrangements for a parley with these Indians
at Quabaug, the English party was set upon in ambush. Only
half of them escaped, and Captain Hutchinson was mortally
wounded.[17] About the same time the Nipmucks were emboldened to attack the settlement at Mendon.[18] Swiftly, other
attacks followed on the western settlements of the Bay, and
the Boston authorities recalled Captain Henchman and his
forces from Plymouth to aid these frontier settlements. A sinister
silence fell over the western frontier during the first part of
August. At the English outpost at Squakheag the silence was
unbroken except for the soft bleating of the sheep and the
lowing of the cattle—then suddenly these sounds were no longer
heard: the sheep and cattle had disappeared.[19] For the scouts of
John Pynchon at Springfield this meant one thing, the Indians
had made a raid to replenish their food supply. The frontier
braced itself for the renewal of hostilities.

Philip with a small band of Indians from his own tribe soon
appeared in Nipmuck country, and other Indians strange to that
part of the country were noticed among the Nipmucks and the
Pocomtucks. The theater of war had shifted. The Bay sent forces
under Captains Beers, Lothrop, and Mosely to aid the Massachusetts troops already in the vicinity—with headquarters at
Hadley. The River Colony also had a motley force of frontiers-
men and Mohegans in the field, with Major Pynchon the commander in chief. Brookfield was attacked early in August and
assaults on other towns on the western frontier of the Bay
followed within the course of a few weeks. Though a large force
of Connecticut and Massachusetts troops continued to comb the
Valley, the elusive savages were always one step ahead of the
English. When a force was sent out to subdue a Pocomtuck
fort, it was found abandoned with only the dead body of a
sachem who had opposed the younger war faction of the Indians. Ambuscades took the lives of two Massachusetts captains,
Beers of Watertown and Lothrop of Ipswich, and nearly wiped
out their entire companies. The folklore of the terror created

by the visitation of the red man on these westerly settlements—
the massacre of "Bloody Brooks," the appearance in person or
ghost of William Goffe, the regicide, directing the defense of
Hadley, or the tales of escape and captivity—have been the
subject of many accounts[20] and need not be repeated here. It is
only important to note that the war had shifted within a few
weeks after the uprising of Philip's small band in Plymouth to
the rebellion of the more powerful tribes of Nipmucks and
Pocomtucks on the River. While Plymouth continued to patrol
her own bounds for hostile Indians, the Bay and River colonies
had deployed a large number of troops to patrol the River and
bring an end to the terrorizing of the Valley settlements.

When the initial outbursts of Indian hostilities had subsided
in Plymouth, Governor Winslow wrote the governors of the
other two confederate colonies, informing them that while "it
pleaseth God to keep us still under the rod, our enemy keeping
themselves cloase within the most hideous swamps they can
fine," it was a suitable time to convene the Confederation. Thus
exercising their right according to the Articles of Confederation,
members of the Plymouth Council issued a call for a meeting
of the Confederation.[21] An emergency session, however, did not
convene in August, probably due to the closeness of the regular
triennial session in September and also because of the sudden
outbreak of hostilities on the western borders of the Bay, which
demanded the full attention of the Massachusetts Council. The
military nature of the colonial governments during this period
has been noted—control of the war being virtually in the hands
of the colonial councils of magistrates, the Puritan solution for
the exercise of executive powers. Even in the more liberal colony
of Connecticut the Council waxed supreme, but it was the only
one of the three confederate colonies to give to the governor
alone a semblance of executive responsibility.[22] Governor Winslow of Plymouth,[23] however, would soon be appointed by the
United Colonies as commander in chief—the first intercolonial
fusion of consultative powers (on the intercolonial level Winslow
was a member of the council of Commissioners of the United
Colonies) and actual military powers. The session of the Confederation convening in September was the super-war council
for the colonies.

The second meeting of the Commissioners, not counting their
brief extraordinary session of 1673 at Hartford, was underway

at the appointed time, the first Thursday in September. Since the colonies were already engaged in fighting the war their own way, combining forces when necessary, a meeting of the Commissioners coming several months after the start of hostilities was considered by some to be too late to be of value.[24] Yet the Confederation was expected to provide a unified system of command for forces of the colonies when they were acting jointly,[25] and to help bring about a treaty with the Mohawks.[26]

The first act of the Commissioners was to accept their constitutional responsibility of coordinating the efforts of the colonies in this war.[27] While the Commissioners gravely turned their attention to the distressing conditions on the frontier, the Bay Colony declared a day for "publick humiliation, with fasting, and prayer, thoroughout this whol Colonie," remembering the "distressed state of the rest of the Colonies confederate with our selves;"[28] and the Deputy Governor at Hartford prayerfully wrote Governor Winthrop, who was attending the Confederation as a Commissioner from Connecticut, that "the good Lord guide the Comissioners to a right order standing of the foundations of the war" and that he was "apt to thinke that the Comissioners have a price in their handes," which could "be no wayes better improved, then to purchase so many foreskins of these Philistines now in hostility."[29] The Commissioners faced a most serious task: directing the great war for securing the Promised Land for themselves—which called forth the great leadership of such as Winthrop,[30] Richards, Danforth, Stoughton, Winslow, and Hinckley.

True to the Puritan penchant for justification of all acts, the Commissioners from Plymouth presented a "Narrative" of the opening of hostilities in Plymouth and the subsequent measures of the colonies to put down the uprising.[31] With the reading of this narrative, grounds were declared to exist for carrying on the war because it was both "Just and Nessarie" and "in its first Rise a defensive warr," and therefore should be "bourne and payed as is agreed in the articles of Confederation."[32] The Commissioners of the United Colonies met in almost continuous session until April, 1676, most of which time, however, was more as an open military conference of colonial leaders and not officially as Commissioners of the Confederation; nevertheless there were intermittent official sessions.

The first phase of this long session may be assumed, from the

sketchy records at this time, to have been held from September 9
October 2 (O. S.). During this period orders were issued by the
Commissioners to raise one thousand soldiers to serve as a ready
reserve for the service of the United Colonies, especially for occasions arising in the "Westerly Plantations." Two hundred of
these troops were to be raised immediately, and provisioned
for fourteen days: the total number of troops to be deployed on
the River to be five hundred. But an important stipulation was
made by the Commissioners, which would later become a
cause of dissension, namely that

> these Soldiers are not to bee fixed in any garrison, but to
> bee vigorously emploied in a fielde Army for the pursuit
> of the Enemy as God shall give opportunity: And there-
> fore they are not by any Authority to bee called off from
> those plantations but by speciall Order of the Commis-
> sioners or by the joint advice and consent of their own
> Councill of Officers, when they shall see it necessary upon
> the removall of the Enemy elsewhere, to march to any
> other place of the United Colonys for theire more Speedy
> releife and the distressing of the Enemy.[33]

A blank commission was issued for a "commander in cheife
over the forces of these united colonies," to be appointed by the
colony where the military action was taking place. The commander in chief was to abide by the "most approved rules of
Military discipline and lawes of war and observing such Instructions as you shall herewith receave from us, or as you shall afterwards receave from us or from the three Generall courts of these
united Colonies, equally concurring."[34] Major John Pynchon
was the first to have this honor of commanding the united forces
on the River, but because of the burning of Springfield by the
Indians, Pynchon was disheartened at the great damage he
sustained as a large landholder of the town and, wishing to be
with his family, tendered his resignation. Captain Samuel Appleton, a fiery soldier from Essex County, was immediately appointed to succeed Pynchon to the generalship of the River
army.[35]

The confederate army during October was extremely active
in the Valley. The Indians were heavily defeated when their
attack on Hatfield was repulsed. Phillip's band soon went into

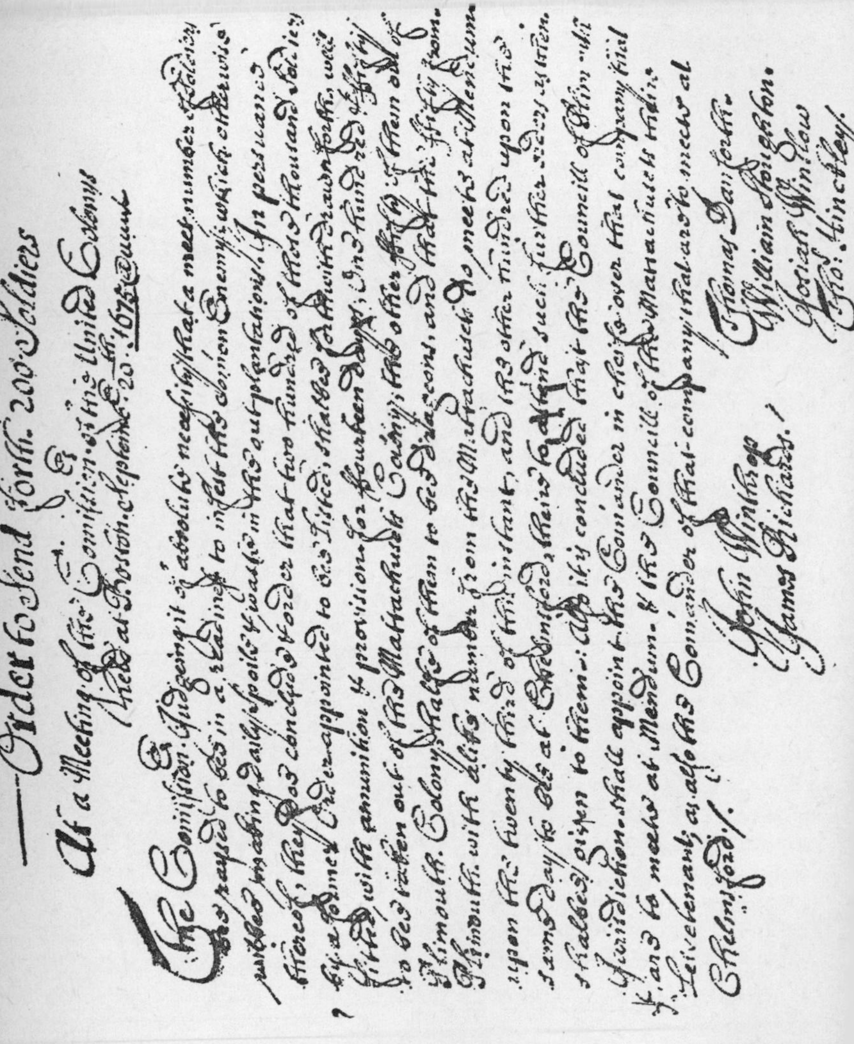
Order to Send forth 200 Soldiers

At a Meeting of the Comission of the United Colonys
held at Boston September 20th 1675 Annum

The Comission Judgeing it of absolute necessity that a meet number of Soldiers bee rayseed to bee in a readiness to infest the comon Enemy, which otherwise will bee making daily spoils & waste in the out plantations. In persuance thereof, they doe conclude & order that two hundred of those thousand Soldiers by a former Order appointed to bee listed, shall bee forthwith drawn forth, well fitted with amunition & provision for fourteen dayes; One hundred & fifty to bee taken out of the Mattachusets Colony; the other fifty of them out of Plimouth Colony, halfe of them to bee dragoons, and that the fifty from Plimouth with a like number from the Mattachusets to meete at Mendum upon the twenty third of this instant, and the other hundred upon the same day to bee at Chelmsford, there to attend such further orders as then shall bee given to them. Also it is concluded that the Councill of Plim: with Jurisdiction shall appoint the Comander in cheife over that company that are to meete at Mendum, & the Councill of the Mattachusets their Leivetenant; as also the Comander of that company that are to meete at Chelmsford.

John Winthrop
James Richards.
Thomas Danforth.
William Stoughton.
Josiah Winslow
Tho: Hinckley.

Conn. Archives

retirement near Albany for the winter and the Indians practically disappeared from the Valley. A problem was then posed for the confederate forces. Should they set up garrisons to protect the frontier settlements or keep an army in the field, rooting out the enemy? Captain Appleton felt that the Massachusetts Council should revise that part of the "Honord Commissioners order, which strictly prohibite the fixeing of any of our souldiers in garrison"[36] The Connecticut Council had different ideas, and fearing attacks on the lower settlements of the River ordered Major Treat to detach himself from Appleton's army. This raised a furor between the two confederated colonies, each accusing the other of violating the orders of the Commissioners: the Massachusetts' interpretation was that the River Colony should keep its force subordinate to Appleton, assisting him in garrisoning the western Massachusetts towns, whereas Connecticut was afraid if the Indians were not crushed outright they would be in a position to attack the Connecticut settlements. The situation was so serious, tending to preclude cooperation in any future operations, that during the period of adjournment of the Confederation during most of October, Wait Winthrop, the son of the governor, was appointed by the River Colony to replace James Richards in the Confederation. Wait Winthrop was expected to use all his efforts to commit the Commissioners against the policy of garrisoning the settlements and instead to secure the raising of a large expedition.[37]

Wait Winthrop took a few days longer than expected to join his father at the Confederation summit, and while waiting for him to appear, the Commissioners from the other two colonies took advantage of the situation to put through a resolution condemning the withdrawal "of their brethren of Connecticott in a time of so great extremity" as an "absolute violation of the maine ends of the Articles of Confederation."[38] But it was soon obvious that to garrison every town would be a serious drain on the troops and resources of the colonies, and would leave them vulnerable to a large scale Indian attack.

The time was at hand for raising a large expedition. The Narragansetts, long a sore spot to the English, provided a suitable target, especially since they were thought to be "deeply accessory" to the "present bloody outrages of the Barbarous Natives."[39] Since the Indians were not now active on the River or in Plymouth, this great tribe might be crushed before they could ally themselves with Philip's band or the River Indians. The Commissioners, therefore, ordered that another force of a thousand men be raised and kept in combat readiness until the time to march at one hour's notice to a place of rendezvous, and from there to march into the Narragansett country.[40] Each colony was charged with providing these troops with the necessary arms and equipment, and sending them to the places of rendezvous: the Connecticut forces at Norwich, Stonington, and New London; the Plymouth and Massachusetts forces at Rehoboth, Providence, and Warwick. Final orders for this combined army were to be issued on or before the tenth of December.[41] The Commissioners unanimously agreed that Josiah Winslow, the governor of Plymouth, should be the commander in chief of this expedition, with the second in command to be nominated by Connecticut while the army would be in that colony. The three subordinate officers to Winslow were three majors from each colony of troops already in the field: Appleton, Talcott, and Bradford. Winslow, however, was "disabled in Body" at the time, and it was then proposed that the commander in chief should be from the colony in which the war was prosecuted; since the brunt of the war was in western Connecticut at this time, then the commander in chief would automatically be the commander of the Connecticut forces, Major Treat. But the rivalry was such between the Massachusetts and Connecticut troops that for the sake of harmony it was thought wiser to install a Plymouth commander. Winslow, however, was soon able to assume the generalship of this united army, and preparations were made immediately to employ it against the Narragansetts.[42]

The Commissioners desired that the blow against the Narragansetts be struck without waste of time, even in the dead of winter. The element of surprise was essential. The Commissioners reasoned that if they waited until spring the Indians might rise "as one Man," when "they should have the leaves of the trees to befriend them," and could work much destruction before being stopped. If the Commissioners adopted a wait-and-see policy with the Narragansetts, these Indians could gather all their forces together in the meantime and "on a sudden, on any occasion" could "spread themselves like Grasshoppers all over the Country."[43] The loyalty of the Narragansetts was most doubtful at the time of the opening session of the Confederation,[44] as it had been for over a generation. The colonists even viewed with suspicion their Indian allies, the Mohegans and the Pequot-praying Indians, and in the passions of war committed grave injustices to friendly Indians.[45] The only way to remove the threat of the powerful Narragansetts was to beat them to the draw. The Commissioners, therefore, desired the utmost haste in the preparation of the expedition under cover of complete secrecy.[46]

The Commissioners of the United Colonies had now given orders for two armies in two different sectors, involving a total of 2,000 men—a very great number at that time. Indeed, the colonies soon experienced difficulty in raising so great a force. The Massachusetts Court, "taking into consideration the great disappointment the country hath suffered by reason of non appearance of souldiers impressed for severall expeditions," exacted a fine on soldiers not appearing for duty; and if "their neglects or refusall be accompanied with refractorines, reflection or contempt upon authority, such persons shall be punished with death or some other greivous punishment."[47] One soldier in the Bay was even imprisoned for slandering the President of the United Colonies, Thomas Danforth.[48]

It was soon discovered that maintaining two large armies in the field was an impossible task. Samuel Appleton, who had expected to be appointed as the Commanding General for the Narragansett expedition, was still embroiled in the dispute with the Connecticut authorities in his determination to garrison the western settlements. Appleton thought there should be only one army and one commander in chief; but since the Commissioners provided for two military sectors, he would do all he could to maintain the authority of the Commissioners in the western sector. Hurling a direct challenge to the Connecticut War Council, Appleton, appealing to the "intanglements in our treaty of our Confederates," issued a proclamation that "whatever officer or officers shall draw off any forces out of this Jurisdiction without order from the Commissioners, or the Joynt Counsel of the chiefe officers, and license of the Commander in chief of the army: their soe doing is a breach of the Articles of Confoederation of the united Collonyes."[49] Thus Appleton was insisting upon commanding the Connecticut force under Treat, which the River Colony had called home to protect the Connecticut settlements rather than those of the Bay. The Connecticut

Council informed Appleton that the main objective of the Commissioners' orders was to provide for a "vigorous pursuit of the enemy and soe as a confederate army to be kept together in joynt Councill," and the actual management to be left to the "respective Councils of the Collonyes."[50] Major Treat's force was permitted by the Connecticut Council to move down the River away from the inter-colony headquarters at Hadley. Major Appleton, who commanded all the united forces in the western sector only so long as the troops of the other colonies were within the Massachusetts boundary, could not claim authority over the Connecticut troops once they were removed. All the Massachusetts commander could do was his "speciall duty"— a "studious Indeavour to respect and attend the act of the Commissioners." Therefore he granted "permission" for Treat to withdraw, with the exception, however, that "noe orders from or by the Commissioners" should come to the contrary.[51] But while the differences in military strategy were being aired by Major Appleton and the Connecticut Council, the Commissioners did not intervene.[52] Major Appleton, becoming thoroughly confused as to what policy to follow and finding that the towns did not want the burden of supporting a large force in their midst, left only token garrisons in the frontier towns under the charge of town commissioners of war. Thereupon he returned homeward to Ipswich with most of his troops.[53]

The war in the western sector was thus at a standstill. When the attack on Hatfield failed, Philip's Indians began to take refuge with the Narragansetts.[54] The Connecticut and Massachusetts forces had separated from a unified command, and Major Appleton had now returned with most of his troops eastward. The Commissioners' call for a second army of one thousand troops was filled from the ranks of the original force under Appleton and Treat. Since the Narragansett expedition was to be an operation in the eastern sector, Plymouth was also to provide assistance. As soon as Appleton returned home he was summoned to lead the united expedition against the Narragansetts.[55] Preparations moved swiftly and with coordination for an attack upon the Narragansetts. Undoubtedly, the natives, looking to past experience, were not expecting that a large confederate army could be quickly put in the field. No qualms in the Puritan conscience were felt against the intention of the magistrates of the colonies, lawfully now under the New Testament, "to wage war upon just and necessary occasion."[56] The Commissioners of the United Colonies themselves felt that "god calls all the colloneys to use their utmost indeavour to defend his Majestys intrest and their owne."[57] On November 29 the Commissioners published an order that each colony was responsible for supplying its soldiers for two months in the field, taking into consideration the "extremity of the winter season."[58] By December 19, the last day specified by the Commissioners before the expedition was to set out, no word had been received from the Narragansett sachems about complying with the English demands for surrendering hostile Indians harbored by them.[59] The powerful tribes of the Narragansett Country at last would be taught a lesson.

After consultation with Governor Leverett in Boston, General Josiah Winslow, commander in chief of this expedition from the United Colonies, marched with his able assistant, Captain Benjamin Church, an early master of guerrilla warfare,[60] to Dedham Plain where he took command of the Massachusetts troops. This force of six companies was formally turned over to Winslow on the eve of the tenth by Major-General Denison of Massachusetts,[61] and the Bay forces, now under the command of General Winslow, the supreme commander, and his staff, marched to Woodcock's garrison at the present site of North Attleboro,[62] where they spent the night. The next day this Massachusetts contingent of the confederate army reached Seekonk, where, as in the early Plymouth campaign against the initial uprising of Philip's Indians, they were met by a sloop from Rhode Island.[63] Captain Mosely's company with Benjamin Church and Joseph Dudley, members of Winslow's staff, embarked upon this sloop, and the others coming by land and ferry arrived at at the head of the Bay, at Providence. There the Massachusetts force was joined by the Plymouth contingent of two companies. Captain Mosely's company, however, in Richard Smith's sloop by-passed Providence and was brought directly to Wickford. The combined forces at Providence sought to capture a Narragansett sachem in the vicinity, but vainly combed "Pumham's Country" all the Sabbath Day. The Indians managed to elude the English.[64] On the thirteenth the combined force from Providence joined with Captain Mosely's troops at Smith's Landing at Wickford. It was learned there from the new arrivals that Captain Mosely had already begun the campaign against the In dians by capturing forty Indians, one of whom proved to be a very valuable guide. With the juncture of the Plymouth and Bay troops now accomplished, the confederate army was ready to attack the Narragansetts in their stronghold, with the exception of the Connecticut contingent, which had not yet arrived in the Narragansett country.

While the Connecticut troops awaited the order to march,[65] General Winslow took all of his force from Smith's garrison, leaving only Captain Oliver[66] and his company to defend the garrison, scanning the woods, capturing a few Indians, and burning wigwams of the natives. Signs of the presence of numerous Indians were everywhere, and every stump or tree possibly concealed a lurking savage. The shooting down of English stragglers only testified too well to the hostile intent of the savages. On the fifteenth the army spent most of the day in an unsuccessful parley with an Indian who had been friendly with the English and now claimed to represent the Narragansett sachems; soon after this envoy departed, some of the English troops suffered several casualties in an ambush by the Indians. On the sixteenth, Captain Prentice's cavalry company rode out to the Pettasquamscut garrison, which was the expected rendezvous with the Connecticut force, but found that the Indians had completely destroyed the garrison and massacred all but two of its defenders. The River troops had not yet arrived and the morale of the united army sank to a low depth.

There was rejoicing in the camp of the confederate army the next day. News of the arrival of the Connecticut regiment under the command of Major Robert Treat greeted the despondent ears of the united army. On the eighteenth, at the site of the smouldering ruins of the Pettasquamscut garrison, the muster of the Army of the United Colonies was held,[67] and General Winslow, "in compliance to the order" of the Commissioners of the United Colonies, took over as the "Cheife commander and Generall of the united amongst all the colonies."[68] The addition of the Connecticut contingent, consisting of about three hundred English and one hundred and fifty Mohegans,[69] brought the confederate army to over a thousand men, the largest military force yet raised in New England. General Winslow could now get on with his bloody mission. A small garrison was left at Wickford; the army was released of the burden of its some fifty Indian captives when these Indians were sold to Captain

Davenport.[70] With provisions low and the men impatient, the bitter cold of mid-December setting in, General Winslow decided to attack at daybreak, the objective being a fortified Narragansett village some eighteen miles away, where it was rumored that a great gathering of Narragansetts had come to spend the winter.

There was little sleep for the Army of the United Colonies on the Sabbath eve of December 18. The weather was bitter cold, and when the bleak dawn came on the 19th there was a blinding snowstorm to greet the weary New Englanders. At five o'clock this Sunday morning, the confederate army began its march upland towards the Narragansett fort, guided by its Indian informer along a circuitous route, in order to prevent being ambushed. The march was steady. The troops filed through the wilderness in the order that they would meet the enemy: first the Massachusetts troops of Mosely and Davenport, followed by the other Bay troops, Major Treat's troops, with the Plymouth force bringing up the rear. At one o'clock in the afternoon the makeshift fort of the Indians on an island surrounded by a frozen swamp was sighted.[71] The Indians had built palisades and had felled many of the cedar trees to impede an assault by the English; but one accessible point was soon found by the English. The Massachusetts forward troops immediately stormed the fort through this unfinished gap in the palisades, but were repulsed with heavy fire. Finally, with all the Massachusetts troops massed together, a great cry went up that the Indians were fleeing, and the Bay forces stormed the fort. The Indians, however, by firing from blockhouses in strategic positions were able to inflict heavy damage on the English, especially on the Connecticut troops, who made the second assault on the fort. Great carnage was inflicted by the confederate army, who themselves suffered heavy casualties. The fort was soon aflame; after three hours of heavy fighting little life, except for the battling warriors who remained to hold their ground, was left among the embers of this once great stronghold. But the English sensed the danger of countless savages lurking nearby in the forest—nightfall was at hand, and therefore it was ordered to "Sound a Retreat." Though victory was theirs, the English could not risk encamping overnight amidst this bloody scene, surrounded by hostile Indians, and with their base of supply sixteen miles away.[72]

Hardly had the retreat sounded when the confederate army was under attack by some thousand savages from the forest, a sortie, however, that was soon repulsed after an hour's fight. The confederate soldiers, hastily throwing their dead into one pit,[73] resumed their weary march back to the garrison at Wickford amidst a heavy falling snow, lighted by reddish gleams from the burning fort. That night several of the companies became separated from the main group, but by the afternoon of the 20th the united forces were drawn up at the garrison in Wickford. The casualties of the English were high, given by one contemporary at two hundred and seven—approximately one fifth of the entire English army. But the savages sustained a far greater loss. Their winter quarters were totally demolished; their dead estimated at six hundred men, women, and children.[74] It is a bit of irony that Ninigret, once the fearful Niantic sachem of twenty years before, whose threatened hostility had prompted the unsuccessful coercive policy of the Commissioners to bring him to terms, did not aid his Narragansett brethren against the English. Now old and feeble, a vestige of the past, he came after the battle to bury the dead.[75]

The battle fought on the frozen Narragansett swamp on December 19, 1675, between the joint forces of the United Colonies and the Narragansetts and remnants of lesser New England tribes has gone down as the most bloody battle in New England before the American Revolution. The justice of dealing such a crushing blow to a tribe not openly hostile to the English will always be questioned. But any fair estimate must consider the viewpoint of the times. That the Narragansetts continued to frustrate the demands of the colonists and their Commissioners of the United Colonies is certainly not a justifiable basis for the destruction of a people. But the Narragansetts harbored enemies of the English—Indians who had brutally murdered Englishmen, with less grounds for retaliation, which motivated the Indians of the later American frontier. Moreover the Narragansetts were openly preparing for war, and it was a question of time who would strike first, and in the days immediately preceding the English attack, Narragansett raiding parties had visited destruction upon several English outposts. War is a bloody and brutal business. The Puritans entertained no romantic notions of war. It was an unpleasant duty and hardship for them; but when no other course but to wage war was left open to them, the Puritans accepted it with harsh realism and there was no greater glory than giving one's life to triumph over the leagues of the devil in the Promised Land.

One important result of the Narragansett expedition was that it fixed in the colonial mind that the council of war was the form which intercolonial cooperative action should take. The councils of magistrates and the various war councils of the colonies took charge of carrying on the war. Members of these councils on the colony level, two from each colony, served as Commissioners of the United Colonies: in effect a super-council of magistrates from the confederate colonies. The work of the Confederation was no longer legislative or deliberative, but rather executive in nature—that is, the conduct of war. The contemporary view, then, the "Commissioners of the United Colonies, sitting in Councel"[76] is most significant. Instead of assuming the role of the first Confederation, that of a primary organ of government providing united policy and laws for the confederate colonies, the revised Confederation concerned itself with the direction of the war in imitation of the colonial councils, the nearest semblances to executive authority in the colonial governments at the time.

After the Narragansett Swamp fight, the Massachusetts and Plymouth forces continued in the field, billeted at the garrison in Wickford. The Connecticut troops, however, returned to Stonington. The English wounded were transported to Rhode Island for better care than could be given in the field.[77] For the next several weeks, minor skirmishes took place in the Narragansett country, engaging the united forces remaining there.

On Christmas Day, 1675, the Commissioners of the United Colonies resolved to continue a vigorous prosecution of the war. Because the "Lord calls alowd to a speedy and vigorous prosecution of the warr," it was ordered that one thousand more men be raised. The "Severety of the Season" and the number of wounded soldiers prevented sending out another expedition right away.[78] Time would also have to be allowed for recruiting the new levy. The Commissioners, undoubtedly wondering if their own meeting would continue indefinitely,[79] asked that the new recruits be supplied immediately.[80] But the colonies had enough of large-scale expeditions for the present, and Connecticut, the colony which had suffered the most casualties according to its proportion, served notice that for the remainder of the winter its troops would be used for "guarding frontiers" from the enemy.[81]

Four days after the Swamp fight, the Narragansetts sent envoys to sue for peace, asking permission to move to higher ground, and since the English forces were weakened because supplies had failed to arrive from Boston and the Connecticut troops had withdrawn, this request was granted, even though it was suspected that the Indians were seeking to gain time.[82] Not long after these negotiations, the first reinforcements ordered by the Commissioners began to arrive. Appearing first at the headquarters of the confederate army was a Massachusetts force under Captain Samuel Brocklebank of Rowley,[83] but these recruits were ill equipped to fight. Eleven of the men of the company had frozen to death on their march to the confederate headquarters and they "brought many others sick and disheartened."[84] Other reinforcements were slow in coming, and the confederate army was forced to welcome volunteers from Rhode Island.[85] The Commissioners, still sitting as a council of war in Boston, ordered General Winslow to put his army into action by January 20.[86] The role of the Commissioners as a council of war is further attested by the fact that General Winslow, the commander in chief of the confederate forces in the field, retained his seat in the meetings of the Commissioners,[87] apparently having returned from the field of battle for the Christmas Day session of the Confederation.

But the Connecticut troops could not recuperate from the wounds of battle as quickly as the Commissioners desired,[88] and, therefore, it was not until January 28 that the Connecticut troops retraced their march from New London to the rendezvous of the Army of the United Colonies. Along with the Connecticut troops was the old friend of the English, Uncas of the Mohegans, who brought with him "some Companies of his own Indians to the Assistance of the English."[89] A fair estimate of the strength of the confederate army with these reinforcements was between 1000 and 1400,[90] still quite a substantial fighting force for the Puritan colonies to keep in the field. An Indian spy was sent by the authorities from Boston to spy on the enemy, but he aroused such suspicion among his people that he could not return direct with his information for fear an "Indian would have borrowed my knife, another my hatchit."[91] Except for several raids to drive the Indians from their rock fortifications, the confederate army was to remain inactive against the expectations of the Commissioners. Because of the intense cold and the "Scarcity of Victuals," some of the Connecticut men and the Mohegans were dismissed.[92] The period of delay during the winter caused apprehension throughout the United Colonies. Philip's Indians[93] had set up camp near Albany, a safe distance from the Puritan army. With the western Indians again growing restless, the frontier towns were having a hard time without the aid of colony wages for soldiers to maintain their garrisons.[94] Public unrest again gave vent to criticism of the Puritan authorities; this time placards appeared threatening death to the President of the United Colonies, Thomas Danforth, and Major Gookin, as "trayters to their king." Needless to say the culprits were soon apprehended.[95]

The councils of the United Colonies became more and more impatient over the inactivity of the united forces in the Narragansett country, and in early March the Massachusetts Council ordered that two or more persons be sent posthaste to the Army in order to give "their best advice."[96] This was undoubtedly occasioned by a lapse in the continual session of the Confederation. The Plymouth Commissioners had failed to appear, and it was declared that their absence "doth obstruct," according to the Articles of Confederation, the carrying out of the Commissioners' duties.[97] General Winslow, who was also the governor of Plymouth, perhaps can be excused. Nevertheless, the faltering again over procedure, as in times before, marked in this time of crisis the end of the effective supervision of the Commissioners. The Massachusetts Council, "to the great Surprise of many People," decided to intervene. The garrison of the united forces in the Narragansett country was ordered by the Council in Boston to be abandoned,[98] an act usurping the authority of the Confederation. But the Commissioners were in no position to contest this action since they did not have a quorum, and such a position would probably not have been taken had they been so inclined. The Commissioners of the United Colonies were dedicated to the principle of military expediency—their one aim to crush the enemy as quickly and as completely as possible; they no longer cared one whit about constitutional argument.

The great hour of the second Confederacy was over. The reins for the direction of the war were left to the lesser councils,

rather than to the supreme council of the colonies. But the glory
of this second New England union was the rallying of all New
England in a unified campaign against the Indians and the
swift sending of a great confederate army against a great host of
the enemy, defeating them outright. Also, in the course of things,
federal control was demonstrated as the best means in seventeenth century America for the effective direction of intercolonial military action. After control of the war had left the
hands of the Commissioners, they continued on in an informal
and advisory capacity, and the date that they broke up is not
known. Governor Winthrop, however, was purportedly attending a session of the Commissioners when he died in Boston,
the first week in April. The Commissioners urged a vigorous
prosecution of the war to the end,[99] but their advice went unheeded and no large scale operations were undertaken for the
rest of the winter.

Before disbanding, the confederate army went in pursuit of
the Indians fleeing toward the Nipmuck country. Wigwams
were burnt and a few captives taken, but the supplies of the
English force soon ran out, and the forces of the three colonies,
at the time of the order from the Massachusetts Council, returned home. The straits of the confederate army were so bad in
their pursuit of the Indians that they were compelled to eat
their horses and ground nuts,[100] which has earned the epithet in
history of "The Hungry March." This was the last maneuver
of the Army of the United Colonies, which had contributed so
tremendously to the "united endeavours" of the Puritan colonies; it could be written less than a generation later that "the
evident hand of Heaven appearing on the side of a people,
whose *hope* and *help* was alone in the Almighty Lord of Hosts,
extinguished whole *nations* of the salvages at such a rate, that
there can hardly any of them now be found under any distinction upon the face of the earth."[101]

The breaking up of the confederate army, leaving only garrison posts to guard the frontiers, was a blunder which merely
encouraged the Indians to further depredations. The contagion
of vengeful Indian raids now spread simultaneously through all
the confederate colonies. The brutal massacre at Lancaster,
only thirty-five miles west of Boston, which has been luridly
told by the wife of the minister of the town in the account of
her own miraculous escape,[102] aroused fresh horror among the

colonists. Other settlements in the Bay were attacked. In the spring in the very area where the Indians had received their disastrous defeat at the Great Swamp, the savages were emboldened to make raids on the English. Fearful that a general outbreak of hostilities in the east was in the making, Captain Peirce, with a mixed company of Englishmen and friendly Indians, set out in pursuit of the raiding parties. But the whole English company was met in ambush, and completely wiped out, save for one Englishman and a dozen of the Indians. On the same Sabbath day a savage band spent its fury on an English group in Springfield on the way to worship. The fall of "Captain Perse and his coragios Company" once again aroused union desire to harry once and for all the disciples of the devil out of the Promised Land:

> The Vials of thy wrath appear for thine
> Let all the poure of heven and earth Combine
> Let hell know it is Curbed by poure devine
> Iff this bee dun they miht with great discretion
> that thy Comand and staf be in our nation
> by such a prudent politick Contrivanc
> wee may Expect the varments ferst Conivanc.[103]

In the Connecticut Valley a union force of Connecticut and Massachusetts troops was again organized at Brookfield, the command of which fell to Major Savage of the Bay, since he was the ranking officer in the colony where the operations were to be held.[104] Meanwhile Plymouth was trying to secure the aid of Massachusetts in sending a "flying army" into the field, as was "consonant to the last conclusion of the Commissioners of the united colonies," but the proposal only invited a rebuke from the Bay criticizing Plymouth for withdrawing its forces from the earlier confederate army and not joining with the troops from the other two colonies in the western section.[105] Connecticut, however, after the news of the massacre of Peirce's troops, consented to join with Plymouth in pursuit of the enemy, dispatching a hundred volunteers to scour the Narragansett country.[106] Things had quieted down enough to afford these troops—all the "present souldiers" were in ready status rather than actually in the field during these first weeks of April.[107] The Connecticut expedition in Plymouth Colony and the Narragansett country had immediate results in defeating a party of Narragansetts at Patuxet. Canonchet, their great sachem, was captured and put to death, an irreparable loss to the Narragansetts. The Connecticut force continued in the field, dealing several other defeats to the eastern Indians, but eventually the whole force of Captain Wadsworth of Milton was ensnared near Sudbury and virtually wiped out. Thus the colonies adopted the policy of pursuing the enemy wherever he appeared. There was not as much intercolonial cooperative action as would have been expected were the Commissioners still at the helm; yet the several armies afforded mutual assistance when necessary. The conduct of the war was now on a scattered basis, with small companies of troops pursuing bands of Indians. Because the Indians had already met a great crushing blow in the Swamp Fight, such a flexible system was better than putting a large cumbersome army in the field, which the Commissioners would have probably done.

As spring advanced, a great gathering of Indians was reported on the upper Connecticut River at Peskeompscut, an encampment at Turner Falls. Here was the opportunity the United Colonies had awaited since the fortune of finding the great body of Narragansetts pent up in one dismal swamp. The Indian gathered at Turner Falls represented the core of the western tribes, the Pocomtucks and the Nipmucks, who had never been decisively defeated by the English, although the Pocomtucks had long fought off the hostility of the Mohawks. If the English could deal a crushing blow to these Indians as they had in the eastern sector at the Great Swamp Fight and in subsequent mopping up operations, then the great uprising would end, and disheartened Indians everywhere in New England would sue for peace. Stationed at the towns of Northampton, Hatfield, and Hadley were four Connecticut and four Massachusetts companies.[108] Other frontier towns were but ghost towns, evacuated because of possible Indian raids, now that leaves were again on the trees.

During the first part of May, the Connecticut Council encouraged peace negotiations with the Valley Indians, but the terms, such as the Indians "shal submit ever to live under the English Government," did not prove attractive to the savages who were willing to fight unto death.[109] While Connecticut continued with the policy of inaction and negotiations, Massachusetts itself decided to send a force to destroy this camp of the Indians at their fishing grounds on the upper Connecticut. A Bay force from the garrisons at Hatfield and adjoining settlements was called out to make a surprise attack on this great encampment of the Indians, even though the English force would be far outnumbered. The ideal time for attack was found. The Indians, having gorged themselves on a great feast of fish and stolen English cattle, were, after an evening storm, asleep in their shelters. The English force, under Captains Turner and Holyoke, at daybreak caught the enemy camp so completely by surprise that they were able to inflict great slaughter—many of the savages were drowned by jumping into the swift current of the stream. Several hundred Indians lost their lives, while only one Englishman was killed. But this great victory was marred by the return of the troops to their garrison, during which time they became panicky over the rumor that the terrible Philip had gathered around him more than a thousand Indians. When attacked by a band of Indians, the English force, gripped by fear, suffered heavy casualties before they reached Hatfield. Nevertheless, the defeat of the Pocomtucks at the Falls was a decisive blow, and with a little vigor the colonies could put down the rebellion once and for all.

After the Falls fight, Governor Leverett of the Bay wrote the Connecticut Council, pointing out that it was "most meete spedly to execute the War in all Places," and therefore requested that a mixed company of Connecticut men and Pequot and Mohegan Indians join the Bay force at Hadley for an united effort against the enemy. It was also requested that, as "Loving freinds and Confederates," a force be again sent to the aid of Plymouth in mopping up operations in the Narragansett country.[110] Accepting this call for a joint effort in the Valley, the River Council ordered Major John Talcott to divide his force at Norwich, and then join the Bay troops at Hadley, while Captain Denison, with seventy men, was "to hunt the Narrogancett country" as he had done the previous month.[111] Although Talcott did not form a junction with the Massachusetts troops on the way from Boston under Captain Henchman, he did arrive in time at Hadley to repulse the last great assault of the western Indians upon that town. The seven hundred Indians making this attack had expected a defenseless town, and their defeat was demoralizing. After several lesser encounters by the forces of Talcott and Henchman, the war in the west was over. Major

Talcott received broad powers from the Connecticut Council with his own council of war "to move and act in the pursuit and prosecution of the enemie, as God shall direct them" in either the River or the Narragansett country.[112] But in the hour of victory, the authorities on the River could not be magnanimous, and in July, with virtually no signs of Indian hostility left, Major Talcott was further urged on "to dispoyle the estate as to destroy the persons of all Indians in hostility against the English."[113]

The whereabouts of King Philip had been somewhat of a mystery throughout the war. It was known that he had fled to the vicinity of Albany; yet at almost every great battle he was reportedly seen leading the Indians on. It is unlikely, however, that Philip ever took part in any of the battles after the opening of the war in Plymouth. With a small band he had taken refuge in the West. Fortunately the English inherited the friendliness of the Mohawks for the Dutch, and the "Keepers of the Eastern Door of the Longhouse" dealt Philip's band such a decisive defeat that in the summer of 1676 he was forced to seek refuge in his original hunting grounds in Plymouth Colony. Many of his own Indians began surrendering *en masse* to the Plymouth authorities.[114] It was only a matter of time before Philip would be hunted down like a dog and slain. The moment came on August 22, when Captain Church, at the head of a Plymouth company that had been searching the woods for Philip, at last came upon this "pestilent Ringleader" and slew him on the spot. His head, taken to Plymouth on a day appointed for Thanksgiving, was displayed upon a pole. Thus, in the words of a tract of the times, the "Warr in New-England" was "Visibly Ended."[115] Though the contagion had spread, starting fresh hostilities on the northern frontier,[116] it had with finality been checked in the three confederate colonies. The aftermath of war only brought again intercolonial disputes over war debts, conquered lands, and the boundaries of the colonies.

The New England Indian was the loser in his last attempt to reverse the process of attrition. The poor "heathen Malefacts, men, women, and Children" who were not "Sentenced and condemned to perpetuall Servitude,"[117] faced a life of deprivation and poverty, with the loss of the spiritual and physical factors with which they had been able to resist the English advancement. In a letter to the king, justifying its claims to the

Mount Hope lands, Plymouth Colony wrote: "Wee begun not a war with them, so neither have wee, nor the confederate Colonys failed to improve our utmost abilities to maintaine your Majesties interest and our own, against their unjust and insolent intrusions."[118]

Because of the multitudinous problems arising from the war, an attempt was made on the part of Massachusetts to call a session of the Confederation in September, 1676, but the Connecticut Governor, ascertaining the views of the magistrates without calling the council together, felt that since "it not being the Trieniall yeare" there was not sufficient business to call a special session of the Confederacy.[119] The Commissioners, however, had overdone their welcome during the war. They had served as a useful body in directing the early phase of the war and the Narragansett expedition. But after power passed to the lesser councils, the Commissioners merely stayed on as individual members of their colonies in an informal conference. James Richards, the Connecticut Commissioner, was still in the Bay during the summer of 1676.[120] If the Confederation had properly adjourned itself when a quorum was not established in the spring of 1676, it might have been reconvened in the fall. The long continuous session of the Confederation from September, 1675, to April, 1676, was in the form of a war council—when that function devolved on the individual colony councils the Confederacy had ended its usefulness. To call a special session now with the war ended would serve no practical purpose.

After the war, the individual colonies prepared the accounts of their expenditures incurred during the war and submitted them to the Commissioners, so that the Commissioners could determine whether the colonies shared the burden of war as apportioned by the Articles of Confederation. Not only was there the expense of paying for the soldiers and the various commissaries designated by the colonies, but there was also the expense of poor relief and compensation to injured veterans.[121] The colonies helped to liquidate their accounts by selling the conquered Indian lands.[122] Taxes were levied, in the same way the colonists had learned in England, by a single poll or property tax, which was doubled or trebled according to the demands of the war emergency.[123] For towns that suffered the brunt of war generous abatements were granted by the Massachusetts Colony.[124]

When the Commissioners reconvened in their triennial session in September, 1678, they took upon themselves the responsibility of supervising the colonies in the liquidation of war debts. The cost of the war as disclosed from the accounts submitted by the three colonies was: Massachusetts, £46,292; Plymouth, £11,743; and Connecticut, £22,173. The Commissioners, by written vote, however, refused to accept the Massachusetts account because some of the items listed were incurred outside of the limits specified by the Commissioners.[125]

But a special session was held in March of 1679 at Plymouth for the purpose of settling the defects in the accounts, and to dispose of other business concerning the war. At this meeting, in order to balance the accounts, Plymouth was ordered to pay Massachusetts £1000 and Connecticut to pay General Winslow £32. With this done the colonies would be "for ever acquitted from further claimes or accoumpts," providing that each colony would take care of other debts that might have been incurred within their own jurisdictions. Likewise, each colony (unlike the Pequot War there were now Indian lands in each of the three colonies) could dispose of lands and profits within its own jurisdiction "without Lett Disturbance or claime of from or by each others."[126] The only other important business of this meeting was a "full Debate" on the erecting of English schools among the Indians, but no action was taken.[127] Nothing was done about a request from Roger Williams in 1677 for the Commissioners to intervene in preventing encroachments on lands belonging to the Indians.[128]

The glorious days of the New England Confederacy had passed. There had been an undercurrent of insubordination to the Puritan authorities in all walks of life. One manifestation had been the rivalry between Major Appleton and the Connecticut Council during the early phase of the war in drawing off the colony's contingent from the united force without permission from the Commissioners. Many factors were breaking down the walls of uniformity: non-Puritan immigration, the spread of the franchise, royal policy, greater contact economically with the outside world, and controversies over religious doctrines, to name but a few. The Confederation was founded on the desire for uniformity and for mutual defense of the Puritan states. The second Confederacy was revived with full force along less rigid constitutional demands than the first. But the necessity for a united effort to put down the great uprising of the savages of all New England—a conflagration which threatened to cut off the expansion of the United Colonies and thereby confine them to their ports on the coast and the River—called forth the Commissioners as a supreme military council. In an unprecedented session, spreading over a period of six months, the Commissioners, with the commander in chief of the united army retaining his seat in the Confederation, ably performed the task of directing the war. The high point of this intercolonial council was the swift dispatch of a confederate army to attack the Narragansetts in their winter quarters. In bitter cold and a blinding snowstorm this act was accomplished, and it spelled the ultimate collapse of the Indian revolt. But a period of inactivity and isolated raids in each of the three colonies forced the colonies to go their own way, following the direction of their own colonial councils rather than of the Commissioners. With the dispersal of the troops, the war was finally brought to an end. Massachusetts, however, found a fresh uprising in the northern settlements, which the other two colonies disowned, to the detriment of the Confederation. Nevertheless, the long, often informal, session of the Confederacy during the holocaust of King Philip's War served to implant in the colonial mind the image of an intercolonial war council as the form for cooperative action.

---

[1] Palfrey, *op. cit.*, III, 155-7. Palfrey's two chapters on "Philip's War" is a good digest of the many printed tracts on the war. A recent and well-written account which makes good use of the local records (Douglas E. Leach, *Flintlock and Tomahawk* (N. Y.: The Macmillan Co. 1958), overemphasizes the role of Philip as a leader in the general uprising.

[2] Memorandum of James Richards, 1675 Winthrop Papers, MHS, XVII, 76.

[3] See Leonard Bliss, Jr., *The History of Rehoboth* (Boston: 1836) and W. J. Miller, *King Philip and the Wampanoags,* (Providence: 1855).

[4] For the sharpest criticism of Philip's abilities and that he was lacking in courage see Grindall Reynolds, "King Philip's War: with Special Reference to the Attack on Brookfield," *AASP*, New Ser., V, 77-95; in the same vein see Sylvester Judd, *History of Hadley*, (Northampton: 1863).

[5] Leverett to Winslow, 23Jun75, Misc. MSS, Boston Atheneum.

[6] CA, Boundaries (N. Y.), II, 29, 31; *CCR*, II, 261-3, 569-74, 578-86; Samuel Hart, "Saybrook in the Early Days," *Papers of the NHCHS*, VII (1908), 126; MA, II, 193; Winthrop Papers, MHS, IA, 155, 12Jul75.

[7] See Arthur J. Weise, *History of the City of Albany*, (Albany: 1884), pp. 163-4.

[8] For the cooperation of the New Hampshire towns, see Joseph Dow, ed., *History of Hampton, N. H.*, (Salem: 1893), I. Soldiers from eleven towns were drafted in Plymouth, and the Commanding General was allowed 6s. a day. (Bowen, *op. cit.* (Rehoboth), I, 16; Prince, *op. cit.*, p. 96.)

[9] "The Present State of New England," Drake, *op. cit.*, p. 132.

[10] Cudworth to Winslow, 27Jun75, Boston Atheneum, Misc. MSS.

[11] "The Present State of New England," *loc. cit.*, pp. 137-8.

[12] Coddington to Gov. of N. Y., 21Jul75, F. Hough, ed., John Easton's *A Narrative of the Causes which led to Philip's Indian War* (Albany: 1858), pp. 62-3; Mather, *Magnalia*, II, 562. Coddington to the Commissioners of the U. C., 23Jun75, in E. Williams, *op. cit.*, pp. 72-3; See also Chapin, *op. cit.* (Privateering), p. 49. Williams wrote: "that all the Colonies were subject to one K. Charles, and that was his pleasure, and our dutie and engagement, for one English man to stand to the death by each other, in all parts of the world." *(MHSC* 4:VII:299-302, Ltr to Winthrop, 25Jun75.)

[13] Leverett to Winslow, 17Jul75, Winslow Papers, MHS, I, 94; Bowen, *op. cit.* (Rehoboth), III, 56.

[14] *Ibid.*

[15] Rev. James Fitch to John Allyn, Jul75, CA, Colonial Wars, I, 10.

[16] George M. Bodge, *Soldiers in King Philip's War*, (Leominster, Mass.: 1896), p. 29.

[17] "Capt. Thomas Wheeler's Narrative," in Joseph I. Foot, *An Historical Discourse*, (West Brookfield: 1843), pp. 31-47.

[18] As a result there was a lapse in the town records from 1675 to 1680. John G. Metcalf, *Annals of the Town of Mendon*, (Providence: 1880), p. 62.

[19] See Herbert C. Parsons, *A Puritan Outpost*, (New York: 1937), p. 40.

[20] The story is told interestingly in many of the histories of the early towns, e.g., Hatfield (Wells), Greenfield (Thompson), Deerfield (Sheldon), and Springfield.

[21] Winslow to Winthrop, 29Jul75, *MHSC* 5:I:429; Leverett to Winthrop, Winthrop Papers, MHS, XIV, 141.

[22] Viz., "to take the command of the Militia into your hands and martiall and dispose of them as you shall Judg best . . ." Winthrop Papers, MHS, X, 22.)

[23] ". . . a moderate man," in the words of a Rhode Island settler, and Winthrop, "a very good sober man." (Account of Wil. Harris, Bancroft and Transcripts (N. E.), II, 295, NYPL.

[24] Jones to Leete, 27Aug75, Judd Transcripts, Misc. MSS and Conn. MSS, I, Forbes Lib.

[25] Conn. Commissioners to Maj. Treat, 30Aug75, CA, Colonial Wars, I, 18.

[26] Winthrop to the Gov. of N. Y., 27Aug75, Winthrop Papers, MHS, V, 150.

[27] *PCR*, X, 364.

[28] Council Order for a Fast, 17Sep75, MA, X, 18.

[29] Leete to Winthrop, 23Sep75, *Winthrop Papers, MHSC* 4:VII:579.

[30] Thomas Stanton, the Indian interpreter for the Confederation, at this time

directed his correspondence to the Commissioners to Winthrop first. (25Sep75, Winthrop Papers, MHS, XVIII, 140).

[31] *PCR*, X, 362-4.

[32] *PCR*, X, 365.

[33] CA, *Colonial Wars*, I, la-f.

[34] MA, LXVIII, 8; *PCR*, X, 457.

[35] Willys Papers, Council of Conn. to the Commissioners, 7Oct75, CHS; Corres. q. in Waters, *op. cit.*, pp. 166-9.

[36] Appleton to Gov. Leverett, 12Oct75, q. in Waters, *ibid.*, pp. 170-2.

[37] Misc. Corres., MA, LXVIII, 10, 11a, 29, Winthrop Papers, MHS, X, 36; XVII, 74; X, 26; Waters, *op. cit.* (Ipswich), pp. 174-85.

[38] MA, II, 363; *PCR*, X, 456.

[39] *PCR*, X, 357-8; Willys Papers, I, 53, CHS.

[40] The breakdown in soldiers to be supplied was: Massachusetts, 527; Plymouth, 158; and Connecticut, 315. 500 were to have "longe Armes." (p. 365.)

[41] Old Style dating will be used in the chronology of the Narragansett expedition because of the importance of certain days, such as Christmas Day, the sabbaths—which requires the original dating.

[42] MA, LXVIII, 39, 53; *MHSC* 3:I:66-8; CA, Colonial Wars, I, 24; *MCR*, V, 69, 73; *PCR*, V, 184ff.

[43] William Hubbard, *The History of the Indian Wars in New England*, No. 3 of Woodward's Historical Series, (Roxbury: (1677), 1845), I, 134-5; Mather, *Magnalia*, II, 566-7.

[44] Smith to Winthrop, 4Sep75, in D. B. Updike, *Richard Smith*, pp. 110-1.

[45] The New Englanders "felt ourselves assaulted by unknown numbers of *devils in flesh* on every side of us." (Mather, *op. cit.*) Leverett to Winslow, 6Jul75, Misc. MSS, Boston Atheneum; A. W. Lauber, *Indian Slavery in Colonial Times*, (New York: 1913), p. 114. Eliot, in December, felt compelled to write the Corporation that "I must change my ditty now" because of the "lamentation over the work of Christ among our praying Indians," resulting from the sufferings endured since they were removed from their homes to an isolated island. For the English destruction of a friendly plantation of Wamesit Indians, see Henry A. Hazen, *History of Billerica*, (Boston: 1883); for the Eliot letter to Boyle, 17Dec75, see Ford, ed., *op. cit.*, pp. 52-55.

[46] CA, Colonial Wars, I, 27.

[47] *MCR*, V, 78-9.

[48] MA, LXVIII, 159, 12Mar75/6.

[49] Appleton to Gov. Leverett, 10Nov75, q. in Waters, *op. cit.* (Ipswich), pp. 186-90; MA, LXVIII, 54a. When the Commissioners ordered the raising of the Narragansett expedition, the Connecticut Council informed Commissioner Winthrop that they could send no one "to attend the business" at Boston and to apoint whomever he liked there to implement this policy. (Ltr of 2Nov75, Winthrop Papers, MHS, X, 28.)

[50] MA, LXVIII, 56.

[51] MA, LXVIII, 61, 63, 63a.

[52] Appleton to Leverett, 19Nov75, q. in Waters, *op. cit.* (Ipswich), pp. 195-6.

[53] *Ibid.*; MA, LXVIII, 66.

[54] "The Present State of New England," Drake, *op. cit.*, pp. 186-7.

[55] Waters, *op. cit.* (Ipswich), pp. 196-7.

[56] Mather, *Magnalia*, II, 201.

[57] Commissioners of the U. C. to Gov. Coddington, 12Nov75, MA, LXVIII, 55.

[58] Willys Papers, CHS, I, 54, 17Nov75.

[59] Concerning the Narragansetts, "that which the Commissioners looke upon as the cheife matter, is that they doe not deliver up those Wapanages according to their agreement signed by the sachem, and delegates of the commissioners." (Winthrop Papers, MHS, V, 154, 12Nov75.)

[60] Church's mixed band of English and friendly Indians is credited with breaking down the well-regulated military system of Plymouth. (See Leach, *op. cit.*, pp. 359-61.) The general use of snaphance weapons for the first time, during King Philip's War, rendered the English more formidable to the Indians. (See Harold L. Peterson, "The Military Equipment of the Plymouth and Bay Colonies," *NEQ*, XX (June, 1947), 197-208; Charles W. Sawyer, *Firearms in American History*, (Boston: 1910); and for the general system of New England defense, Osgood, *op. cit.*, I, Chap. 13.) Privately owned arms, subject to requisition by the colonies, were actually a sort of public property. (See Morison Sharp, "The New England Trainbands in the Seventeenth Century," Unpub. Ph.D. Dissertation, Harvard Univ., 1938.)

[61] Bowen, *op. cit.* (Rehoboth), II, 47; John E. Morris and George W. Ellis, *King Philip's War*, (New York: 1906), p. 144. For a general account of New England's Indian Wars see Herbert M. Sylvester, *Indian Wars of New England* (Boston: 1910), 3 Vols.

[62] Bowen places this site at Rehoboth; Morris and Ellis at North Attleboro; and Bodge at Attleboro.

[63] Coddington to Winslow, 15Dec75, Winslow Papers, I, 100; Bodge, *op. cit.*, p. 180.

[64] For a contemporary account of the troop movements in the Rehoboth-Providence area, see the letter of Rev. Noah Newman to John Cotton, 10Dec75, Bowen, *op. cit.*, II, 48-9.

[65] At the expense of the towns. (E.g., *Groton Records*, p. 52.)

[66] Capt. James Oliver of the Third Massachusetts Company at one time had been given the responsibility in the Bay for providing lodgings for the visiting Commissioners of the United Colonies in Boston. *(MCR*, IV, Pt. 2, 75.)

[67] For the "Roster of the Officers of the Army of the United Colonies" see Bodge, *op. cit.*, pp. 182-4. For statistical information on King Philip's War this is a very valuable book.

[68] Winthrop to Treat, Winthrop Papers, MHS, V, 155, 18Dec75; MA, LXVIII, 87a; Treat to Comm. of the U. C., 4Dec75, Winthrop Papers, MHS, XIX, 74. The Commissioners had ordered that General Winslow be attended by "a sufficient Lifeguard."

[69] Bodge, *op. cit.*, p. 182.

[70] *Ibid.* From the Bay's viewpoint the Narragansett expedition was justified by the "articles of confoederation" which called for assistance from the United Colonies to aid a colony in trouble. (Viz. Plymouth's crusade to crush Philip's Indians.) (MA, LXVII, 247). But the Commissioners were suspected by the Rhode Islanders for wanting to use a conquest of the Narragansetts as grounds for asserting their claims to the Narragansett Country. *(RICR,* II, 556-7.)

[71] It seems that all Indian battles in New England took place in swamp areas, which is explained when "swamps" at that time did not necessarily denote marshy ground but any flat lands, which were covered with wooded growth and escaped fires set by the Indians. (See J. H. Temple, *History of Northfield,* (Albany: 1875), p. 21.

[72] Bodge, *op. cit.,* pp. 185-90.

[73] Sewall, *Diary,* 19Dec75, *MHSC* 5:V:11. Drake, ed., "The Continuation of the Present State of New-England," *op. cit.,* p. 183.

[74] *Ibid.,* p. 185.

[75] Various authors have given the site of the swamp at different places, though in the same vicinity: South, West, or North Kingston, R. I.

[76] e.g., Drake, ed., *op. cit.,* p. 178; or "our Authority then in Councel." (p. 177).

[77] Drake, *op. cit.,* pp. 184-5; Bodge, *op. cit.,* p. 199.

[78] MA, LXVIII, 105; Willys Papers, I, 54, 229; Winthrop to Leete, 25Dec75, Winthrop Papers, MHS, V, 189; Bowen, *op. cit.,* II, 43-52. Rehoboth made a distinction between the soldiers "that went to Nariaganset" and those raised by this order who served" under Major Bradford."

[79] Winthrop was planning a trip to London. (Winthrop Papers, MHS, V, 157.)

[80] MA, LXVIII, 108.

[81] Leete to Winthrop, 20Jan75/6, MHSC 4:VII:582.

[82] Drake, ed., *op. cit.,* pp. 194-5.

[83] Bodge, *op. cit.,* p. 201.

[84] Drake, ed., *op. cit.,* p. 195.

[85] Williams, E., *op. cit.,* (Coddington), p. 76.

[86] MA, LXVIII, 111; CA, Colonial Wars, I, 31, 32; Richards to Winthrop, 5Jan75/6, Winthrop Papers, MHS, XVII, 76.

[87] The orders of the Commissioners of December 25 and January 6 bears the signature of Winslow.

[88] Palmer to Winslow, 16Jan75/6, *MHSC* 1:VI:89-90; also letters of Allyn and Richards to Winthrop, 12Jan75/6 and 13Jan75/6, Winthrop Papers, X, 30 and XVII, 77.

[89] Drake, ed., *op. cit.,* p. 195.

[90] A contemporary estimate has it as high as 1600. *(Ibid.)*

[91] Report of 24Jan75/6, Misc. MSS, MHS, III.

[92] Drake, ed., *op. cit.,* p. 197.

[93] One writer has noted that there is no proof that Philip ever took part in any action with the western Indians, who even threatened to take his head to the English. (Sheldon, *op. cit.* (Deerfield), pp. 81-2).

[94] S. Judd., *op. cit.* (Hadley), p. 191.

[95] MA, XXX, 193 and 193A.

[96] MA, LXVIII, 154B; Conn. Council to Winthrop, 16Feb75/6 and Richards to Winthrop, 18Feb75/6, Winthrop Papers, MHS, X, 31 and XVII, 78.

[97] Mass. Council to Conn. Council, 13Mar75/6, MA, LXVIII, 157.

[98] Drake, ed., "A New and Farther Narrative of the State of New England," *op. cit.*, p. 216.

[99] *PCR*, V, 184-5.

[100] Ellis and Morris, *op. cit.*, p. 163.

[101] Mather, *Magnalia*, II, 582. In February, the Commissioners issued another call for troops to be sent against the Indians around Brookfield, the total for the three colonies being six hundred.

[102] Mrs. Rowlandson's "Narrative" of her captivity is printed in Charles H. Lincoln, ed., *Narratives of the Indian Wars*, Vol. XIV of the *Original Narratives of Early Amer. Hist.* (New York: 1913).

[103] Printed in Bowen, *op. cit.*, II ,36-7.

[104] Ellis and Morris, *op. cit.*, p. 180.

[105] MA, LXVIII, 177, 187, 196.

[106] CA, *Colonial Wars*, I, 202-4.

[107] Drake, ed., *op. cit.*, p. 230.

[108] Palfrey, *op. cit.*, III, 193.

[109] *CCR*, II, 438-40. At times the entire membership of the Connecticut Council was comprised of men who had all served as Commissioners of the United Colonies; e.g., the 24Feb75/6 meeting, consisted of Leete, Talcott, Allyn, Richards, and Willys—the Commissioners in Boston at the time representing the colony were the father and son combination, Gov. John Winthrop and Wait Winthrop. (*Ibid.*, p. 411.)

[110] CA, *Colonial Wars*, I, 75; Jones to Leete, 2May76, Willys Papers, CHS.

[111] *CCR*, II, 449.

[112] *CCR*, II, 455.

[113] *Ibid.*, p. 460; Leete to Talcott, 15Jul76, Willys Papers, CHS, I, 61. Governor Leverett of Mass. was busy writing the home government at this time of the course of the war. (Bancroft Transcripts, 15Jul76, II, 383-394, NYPL.) For his services during the war he was later knighted.

[114] Drake, ed., *op. cit.*, pp. 242-3. It was the habit of the Mohawks to make raids on the New England Indians, friendly and unfriendly to the English, but it is doubtful if they ever had an "extended occupation of any portion of New England." (Charles C. Willoughby, *Antiquities of the New England Indians* (Cambridge: 1935), p. 198.) The New York governor was engaged in a policy encouraging the Mohawks against the French, expecting therein the cooperation of New England. (Council of Conn. to Council of Mass., 20Jul66, Misc. MSS, Boston Atheneum.) See in this connection, Ruth Higgins, *Expansion in New York*, (Columbus, Ohio: 1931).

[115] Drake, ed., *op. cit.*, pp. 287-93.

[116] Council of Mass. to Winslow, 20Aug76, Winslow Papers, MHS, I, 103; rea-

sons given for the outbreak of hostilities in the northern settlements have been
given as: (1) dependency of the Indians for hunting guns from the French;
(2) refusal of the Confederation to aid these Indians against the Iroquois;
(3) conversion to Catholicism; (4) revenge against certain traders. A. D. Parker, *History of Pemaquid,* (Boston: 1925), pp. 129-31.)

[117] Misc. MSS, III, 6Nov76, MHS.

[118] Stevens Transcripts, IV, 445, John Carter Brown Library, 13Jul77.

[119] Rabinowitz Collection, Add. 4, 20Aug76, Yale University Library.

[120] *Ibid.*

[121] E.g., see Josiah Paine, *A History of Harwich* (Rutland, Vermont: 1937).
Fairfield was the leading town in Connecticut as a supply depot for the army of
the United Colonies. (See Lynn W. Wilson, *History of Fairfield County, Conn.*
(Hartford: 1929.)

[122] For Plymouth and the Mount Hope lands see Frederick Freeman, History
of Cape Cod (Boston: 1860), I, and Samuel Deane, *History of Scituate* (Boston: 1831).

[123] See D. R. Dewey, *Financial History of the United States* (New York:
1915).

[124] D. R. Dewey, "Economic Organization, 1620-89," *Commonwealth History of
Massachusetts,* ed. by A. B. Hart (New York: 1927), I, 416.

[125] *PCR,* X, 367, 402-3.

[126] *PCR,* X, 367.

[127] *Ibid.,* p. 368.

[128] Roger Williams to the Commissioners, *Letters of Roger Williams,* ed. by
J. R. Bartlett, *Publications of the Narragansett Club,* 1:VI: 393-4.

CHAPTER XIV

Dominion Interlude

After King Philip's War, in the words of that doughty divine Cotton Mather, there ensued a "Lamentable Decade." It was a time when new attacks were made upon the Puritan governments of the colonies, resulting in the revocation of the Massachusetts Charter. The Indians on the northern frontier continually wrought havoc on the outlying settlements of the Bay. In religion and public affairs, the Puritan oligarchy was beginning to be on the defensive; the times called for greater freedom of movement and expression. But the saddest event, in the eyes of the New England Puritans, was the effecting of one of their great fears, ever present since the founding of the Puritan colonies: the setting up of a governor-general over the colonies. This attempt of the Stuart government to consolidate the New England colonies and New York under one administration was doomed from the start, for the colonies, though experienced in cooperative action, were too much states-unto-themselves to be brought with the stroke of a pen into one hierarchy of government.

The Andros Regime of 1686-9 was so resented in New England for its arbitrary government and its attack upon the settled institutions of the colonies that after the Revolution of 1689 the colonists sought to erase all semblance of the Dominion government from their memory. The Dominion of New England was to be but an interlude in the state of things—a three year void. In all, the period from the end of King Philip's War to the fall of the Dominion government in 1689 is a period of little activity on the part of the Confederation. Three triennial meetings were held in 1678, 1681, and 1684, and one special session in 1679. The meetings were perfunctory; the main business was the apportionment of the war debt of the colonies. The special session of August, 1679, was not an emergency session in the real sense of the term. In the summer of 1679, a letter had been received from the king directing the colonies to submit an ac-

314

count of the progress of the Indian war. The Commissioners, therefore, met in August, and drafted a reply from the United Colonies to the king's letter. Among the points that the Commissioners discussed were the necessity of the war; the taking over of Philip's lands at Mount Hope and the Narragansett lands in Connecticut; and declaring invalid the recommendations of the royal commissioners in 1664-5. The Commissioners took it upon themselves to defend the Confederation in general.[1] But calling the attention of the royal government to the Confederation did more harm than good for it reminded that New England still operated in many ways contrary to the intentions of the home government.

The meeting of the Commissioners at Boston in 1681 did little more than settle minor claims arising out of the war. The session of 1684 at Hartford, the last of the triennial meetings, likewise did little serious business. This was the last meeting in which records of the meetings of the Commissioners found their way into the official "Acts of the United Colonies," and which New England historians have erroneously believed to have been the last meeting of the Confederation. In the sense that the Andros regime put a period to the regular triennial meetings and the session of 1689 was an unsuccessful attempt at revival, this may be considered the end of the Union of 1672, as the meeting of 1667 was the end of the Union of 1643. Thus it was fitting that at the 1684 session, the Commissioners in their final act, symbolically reminding the colonists of the manifold favors of divine Providence on their Confederation, declared a day of public thanksgiving.[2]

Meanwhile the New England colonies were falling again into royal disfavor. Complaints were lodged in England against the authorities of New England, especially those in Massachusetts, for evasion of the Navigation laws and the hesitant allegiance to the royal government. A new generation was appearing in the United Colonies—no longer were the main ends of government to preserve the old order in ascendancy; the colonies now were demanding a share in world commerce, a longing contrary to the imperial policy of the home government. For the present, England would not interfere with intercolonial trade, but when enumerated articles were shipped directly to English ports and articles in exchange came back to the colonies passing through other than English ports, then the plan of fitting the New England colonies into their part in the English trading empire went awry. English colonies in America could not be permitted to go their own way without regard for the policy of the home government.

Up to the time of King Philip's War, little was done to bring about the enforcement of the Navigation laws. In 1675 the Lords of Trade appointed a special committee of the Privy Council to succeed the previous Council for Trade and Plantations, whose purpose was to look into the complaints of English merchants that the English Navigation laws were violated by the Bay Colony.[3] This committee of the Lords of Trade drew up a set of inquiries to determine the extent to which New England should fit and was then fitting into the royal commercial policy. The inquiries were submitted to the Commissioners of Customs, who returned the answer that New England was "equally subject with the rest to those laws which related to the plantation trade," and that they had been ignoring the Acts of Trade and Navigation. It was recommended that the governors of the colonies should take oaths for enforcing these laws and also that bonds be required of shipmasters to insure their abiding by the trade acts. The report of the Commissioners of Customs, in effect, demanded more stringent enforcement machinery.[4]

In order to get a clearer view of the situation in Massachusetts, Edward Randolph was sent to the colonies by the King as a special agent to deliver a letter of the King and to conduct further investigations. Included in the instructions to Randolph was the ascertainment of "where the Legislative and Executive Powers of the Government of New England are seated." Furthermore, viewing with alarm the union sentiment in the colonies, Randolph was to find out in the Bay "how they do att present correspond with the confederate and other Collonies." Massachusetts was required to send agents to the home government in defense of the complaints lodged against the colony.

The Randolph mission, however, was frustrated from the start. Governor Leverett of the Bay, a leading member of the country-conservative party, which embraced most of the old-line Puritans, staunchly resisted Randolph's efforts in every possible way. Shipping was arranged to depart without Randolph's inspection. The answer to the King's letter was sent to England by other hands than Randolph's. While in New England, Randolph's dislike for the Puritan orthodoxy was further inflamed by reports he received from the various groups of malcontents. It is no wonder then that on his return home he presented biased and exaggerated reports against the Bay Colony, losing no opportunity to depict the government as arbitrary, and contrary to the laws of England. The government of Massachusetts was criticized on every point, with the general theme of the report placing the General Court as the supreme authority in the colony as against due subservience to His Majesty's will. The Randolph report was careful not to indict all the United Colonies, but instead, skillfully played upon the resentment of the other English settlements towards the Puritan rule at the Bay. The Confederation, therefore, did not come under indictment in this report. The only reference to the Confederacy was a favorable mention of the liberal governor of Plymouth, Josiah Winslow, "a person eminently popular and beloved in all the colonies of N. E. and was generall of the united forces against the Indians." The discontent among the people and the antagonism of the other colonies toward the Bay was greatly exaggerated by Randolph, and exploited to the full in an attempt to show adequate grounds for "settling a general government over the whole country, without which it is feared civill wars will in a short time breake out between the colonies, the government of the Massachusetts dayly imposing and incroaching upon their neighbours."[5]

As requested in the King's letter, the Massachusetts General Court, though not until after much delay caused by the shrewd old soldier-governor, John Leverett, decided to send two agents to England to represent the colony against the charges levied against the Puritan Commonwealth. Chosen for the mission was a Commissioner of the United Colonies, William Stoughton, and Peter Bulkeley, later elected to that office. Stoughton, despite his arch-Puritanism was a wise choice by the magistrates. He had resided in England, and as a member of the clergy could keep himself well above polemic entanglements.

When the Massachusetts agents, however, were summoned to appear in the Council Chamber at Whitehall, they stated that the only authority invested in them by the Massachusetts Colony was to answer questions concerning the Mason and Gorges boundary claims. Concerning the laws of the colony, oaths of allegiance, coining money, or harboring the regicides—questions long of interest to the Stuart regime—and the enforcement of the Navigation Laws, the Massachusetts envoys could not speak officially for the colony, although they ventured their private opinions. Thus the efforts of the Lords of Trade to get a firm statement of the Massachusetts position failed, and the Bay again had performed one of those maneuvers designed to show acquiescence to royal authority, but in such a way as not to put any strain on its own commonwealth government. Yet, the recalcitrant attitude of Massachusetts was evident, and it made the bringing of the New England colonies under more direct control of the home government even more urgent. This course was aided by an attempt to lump the New England colonies with the royal colony of New York, receiving an impetus from Andros's assertion that the Duke's colony "have kept good neighbourly Correspondency" with the New England colonies.[6] The Massachusetts agents were informed that the King would not treat his own subjects as "foreigners," but expected strict conformity with the English Acts of Trade. The Royal government might go along with the request of the Massachusetts agents to amend their charter to cover the so-called abuses of the colonial government, such as the coining of money—colonial self-government in itself was not particularly objected to—but the undermining of the British trading empire would not be permitted.[7]

In 1678, the Lords of Trade again considered the Massachusetts question, this time recommending that *quo warranto* proceedings be initiated against the charter. What really angered the Bay was the appointment of its enemy, Edward Randolph, as Collector of Customs in New England. Randolph, instead of receiving his salary from the revenue collected in the colony where he served, as was the habit for the other commissioners, was to receive his salary from the English government—the first time the royal government had ever practiced maintaining a fixed civil list in the colonies, a factor in the next century in bringing about the American Revolution. But also alarming to the Puritan party in New England was the declaration that "their Lordshipps, from these Dissentions among the Colonies, inferr the great necessity there is for His Majestie to appoint some General Governor, or some Supreme Authority over them."[8]

For over a year the "Collector, Surveyor and Searcher of His Majesties Customes" remained in Boston, sending detailed re-

ports to the home government of the violations of the Acts of
Trade by the Massachusetts colony. When he tried to enforce
the laws, he met opposition from all sides—from the courts, the
government and the people, the general effect of which was to
nullify the acts of trade in Massachusetts.[9] In 1680, Randolph
tersely summed up his grievances against the Bay authorities,
all of which purported to infringe upon the prerogative of the
King. By extending their company charter into that of a political
state, the Bay founders had acted as "usurpers"; furthermore,
they had formed a commonwealth, denying appeals to England
and were not taking the oath of allegiance; the regicides had
received protection; the Bay had established its own mint;
English subjects were put to death because of religion; Massachusetts had resisted royal authority in New Hampshire and
Maine; oaths of fidelity were taken to the Massachusetts government; and the acts of trade and navigation were violated.[10]
When Randolph again returned to his post in the colonies,
further complaints were lodged against the Bay for the obstruction of the enforcement of the acts of trade and the competition
of the Bay in insisting on using its own officers for the collection of custom duties. Writing in 1682, Randolph declared that
"till this government be thoroughly regulated, all that his Majestie commands will signify nothing," and this "independency in
government claimed and daily practised" was "one chiefe occasion of the many mutinies and disturbances in other his Majesties forreigne plantations."[11]

Although a new governor was elected in the Bay in 1679 in
the person of Simon Bradstreet,[12] who had long experience as a
Commissioner of the United Colonies and unlike his predecessor was a moderate, the extreme party continued to stir up
enough popular sentiment to frustrate the efforts of Randolph.
His Majesty's commissioners continued to lose cases in the
Massachusetts courts, and on one occasion one of Randolph's
deputies was imprisoned for failure to pay a suit brought against
him, which the deputy had lost.[18] Massachusetts seemed to be
following the fortunes of emerging Whiggism in Britain—if a
crisis again developed there as it had in Cromwell's time,
they could go their own way without interference from the
home government. But Massachusetts was too long in playing
its hand, and in 1684, after refusal to plead when a writ of *scire
facias* was served upon the governor and company, the charter

was annulled. Massachusetts, like its lesser neighbor at Plymouth, now lacked a legal existence. The way was now cleared to set up royal government in the colony, and possibly to combine the original confederate colonies with the other New England settlements and the province of New York. One of the first acts in setting up a new Massachusetts government would be to appoint a royal council.[14] Yet, for over a year, no immediate action was taken to supersede the Puritan government of the Bay, and Massachusetts, probably counting on a change in royal policy due to Whig pressure to leave her government and that of the Confederation alone, proceeded to elect Commissioners of the United Colonies as usual for the years of 1685 and 1686.

While the Bay colony was sustaining attacks on its charter government from abroad, a real menace to the lives of the colonists was spreading on the northern frontier. No sooner was King Philip's War terminated, than the Abenakis and Saco Indians with the aid of French arms were raiding the outlying settlements on the Maine and New Hampshire frontiers. During the fall of 1675 the savages encountered little resistance in massacring the defenseless settlements in this area. The United Colonies were slow to react to this uprising—still smarting under the expenses and vagrancy problems of King Philip's War[15]— and the Confederation never did "own" the war in the north. Yet the Bay was well aware of the distresses on the frontier, with refugees pouring into Boston and Salem every day.[16] A Massachusetts force under Major Waldron was sent to the northern frontier to seize leaders of the hostile Indians, but when the Indians were gathered for a treaty, the Massachusetts commander indiscriminately seized two hundred of the savages and transported them back to Boston, where some were tried and executed, others sold into slavery.[17] Needless to say, such arbitrary policy only served to inflame the border war anew. In 1677, another Massachusetts force was dispatched for the relief of the frontier, but in a number of engagements with the Indians suffered heavy casualties. The Governor of New York, seeking to "mayntayne a reciprocall good correspondence" with the New England colonies[18]—better interpreted to mean looking after His Majesty's interests—sent a force to Pemaquid, built a fort there and secured the release of some English captives. In the spring of 1678 the Indians were finally brought to terms, but throughout the following decade there remained an uneasy peace, and the Massachusetts colony continued to keep soldiers on patrol on the northern frontier.[19]

As for the defense of the New England colonies, Edward Randolph, leaving no stone unturned in recommending in his reports to the king ways to bring "the subjects there to their obedience and loyalty to theire Soveraign,"[20] presented his plan "for the present Security of that Country from forraigne or Indian invasion untill his Majesty shall please to appoint a General Governor." Randolph proposed that Josiah Winslow, "late General of the forces of the united Colonies in the Indian Warre," be appointed "his Majestys Major General of that whole plantation." The names of John Winthrop, Denison, Bradford, Treat, and Talcott, men who had served as Commissioners of the United Colonies, among others, would be "constituted Deputy Liewtenants by his Majestys Commission to settle the Militia of the Several Colonies, and to give out Commissions for the future only in his Majestys Name."[21] Such a royal military council for the colonies would then replace the Commissioners of the Confederation. But for the appointment of a royal council for the colonies, Randolph would have to wait until the establishment of the Dominion government.

The "Indian Worke," the cement of union of an earlier Confederation period, now labored under severe encumbrances. The number of praying Indians decreased in proportion to the general extermination of their hostile brethern. After King Philip's War, the praying Indians of Massachusetts were settled in four plantations: Natick, Ponkapoag, Hassamesit, and Wamesit—and only a few years since, Daniel Gookin had boasted of fourteen praying plantations! Even these poor savages were under severe restrictions. On sight of an Englishman they were to lay down their guns, nor could they "travaile the woods" with guns unless given a certificate by the Bay Indian commissioners, Major General Denison or Major Gookin.[22] The Pequot governors were continued in Connecticut and even subsidized in order that they might provide their following with adequate defense against hostile Indians, particularly from roving bands of the Iroquois.[23] Yet there were still several accomplishments in the "Indian Worke." Because of the scarcity of Indian Bibles,[24] Eliot's Indian Bible went into a second edition.

The role of the Commissioners of the United Colonies as agents in New England for the administering of the Corporation funds, however, rapidly decreased. Daniel Gookin continued to work with John Eliot, the former being intrusted with civil supervision of the praying Indians, while the latter continued to administer to their spiritual welfare—their cooperation being evidenced by their addressing correspondence jointly to the Massachusetts General Court.[25] The Corporation in London, however, became more and more concerned over the administration of the funds for the missionary work in the colonies. The "profit and improvement" of the funds sent over was "soe small" that in 1684 the Corporation demanded to know precisely in whose hands the funds were now intrusted.[26] In 1685, instead of addressing their correspondence to the Commissioners of the United Colonies, as they had been accustomed to do before the proceedings against the Massachusetts Charter were initiated, the Corporation now singled out by name the Commissioners— namely, Stoughton, Dudley, Bradstreet, Bulkeley, and Hinckley "or some of them."[27] The Corporation had hopes of Indian scholars under their auspices continuing at Harvard,[28] but were greatly disappointed in 1685 to learn that only one Indian scholar was then maintained at the College.[29]

That ubiquitous investigator-customs official of the king, Edward Randolph, did not like what he saw in the Commissioners' administering of the Corporation funds.

I have taken care to inform myself how the Mony sent over hither for the Company of Evangelizing Indians in New England is deposed of; Here are seven persons called Commissioners or Trustees, who have the sole manage of it. The chief of which are Mr. Dudley our President a man of a base servile and Antimonarchial Principle; Mr. Stoughton of the old Leven; Mr. Richards, a man not to be trusted in publick business; Mr. Hinckly, a Rigid Independent, and other like to these.

Randolph's main grievances were probably due to the control by the Massachusetts colony in disbursing the funds, which were used to the advantage of the Boston merchants, and also the employment of the funds for promoting Puritanism, whereas Randolph felt that the Anglican church should have a foothold in the New England colonies. Randolph, therefore, reminded "your Grace of your promise to me when in England; that a

Commission should be directed to some persons here unconcerned to Audit and report their Accounts of that Mony." Furthermore, "we want good Schoolmasters, none here being
allowed or but of ill Principles; The mony now converted unto
private or worse Uses, will set up good and publick Schools,
and provide a maintenance of our Minister who now lives upon
a small Contribution."[30] But the fame of one man kept the
"Indian Worke" alive for a while longer. Wrote Samuel Sewall in
February, 1686, "The best news that I can think to speak of from
America, is, that Mr. John Eliot, through the good hand of God
upon him, hath procured a second Edition of the Bible in the
Indian Language; so that many Hundreds of them may read
the Scriptures."[31] Thus the "Indian Worke" gradually faded
out,[32] the label of the Confederation was no longer upon it,
though the personnel of the Confederation still controlled the
funds. It was the sign of an end of an epoch—more than closing
the pages on the Puritan monopoly on evangelizing the New
England Indians. When John Eliot died in 1690, it was the year
that the New England Confederation distinctly gave up the ghost.

Intercolonial cooperative action[33] after King Philip's War
to the time of the coming of the Dominion government was
manifested in several forms other than the perfunctory meetings of the Commissioners during this period: first, in the negotiating of Indian treaties, and second, in the attempt to settle
land disputes. A treaty with the Mohawks brought the relationship of the New England colonies with the neighboring
colony at New York closer because of the need to present a
united front to the western Indians.

In the fall of 1677 a war scare again gripped the settlements
in the Connecticut Valley. Hatfield and Deerfield were raided
by a renegade band of Pocumtucks, which the colonists had
at first taken to be Mohawks.[34] The Mohawks, however, did
raid the friendly Indians of New England, and therefore stirred
the ire of the United Colonies, who felt the responsibility to
protect their Indian allies. The Connecticut Council, which had
previously concluded a treaty with the Mohawks, having ignored Governor Andros's proposals to proceed jointly,[35] alerted
the militia of the colony.[36] Massachusetts commissioned two
men to join with the other colonies for concluding another treaty
with the Mohawks and securing the return of captive friendly
Indians.[37] Finally, John Pynchon of Springfield was sent to

Albany, in the pay of Massachusetts,[38] where the previous treaty with the Mohawks was reaffirmed.[39] But the idea of a joint regulation of the frontier, though the colonists enacted commercial regulation with the Indians such as the granting of licenses, had not yet materialized,[40] and the English settlements continued to sprout upon the hunting grounds of the Indians without restraint of the colonial governments. Efforts to call a special session of the Confederacy in the spring of 1679 to treat with the Mohawk situation[41] failed to convene the Confederation, probably because it was known that Governor Andros wanted to attend a meeting of the Commissioners in person[42] and it was thought wise that he not become too familiar with union sentiment in the New England colonies, which he could exploit in bringing about a consolidation of the colonies.

A thorn in the flesh of the Commissioners in this twilight period of the Confederation was their indebtedness to the Rhode Island colony incurred during the war. Mention has been made of the Ishmael colony eagerly providing transportation for the united forces and caring for the wounded of the United Colonies— all of which was undertaken at the expense of Rhode Island. Like the other colonies, Rhode Island found that to cover the cost of the war "moneys will be drawn like blood from many amongst us."[43] The claims against the United Colonies for reimbursement, however, fell upon deaf ears as to both the colonial governors and the Commissioners of the United Colonies.[44] A suit in Connecticut by a person treating a soldier wounded while in the service of Major Pynchon was settled by the Commissioners, who apportioned the payment of the award among the confederate colonies.[45] But the persistent efforts of the Rhode Island governor, Peleg Sanford, came to naught in spite of his beseeching the Plymouth governor and Commissioner of the United Colonies, Thomas Hinckley, to remember the "great disbursement in the year 1675, by General Winslow's order, for the preservation of the wounded men of the Confederate Army." It was requested that at least Plymouth Colony pay its share.[46]

King Philip's War had postponed the land controversies among the colonies, not only because the war effort had been the main concern of the colonies, but also because settlers for defensive purposes had left their frontier lands. With the Indian menace now removed, the colonial boundaries needed defining.

Jurisdiction over such areas as the King's Province, Maine, and New Hampshire likewise required a settlement, and the defeat of the Indians raised the problem of disposing the newly acquired lands among the confederate colonies. In 1679, Massachusetts lost its jurisdiction over the New Hampshire towns, when a royal commission was appointed to administer the government there. The Bay, however, was more fortunate in asserting its claims over the Province of Maine, since the Colony had shrewdly bought out the Gorges heirs, thus making the Bay Colony the legal proprietor of the Province, which arrangement lasted until Maine became a state of the Union in 1820. Nevertheless, at this time the royal government refused to recognize governmental rights of the Bay over this northern province, keeping the situation in abeyance until dominion government could be established for all New England.[47]

The settlement of land controversies resulting from the war was of greater contention to the confederate colonies. At first it was proposed that a special session of the Confederacy be called in 1677, to take in commissioners from Rhode Island[48] to settle the claims on the Indian lands "according to the Articles between the Confederates." The special session, however, was not convened, nor were the land disputes seriously considered at the regular triennial session of the Commissioners in 1678. Meanwhile, speculation in the conquered lands of Mount Hope and the King's Province in the Narragansett country ran rife.[49] The activities of the Atherton Company, with the former Massachusetts Commissioner and future governor Simon Bradstreet at its head, were in full swing. This land company afforded the only hope for the Bay and River colonies to keep a foothold in the Narragansett country.[50] It was hoped thereby that claims of Plymouth and especially Rhode Island would be nullified when the settlers under the Atherton Company's auspices would choose to join with either Connecticut or Massachusetts. The three confederate colonies, however, cooperated in unanimously declaring that Rhode Island settlers in the conquered lands were intruding upon the jurisdiction of the confederate colonies—as was especially evidenced in the letter of the Commissioners to the King at their special session in August, 1679.[51]

The Atherton Company, as they had done before King Philip's War, depended upon the authority of the Commissioners of the

United Colonies to assert the claims of the Company to the lands in the Narragansett country, which was constituted the King's Province by the royal commissioners in 1664-5 and was then placed under Rhode Island officials until final determination by the Crown—an act now thought invalid by the United Colonies because these Narragansett lands, based upon Indian deeds, were conquered by the forces of the confederate army. For the encouragement of settlers to take up lands under the auspices of the Atherton Company, an advertisement appeared in Boston —probably the first enticement offered by land-jobbing companies, which were to become identified with the disposal of the public domain for over two centuries.

> Whereas, the lands of Narragansett, and Niantick countryes, and parts adjacent, are places very pleasant and fertile, fit and commodious for Plantation, and several townships; the true and legal right whereof belongs to certain gentlemen in New England (the most part of them dwelling within the Colony of the Massachusetts), by purchase from the chief Sachims, that were sole proprietors of the same, and was sinc allowed and approved by the Honoured Commissioners, or the United Colonies, and recorded in the Book of Records for the Colony of Connecticot, under which government and jurisdiction the land aforesaid lyeth.
>
> These are therefore to certifie and inform all Christian people, that are willing, or may be desirous to settle themselves in a regular way of townships on the said lands, that they may please to apply themselves to the subscribers hereof in Boston, who are by the said gentlemen, the proprietors, chosen and appointed a Committee to act in any of their concerns touching the premises; with whom all such persons may treat and agree on very easie and reasonable terms.[52]

The reference to the authority of the Commissioners of the United Colonies at this late date is of interest in showing that, despite mounting criticism against the governments of the confederate colonies for their independency, they were willing to infer that their Confederation had powers transcending those of the royal prerogative.

Connecticut Colony then directly challenged the right of Rhode Island officials, acting under royal authority, to exercise jurisdiction over the Narragansett lands. Richard Smith and Jeremiah Bull were appointed commissioners for Wickford—a settlement likewise claimed by Rhode Island.[53] When a special commission, made up largely of men who were elected to the Commissionership of the United Colonies, met at Patuxet in 1677, the claims of Connecticut to the lands in the vicinity were upheld by this special court. Rhode Island, through its agents in London, made a vigorous effort to upset this decision, "Judged by incompetent Judges of the united Collonyes who formerly plundered them."[54] When the Commissioners of the United Colonies met in August, 1679, to answer the King's inquiries, they asserted that the Mount Hope lands acquired during King Philip's War belonged to the jurisdiction of Plymouth and the Narragansett lands belonged to Connecticut. The Rhode Islanders, however, did not sit idly by, and even went to the extent of ordering the arrest of Connecticut officials appointed for the disputed territory[55]—all of which caused the River Colony to provide a more flexible basis for the regulation of the militia by delegating greater power to the county sergeant-majors. If force should be needed in the Narragansett country, the militia would be in readiness.[56]

At last the tension was relieved when the royal government in 1683 appointed a commission to conduct a hearing on the Narragansett lands, which was to report its findings to the Privy Council for final determination of the controversy.[57] This commission, however, was one sided, containing men who were definitely known to favor the position of the River Colony, with even several of the members coming from the Atherton Company. Thus it is not surprising to find the report of these commissioners setting aside the claims of Rhode Island, granting Connecticut Colony jurisdiction, and confirming the "propriety of soil" to the Atherton Company.[58] The Commission also set aside the claim of the patent issued to the Duke of Hamilton a generation earlier, which Edward Randolph had defended.[59] Royal policy, unlike the work of the royal commissioners in 1664-5, had now gone against the Rhode Islanders, and favored the landed parties in both Connecticut and Massachusetts, in effect vindicating the position of the New England Confederation in its earlier decisions to uphold the landed interests of the

United Colonies in the Narragansett country. The reason that the English government supported the position of the two confederate colonies may have been the desire to create a climate of opinion that would support future attempts to bring the colonies under more direct control.

The new government of Massachusetts after the vacation of its charter was to consist of a president and a council of sixteen members, with the boundaries of the Bay Colony now including New Hampshire, Maine, and the King's Province. Joseph Dudley, a former Commissioner of the United Colonies and a moderate, was named President of the Council; no provision was made for continuing the House of Deputies. A conspicuous omission in the Council was Thomas Danforth, the acknowledged leader of the orthodox party.[60] Although the new government was less amenable to the people, several innovations commended it, such as the provisions for a chief justice in the form of the deputy president and for the probate courts.[61] Whether the creation of Massachusetts as a royal dependency was originally intended as a temporary expedient[62] is open to question. Nevertheless, the advantages of a more general union of the colonies were soon apparent. Such a union would enable greater enforcement of the acts of trade, and, assuming the role of the former Confederation of the colonies, would provide for the common defense. It would be a convenient time for the home government to unite the New England colonies: *quo warranto* proceedings were under way against the Rhode Island and Connecticut charters, and the Plymouth Colony still had no basis for their corporate government. A foreboding of confining the New England colonies to dominion status was found in President Dudley's inauguration address. Always a union man —himself a former Commissioner of the United Colonies as was his more strait-laced father, who a generation before had given valuable service to the New England Union—Dudley declared that he and the new Council would "take the charge and management of this His Majesties Territory and Dominion of New England" for the "happy increase and advance of these Provinces, by their more immediate dependence upon the Crown of England" and a "sober loyall and dutyfull dimenour towards His Majestyes Government here," the "plainest path unto your own happiness."[63]

The Stuart policy of centralizing government in the colonies under more direct control of the home government had a very real basis, because of the danger of aggression from their French neighbor to the north.[64] But other practical reasons existed for wanting to consolidate the governments of the colonies. First of all, there was the very great expense of maintaining separate royal governments in the colonies; the colonies not sustain the expense of the many English officials required to come to the colonies. Furthermore, there would be needed effective enforcement of the trade acts and development of naval stores in the New England colonies.[65] The conciliatory policy of President Dudley, and his rivalry with Randolph, was impeding the work of the new government in the Bay, especially Randolph's collection of custom duties. It was not surprising then that as early as June, 1686, Sir Edmund Andros was commissioned Governor of the Dominion of New England, with powers including those of Captain General of all military forces of the Dominion and Vice Admiral of the English navy. The new governor would preside over a territory embracing all of the confederate colonies, Rhode Island, New Hampshire, Maine, and the disputed Narragansett country. Like the Dudley administration in Massachusetts, the Dominion governor was to preside over a council made up of the leading prerogative men in the colonies. Thus the proposals of Randolph in 1681 were put into effect. This bitter opponent of the Puritan oligarchy had written that the appointment of a Governor General over "all the Colonies being 5 in number[66] united under one generall Government" would be more "servicable to the Crown, and the better enabled to secure themselves and Neighbouring Plantations against any forreign Invasion or Domestick attempts; all of them at present being independent, not one Government haveing authority, or Influence upon another in Civill or Military Affaires."[67] Though the courts of election had already elected Commissioners of the United Colonies for 1686, the establishment of royal government in Massachusetts and subsequently dominion government for the colonies, served sharply to cut off the Confederation. Naturally, with the colonies brought under imperial control and a consolidated administration replacing the cooperative union of the colonies, the New England Confederation could not exist. To have done so would have been rebellion. Thus no Commissioners were chosen during the period of the dominion government from any of the three colonies.

On a bleak December day in 1686, the head of the Stuart contrivance for the Dominion of New England, the paper union of all His Majesty's colonies in the Canaan of the New World, arrived in Boston with two companies of English troops, the first ever to be stationed in America. The arrival of the "Captain Generall, Governour of New England" was a gala occasion. When the Governor had landed he was met by a great crowd of Boston merchants and many other citizens, and all the militia of "Horse and Foot" were drawn up to honor the new Governor. But Governor Andros was not one to be delayed by pomp and circumstance; he had a serious and difficult task, to transform completely the governments of the New England colonies, which could only be done with speed, before an opposition party could be organized. Thus he proceeded immediately to the Town House, the scene of the former government and of the meetings of the Commissioners of the United Colonies when in Boston, where his commission of June, 1686, and subsequent instructions were read. A Council for the colonies was summoned to meet nine days later,[68] and for those officials already present, the oaths of allegiance and office were administered.[69] But the first meetings of the new Council were thinly attended, and of the twenty-six members of the Council, hardly more than six or seven ever appeared, and these being recipients of the Governor's patronage, such as the former Commissioners of the United Colonies, Dudley and Stoughton, who were both appointed judges of the "Superior Court."[70]

The Dominion of New England afforded a sharp contrast to the previous self-governing colonies. The only constitution was that derived from the commission and various instructions to the new governor,[71] which struck at the very heart of local self-government and confined all powers in an administrative agency, without recognition of the right of people to legislate in their own affairs. In effect, the Andros government was to be absolute, invested with full authority to enact laws, levy taxes, and control the militia of the colonies. Andros was authorized to regulate the value of foreign coinage in the colonies,[72] the right of the Bay to continue minting its own coins being disallowed. All laws were to be sent to England for approval,

and those disallowed by the King in Council were to be void
in the colonies.[73] An alien feature to the laws of New England
was the requiring of a quit rent of two shillings and sixpence
per hundred acres on all lands to be disposed in the future.[74]
"Liberty of Conscience" was to be permitted to all religions, but
with special emphasis upon "the exercise of Religion according
to the Church of England."[75] Another point of contrast with the
former government was the placing of New England on a permanent military basis, whereas formerly the colonies would invest
supreme military authority in the colonial councils or the Confederation for the temporary duration of an emergency. But
now, with the government under continual control of the Governor-General, the supreme commander of the military forces
of the colonies and his administrative council, all affairs of government could at any time be subject to the military arm.
Andros recognized the value of maintaining a strong grasp on
the military forces in order to bring about effectively the consolidation of the New England governments—using the pretence
of threatened invasion from the French in Canada.[76] A vital
part in the consolidation of the military resources of the colonies
was the establishment of military depots "for receiving and
keeping of arms, ammunition, and other public stores."[77]

But the coming of Governor Andros to organize the governments of Massachusetts, New Plymouth, New Hampshire,
Maine, and the Narragansett country under one administration
still left the envisioned dominion of the northern colonies incom-
plete. To round out the Dominion of New England, the submission of Connecticut and Rhode Island had to be obtained.
Although neither of the two colonies would surrender their
charters to Andros, Rhode Island readily acquiesced in the new
government by sending its five members to the Andros Council.
The River Colony, however, remained obstinate; and, although
the surrendering of its charter was not essential to the dissolu-
tion of the colonial government,[78] Governor Andros took the
position that such action was necessary as a visible sign of submission. Three writs of *quo warranto* were served on the Connecticut colony to surrender its charter, but they were of no avail.[79]
Pressure was brought to bear on Connecticut—even Governor
Dongan of New York advised the Colony's submission, and
indeed, there was little left to do unless Connecticut should take
its chances in court, with very little chance for success, since

the Massachusetts and the City of London charters had already been vacated.[80]

Governor Andros, to demonstrate his policy (he still harbored a special grievance against Connecticut for that Colony's refusal to allow his contingent of New York troops to participate in the war of the United Colonies against Philip's Indians) decided in October, 1687, to travel down to Hartford and compel the recalcitrant River officials to submit formally to his dominion government. Little notice was given to the Hartford authorities of the coming of the Andros expedition from Boston, and therefore there was not much that could be done except to welcome the dominion governor and his entourage upon their arrival.[81] Andros soon attended a meeting of the General Court, and while a debate was ensuing, with the Connecticut Charter lying upon the table, the lights of the chamber were suddenly extinguished. When the lights came on again, the Charter had vanished. Many a story has been written about the disappearance of the Connecticut Charter—that it was whisked away to the famous Charter Oak, and there remained until popular government was restored in the colony—and many guesses have been made as to who was responsible for this daring maneuver—Allyn, Talcott, Treat, or Wadsworth. Some have doubted the authenticity of the episode altogether. But such discussion is not within the scope of this work; it suffices to note that in any event Governor Andros did not secure the Charter. Nevertheless, he had accomplished for the time being the main object of his mission, for he successfully secured the submission of the Colony. The General Court immediately ceased its jurisdiction, and ordered that the Colony, "being annexed to the Massachusetts and other colonys," proceed "under his Excelencies Government."[82] Three weeks later the Dominion Council declared that the laws of the Council were now in force in the River Colony.[83] In April, 1688, the jurisdiction of the Dominion was extended to embrace New York and the Jerseys—with this last addition considered as one colony. The Dominion of New England covered in one union eight of His Majesty's colonies, a solid phalanx on the northern seaboard.

The powers of the Dominion Governor were now quite formidable. He was to preside over a Council of forty-two members from the representatives of the colonies forming the consolidation. The governor had authority to suspend a Councillor or any members of the militia simply by showing sufficient cause. With only five members making a quorum in the Council, there was virtually no restraint upon the influence of the Governor, who could always count on a loyal few to carry through his policy. Even that odious practice of giving to provincial governors the "power of the press" was initiated, by which all printing had to be licensed by the government.[84] Such an arbitrary government was obviously an anachronism in New England affairs. If Andros had been as wise a politician as he was an able administrator of Stuart policy, he might have had a fair degree of success in consolidating the New England governments on a permanent basis. Playing for the support of not only the prerogative men but also for the moderate party men such as Bradstreet and Stoughton, Governor Andros could have built up real support for the government. He would also have had to be careful not to interfere too directly with the settled institutions of the New Englanders. But resorting to his training as Governor of the province of New York, Andros made the tragic blunder of trying to institute government alien to the New Englanders—of which there could have been no greater error in judging the temperament of a people who on their own had constructed a confederate government.

The Dominion Governor soon found that exercising his authority was an entirely different matter from what it had appeared on paper. Concentrating his efforts on the Bay Colony, the Andros Council proceeded to levy taxes without the consent of an assembly of the people. Public fees were increased, those of the probate some twenty-fold. Town meetings were allowed to meet but once a year. Writs of intrusion forced the landed proprietors to engage in expensive suits to defend their titles; the claims of the Atherton Company in the Narragansett country were again invalidated, as "having been based upon grants extorted through terror from the Indians by the illegal acts of the United Colonies," and Rhode Island was again for the third time given jurisdiction over the King's Province.[85] Many grievances mounted against the Andros government, some of which were merely distasteful to the Puritan manner of doing things. But the investment in the colonial executive of sole powers of taxation, the infringement upon the land system of the colonies, and the regulation of town government aroused the resentment of all the New England colonists, to whatever faction they belonged.

Governor Andros had little time to expand his experiment in consolidation outside the Bay Colony. The protests there had shown that he would have to proceed more cautiously. But meanwhile his time was consumed inspecting the governments under his rule and in raising forces to put down an Indian uprising, again spreading on the northern frontier. The advantages of consolidation from a military point of view were seen when Andros personally headed an expedition of some seven or eight hundred troops to the Maine settlements—a protection to this frontier which the New England Confederation after King Philip's War was unable to afford, and would be unable to do again when the reins of Dominion government would be severed.[86] But the Andros expedition only added to his unpopularity, and he was even accused of creating a war in order to build up his military control.[87]

The Indian problem thus averted the Dominion government from meeting a real test in domestic policy. As for the land grants requiring the payment of quit rents, not more than twenty were actually passed during the entire Andros administration,[88] to give an indication of how little the process of royalization of the New England colonies had progressed. Andros's attention was further distracted by the pressure put on him from New York for a joint expedition of the Dominion colonies against the French in Canada.[89] Nor was there much time to revive the missionary work among the Indians, which had been the province of the Commissioners of the United Colonies. The Lieutenant-Governor of the Dominion, Francis Nicholson, who resided at New York, took it upon himself to visit several of the plantations of praying Indians, but used the opportunity to draft the Indians into military service.[90] Although Eliot, lingering on to the last days in his worldly home, felt that "the work in general seemeth to my soul to be in and well toward a reviving," he sensed that he was "drawing home,"[91] which also might have been said of the "Indian Worke" as a whole.

Hardly had Andros returned to Boston from his unfruitful expedition against the northern Indians, than a wave of popular indignation greeted him. Tidings of the landing of William of Orange had reached the New World. The Governor tried unsuccessfully to keep the news from the populace, but the long-awaited overthrow of the Stuart monarchy, accomplished without the shedding of blood, was too great an occurrence in the Puritan colonies to be for long kept secret. The news of the "Protestant Wind" bringing the Prince of Orange (New Englanders through their Puritan heritage had always entertained a closer tie with the Dutch than did their brethren back home) served as a spark to raise the colonists in the Bay in rebellion against the hated regime. The organization of government during the course of the rebellion was in many ways similar to the course of action followed by the American patriots during the era of the Revolution.

On that fateful day of April 18,[92] the very day that the second rebellion began in 1775 in the British march to Concord, about nine o'clock in the morning, the sound of drums echoed throughout the town of Boston. A crowd of townspeople began to crowd about the Town House, eagerly awaiting word from the leading citizens, who as members of Andros' Council were known to be unsympathetic to the Dominion government. About noon a "Declaration of the Gentlemen, Merchants, and Inhabitants of Boston and the Country adjacent" was read, meeting the approval of the people. Like the Declaration of the following century, it enumerated grievances against the arbitrary rule of Andros and conciliar government as a whole.[93] The peroration of this Declaration of the right of revolution, with its expressions of a latent nationalism, is deserving of quotation:

We do therefore seize upon the persons of those few ill men which have been (next to our sins) the grand authors of our miseries; resolving to secure them for what justice orders from his Highness, with the English Parliament, shall direct, lest, ere we are aware, to find (what we may fear, being on all sides in danger) ourselves to be by them given away to a foreign power, before such orders can reach unto us; for which orders we now humbly wait. In the mean time, firmly believing that we have endeavored nothing but what mere duty to God and our country calls for at our hands, we commit our enterprise unto the blessing of Him who hears the cry of the oppressed; and advise all our neghbors, for whom we have thus ventured ourselves, to join with us in prayers, and all just actions, for the defence of the land.

The leading men in the revolution of both the moderate and old guard factions put in an appearance at the Town House during this dramatic episode, among whom were counted the former Commissioners of the United Colonies—William Stoughton, Thomas Danforth, Simon Bradstreet, Wait Winthrop—and a new political figure in the Bay, a Commissioner during the revival of the Confederation, Elisha Cooke.[94]

Andros and his retainers took refuge in the castle fort in Boston harbor, but were soon compelled to surrender, and were held as prisoners. Thus, with one easy stroke, rebellion was smoothly accomplished in New England. It has been pointed out that the New England colonies would have revolted against the Andros government whether or not the Glorious Revolution had taken place in the mother country. Evidence given for this position is the careful framing of the "Declaration," which must have taken more than several days during the fury of revolt to have been drawn up.[95] The reasons given for the justification of the revolution in New England, the attempt of Andros to stifle the news of the landing of William of Orange in England and the popular furor over Andros's Indian expedition,[96] only ignited into flames the rebellion that was smouldering under real economic and political grievances.

The New Englanders sought to cover up all traces of the brief period of the Dominion of New England. It was to be nothing more than an unpleasant memory. The records of the Andros Council were slashed from the official records of the colonies, and the new records of the established colonial governments read as if nothing had happened during the sixteen months of the Andros regime, the time that Connecticut was included in the Dominion, and twenty-eight months for the Massachusetts Colony. Connecticut immediately re-established its charter government, pointing out that it was never revoked, though there was "an interruption to our government" due to the brief dominion status of the colonies.[97] Since Connecticut had felt the brunt of

Andros' policies very little, the freemen of the colony had no difficulty in reconvening a court of elections in May and renewing their former government.[98] Plymouth, likewise, soon had its previous government in operation again. But in the Bay, four years of Council government under President Dudley and then under Andros had effected a real severance of the colonial government. To get back on its feet a gradual policy had to be followed: first, as in a later Revolution period, a Council of Safety of the prominent men of the Colony delegated to themselves interim authority of government. The venerable former Governor and Commissioner, Simon Bradstreet, was chosen president of this body; and Wait Winthrop, now of the Bay Colony, who had served as a Connecticut Commissioner with his father during the latter's last year of life, was placed in command of the militia.

From the Massachusetts Council of Safety would emerge the re-establishment of the Colony government and a brief revival of the New England Confederation, both of which would soon be replaced by a new imperial arrangement whereby the one-time Puritan Commonwealth would become a royal colony and Plymouth would cease to exist as a separate colony. But the road to subsequent union of the American colonies was now to be trodden in an ever widening sphere of intercolonial cooperative action. Though the Andros government and succeeding generations failed to contribute in depth to an emerging consciousness for union, the desire for the enlargement of the sphere of cooperation, now embracing all of the New England colonies and New York, was a very definite contribution. Thus the Dominion of New England was more than an unfortunate interlude or interruption: it increased the horizons for American union.

---

[1] *PCR*, X, 407-9.

[2] *PCR*, X, 410-12. This recommendation was carried out after a delay. (*MCR*, V, 463.)

[3] English commercial regulation in relation to the American colonies is one of the few phases relating to seventeenth century America that has received the light of modern research, and therefore will not be dealt with in depth in this chapter. For the background of the maneuvers leading to the vacating of the Massachusetts Charter, see Palfrey, *op. cit.*, III; George L. Beer, *The Old Colo-*

nial System, 1660-1754, Pt. 1, II; and Viola F. Barnes, *The Dominion of New England: A Study in British Colonial Policy,* (New Haven: 1923), Vol. XI of *Yale University Historical Publications.*

[4] Report of the Commissioners of Customs, 12May75, Bancroft Transcripts (New England), II, 303-311, NYPL.

[5] The documents and letters relating to this investigation are found in Robert N. Toppan, ed., *Edward Randolph . . . Letters and Official Papers,* Vol. XXV of the *PPs,* (Boston: 1898), II, 192-268.

[6] Documents and letters in Toppan, ed., *op. cit.,* pp. 274-320.

[7] *Ibid.,* pp. 282-3; Beer, *op. cit.,* pp. 270-3 .

[8] Toppan, ed., *op. cit.,* III, 19-34; Edward Randolph, "A short Narrative of my proceedings," *Andros Tracts,* Vol. VII of the *PPS* (1874), III, 226; Beer, *op. cit.,* pp. 275-7.

[9] Beer, *op. cit.,* pp. 282-4. The situation in Connecticut was different since that colony owed its charter to the Stuart government, and "after above forty yeares sweating and toyle in they wilderness . . . we have neither Leasore or ability to Lanch out in any considerable Trade at Sea, haveing onely a few smale vessells to carry our corne Hoggs and Horses unto our Neighbours of Yorke and Boston." (Ltr to his Majesty's Commissioners of Customs, 24Jan80/1, CA, Foreign Affairs, I, 24.)

[10] "Representation of the Bostoneers, 1680," *Hutchinson Papers,* Vol. III of the *PPs,* II, 265. Also "Printed Laws of New England contrary or Disagreeable to Laws of England," *Andros Tracts, op. cit.,* pp. 13ff.

[11] *Hutchinson Papers, op. cit.,* p. 281.

[12] An "old man, quiet and grave . . . dressed in black silk" was the observation of a visiting Dutchman. [For further description of New England at the time, including an interesting account of a militia drill, see Jasper Dankers and Peter Sluyter, "Journal of our Voyage from New Netherland," *Memoirs of the Long Island Historical Society,* (Brooklyn: 1867), I, 369, 378, 389-90.]

[13] Beer, *op. cit.,* p. 300.

[14] "Measures to be taken after vacation of Charter," Toppan, ed., *op. cit.,* III, 324-6; "Exemplification of the Judgment for Vacating the Charter of Massachusetts Bay," *MHSC,* 4:II:246-78. Instead of actual disallowance of colonial laws the royal government was beginning to use a more positive method, the issuing of instructions, which in superseding previous measures were really "dormant disallowances." (C. M. Andrews, "The Royal Disallowance," *AASP,* XXIV, 342-62. For a complete survey of the practice of sending colonial agents to London, see James J. Burns, *The Colonial Agents of New England* (Washington, D. C., 1935).

[15] In Milford, the "extreordenary expense" of supplying the army with food while stationed at New London was typical of burdens placed upon the towns. (Fenn to Winthrop, 22Feb76/7, Winthrop Papers, MHS, XIII.) Refugees increased the problem of vagrancy. For reasons for having tight qualifications for newcomers, see Channing, *op. cit.,* I, 428. The Commissioners of the United

Colonies expressed appreciation for aid received from Rhode Island during the war, but the "Hospitall" for wounded troops provided by Rhode Island was considered a poor exchange for the "House of Correction" provided them by the United Colonies. (Hough, ed., op. cit., pp. 132-4.)

[16] *New Hampshire Historical Society Collections*, III, (1870), 101-2.

[17] Friendly Indians, such as the Mohegans, would often sell captive Indian children to the English. (E.g., Ind. Deeds, Unbound, CHS, 9Jan77.)

[18] Winthrop Papers, MHS, X, 70.

[19] See Nathaniel Adams, *Annals of Portsmouth*, (Portsmouth: 1825), pp. 60-63; George W. Chase, *The History of Haverhill, Mass.*, (Haverhill: 1861); for the destruction of Groton, see S. A. Green, *Early Records of Groton* (Groton: 1880).

[20] "The case upon the patent of the Corp. of Mass. Bay," New England and New York MSS, 28Oct77, MHS.

[21] Toppan, ed., *op. cit.*, III, 40. Either Randolph was unmindful of Winthrop's death, or meant his son, Wait Winthrop.

[22] Nathaniel Bouton, ed., *Documents re New Hampshire*, I, 348. Uncas and the Mohegans reaffirmed their "long friendship" with the English. (Willys Papers, CHS, II, 13Aug77; CA, Indians, ser. 1, I, 34, 14May78.)

[23] CA, Indians, ser. 1, I, 31; *CCR*, II, 500-1.

[24] Even none could be found at the Boston booksellers. (Dankers and Sluyter, *op. cit.*, 382-3.

[25] MA, XXX, 285, 20Aug84.

[26] Winship, *op. cit.*, p. 203.

[27] *Ibid.*, pp. 206-8.

[28] For the poverty of the College at this time see Andrew McFarland Davis, "The Early College Buildings at Cambridge," *AASP*, New Ser., VI, 323-49. Some relief was obtained from the Bay which exempted estates of the College Corporation and its officers up to £100 per person. *(MCR*, IV, Pt. 2, 537, 8Oct72.) It is interesting to note, since this study has emphasized the influence of the Dutch upon the Confederation, that even the "Rules and Orders" for a professorship in Divinity in Harvard was copied after the methods of the "professors in the Universitys of Holland." Printed in Josiah Quincy, *History of Harvard*, p. 535.

[29] Winship, ed., *op. cit.*, pp. 206-8.

[30] Randolph to the Archbishop of Canterbury, 27Oct86. *Andros Tracts*, III 18-9.

[31] *Letter Book, MHSC* 6:I:22.

[32] For a severe indictment of the treatment of the New England Indians, "the desolations caused by promiscuous slaughter, starvation, sickness, and the slave-business," see Frederick Freeman, *Civilization and Barbarism* (Cambridge: 1878).

[33] In July, 1684, the colonies of Virginia, Maryland, Massachusetts, and New York were represented at a conference at Albany. The purpose of the meeting

was to conclude a treaty with the Indians. Massachusetts, however, was represented by a New Yorker, Stephanus Van Cortlandt.

[34] Wells and Wells, *op. cit.*, pp. 88-95.

[35] Misc. MSS, MHS, III, 24May77; Willys Papers, CHS, II, 5Apr77; CA, Col. Wars, I, 140.

[36] *CCR*, II, 506-7.

[37] CA, Colonial Wars, I, 138.

[38] See Mason A. Green, *Springfield, 1636-1886* (Springfield, Mass.: 1888).

[39] *Ibid.*, p. 199.

[40] Ronald O. MacFarlane, "Indian Relations in New England, 1620-1760: a Study of a Regulated Frontier," *Harvard University Summaries of Theses,* (Cambridge: 1934), pp. 167-70.

[41] MA, LXIX, 222.

[42] *PCR*, X, 404.

[43] Williams to Hinckley, *Hinckley Papers, MHSC* 4:V, 4Oct78.

[44] Sanford to Hinckley, 27May82, *Hinckley Papers, MHSC* 4:V:67-9.

[45] Willys Papers, CHS, II, 10. Meeting of the Commissioners, 6Sep81.

[46] Sanford to Hinckley, 1Jun82, *Hinckley Papers, op. cit.*, pp. 69-70.

[47] Farnham, ed., *Documentary History of Maine*, VII, 15Mar78.

[48] R. R. Hinman, ed., *Letters from the English Kings and Queens . . .*, (Hartford: 1836), p. 101, 17Aug77, Winslow Papers, I, 107, MHS, 23Aug77.

[49] MA, III, 26; Reynolds to Winslow to Mass. Council, 15Sep78 and 20Feb78/9, resp., Winslow Papers, MHS, I, 111 and 112.

[50] See Leach, op. cit., pp. 115-6.

[51] CA, Foreign Affairs, I, 15; MA, II, 205; Misc. MSS (Allyn), 25Jul79, NYHS; Winthrop Papers, MHS, X, 34, Allyn to Winthrop, 1Aug79; *MHSC* 1:V:220-9; Irving B. Richman, *Rhode Island,* (New York: 1902), II, 211.

[52] *RICR*, III, 10.

[53] *CCR*, III, 32.

[54] *Harris Papers, RIHSC*, X, 180-1, 234; R. I. Archives, Boundary Settlements, R. I. and Mass., I, 4; Sainsbury, ed., *Calendar of State Papers,* IX, 587, Stevens Transcripts, IV, 453, John Carter Brown Library. In 1675 the governors of the colonies bordering on Rhode Island were requested to appoint a commission to "hear all differences" relating to the land controversies. (Hinman, *op. cit.*, 4Aug75, p. 98).

[55] *CCR*, III, 286-90.

[56] *Ibid.*, pp. 61-3.

[57] *Ibid.*, p. 320.

[58] *Ibid.*, p. 321, *RICR*, III, 40-5.

[59] See Elizabeth H. Schenk, *The History of Fairfield,* (New York: 1899), I, 221. In Rhode Island's view, the 7,000 acres of Mount Hope lands were within the limits of the Rhode Island charter and the King's Province, "notwithstanding the United or Confederate Collonys (as they tearme themselves) have endeavored to insult over your loyall people, and have forbidden us the exer-

cise of your Royall pleasure, as to the government thereof." *(RICR, III, 43-6.)*

[60] Danforth, while President of Maine, appointed by Massachusetts, received generous portions of lands for his service. (E.g., Baxter, ed., *Documentary History of Maine,* IV, 414.)

[61] Everett Kimball, *The Public Life of Joseph Dudley,* (N. Y.: 1911), p. 30-1.

[62] The Dudley administration was only intended to be temporary.

[63] MA, Council Recs., II, n.d. No attempt was made by the Dudley administration at this time to interfere with local government. (MA, Council Recs, II, 35.) But licenses from "some of his Majesty's Councill, or any two Justices of the peace" were needed for trade in "strong Liquor" with the Indians. *(Ibid.,* II, 44. 8Jun86.)

[64] See Edward Channing, "Col. Thos. Dongan, Gov. of N. Y.," *AASP,* XVIII, 336-345. That the French always entertained a dread of a united New England may be ascertained from Father Druillettes's statement in 1650-1: "I suppose it a thing perfectly assured that the English of the four united colonies—to wit, Boston, Plymeouth, Kenetigout, and Kwinopeia (New Haven)— are very well equipped for exterminating the savage nations." *(Jesuit Relations,* XXXVI, 105.)

[65] Barnes, *op. cit.,* pp. 29-31. For the steady increase in the prosperity of the colonies since the forming of the first Confederation in 1643 as a factor in bringing about consolidation, see Hermann F. Clarke, *"John Hull, Colonial Merchant," AASP,* XLVI (1936), 197-221.

[66] Massachusetts, Plymouth, New Hampshire, Maine and the Narragansett country.

[67] Randolph to Jenkins, 30Apr81, Toppan, ed., *op. cit.,* (A. T. S. Goodrick, ed. of Vols. VI and VII), *PPS,* VII, 89-94. In reference to the Indian Worke, which Eliot wrote of in 1686 as "nothing new but lamentations." *(MHSC* 1:III, ltr to Boyle, 29Aug86.) Dudley showing his union sympathy wished the Confederation could better deal with the funds when they would be sent over and appoint "general agents" to supervise the problems of trade, etc. *(CCR,* III, 311-2.)

[68] MA, Council Records, II, 106, 20Dec86; Larabee, *Royal Instructions,* I, *passim.*

[69] *Ibid.* (Larabee), No. 72.

[70] Palfrey, *op. cit.,* III, 519-20.

[71] Barnes, *op. cit.,* p. 40.

[72] See Andrew McF. Davis, "Andros's Proclamation Money," *ASP,* New Ser., XIII, 500-8.

[73] Larabee, ed., *Royal Instructions,* I, No. 209.

[74] Toppan, ed., *op. cit.,* III, 334; Barnes, *op. cit.,* p. 41.

[75] *Ibid.* Randolph was always critical of retaining in the Council members of the "late Government," whom he thought took advantage of the "liberty of conscience" to "retain their old principles." (Stevens Transcripts, III, 214, John Carter Brown Library.)

[76] For the designs of French Canada on the English colonies, see George Stanley, and Harold M. Jackson, *Canada's Soldiers, 1604-1954*, (New York: 1954), pp. 31-89.

[77] Larabee, ed., *op. cit.*, #572.

[78] Charles J. Hoadley, *Hiding of the Charters*, (Hartford: 1900), p. 21.

[79] *CCR*, III, 375-88; A. C. Bates, "Expedition of Sir Edmund Andros," *AASP*, (Oct., 1938), 276-99.

[80] L. Welles, *Loss of the Charter in Conn.*, (New Haven: 1918), pp. 110, 127-8.

[81] For summaries of the Dominion period see Charles M. Andrews, *The Fathers of New England*, Vol. VI of the *Chronicles of America Series*, (New Haven: 1919) or Ch. XIII of Osgood, *op. cit.*, III.

[82] Larabee, ed. *op. cit.*, No. 18; *CCR*, III, 248.

[83] MA, Council Recs., II, 154.

[84] Palfrey, *op. cit.*, III, 561-2; C. A. Duniway, *Development of Freedom of the Press in Massachusetts*, (1906), p. 64.

[85] Samuel G. Arnold, *History of the State of Rhode Island*, (New York: 1859), I, 498-502.

[86] *Province and Court Records of Maine*, Introd., *passim;* Samuel A. Drake, *The Border Wars of New England*, (New York: 1897), pp. 9-11.

[87] John Palmer, "The Revolution in New England Justified," *Andros Tracts*, I, p. 73; Parker, *op. cit.* (Pemaquid), p. 149. For an enumeration of grievances against the Andros government, see Toppan and Goodrick, eds., *op. cit.*, VII, 342-4.

[88] Osgood, *op. cit.*, III, 408. The protest of the New Englanders was not against taxes as such (the Confederation had levied taxes on a proportionate basis), but rather against usurped power. (See Charles H. J. Douglas, *The Financial History of Massachusetts to the American Revolution*, Vol. I of *Columbia University Studies . . .,*(New York: 1892), pp. 22-3, 51.)

[89] O'Callaghan, ed., *The Documentary History of New York*, I, 273-4. Council held at Fort James, 13Mar87/8.

[90] Huntoon, *op. cit.*, p. 20. In 1691, Captain Prentice was petitioned by the praying Indians to become their superintendent upon the death of Daniel Gookin, who had served in that capacity during the Confederation period. A committee was appointed concerning the "mookegan Lands" to "take care of the said Lands that the Indians be not wronged in theire rightfull possessions." (Emmet Coll., No. 4919, NYPL.)

[91] Eliot to Boyle, 7Jul88, *MHSC*, 1:III:187. Randolph had proposed a "Romanist Mission" in the "Indian Worke." Also: "I feare much of this Stock has been imployed to oppose his Late Majestie prosecuting their charter." (Toppan and Goodrick, eds., *op. cit.*, VI, 240-7.)

[92] Old Style.

[93] Palfrey (Vol. III) has an excellent summary of the contemporary tracts, on the events of the Revolution in New England and I have found it not necessary for the purposes of this study to go much beyond his narrative. The following quotation in the text is quoted in Palfrey (III), pp. 578-9.

[94] Albert Matthews, *Notes on the Massachusetts Royal Commissions, 1681-1775*, (Cambridge: 1913), pp. 15-20. The invective of the Declaration reflected the pent up bitterness of the New Englanders; e.g., condemning the "illegalities . . . done by these Horse-Leaches in the two or three yeares that they have been sucking of us . . . Doubtless a land so ruled as once New England was, has not without many fears and sighs beheld the wicked walking on every side and the vilest Men Halted." (Stevens Transcripts, III, 250, John Carter Brown Lib.)

[95] See Osgood, *op. cit.*, III, Ch. XIV.

[96] *The Revolution in New-England Justified, Force Tracts*, V, No. 9.

[97] Gov. and Council of Conn. to James Porter, 3Jun89, *CHSC*, XXIV, 26.

[98] *CCR*, III, 250.

CHAPTER XV

Remnants of Confederation

At no other time before the period of the American Revolution was there greater affinity for union among the colonies than during the brief years of 1689-91. During this time the New England Confederation was revived for a brief spell, and intercolonial cooperative action for military purposes branched out through all the New England and Middle Colonies, as was evidenced by the New York Conference of 1690, which led to the fiasco of a joint expedition to Canada. These two years are most important in showing the progress of the evolution of the federal principle in America. With "sad distractions" once again because of the brief transition of government in the homeland, the colonists, faced with providing for their own common defense, took the reins of government into their own hands. The course they took was the most natural one. Without hesitation, the colonists resorted to intercolonial union, which is evidence that their combining in time of stress was the accustomed mode of action. The premise of federalism, cooperative action, was now firmly established. It remained for the future for the common ties of heritage and purpose to give rise to a buoyant nationalism that would cement the colonies into a permanent federal union.

For many days after the overthrow of the Andros regime, the excitement of rebellion continued in the Bay Colony; the "Sword yet continued in every Man's hands, and for divers weeks, the Colony continued without any pretence to Civil Government."[1] A general court was convened on the basis of the governor and assistants chosen by the freemen in 1686,[2] the last election before Dudley assumed the presidency of the Council government. All that was accomplished at this five week session of the General Court was to declare the previous laws of the Colony according to their original charter to be in effect provisionally until further word from the new government in England. It was expected that, because of the triumph of Whiggery in England, a new charter would be given to the colony. Increase Mather was already negotiating a charter,[3] and such critics of the Andros government as William Phips, who felt Andros had usurped the powers of his office of provost marshal general, and Richard Wharton,[4] Samuel Sewall, and Elisha Hutchinson were giving Mather able assistance in winning friends for the Bay Colony.[5]

Meanwhile the tomahawk was unleashed with renewed fury on the northern frontier, with the "sack of Dover" encouraging the savages to spread their hostilities; on the western frontier near Albany the French were inciting the Indians to attack the English settlements. Connecticut hastened to send a contingent of troops to the Albany vicinity to reinforce the New York troops garrisoning that frontier.[6] A call was issued by the authority of the King that in case of an all-out Indian offensive in New Hampshire, the "assistance" of all the "neighboring colonies" should be provided, that "due provision may be made to oppose and repel them."[7] Volunteers were ordered raised in the Bay Colony, mostly from the friendly Indians, to be dispatched to the northerly settlements under the command of that military adventurer, Benjamin Church.[8] For this proposed expedition of a mixed band of English troops and Indians, the Bay Colony sent messengers to the two former confederate colonies, Connecticut and Plymouth, for their "advise and assistance."[9] This request was to touch off again negotiations for convening the Commissioners of the Confederation for a fall session. Five years had lapsed since the last session of the Confederation —the time for the regular triennial meeting had unfortunately fallen during the Dominion government.

Almost without exception, all sketches of the New England Confederation state flatly that the Confederation ended in the year 1684, that the Dominion of New England forever ended the New England Confederacy. Herbert L. Osgood, some fifty years ago in his able history of the colonies, stated the Confederation ended in 1684. But such was not the case: the Confederacy was revived, and one of the fruitful pieces of the research for this study has been the reconstruction of this renewal of the Confederation. The brief appearance of the New England Union—itself a specter of the past—demonstrates that combining had become a natural tendency and the colonies had acquired a taste for union that was to find other channels of cooperative action in the future.

Not long after their first letter desiring the cooperation of

Connecticut and Plymouth in an expedition against the northern Indians, the Massachusetts authorities requested their former confederates, for the "joint and vigorous prosecution of the common enemy," to send Commissioners to Boston, "according to the rules of our ancient union and confederation."[10] Governor Robert Treat of Connecticut gladly received the Bay proposal for the revival of the Confederation: "our Neighbourhood and correspondence begins to revive again, in its ancient and proper forme, after so great and threatening an eclipse", that "you cannot but assure yourselfs that we bear our share as become Bretheren" in "both intestine and foreigne disquietments." Although the Connecticut General Court had not yet designated men to serve in the capacity of Commissioners, they were "willing in the season of it to revive the ancient confederation of the colonyes." Concluding his letter, the Governor of the River Colony wrote: "If you shall see cause to signifye to us, the Highest you will give by the pole, or to send some Gentlemen from your selves to treat with them, we shall not be wanting to assist without influence in what shall be rationally desired of us."[11] The Court then proceeded to elect two men, William Pitkin and Samuel Mason, though not officially given proper title as Commissioners of the United Colonies, to "treat with those of Massachusetts and Plimouth to consult of such rules and methods as shall be judged most proper" for the "preserveing" of their "Majesties subjects."[12]

In August of 1689, Plymouth elected two Commissioners of the United Colonies to serve for the remainder of the year, Thomas Hinckley and John Walley. They were to inquire into the "grounds" of the war and see that the colony bore its due proportion with their "friends and ancient confederates of the Massachusetts and Connecticut," and if necessary to broaden the union with "any other of their majesties colonies that may be concerned therein."[13] Meanwhile the Bay Colony issued an order for the raising of six hundred troops for an expedition against the northern Indians,[14] a force larger than originally intended. On the western frontier, in order to renew a treaty with the Mohawks, all three confederate colonies joined in sending special commissioners[15] to a conference with the heads of the Five Nations at Albany, which secured from this great league of tribes a profession of friendship to the English.[16]

Ten days after the Plymouth resolution to send Commissioners to a meeting at the summit of the United Colonies, the Bay Colony followed suit, and appointed the reactionary Thomas Danforth, recently reinstated as President of the Province of Maine, and the former physician, Elisha Cooke, to attend a session of the revived Confederation.[17] The Massachusetts Commissioners were elected during one of the several conventions of freemen[18] held during 1689 under the auspices of the Council of Safety, which functioned during the emergency period as the supreme authority in the Colony. It is interesting to note that while the Puritan colonies were preparing to revive their confederacy, the Maryland Assembly was soliciting from the English colonies in America a declaration of closer cooperation and mutual concernment.[19]

The Commissioners of the three United Colonies met on schedule during the first week of September at Boston.[20] The occasion was not unlike the meeting of 1670, when the Commissioners sought solely to repair the crumbling walls of the Confederacy. But it is interesting to note that the Commissioners of 1689 showed little concern over drawing up a new Articles of Confederation. Since King Philip's War, the idea of colonial union was put on the basis of military expediency; and there was little interest in establishing an intercolonial constitution, except among orthodox Puritans who wished to retain their influence over government.[21] But was the meeting of the delegates from the three colonies a bona fide session of the New England Confederation? Undoubtedly the three Puritan colonies thought of this meeting as a revival of the Confederation, as evidenced in the naming of the six Commissioners; and the proceedings of the Commissioners has all the earmarks of the Confederation operating under the Articles of 1672.

Even historians who have not made use of the manuscript material of the period should have been able to conclude from Church's *History* and the colonial records that the Confederation was revived. From these sources it may be deduced that the procedure of the Articles of Confederation was followed. For instance, the Boston meeting was attended by six Commissioners, two each from each confederate colony: Massachusetts, Plymouth, and Connecticut.[22] A president was chosen from the host colony in the person of Thomas Danforth, twice before President of the United Colonies.[23] The two Commissioners from Plymouth were expressly chosen as Commissioners of

...of the last meeting of the Commissioners: evidence that the Confederation was revived in 1689.

Mass. Archives

the United Colonies, and the Commissioners from the other colonies, though with more loosely worded commissions, coming from the magistrates and as general officers of the colonies, left no doubt that they were attending as Commissioners of the Confederation.[24] Furthermore, the convening of this session occurred at the prescribed time of the regular meeting of the Confederation (September), though the Dominion government had interrupted the triennial sequence; and relying again upon Major Church's narrative, his commission was issued at this meeting "pursuant to an agreement of the Commissioners of the United Colonies."[25] Thus from the scant printed sources there is sufficient evidence to show the revival of the Confederacy in 1689. But from the manuscript sources, as was the case of the long session of the Confederacy during King Philip's War, one receives a much more complete picture and an understanding of the main role of the Commissioners as a super-colonial council of war.

One of the first acts of the Commissioners at this final session was to examine the grounds for waging war against the northern Indians. After reading a narration of the causes of the war—it will be remembered that the same procedure was followed when the Commissioners took over responsibility for the conduct of King Philip's War—the Commissioners declared that the war was a "just" war, and, in the light of the Puritan conscience, was to be prosecuted jointly as a defensive war.[26] It was, therefore the "duty of all their Majestyes Subjects in New England to prosecute the same."[27] The Connecticut Commissioners on the spot bound the River Colony to a contribution of two hundred men, as their fair proportion according to the Articles, to aid the Massachusetts-Plymouth expedition then in preparation for the northern campaign.[28] Major Church of Plymouth was acknowledged commander in chief by the Massachusetts Council, with Captain Simon Willard (the younger) of the Bay placed second in command[29] The commanding general of this confederate expedition was to provide a continual flow of intelligence, at his discretion, to either the Massachusetts Governor and Council or to the Commissioners of the United Colonies.[30] The English force, however, set out for Falmouth before the two hundred troops pledged by the Connecticut Commissioners could be added to the force. Though wandering around somewhat aimlessly, Major Church and the confederate troops were able to rout the enemy at the battle of Brackett Field, near the present site of Portland.[31] With the Indians pursued for some distance, this first joint expedition came to an end.[32]

Meanwhile, the Commissioners at Boston continued their deliberations on the best means of putting down the Indian insurrection. Their recommendations were all of a military nature. The war was to be vigorously prosecuted; Maine and New Hampshire would be called upon to perform their share of the burdens of the war—these settlements already were bearing the brunt of the war, being the scene of the hostilities and left unprotected at the collapse of the Dominion government. Having learned from the experience of King Philip's War, the Commissioners ordered that if for some reason the Confederation should be interrupted the Massachusetts Council should "give such instruction and farther directions to the cheife commanders and make such farther supplys to the army that they see meet and necessary"—thus allowing for the war powers of the Commissioners to devolve officially upon the lesser Council.

On September 21, the Confederation decided to adjourn until October 28. The Commissioners were given a little homework: before the next session reconvened, the Commissioners of each colony agreed to return with a list of all the male inhabitants between the ages of sixteen and sixty, the age limits for conscription established by the Articles of Confederation. Moreover, the Commissioners ordered all company commanders to report on a muster of all troops within their commands. The Commissioners took a more active interest than ever before in providing for a commissary for the troops in the field; since most of the troops were from the Bay, Plymouth and Connecticut were charged with sending supplies to the frontier. A most significant step was taken in the direction of putting the Confederation back on a constitutional basis when the Commissioners ordered that before they reconvened in October the general courts should specifically instruct them to "act as Commissioners of the united Coloneys and to attend the first articles of Confederation."[33]

The Confederation had been given a brief respite, and used its time to take swift action in sending the joint expedition against the Abenakis. Even the arch-enemy of New England Puritanism, Edward Randolph, in reports to the Lords of Trade, on several occasions called attention to the role reassumed by the Commissioners of the United Colonies.[34] But re-establishing the Confederation on a permanent basis among the three original confederates was out of the question. The times called for an expansion of cooperation among the colonies, and in view of the imperial policy of the home government the colonists dared not proceed beyond military cooperation—thus not requiring the reaffirming of their former, virtually independent Union under the Articles of Confederation. As had been the baneful experience of former times, events of great moment occurred during the recess of the Confederation, which forced the colonial authorities to take measures that in effect served to by-pass the Confederacy.

It was not by coincidence that a request came from a committee at Albany, asking of the Connecticut Colony two hundred troops for reinforcing the western frontier at Albany.[35] The number could be raised by order of the Commissioners of the United Colonies, but not deployed on the northern expedition. Even the Massachusetts Colony was putting pressure on the Connecticut Council to make use of these troops by sending them to Albany. The matter, Governor Bradstreet wrote, should be referred to the Commissioners of the United Colonies, but there was not time for that, "forasmuch as it may be too long a delay for the Commissioners of the several Colonys to meet." The Connecticut authorities were urged to go ahead and send this contingent; they would thereby be performing their obligations as a member of the Confederation in the western sector as Massachusetts and Plymouth were now doing against the northern Indians.[36] To secure approval for this policy from the third confederate, Plymouth Colony, the eighty-seven-year-old Governor of the Bay addressed a similar letter to the Plymouth Council. Governor Bradstreet again called attention to the delay that would ensue if they waited for the reconvening of the Commissioners, that it would be best to let Connecticut go it alone in sending a New England force to the relief of the Albany region—any additional expense could be borne in "due proportion by all the Colonies."[37] These letters had a profound effect in underscoring the view that military cooperative action did not have to be channeled through a revival of the old Confederation.

Another maneuver distracted attention away from the Puritan

Confederation. Governor Bradstreet, himself a member of the
moderate faction, appears to have been a prolific letter writer
during the interim between sessions of the revived Confederation.
He invited commissioners from the settlements of Maine and
New Hampshire to sit in with the Commissioners of the United
Colonies.[38] Since the Confederation was functioning as a Council of War, it was only fair to include in the direction of the
war representatives of the settlements most affected by its rav-
ages. But to mix in with the exclusive intercolonial council of
magistrates delegates from faraway frontier settlements was
clearly a violation of the character of the Confederation. To admit these local officials, even though commissioned to represent
several towns, would be the same as allowing deputies to the
lower chambers of the colonies to sit among the ranks of the
Commissioners—a practice strictly forbidden since the early
days of the Confederation because the Puritans regarded the
Commissioners as general officers. A reply was soon made to
Governor Bradstreet's invitation from the leading men of the
frontier setlements, regretting that they did not have time to
appoint Commissioners to attend the session reconvening in mid-
October, but for a future session they would be glad to send
Commissioners.[39] Thus for a few days longer the Confederation
was spared the corruption of its ranks.

When the Commissioners reconvened, they set themselves to
the business they had planned for themselves before their adjournment in September. Lists were again ordered to be made of
persons in military service and the places where troops were
garrisoned. As an immediate result of the Commissioners' proposal for discharging troops, the Suffolk regiment was discharged
from active service. But alas! the work of the Commissioners
during this session bore only the Commissioners' signatures of
the Plymouth and the Massachusetts colonies.[40] The Commissioners from Connecticut were no longer in attendance—the first
sign of the Confederacy moribund under the Articles of Confederation; the acts of only four Commissioners would not
have been considered valid. Meanwhile, the inhabitants of New
Hampshire made good the opportunity afforded them by Governor Bradstreet's invitation to send commissioners to the
meetings of the Confederation. At a town meeting at Dover, it
was certified from the votes of the town and of Portsmouth

that William Vaughn had received the majority of the votes "for the joyning with the Commissioners of the United Colonies, and to join with the rest of the Representatives of this Province, in giving such instructions to the said Commissioners as shall be thought meet, for the vigorous management of the present war."[41] The Province of New Hampshire was now receiving recognition as an independent government, sending its own representative to the seat of the intercolonial council. Before the new Commissioners arrived, the four Commissioners from Plymouth and Massachusetts[42] continued with the work of the Confederation. During November, in compliance with the order of the Commissioners of the United Colonies, the forces on the northern frontier were drawn off from the pursuit of the enemy, a part of them being retained to maintain garrisons and the remainder sent home for discharge.[43]

News of the declaration of war between England and France was the occasion for the last meeting of the Commissioners of the United Colonies. At this session in Boston on December 16, 1689, the Commissioners—five of them, two each from the two original confederate colonies, and the new Commissioner, William Vaughn, from New Hampshire—ordered that the King's Declaration of War be published throughout the colonies, that "due care be taken that the Militia be well settled, and the fortifications in the sea port townes be fit for service." The Commissioners proposed that the Massachusetts Council which was sitting at the same time as the Commissioners name a committee to "inquire" into their relation with the French at Canada, and to make their report to "the present Convention" (as the Commissioners, dismissing hopes of re-establishing the old Confederacy, now termed themselves) or in their absence to the Massachusetts Council.[44] On the same day, Elisha Cooke, the Commissioner from Massachusetts, was voted by the Bay Council and Representatives to join Increase Mather and the other agents in London, where they had been negotiating a new charter for the Colony.[45] Thus the ranks of the Commissioners of the Confederation were further depleted. This was the last day that delegates from the New England colonies met in the style of the New England Confederation: from this time on the Puritan Union of 1643 and 1672 was to be but a proud memory. Only Plymouth, struggling to maintain its independent existence from the Bay, continued to expressly name Commissioners of the United Colonies[46] in the vain hope that their ancient union might once more become a reality.

While waiting for William III to define the status of the colonial governments, the affairs of government in the colonies were virtually at a standstill. The New Hampshire settlements suffered from this transition more than any of the other colonies, for with the united troops withdrawn their scattered towns were caught with only tiny garrisons to defend them against attack. Would they remain a separate royal province or be returned to the fold of the Bay Colony, with whom they maintained close ties of family and social outlook? The home government, though a new Committee on Trade and Plantations had been appointed from the Privy Council, was cautious in regard to colonial affairs. Moreover, the ascendant Whig party leaned more favorably towards colonial legislative autonomy than towards the policy of the Stuarts, which had attempted regional consolidation of all the colonies.[47] The Massachusetts authorities likewise were hesitant to interfere with the government of the New Hampshire towns, since under the Dominion they had been constituted a royal province.[48] But Indian depredations continued, and the tiny northern settlements were left with little choice except to form their own government. A convention was therefore held, attended by twenty-two delegates from the four province towns, and a President and lesser officials were elected.[49] It was decided to cast their lot with the Puritan colonies, as had been demonstrated in December when these towns sent a Commissioner to the Confederation. The province towns soon went one step further, and asked to come under the jurisdiction of the Bay for protection until "his Majesty's will" would be known. The Massachusetts Council complied by setting up a committee, including former Commissioner Vaughn, to provide for civil and military organization under the Bay authority.[50] Massachusetts, still with only provisional government, though more reluctantly than in the earlier times of the Confederacy, found herself again in the driver's seat for securing a coordinate defense of the New England colonies.

The French designs on the English colonies in America were laid bare when Count Frontenac returned to the governorship of New France. It was the object of French policy to win the friendship of the Iroquois—for several generations the French had tried unsuccessfully to win the allegiance of this powerful Indian confederacy, but had failed because of rivalry over the fur trade and the indiscreet policy of the French governors. The Mohawks, who had been traditional allies of the English though they had no misgivings over attacking Indians friendly to the United Colonies, were now standing aloof as the great struggle shaped up between the peoples of the two nations of white men. The French governor hoped that by a strong display of force against the English, the Mohawks would be overawed into throwing in their lot with the stronger of their two big brothers. But a strike against the English called for promptness and surprise. Frontenac thus devised his famous plan for a three pronged attack on the English settlements: from Montreal, a war-party was to strike at Albany; from Three Rivers, another motley force of Indians and white men to strike at the New Hampshire settlements; and the third to set out from Quebec and attack the Maine settlements.[51] The Abenakis were already striking terror on the northern frontier; but it was the surprise attack on Schenectady in the dead of winter, the complete wiping out of the settlement, including a contingent of Connecticut troops, that once again, as in Philip's time, spread the alarm throughout the New England colonies.

In March, 1690, the Massachusetts General Court issued a call for an intercolonial congress, which went even beyond the Consolidation of 1686-9, and invited commissioners to attend from the colonies as far south as Virginia and Maryland. The purpose of this conference would be to "Advise and Conclude on Sutable Methods in Assisting each other for the Safety of the whole Land."[52] A committee headed by Robert Livingston, town clerk by appointment of the former governor, only a day later was appointed at Albany to "Consult what might be Expedient for the Carrying on the warr unanimously" with a "Comittee for New England."[53] Until the massacre at Schenectady, the government of New York Colony was split into two parts, the result of the overthrow of the Dominion government. Jacob Leisler, a trader at New York, seized power in that town in demagogic fashion through manipulation of the train bands of the town; at Albany the faction headed by Mayor Peter Schuyler still ruled. But the French attack on Schenectady forced Albany to submit to Leisler's rule. Thus, after a week had passed since the initial call for a congress,[54] Governor Bradstreet addressed Leisler as head of the provisional government of New York—expressing the desire "that there may be an Uniting and combining as one to withstand and Oppose the common Enemy" and for sending an expedition against the French there might be a "joint concurrance and Assistance of all the Governments in these their Majesties Colonys."[55] On the same day, the aldermen of Albany were informed that their "Neighbours and Confederates of Connecticut" were sending troops to reinforce the fort at Albany.[56]

Although it was originally proposed that the intercolonial congress be held at Rhode Island[57]—a far cry from the earlier attitude of the Bay in refusing the Ishmael colony membership in the Confederation—the New England colonies were prevailed upon to send commissioners to New York the last Monday in April.[58] Massachusetts was the first of the three confederate colonies—little interest was aroused in Rhode Island—to name commissioners for the New York conference. William Stoughton and Samuel Sewall, two ministers who had relinquished the cloth for public service, the former having served as a Commissioner of the Confederation, were named commissioners to represent Massachusetts at the conference.[59] Plymouth, because of its "scattered living" and the "extreme strait of time," found it impossible to call a general court or council, "in whose power it is, according to our constitution, to commissionate men to act and conclude in matters of so public," avoided naming special commissioners. Instead, Major John Walley, then serving as "one of the commissioners for the United Colonies," was sent. It was felt that Walley, in his capacity as Commissioner of the Confederation, was best suited from among the officers of the Colony to "consult and advise about the weighty affair."[60] It was not unusual for Plymouth to hedge in investing plenary powers to commissioners, as was evident at the time of the forming of the New England Confederation; and it may have also been thought best to flaunt the authority of the defunct Confederation about so that it would not be forgotten that Plymouth had entered this compact as a free and independent colony, whose political integrity was guaranteed. From Hartford, Major Nathan Gold and William Pitkin, the latter having served in the Confederation, were sent to New York to represent the River Colony.[61]

The Congress convened on the first day of May (O.S.). Jacob Leisler and P. D. Lanoy, the mayor of the city of New York, represented New York Province. Only the commissioners appointed from the three former confederate colonies were represented from the other colonies. Virginia and Maryland hesitated to send commissioners because of the dubious authority in their governments while waiting for an expression of His Majesty's will. Like the northern colonies, (the usurpation in New York by Leisler being an exception), the provisional governments in the southern colonies dared to proceed only cautiously—united action for them was a new step. Moreover, the southern colonies were distant from the Hudson and Mohawk Valleys, and since their settlements were more widely scattered, they could not concentrate military action as readily as the northern colonies.[62] It is significant, however, to note that observers, not in the official capacity as delegates, attended the conference from Maryland, thereby, at least, giving the conference a general character.[63]

The meeting of the New York Congress was brief, lasting only several days—perhaps the New Englanders did not want to associate too long with the rebel Leisler for fear they might be thought to condone his actions. The commissioners from the colonies came to unanimous agreement. A two-pronged invasion of Canada was proposed. Eight hundred and fifty-five troops were to be raised from the five colonies, Maryland included.[64] Leisler, the mentor of the conference and as acting Lieutenant Governor of New York, was to appoint the commander in chief of the land forces upon the recommendation of the Bay and River colonies. The objective of this united expedition was to take Quebec, which would be attacked by both the overland and naval forces. It was assumed that the primary responsibility of the naval expedition would rest with the easternmost colonies of Massachusetts and Plymouth, whereas Connecticut would supply the largest contingent of New England troops to join the expedition setting out from New York.[65] Connecticut, therefore, was afforded the opportunity to appoint the commander in chief of the overland expedition. Fitz-John Winthrop, a direct descendant of the two prime movers of the New England Confederation of two generations, was named by the Connecticut Council, with the appointment receiving approval from the other colonies.[66] The preparations for the joint attack was thoroughly enmeshed in confusion and misunderstanding. The two eastern colonies refused to send their quota of troops to join the land force until their naval expedition should meet success at Port Royal, which forced a reallocation of the troops to be furnished by New York and Connecticut for the overland expedition—raising the quota for Connecticut to three hundred.[67] But before proceeding with this ill-planned and ill-fated cooperative attack on New France, the last such action to bear any stamp of the Confederation, mention might be made of a half-hearted attempt in the summer of 1690 to rejoin the Puritan colonies, this time with Rhode Island, into confederate union.

That the idea of renewing the Confederation was still remotely in the minds of the colonists may be traced in several actions of the legislatures of the former confederate colonies. On July 27, 1690, the General Court of Massachusetts addressed letters to Plymouth, Connecticut, and Rhode Island requesting a meeting in August of representatives from these colonies, who would be "fully empowered and instructed to conclude" in all matters relating to the common safety.[68] Previously the Plymouth Court had granted her Commissioners of the United Colonies, still elected annually, permission to treat with other "commissioners from the other Colonies and Governments."[69] The River Colony, having elected commissioners for the New York Conference, showed that it favored cooperative action, but it remained silent on re-establishing the Confederacy. Nevertheless a meeting of New England Commissioners, two from each colony in the custom of the Confederation, was taken seriously by the Massachusetts and Plymouth colonies, and a conference was arranged for the last day of July at Boston.[70] Major Walley and Governor Hinckley of Plymouth, as Commissioners for Plymouth, arrived at the appointed time. Samuel Sewall of the Bay also appeared, but Commissioners from Connecticut and Rhode Island failed to show up, and the meeting came to naught, except for some discussion over the number of troops to be contributed by the Bay and Plymouth colonies for the northern expedition.[71]

Why Connecticut refused to go along with a meeting of the New England colonies in the summer of 1690 is difficult to explain. It is true there was some resentment over the refusal of the other former confederates to hold back their quota of troops promised at the conference in New York, thereby throwing the whole responsibility of supplying New England troops for the overland expedition upon Connecticut. Probably it was felt, having learned from past experience in dealing with the

other Puritan colonies, that all that could come of a meeting of
the New England colonies at this time would be an attempt to
get larger commitments of troops from each other. Connecticut
could have profited much by a renewal of the New England union. A move had been afoot to unite Connecticut with the Province of New York, which at this time of re-establishing the colonial governments was exerting more pressure than ever.[72] A way
to discourage "union of Connecticut with New York" would have
been to declare openly an alliance of the New England colonies.
From an administrative point of view, in order to coordinate the
attack on Canada, an intercolonial board was needed for the duration of the war—which, now lacking, the colonies proceeded
with their preparations without any central control. Rhode
Island, continuing to receive urgent appeals from the Bay to
join in the intercolonial expedition against Canada,[73] professed
little interest in an expedition against the French and Indians;
in any event, since they were a small colony, "weakly fitted to
oppose an enemy," they would have their hands full setting up
defenses for the port of Newport.[74] More deeply, however, the
Rhode Islanders felt no great obligation towards their former
enemies, the Puritan colonies; indeed, their greatest fortunes,
such as receiving their charter and jurisdiction over the Narragansett country, came when they were most antagonized by the
United Colonies.

Meanwhile the plan for the invasion of Canada received a
jolt of encouragement with the taking of Port Royal by a
Massachusetts expedition under Sir William Phips.[75] This naval
success brought a wave of overconfidence to the preparations for
the joint enterprise against Canada, which could ill be afforded
in view of the many difficulties facing such an expedition. As
summer came, the colonies each went its own way in meeting
their commitments for the expedition against Canada. The
greatest encumbrance to organizing the expedition was the personal jealousies and feuds. Leisler's deputy, Jacob Milborne,
who had compelled the surrender of Albany to Leisler's men,
was unacceptable to the Albany faction to head a contingent of
New York troops.[76] Although the appointment of Fitz-John
Winthrop as commander in chief of the land expedition met
the approval of all concerned, and Leisler forwarded a "blank
commission" for that office to Albany,[77] the acting head of New
York Province became impatient waiting for the arrival of the

New England troops, writing Governor Treat that "it is high tyme to betake them to the March."[78] But when General Winthrop did arrive at Albany, in mid July, he found that Leisler had accomplished little himself, the New York contingent not having been raised according to the quota assigned the Province. At Albany, wrote the New England commander, "I found all in Confusion the designe Against Canada poorely Contrived and little prosecuted."[79]

The colonies appointed their own commissaries for supplying the united army. In Massachusetts, the Council named three "Commissioners for the War" to impress provisions "with assistance of a Constable."[80] Plymouth, finding that in the Phips's expedition to Canada against Port Royal and the one now in preparation the councils of war had replaced the Confederation, looked for other means whereby her Commissioners of the United Colonies could be put to use. At last there was a way— incidentally, the germ for the later colonial and central commissary departments of the Revolutionary period—the Plymouth Commissioners, general officers of the Colony, were charged with the direction of the outfitting of Plymouth's share of the united forces. The expense on the colonies was great. Massachusetts was compelled to increase its issue of bills of credit nearly sixfold in order to pay the troops engaged by the colony;[81] and Plymouth met much difficulty in meeting the colony's expenses for the expedition, especially with the colony fast disintegrating and some towns refusing to pay the colony taxes—the ratable property of each county was about one-third of the total colony value.[82]

In Plymouth, the "officers and souldiers" for the Quebec mission were to march "at such time and rendevouse at such places as they shall receive orders from one or both of the commissioners of the colony, one or both of which are hereby impowered to grant warrants, to impress vessels, men, armes, and ammunition, or any other thing needed, and can be procured within the colony for this present expedition." The two hundred soldiers of Plymouth, consisting of both English and Indian troops, were to join the Massachusetts and the "other confederated forces," with the Commissioners fitting them with "victualls, provision, and other necesaries, for the said expedition."[83] Thus the war powers of the Plymouth Commissioners were complete, ranging from the control of the commissary to securing the complete mobilization of the colony's resources. This wide grant of authority to the two Commissioners instead of the time-honored Council of War of the Colony was unusual, but it did have reason. In Plymouth the Commissioners were members of the Council of War, and most likely it was felt that, with the colony on the verge of disruption and possibly soon to be incorporated into the Bay, a full attendance in the Council could not be obtained. Therefore, leaving the powers of the full Council to two of its members more easily insured the continuance of government separate from the Bay. The last hopes of the Colony were gambled on keeping the Confederation alive. By investing the Commissioners of the United Colonies from Plymouth with full authority for directing the military preparations of the colony and for deploying the troops, Plymouth sought to remind the other colonies that this was but the proper function of the Commissioners, and the best interests of the colonies would be served if the other confederate colonies should reappoint their Commissioners of the Confederation to conduct the Canadian expedition. Thus were pinned the hopes of the Colony on the Cape—in desperation and in poverty, still abiding in the shadow of the New England Confederation.

The two-pronged attack on Canada, without effective co-ordination, was doomed from the start. The overland expedition, with its first objective to assault Montreal, never got as far as Lake Champlain, where the troops were to be transported into the northern region. Egged on by Leisler's committee at Albany for the conduct of the war, General Winthrop, with a large force of several thousand Englishmen and Indians (the Connecticut contingent numbered two hundred, most of the force being recruited from among the Indians), finally set out in the early fall to conquer Canada.[84] But mishaps occurred at the start of the expedition. Only a few of the expected Indians appeared at the rendezvous; canoes which were to be supplied by the New Yorkers at Albany were not at hand; and sickness and dysentery broke out among the troops.[85] Leisler was enraged at Winthrop's retreat back to Albany, showing so "great contempt" for the colony of Connecticut that the River Colony refused to forward provisions for the troops quartered at Albany, and gave Winthrop authority to return home with his troops if he so desired.[86] To end all future possibility of a cooperative expedition against the French, Leisler rashly ordered the arrest of Winthrop, whereupon the Connecticut commander, and supposedly the commander in chief of all the united forces, was imprisoned. The farce did not last long, for the Mohawks crossed the ranks of the Albany troops and bore off the English commander, under whom they had expected to serve in the invasion of New France. Thus was ended the military cooperation on the western frontier. Needless to say, the court of inquiry called by Connecticut to investigate Winthrop's conduct vindicated him with the highest praise.[87]

The Massachusetts-Plymouth naval expedition against Quebec under the command of Sir William Phips of the Bay and Lieutenant General John Walley of Plymouth[88] likewise met with ill success. Although the English fleet "cannonaded Quebec terribly, both the upper and lower Towns,"[89] landing parties sent against the French were met in ambuscade, the English suffering heavy casualties. Because of the failure of the western expedition against Montreal, strong reinforcements were afforded for the French at Quebec, thus greeting the English with much greater force than had been expected. Sickness and a shortage of ammunition handicapped the naval expedition, not to mention, of course, the "too timely intelligence."[90] With an early winter setting in, the colonials had little choice but to return home. Thus was the disastrous finale of the expedition against Canada and the first general military cooperation[91] of the American colonies. Although the plan to attack Canada, according to the consensus of the times, could not "have been better laid,"[92] the disunity and the bickerings of the colonies over its execution spelled its failure. Instead of bringing the colonies into closer union, the Canadian fiasco produced the opposite effect, making the colonies less dependent on each other—thereby slowing down for several generations to come the growth of American federalism.

In the fall of 1691, at last the Bay Colony was granted a royal charter, an event which dispelled all hopes of reviving the Confederation. The new charter was the result of the persistent negotiations of the Massachusetts agents,[93] and since "all other means of Restoration to our Ancient Liberties failed us,"[94] it was considered under the circumstances the best possible grant that could have been given by a royal government bent on constructing an empire of trade and defense. The new charter—Connecticut and Rhode Island were allowed to continue under their old charters, and New Hampshire was constituted a royal province—embodied a skillful compromise between the forces of consolidation and those of self-government.[95] A destructive blow to Plymouth's effort to revive the Confederation was the incorporation of that colony into the Bay. The jurisdiction of the Bay over the Province of Maine, recently purchased from the Gorges heirs, was recognized. Less welcome was the appointment of the governor by the crown; but even then, though the governor was invested with veto powers, there were important checks on his authority, such as a time limitation placed upon the exercise of the veto, right of the colonial courts to appeal to the Privy Council, a guarantee of annual elections, and the assembly to share with the council through joint ballot the right to appoint members of the council.[96] Now the Massachusetts government instead of having a charter which provided grounds for an assertion of independence found the basis of its government "dependent on the Crown of England," and bound not to make any laws "repugnant" to the laws of England. Oaths of allegiance to the King were required for public office, and all warrants issued were to be in the "King's Name."[97]

The new charter of Massachusetts, although creating the colony a royal province, actually was a victory for the commonwealth-Puritan party in the Bay. The colony was preserved intact in its present territorial limits, and though the landed interests lost out in the long-disputed claims in the Narragansett country, the annexing of the Province of Maine and Plymouth Colony was more than satisfactory. Self-government suffered little by the grant of the new charter. Local institutions were preserved without interference from abroad; and on the colony level the royal council was simply another name for the council of magistrates, and the assembly the same as the house of deputies—even the office of governor did not emerge with clearly defined executive powers, as in former times, except for the veto, which was too enmeshed with the council and assembly. In the words of Cotton Mather, the transition into the status of royal province in the Bay put all the New England colonies on the common ground of royal authority; the "United Colonies" became "his Majesties Colonies." But the royal prerogative was subject to the same limitations as the New England Confederation which it supplanted:

> ... our Colony ... have power to choose Deputy Governour and Assistants and all General Officers ... only the King Reserves to himself, the liberty of sending a general, for all the united Colonies; who nevertheless, will have no power to do any thing in our Colony without the Concurrence of our own Magistrates; nor can any Lawes, bee made, or Taxes Levied, without a General Court.[98]

Even the delivery of this final blow to the Confederacy, the combining of Plymouth and Massachusetts under a royal charter, did not immediately erase all signs of the Confederation. The "separation from so neere a union"[99] forced the colonies to look for other channels for cooperative action. In the late fall of 1691, nearly a month after the granting of the Massachusetts charter—though word of this action had not yet arrived in the colonies—the Bay Colony again addressed the governments of Plymouth, Connecticut, and Rhode Island that because of the "growing Distresses of the Countrey" and the need to raise a "considerable force" these colonies "willingly contribute" their "Assistance."[100] In 1692 the powers of Governor Phips[101] were enlarged to include the office of commander in chief of all the military forces of the "Territory and Dominion of New England," he receiving instructions similar to those issued Governor Andros during the Consolidation period.[102] The course of intercolonial cooperative action would now be confined to military affairs, and the next decade would witness still further attempts of the royal government to establish military cooperation on a dominion basis. With the passing of time, the colonies would learn to rely on their own efforts for mutual defense.

The last vestige of the Confederacy appeared on April, 1693, when William Stoughton, recently succeeding another arch-Puritan, Thomas Danforth, to the lieutenant-governorship, though himself more moderate, wrote the Corporation in England for Promoting the Gospel in the capacity of "a commissioner of the United Colonies." He had been working alone in trying to keep up the "Indian Worke"; William Bradford (the younger), the last deputy-governor of Plymouth, had given Stoughton some assistance, but not much. The missionary work among the Indians, the chief occupation of the Commissioners of the Confederation during the Period of Falling Out was now virtually extinct, due to the "many discouragements during the late uncomfortable revolution and confusions here."[103] But, though the visible signs of the New England Union now disappeared, the New England Confederation was never forgotten, and into the colonial conscience was implanted forever an appreciation of united action.

The New England Confederation through storm and strife, strength and weakness, casting aside and sudden revival, managed to endure for half a century, a testimony to the vitality of the idea of union in the American colonies of the seventeenth century. Like all institutions suited for an age, it came to an end with the passing of that age. Briefly, the United Colonies of New England became an anachronism as a result of the confluence of a number of factors.

The colonies were gradually being fitted into the imperial policy of the home government. England since the Restoration was taking an active interest in the colonies; the American colonies were to take their proper place in a great far-flung commercial empire. All attention was to be directed to the mother country, economically and politically. In such a scheme of things there was no place for a Confederation of United Colonies—if there had been then the royal government would have been tempted to adopt the policy of its Stuart predecessors and consolidate the colonies under more direct control.

With the granting of a new charter to Massachusetts, the Bay Colony became administratively tied to the home government, and could no longer function as an independent state in negotiating a treaty of union. Plymouth, the last bastion of the Confederation, was eliminated by the Massachusetts Charter. Connecticut, enjoying virtual self-government under a royal charter and disillusioned over the lack of cooperation in the recent farcical expedition against Canada, saw no advantages for renewing the Confederacy.

Technically, the Articles of Confederation had long been violated. Even the limit of fifteen years which Massachusetts had tacked upon her acceptance of the Articles of 1672 had long been passed, expiring during the Andros period. Hence, as under the first Confederation, after the Articles had been violated enough times, the Confederation for all practical purposes ceased to exist. To revive the Union would have called forth another great effort of the colonies and the making of a new constitution —a course the colonies could not risk taking for fear of endangering their liberal charters.

The interruption by the Andros regime made the Confederation actually non-existent, if for no other reason than the Confederation was inoperative during this period, thereby contrary to the Articles. After the overthrow of the Dominion government, when a meeting of the Commissioners was held, a movement for making a new constitution did not materialize—a new constitution being requisite for the preserving of the Confederation. Though the Commissioners of the Confederation continued to meet until early December in the capacity of a war council, the admission to their ranks of a commissioner from the New Hampshire settlements violated the "tenor" of the Articles of Confederation, and the breaking up of the meeting shortly afterwards put an end to the brief revival of the Confederacy. The New York Conference, attended by commissioners from New York and men who had served in the final session of the Confederacy, likewise was out of the scope of the old Confederacy.

The twofold purpose of the original Confederation had been to preserve the entrenchment of the Puritan oligarchy in the colonies, a party no longer in control, and to defend the colonies against Indian hostilities, now removed to a distant frontier. The expansion of the New England settlements left the individual colonies more cohesive and better able to look out for themselves, thus diminishing the benefits of union. Moreover, the great Indian uprisings of the 1670's and 1680's had demonstrated that the advantages of confederation were better served by intercolonial councils of war. For the expedition of 1690, the colonists saw little advantage for operating under the New England Confederation—an intercolonial council of war would suffice. Indeed, the only fruits of confederation were those to be had by Plymouth, then gasping to preserve its territorial and political integrity.

The New England Confederacy died hard; but it left firmly ingrained in the consciousness of America, seeds for a sturdy Federalism of the future.

[1] "An Account of the late Revolution," Stevens Transcripts, III, 256, John Carter Brown Library; Bradstreet to Dudley, 13Jul89, Revolution in New England, NYPL, No. 43.

[2] Nourse, ed., *Early Records of Lancaster*, p. 126; MA, CVII, 24.

[3] For a detailed account of these negotiations see K. Murdock, *Increase Mather*, (Cambridge: 1925).

[4] Wharton once sought from the New England Confederation exclusive privileges for a company developing naval stores. (See S. L. Cook, "Governmental Crisis," *Commonwealth History of Massachusetts*, ed. by A. B. Hart, (New York: 1927), I, pp. 570-1. The names of the following men were wrapped up in the land controversies of the time.

[5] Viola F. Barnes, "The Revolution of 1689," *ibid.*, p. 599.

[6] C. Reynolds, *Albany Chronicles*, (Albany: 1906), p. 117. For the course of the war in the northeast, see William H. Fry, *New Hampshire as a Royal Province*, (New York: 1908).

[7] Larabee, ed., *Royal Instructions*, No. 613.

[8] MA, CVII, 162a; Charles W. Tuttle, *Historical Papers*, ed. by Albert H. Hoyt, (Boston:1889), p. 201.

[9] MA, CVII, 167.

[10] Ltr of 17Jul89, quoted in Tuttle, *op. cit.*, p. 203.

[11] MA, II, 210a, 31Jul89. For a contemporary, biting indictment of the renewing of the Confederation and its bringing the colonies into greater debt—i.e., Connecticut having to aid Massachusetts in the war against the northerly Indians—see Gershom Bulkeley, *Will and Doom*, printed in CHSC, III, pp. 201-2,

[12] CCR, IV, 2-3.

[13] PCR, VI, 212; Instructions to the Plymouth Commissioners, 14Aug89, MA, CVII, 262a; Peirce, *op. cit.* (Civil Lists), p .102.

[14] Order of House of Rep., Gov. and Council, *Doc. Hist. of Maine*, IX, 35-7.

[15] Col. John Pynchon, Capt. Thos. Savage, Capt. Jonathan Bull, and Capt. Andrew Belcher.

[16] MA, CVII, 284-289; *Doc. Hist. of Maine*, IX, 38, 52-3; Cadwallader Colden, *The History of the Five Indian Nations of Canada*, (New York: 1904), I, 119; William Smith, *History of New York*, (Albany: 1814), I, 111.

[17] MA, LXXXI, 55.

[18] 23Aug89, CA, Col. Wars, II, 17.

[19] *Md. Archives, 1684-92*, p. 233

[20] Benjamin Church, *King Philip's War (The History of the Eastern Expeditions)*, ed. by H. M. Dexter, No. 3 of the *Library of N. E. History*, (Boston: 1847), II, 11-15.

[21] E.g., as evident in the "Testimony and Counsel of the Rev. John Higginson" of Guilford, *CHSC*, II, 99.

[22] Church, *op. cit.*, p. 11.

[23] *Ibid.*, p. 15.

[24] CCR, IV, 2-3, 10-11; PCR, VI, 212; Church, *op. cit.*, p. 15.

[25] *Ibid.* (Church), p. 8.

[26] MA, XXX, 315; CA, Colonial Wars, II, 20; Willys Papers, CHS, II, 30.

[27] Report of Samuel Mason and William Pitkin, Commissioners of Conn., 21Sep89, MA, XXXV, 4.

[28] *Ibid.*; CHS, Willys Papers, II, 32.

[29] MA, XXXV, 69; CVII, 331.

[30] CA, Colonial Wars, II, 21.

[31] See Drake, *op. cit. (Border Wars*, pp. 39-41.)

[32] Alfred Crocker, "The Colonial Wars," in *History of Barnstable* (Hyannis, Mass.: 1939).

[33] Acts of the Commissioners of the United Colonies, Willys Papers, 21Sep89, CHS, II, 31.

[34] Letters of 8Oct89 and 25Feb89/90, Toppan and Goodrick, ed., *op. cit.*, VI, 296-7, 336.

[35] MA, XXXV, 32.

[36] CA, Col. Wars, II, 22.

[37] Bradstreet to Governor and Council of Plymouth, 5Oct89, *Hinckley Papers, MHSC* 4:V:217-8.

[38] MA, XXXV, 50; Tuttle, *op. cit.*, p. 204.

[39] Tuttle, *op. cit.*

[40] Proposals of the Commissioners of the United Colonies to Gov. and Council of Mass., 25Oct89, MA, XXXV, 63, 63a.

[41] Bouton, ed., *op. cit.*, II, 32; Tuttle, *op. cit.*, p. 205; George Wadleigh, *Notable Events . . of New Hampshire,* (Dover: 1913), p. 94.

[42] Danforth and Cooke (M); Hinckley and Walley (P).

[43] MA, XXXV, 8Nov89; *Documentary History of Maine,* IX, 72-3; 76-7 and V, 12-3.

[44] MA, XXXV, 106; New England and N. Y. MSS, Photostat, MHS; Tuttle, *op. cit.*, pp. 205-6.

[45] MA, XXXV, 104b.

[46] Until incorporation with Massachusetts in 1691. *PCR*, VI, 234, 261.

[47] Unlike the Stuart policy of establishing conciliar government, with the coming of the new King there "was a complete tolerance of the assemblies and a fairly scrupulous respect for their autonomy." (See G. H. Guttridge, *The Colonial Policy of William III,* (Cambridge Univ. Press: 1922).

[48] That the defenses of New Hampshire were neglected was inexcusable. *(Ibid.,* p. 20.)

[49] Wadleigh, *op. cit.*, p. 94; Tuttle, *op. cit.*, pp. 207-9.

[50] *Ibid.* (Tuttle), p. 210.

[51] Francis Parkman, *Count Frontenac and New France under Louis XIV,* (Boston: 1903), pp. 218-9.

[52] *Documentary History of Maine,* V, 52.

[53] MA, XXXV, 343.

[54] 19Mar89/90.

[55] *Documentary History of Maine*, V, 66.

[56] *Ibid.*, p. 69.

[57] *Ibid.*, p. 65.

[58] Rhode Island had its hands full expecting an attack from the French fleet, and New York may have been considered a more central meeting place since the southern colonies were invited. To the New Englanders it was "of absolute necessity that Albany lay down the Cudgels, and submit to York." *(Ibid.*, p. 64.)

[59] *Ibid.*, p. 75.

[60] *Hinckley Papers, MHSC* 4:V:242-3.

[61] Emmet Collection, No. 6847, NYPL.

[62] John C. Hammelef, "British and American Attempts to Coordinate the Defenses of the Continental Colonies . . ." Unpublished PhD. Dissertation, Univ. of Michigan, 1955, Univ. microfilm.

[63] Frothingham, *op. cit.*, p. 91. Invitations were also sent to the Barbados and Bermudas. New Jersey, Pennsylvania, and Virginia refused to associate with Leisler. C. M. Andrews in his *Colonial History* (Vol. III, p. 131) makes an unwarranted observation: "This remarkable effort at colonial cooperation . . . is more noteworthy even than the formation of the New England Confederation because it had no religious motive behind it." Wrote an unfriendly New England observer at the time: "To York they go, and there they enter into a confederation with Leisler in pretence against the French in Canada." *(Gershom Bulkeley, op. cit.*, p. 203.) A tract was circulated at this time, stating questions to be considered pertaining to "Our Union and Subjection," viz.: "Whether the Summer which is now advancing be not like to be the blackest Summer that ever *New England* saw, if by the firmest unity, we prevent it Not?—Whether for one Colony in the Country to go to shake off the other (since united) Colonies, in the assistance, which the common dangers have called for, would not be to invite all kinds of miseries on the whole?" ("Further Quaries upon the Present State of the New-English Affairs," *Andros Tracts*, I, 207-8.)

[64] Viz.: N. Y., 400; Mass., 160; Ply., 60; Conn., 135; Md., 100.

[65] *Winthrop Papers*, XV, 129; *Documentary History of Maine*, V, 93; CA, Col. Wars, II, 57; *Documentary History of New York*, II, 239; *Hinckley Papers, MHSC* 4:V:266; *Pincheon Papers, MHSC* 2:VIII:238.

[66] Winthrop Papers, MHS, X, 50 and VI, 65; CA, Colonial Wars, II, 69.

[67] *Documentary History of New York*, II, 254-5.

[68] *Hinckley Papers, MHSC*, 4:V:267.

[69] Brigham, ed., *Laws of New Plymouth*, 20May90; *PCR*, VI, 250.

[70] MA, XXXVI, 167.

[71] Sewall, *Diary, MHSC* 5:V:326. Increase Mather proposed to Connecticut that they join with the other colonies in sending agents to England, "that all the Colonies in New England might concert." *CHSC*, XXIV, 37.

[72] *CHSC*, XXIV, 47.

[73] MA, XXXVI, 159a.

[74] *RICR*, III, 273.

[75] See Palfrey, *op. cit.*, IV, 49-50. Phips' commission was issued by the Massachusetts Council. (14Apr90, *Documentary History of Maine*, V, 75.)

[76] Willys Papers, CHSC, XXI, 321.

[77] Winthrop Papers, MHS, X, 51, *Documentary History of New York*, II, 203.

[78] *Documentary History of New York*, II, 269 .

[79] Journal of Fitz-John Winthrop, Winthrop Papers, MHS, VI, 172; Willys Papers, CHS, II, 35.

[80] MA, XXXVI, 101.

[81] Dewey, *op. cit.* (Fin. Hist.), p. 21.

[82] Bowen, *op. cit.* (Rehoboth), I, 12-3.

[83] *PCR*, VI, 248-50. A contrast between attitudes of the French and the English in their preparations is afforded in George Chalmers, *Political Annals* (New York: 1868), *NYHSC*, I, 56. The dispute among the English "factions" prevented the "energy of Union."

[84] Winthrop to Schuyler, 23Jul90, Winthrop Papers, MHS, VI, 68; Instructions from Leisler's Commissioners, 31Jul90, *ibid.*, XII, 29.

[85] Nelson P. Mead, *Connecticut as a Corporate Colony* (Lancaster, Pa., 1906), pp. 106-8.

[86] Conn. Council to Winthrop, 9Sep90, Winthrop Papers, MHS, X, 53.

[87] Extract from Ct. Recs., 9Oct90, *Ibid.*, X, 54.

[88] Walley, as did Phips, received his commission from the Massachusetts Council, 11Jul90. (MA, XXXVI, 158.)

[89] *Jesuit Relations*, LXIV, 43.

[90] *Major Walley's Journal*, Mayo, ed., Hutchinson's *History*, p. 467.

[91] By "general" is meant a representation of all the English colonies in America, a step beyond the New England Union.

[92] Cotton Mather, *The Life of Sir William Phips*, ed. by Mark van Doren from the *Magnalia Christi Americana* (1697) (New York: 1929), p. 70.

[93] It will be remembered that the departure of Elisha Cooke, one of the agents, from the meeting of the Commissioners, 6Dec89, helped in the final disruption of the Confederacy, though his actual departure was apparently delayed several months, Winthrop Papers, MHS, XII, 37.

[94] Cotton Mather to Hinckley, 26Feb91, Columbia University Facsimiles.

[95] See E. B. Greene, *Provincial America*, Vol. VI of the *American Nation Series*, ed. by A. B. Hart (1905), pp. 21-3; also an earlier work by the same author, *The Provincial Governor* (New York: 1898), pp. 75-6.

[96] "Second Charter of Massachusetts," 7Oct91, *Select Charters of American History, 1606-1775*, ed. by William MacDonald (New York: 1899), pp. 205-12.

[97] *Andros Tracts*, II, 229.

[98] Cotton Mather, *Diary*, MHSC, 7:VII:142.

[99] Winthrop Papers, MHS, XVII, 14.

[100] MA, XXXVII, 190.

[101] "The Children of Israel were desirous that he should Rule over them." (Increase Mather in *Narratives of the Insurrections*, ed. by Jameson, p. 294.)

[102] Winthrop Papers, MHS, 25Jul92; Larabee, ed., *Royal Instructions*, I, No.

611. In 1694 Phips was constituted "chief commander" in the colonies "to command or Order such Proportion of the Forces of each of Our Colonies" as the royal government saw fit. (Peck Coll., RIHS, I, 14.)

[146] Letter of 14Apr93, printed in Ford, ed., *op. cit.*, p. 79. Ill feeling from the Confederation persisted as late as 25Sep93 when William Pitkin, last Commissioner of the Confederation from Connecticut, drew up a "Narrative of the Service of Connecticut in the Indian Wars," showing the compliance of Connecticut "with Boston and Yorke in articles for a confederate army" but criticized the other colonies for not living up to the "Articles of Confederation" in supplying their proportion of troops and expecting more of Connecticut. *(CHSC, XXIV, 65, 66, 69.)*

CHAPTER XVI

A Legacy for America

The sun shall be no more thy light by day; neither for brightness shall the noon give light unto thee: but the LORD shall be unto thee an everlasting light, and thy God thy glory.

Thy people also shall be all righteous: they shall inherit the land for ever, the branch of my planting, the work of my hands, that I may be glorified.

A little one shall become a thousand, and a small one a strong nation: I the LORD will hasten it in his time.[1]

Several generations had passed since the Children of Israel came to the rocky shores of the new Canaan. Through hardship and peril they had hewn a home out of the wilderness. The Lord had blessed them: He had led them to the Promised Land; in time of want He had given them succor; and He had delivered their enemies into their hands. To the New England Union of their fathers they owed the preservation of their lives, liberty, and their institutions. Harken then unto the glad tidings of Zion!

As the prophet of old spoke of the rising of a "strong nation" from small beginnings, so has been the lesson of history. The early settlers of New England came to the New World to escape persecution and to build for themselves a new home in the land of milk and honey. For the most part they were not disappointed; the opportunities for fisheries, trade, and abundant lands were there for the asking. Like the early Israelites they could now worship together as they had longed to do without restraint; yet they would not tolerate any corruption of their pure religion —the ideal state was a rule of church elders, though there was no actual fusion of church and state. But the theocratic system could not hold a people in check, who themselves were escaping the fetters of authoritarianism. A peculiar mixture, therefore, was the result of the efforts to establish a Bible Commonwealth in the New World. On the one hand was the attempt to preserve unity in thought and institutions; on the other, the very effort to coerce the people along a straight and narrow path stimulated opposition and challenged the hardy spirit of the founders, with the end result of liberalization. Thus was the paradoxical nature of the Confederation of the Puritan colonies. Called into being in order to form a united front for fostering the "True Vine" and deterring aggression from without, the members of the intercolonial league soon became a sounding board for criticism against the rule of the elders, particularly evidenced in the independent opinions of such Commissioners as Hathorne, Bradstreet, Cudworth, Hatherly, and Winthrop, Jr. The New England Confederacy, through its long life, serves as a gauge for measuring the power of the Puritan oligarchy, the planting of seeds of national consciousness, and Puritan conceptions of government.

Because the United Colonies of New England was a general alliance of the individual colony governments and the colonies did not invest the Commissioners with any powers not commonly shared by them, the structure of the Confederacy underlines the ideas of government held by the Puritans. First of all, the Commissioners were regarded as general officers of the colonies —not a picked commission to settle special disputes. An uproar arose in the colonies when the attempt was made to allocate the offices of Commissioner between two factions—witness in Massachusetts the struggle between the popular party in the House of Deputies and the conservative magistrates. Since the Commissioners represented the whole colony in the intercolonial board of Commissioners, it was thought unwise to give the appointment to officers who represented only particular constituencies of the colony as did the deputies. It became requisite, then, that the office of Commissioner of the United Colonies should be elective either by the freemen in a court of election or at least by the appointment of one of the elected general officers of the colony, such as the governor, deputy governor, treasurer, or if these were incapacitated a high ranking magistrate, who, was in effect a general officer elected by both houses. The election by proxy developed as a result of the recognition of the right of freemen to cast their votes for the governor and Commissioners even though they were unable to attend the court of election. Thus was provided the basis of our own electoral system today.

The principle, therefore, that general officers of the colonies should be elected by qualified voters of the whole colony was expanded to the level of intercolonial union by requiring that the Commissioners of the Confederation be general officers. This is the basis for the idea, later reinforced by the conception of the royal prerogative, that the state and National Executive should be founded upon the will of the whole people. The Confederation also brought to the intercolonial level the latent executive powers of the colonies, as evidenced in making the Commissioners, who served on the colonial councils of magistrates, in effect a supreme council for the colonies. The colonial councils, constantly under the threat of war and having to face several war emergencies, exercised executive authority: they issued orders and commissions for the raising of troops and supervised the conduct of war. The governors-in-council were not unlike the king-in-council. On the intercolonial level the governors-in-council—the governor was almost without exception (if he were available) one of the Commissioners from his colony—comprised the board of Commissioners of the United Colonies, thus transferring to this central agency their own exercise of executive authority. Traces of executive powers had begun to emerge in the Confederation—witness the Commissioners' raising a "confederate army" for services in King Philip's War and supervising for several months the troop actions of the New England colonies. Thus in the Confederation were found the germ for later ideas of an intercolonial executive.

Besides conciliar powers, the Confederation developed other Puritan notions of government. Of nearly three score Commissioners only several were drawn from the clergy. This was also the case on the colonial level. Civil government supported and implemented the views of the clergy, but the actual administration of civil government was regarded as distinct from religious or church government. Clergymen who became public servants shed the cloth even though this was not officially required. In the Confederation, the names of John Davenport, John Cotton, John Norton, or the Mathers are conspicuously absent from the roster of Commissioners. The New England clergy resisted entering public office—a notable exception was Increase Mather, who, being one of the most influential men of the colony, was the Massachusetts agent to England. The proper place of the clergy was to exhort the people to know their responsibilities, not direct the actual operation of government for which persons of other callings were better suited. Thus there was a clear demarcation of civil and church government. The decline in orthodoxy during the final years of the Confederacy reflected the diminishing influence of the clergy, not its control. The Puritan contribution to the idea of separation of church and state in America, almost wholly unintentional, is significant.

A strain of Puritanism evident in the Confederation was a regard for higher law. Unfortunately the Puritans too often confused Mosaic law with the more general notions of fundamental law; as is the tendency in any attempt to rationalize such intangibles, they sought justification for their every act. Puritan judges had little trouble settling cases of litigation—there were the ancient laws and current necessity. But when called upon to take action, rather than sit in judgment of others, especially when a course of action was of great moment such as the determination of war, the Puritans sought greater justification than the specific laws and examples of the past. They turned to higher law, the unwritten law of God. Though they searched hard for precedents during the nullification crisis of the 1650's and the Bay Colony felt obligated by the Articles of Union to declare war, a deeper responsibility was found to transcend the specific powers of the written compact. It never occurred to the Puritans to define their references to the higher law or even go beyond Biblical law into the later Lockean or Rousseauian sphere of natural rights. But it is significant to note that their penchant for justification of all their acts—as the records of the Commissioners so often testify—was reaching for a criterion beyond their experience or explanation.

The Articles of Confederation was a manifestation of the Puritan respect for contractual agreements. On an interstate level, this was the beginning of American Constitutionalism. Mention has been made in the first chapter of the Puritan tendency to categorize functions according to particular or general classifications. In creating a constitution for all the colonies, establishing an agency with jurisdiction in matters of common concernment, we see an evolution of federalism from the town and colony level to an intercolonial league. But in creating a federal agency, the Puritans entrusted to it only enumerated powers, which was consistent with their reliance upon the compact in all aspects of life. The principle of delegated powers was to form the basis of the later American Constitution. Compact government under the Puritans also fostered the negative aspects of the compact theory, that of limited government.

The Commissioners of the Confederation professed the high regard of New England Puritanism for the vitality of local institutions. Congregations had migrated to New England and, in turn, splintered to find new homes in the wilderness. Local institutions multiplied, often combining politically as in the cases of the compacts forming the colonies of New Haven and Connecticut. Particularism was strong—witness the Bay Colony, attempting to go its own aristocratic way, being brought into line by the towns and forced to expand its freemanship and to accept in the General Court deputies from the towns. Suffice to say, the Commissioners consistently respected the authority of the colony and town institutions and made no effort to usurp their authority. Indeed, the Commissioners were overcautious; their acts were in the form of recommendations, and wartime orders were left for implementation by the local governments as they saw fit. The Commissioners exercised primarily moral force to keep the colonies along the lines of united policy. Thus vigorous local government, which was to become an honored tradition in New England, was encouraged by the Commissioners not seeking to meddle in the internal affairs of the colonies.

The Confederation guided the New England colonies during the critical period of their establishment. Despite a continual Indian threat there were more than thirty years of peace. This accomplishment alone would be significant. But the Confederation also made visible contributions to the theory of federal government in America and promoted the idea of independence.

Not only was the New England Confederation the first experiment in American federalism and the only federation under the old British colonial system,[2] but it served as a basis for later plans of union. The Articles of Confederation of 1781 and the Constitution of 1787 show traces of influences from the Articles of the first federation of the American colonies.

Penn's Plan of Union of 1697, which was not worked out in detail, embodied some of the principles of the New England Articles of Confederation: for example, the holding of annual meetings and appointing two representatives from each colony. Later in the colonial period the influence of the Confederation is seen in the famous Albany Plan of Union. The Grand Council

was to meet annually and on extraordinary occasions, to choose
a speaker, to have jurisdiction over Indian affairs, and to submit
general accounts annually. Taxation was to be proportionate.
Benjamin Franklin, who drafted the Albany Plan, was known to
have had a high regard for the New England Confederation;
when proposing a draft of a federal constitution in 1775, he
scribbled on it his analysis of the Articles of Confederation of
1643.[3]

Galloway's Plan of Union, a measure whereby the conservatives in 1774 hoped to offset the growing radicalism of the colonies, included features that might have been present had the
New England Confederation been reinstated under auspices of
the royal government. A President-General appointed by the
royal government was to preside over a council of the colonies.
The President and Council were to constitute a part of the British legislature—legislation could be initiated by either the American council or the British Parliament, each having the powers
of veto.

The Articles of Confederation of 1781 bears a strong resemblance to the New England Articles of Confederation. It is
not necessary here to compare phrase with phrase nor the
similarities in the two Articles—the reader can easily do this
himself, but certain features are striking. Most obvious are the
titles of the two Confederations: "The United Colonies of New
England" and "The United States of America." Such phrases
as "mutual welfare" and "firm league of friendship" have their
origins in the first Confederacy. Compare also provisions of the
second League, such as annual appointment of members of
Congress by the state legislatures, the guarantee of two members
in Congress from each state, each state having an equal vote,
and Congress as a court of appeal on interstate boundary questions.

The Federal Constitution, like its New England antecedent,
was a document of enumerated powers, many of which were
found in the earlier document. In the Constitution we see two
Senators representing a state, annual meetings of Congress, the
extradition clause, the privileges and immunities clause, proportionate representation in the House and the powers of taxation
thereof proportionate to the population, and the provision that
no new states are to be formed within a state or by the "junction of two of more States, or Parts of States, without the Con-

sent of the Legislatures of the States concerned as well as of the Congress." That the framers of the Constitution were well aware of the long constitutional development of the colonies and entertained an appreciation of the New England experiment in Union is not too much to assume in view of the high degree of education of many of the founders, the reverence of New Englanders for their ancient union, and that among the founders Benjamin Franklin, John Adams, and Rufus King were known to have expressed an indebtedness to the early Confederation.

The origins of our Constitutional system have been too often slighted. In all the many studies of our constitutional history, practically no mention is made of the New England Confederation. A well-known study on the foundations of American constitutionalism virtually omits the influences of seventeenth century America. Expounders of constitutional law have missed a fertile field of precedents by neglecting colonial history. It was during this period that the New Englanders in working out their own institutions planted the seeds of American federalism, and, in seeking depth to our political institutions, one cannot consider the formative period of American history insignificant because it is "ancient" history. To explain our institutional growth by examining only a century and a half of our history and neglecting the other two hundred years would seem absurd—yet that is what has been done. Historians have been content to work with familiar material or to find security in the usual and tried episodes of history. Moreover, there is a general misconception that there is little left to investigate in the first two centuries of American history; but the opposite is true, as is evidenced by the lack of treatment of the rise of American federalism.

Mention has already been made of the Puritans developing executive powers in the form of their councils of magistrates and the transferring of many of the characteristics of these councils to the intercolonial board of Commissioners of the United Colonies. But the origins of the United States Senate may be traced back also to the executive-advisory councils of the colonies and the intercolonial council of Commissioners. The framers of the Constitution of 1787, both nationalists and anti-nationalists, intended that the Senate should be a council to work with the President, and that the legislative function should be guided by the Lower House. To the nationalists (or federalists) the Senate was an advisory council for purposes of consulting with the President.[4] The anti-nationalists (not necessarily the anti-federalists) expected the Senate to be a sort of council of revision to check the Executive and curb rash actions of the House. Even the heads of the early executive departments, particularly of War and Finance, expected free access to the Senate, which hope, however, was soon disappointed. With the hopes of the founders to make the Senate a council of advice and revision being defeated, the Senate struck out on its own course as the upper House of the Legislature. But the Senate-Council envisioned by the fathers of our Constitution bears a striking resemblance to the Confederation-Council of the Commissioners of the United Colonies.

Under the Constitution, the Vice President presides over the Senate. The Commissioners of the Confederation also chose a president to preside over their sessions. If the Senate had developed along the lines that Washington and other nationalists had expected, the President would have "headed" the Senate by virture of the fact that the Vice President of the Executive Branch presided over the Senate and the President possessed the veto power. Throughout the colonial period, we find a fusion of council and legislative powers in the colonial governments, which matter was not clarified until the working out of the separation of powers embodied in the Constitution. Neither presidential nor cabinet government was ever understood by the American colonies, but it is safe to say that they leaned toward the latter in their experiments in intercolonial union— the lack of devotion to the crown or a chief of state, however, aroused disintegrative forces in any attempt at union.

Briefly the contributions of the New England Confederation to colonial notions of a national legislature may be stated as follows: (1) representation by whole states; (2) equal votes for each state; (3) two delegates from each state; (4) a national forum; (5) power to make treaties with foreign states; (6) war powers, such as declaring war and calling into service of the "Country" the militia of the states; (7) regulatory powers, though without enforcement machinery, in such matters as imposts, Indian trade, or vagrancy; (8) overseeing of Indian affairs of the colonies; (9) a watchdog for the common welfare; and (10) an intrenchment of conservative interests among the majority of its members. Fifty years of representative government under an intercolonial Confederation thoroughly implanted in the colonial mind an appreciation of the advantages of union under a central council. Thus the chief contributions of the Confederacy found later expression in the American Senate. One, however, has to look for precedents for the Lower House in the influence of the House of Commons, the stormy course of the colonial assemblies, and in the negative example of the Confederation of 1781, which had retained too many features of state-supremacy handed down from the earlier Confederacy.

For the origins of the Supreme Court one finds an interesting precedent in the New England Confederation, even through our judicial heritage has come down through the individual colony judicatures and English common law practices. But it is interesting to note that the colonists referred to the board of Commissioners as the "Supreme Court" (Winthrop). What was meant was an arbitral commission to settle disputes arising among the colonies. The decisions of the Commissioners were only good if accepted by the colonies involved—on several occasions, such as disputes over the Connecticut impost and the Narragansett lands, the colonies refused to abide by the decisions of the Commissioners. Except as a board of arbitration, the Commissioners had no appellate jurisdiction. But in several areas the Commissioners exercised special or original jurisdiction. Many a session of the Commissioners, who heard accusations against Indians brought before them, took on the form of a trial. Indians were confined to prison because of the Commissioners' decisions. In the case of Miantinomo, the powerful Narragansett sachem who fell captive to the Mohegans, a death sentence was imposed, though the responsibility for his execution was given to the Mohegan chief. Until the crown established courts in the colonies, the Commissioners also dabbled in the awarding of prizes and in protesting against seizures by the Dutch. During the Dutch War, the Commissioners even conferred upon the inhabitants of Fairfield authority for marque and reprisal. Although a system of judicial review failed to develop—which would have been impossible because the general courts of the colonies retained ultimate authority and the confederation itself lacked legislative powers upon which a review would be passed— the Commissioners did seek to interpret the Supreme Law of the Land, the Articles of Confederation. The debates of the Nullification Crisis of 1653-5 was the first time in American history that the great issue of states rights versus central control was argued before an American tribunal, although, what would seem strange today, the Commissioners argued their cases themselves and then rendered a decision. Nevertheless, the debates over the right of a confederate to nullify an act of the Commissioners binding the colonies to wage war and to secede from the Union called into question all phases of the obligations of the colonies to their compact. This was the beginning of constitutional law in America.

America's first experiment in federal government was also of great negative value. Imperfection points the way for perfection in the future. The bigotry of the Confederacy in matters of conscience and the attempt to make "Unitie our Dutie" served to warn the settlers of the evils of imposed conformity and made them more guarded of their liberties. The New England Confederation also revealed many weaknesses to be corrected in the later course of American federalism, as evidenced in the problems of conflicting sovereignties between the central and state governments. The creation of the Confederacy of 1643 may have been, in the words of Increase Mather, "an act of absolute sovereignty" on the part of the contracting states, but for the Confederation itself there was only a temporary illusion of sovereignty.

The Constitution of 1787 attempted to correct certain deficiencies first revealed by the New England Confederation. Besides setting forth the doctrine of dual sovereignty, which had received tacit recognition in the Articles of 1781, the Constitution gave the Federal Government means of enforcement— particularly, powers to maintain an army and to use military force to compel compliance with national policy. From the first experiment of federal government in America, therefore, each attempt improved upon the one preceding—even today the refining of our federal system is a continual process. However, it was the original experiment which provided the giant step toward the creation of the Federal Union of 1789 by laying the groundwork and setting minds to explore the possibilities of union.

A spirit of independence penetrates not only the New England Articles of Confederation but also the course of the Confederation. At the time of the forming of the Union of 1643 the colonists realized that help and protection could not be expected from the home government which was torn with strife of civil war. The colonists knew also that their survival, prosperity, and the preservation of their way of life depended upon their self-reliance. This history of the Confederation is the history of action of the colonists independent of the mother country. The Confederation, condemned by the Stuarts, was tolerated only as a military expedient because of the inability of the royal government to provide for the complete defense of the colonies. During the Andros regime the Confederation was extinct because it was irreconcilable with the Dominion government; but after the fall of that government, the New England Confederation was immediately renewed. The Confederation at this late date was respected for its military value—it was soon apparent that military cooperation did not have to follow the pattern of confederation. When the colonies of New England were granted liberal charters under the new Protestant king, they were content to abandon their efforts to establish their ancient union. The New England Union had filled a void created by the unsettled condition of the Civil War-Protectorate-Restoration-Glorious Revolution period. Thus for a half a century the advantages of united action without the sanction of the King or Protector were made known on the American continent: the New England Confederacy, conceived in liberty and founded upon a common cause, would remain a beacon light of encouragement to the patriots of the eighteenth century.

We are indebted to the Puritan settlers of England for their settling the wilderness and their appreciation of self-government. In making their homes in new Canaan, the Puritans left a rich legacy to American federalism, implanting into the colonial consciousness an experience in federal union and an example of the capability of the colonists to shape their own destiny. Fifty years of Confederation left a feeling for union and a longing for independence that was never to die.

The New Englander of 1690 would have looked back with a different appreciation of the New England Confederation. The last hearty war-whoop had echoed throughout the New England hills, and there was peace in the land.

[1] Isaiah 60:19, 21-2.

[2] Hugh E. Egerton, *Federations and Unions Within the British Empire*, (Oxford: Clarendon Press, 1924), p 8

[3] *American Political Science Review*, VIII, 393-412.

[4] Early in his administration, Washington was furious as a result of a visit to the Senate. That august body refused to act upon the President's recommendations in his presence and sent his urgent proposals for a national military establishment into committee, of which Washington replied in disillusionment: "no council ever committed anything."

Articles of Confederation, 1643
(*PCR*, IX, 3-8)

WHERAS wee all came into these parts of America with one
and the same end and ayme namely to advance the Kingdome
of our Lord Jesus Christ and to enjoy the liberties of the Gospell
and the same end and ayme namely to advance the Kingdome
in puritie with peace and whereas in our settleinge (by a wise
providence of God) we are further dispersed vpon the Sea
Coasts and Rivers then was at first intended, so that we cannot
according to our desire with convenience communicate in one
Government and Jurisdiction: And whereas we live encom-
passed with people of severall Nations and strang languages
which hereafter may prove inurious to us or our posteritie. And
forasmuch as the Natives have formerly committed sondry
insolences and outrages upon severall Plantations of the English
and have of late combined themselves against us And seing by
reason of those sad distractions in England which they have
heard of, and by which they know we are hindred, from that
humble way of seekeing advise, or reapeing those comfortable
fruits of protection which at other times we might well expecte.
Wee therefore doe conceive it our bounden dutye without delay
to enter into a present Consotiation amongst our selves, for
mutuall help and strength in all our future concernments: That
as in Nation and Religion so in other respects we bee and continue One according to the tenor and true meaneing of the
ensuing Articles: Wherefore it is fully agreed and concluded by
and betweene the parties or Jurisdictions above named and they
joyntly and severally doe by these presents agree and conclude
That they all bee and henceforth bee called by the name of the
UNITED COLONIES OF NEW ENGLAND.
   2. The said United Colonies for themselves and their pos-
terities do joyntly and severally hereby enter into a firme and
perpetual league of frendship and amytie for offence and defence, mutuall advice and succour upon all just occasions both

for preserving and propagateing the truth and liberties of the Gospell and for their owne mutuall safety and wellfare.

3. It is further agreed That the Plantations which at present are or hereafter shalbe setled within the limmetts of the Massachusets shalbe forever under the Massachusets and shall have peculier Jurisdiction among themselves in all cases as an entire Body and that Plymouth Connecktacutt and New Haven shall eich of them have like peculier Jurisdiction and government within their limmetts and in referrence to the Plantations which already are setled, or shall hereafter be erected or shall settle within their limmetts respectively Provided that no other Jurisdiction shall hereafter be taken in as a distinct head or member of this Confederation nor shall any other Plantation or Jurisdiction of any of these Confederates be received by any of them nor shall any two of the Confederates joyne in one Jurisdiction without consent of the rest which consent to be interpreted as is expressed in the sixt Article ensuinge.

4. It is by these Confederates agreed that the charge of all just warrs whether offensive or defensive upon what part or member of this Confederation soever they fall, shall both in men provision and all other disbursements be borne by all the parts of this Confederation in different proportions according to their differrent abillitie in manner following, namely that the Commissioners for eich Jurisdiction from tyme to tyme as ther shalbe occation bring a true account and number of all the males in every Plantation or any way belonging to or under their severall Jurisdictions of what quallyty or condition soever they bee from sixteene yeares old to three-score being Inhabitants there. And that according to the different numbers which from tyme to tyme shalbe found in eich Jurisdiction upon a true and just account, the service of men and all charges of the warr be borne by the Poll: eich Jurisdiction or plantation being left to their owne just course and custome of rating themselves and people according to their differrent estates with due respects to their quallites and exemptions among themselves though the Confederation take no notice of any such priviledg: And that according to their differrent charge of eich Jurisdiction and plantation, the whole advantage of the warr (if it please God so to bless their endeavours) whether it be in lands goods or persons shalbe proportionably devided among the said Confederates.

5. It is further agreed That if any of these Jurisdictions or

any plantation under or in combynation with them be envaded by any enemie whomsoever upon notice and request of any three majestrates of that Jurisdiction so invaded, the rest of the Confederrates without any further meeting or expostulation shall forthwith send ayde to the Confederate in danger but in different proportions: namely the Massachusets and hundred men sufficiently armed and provided for such a service and jorney, and eich of the rest fourty finde so armed and provided, or any lesse number, if lesse be required according to this proportion. But if such Confederate in Danger may be supplyed by their next Confederats, not exceeding the number hereby agreed, they may crave help there, and seeke no further for the present: the charge to be borne as in this Article is exprest: And at the returne to bee victualled and supplyed with poder and shott for their journey (if there bee neede) by that Jurisdiction which employed or sent for them: But none of the Jurisdictions to exceed these number till by a meeting of the Commissioners for this Confederation a greater ayd appeare necessary. And this proportion to continue till upon knowledg of greater numbers in eich Jurisdiction which shalbe brought to the next meeting some other proportion be ordered. But in any such case of sending men for present ayd whether before or after such order or alterration, it is agreed that at the meeting of the Commissioners for this Confederation, the cause of such war or invasion be duly considered: And if it appeare that the fault lay in the parties so invaded that then that Jurisdiction or plantation make just satisfaction, both to the Invaders whom they have injured, and beare all the charges of the warr themselves without requireing any allowance from the rest of the Confederats towards the same And further that if any Jurisdiction see any danger of any Invasion approaching, and there be tyme for a meeting, that in such case three majestrates of that Jurisdiction may summon a meeting at such conveyent place as themselves shall think meete, to consider and provide against the threatened danger Provided when they are mett they may remoove to what place they please Onely whilst any of these foure Confederats have but three majestrats in their Jurisdiction, their request or summons from any two of them shalbe accounted of equall force with the three mentioned in both the clauses of this Article, till there be an encrease of majestrats there.

6. It is also agreed that for the mannageing and concluding

of all affaires proper and concerneing the whole Confederation
two Comissioners shalbe chosen by and out of eich of these
foure Jurisdictions namely two for the Mattachusets two for
Plymouth two for Connectacutt and two for New Haven being
all in Church fellowship with us which shall bring full power
from their severall generall Courts respectively to heare examine weigh and determine all affairs of our warr or peace
leagues ayds charges and numbers of men for warr division of
Spoyles and whatsoever is gotten by conquest receiveing of
more Confederats for plantations into combination with any of
the confederates and all thinges of like nature which are the
proper concommitants or consequents of such a Confederation
for amytie offence and defence not intermedleing with the government of any of the Jurisdictions which by the third Article
is preserved entirely to themselves. But if these eight Comissioners when they meete shall not all agree, yet it is concluded that
any six of the eight agreeing shall have power to settle and
determine the businesses in question: But if six do not agree
that then such propositions with their reasons so farr as they
have beene debated be sent and referred to the foure generall
Courts viz the Mattachusetts Plymouth Connecttacutt and New
Haven: And if at all the said Generall Courts the business so
referred be concluded, then to bee prosecuted by the Confederates and all their members It is further agreed that these
eight Commissioners shall meete once every yeare besides extrordinary meetings (according to the fift Article) to consider
treate and conclude of all affaires belonging to this Confederation which meeting shall ever be the first Thursday in September. And that the next meeting after the date of these presents
which shalbe accounted the second meeting shalbe at Bostone
in Massachusetts the third at Hartford the fourth at New Haven
the fift at Plymouth, the sixt and seaventh at Bostone And then
Hartford New Haven and Plymouth and so in course succes-
sively, if in the meane tyme some middle place be not found
out and agreed on which may be commodious for all the Jurisdictions.

7. It is further agreed that at eich meeting of these eight
Comissioners whether ordinary or extraordinary, they orr six
of them agreeing as before, may chose their President out of
themselves whose office and worke shalbe to take care and direct
for order and a comely carrying on of all proceedings in the

present meeting: but he shalbe invested with no such power or respect, as by which he shall in propounding or progresse of any business or any way cast the scales otherwise then in the precedent Article is agreed.

8. It is also agreed that the Comissioners for Confederation hereafter at their meetings whether ordinary or extrordinary as they may have Commission or opertunitie do endeavoure to frame and establish agreements and orders in generall cases of a civill nature, wherein all the Plantations are interested for preserveing peace among themselves, and preventing as much as may bee all occasions of warr or differencs with others, as about the free and speedy passage of justice in every Jurisdiction, to all the Confederats equally as to their owne, receiveing those that remoove from one plantation to another without due certefycates, how all the Jurisdictions may carry it towards the Indians, that they neither grow insolent nor be injured without due satisfaction, lest warr break in upon the Confederates through such miscarryages. It is also agreed that if any servant runn away from his master into any other of these confederated Jurisdictions That in such case upon the Certyficate of one Majestrate in the Jurisdiction out of which the said servant fled or upon other due proofe: the said servant shalbe delivered either to his Master or any other that pursues and brings such Certificate or proofe. And that upon the escape of any prisoner whatsoever or fugitive for any criminall cause, whether breakeing prison or getting from the officer or otherwise escapeing upon the certificate of two Majestrats of the Jurisdiction out of which the escape is made, that he was a prisoner or such an offender at the tyme of the escape, the Majestrates or some of them of that Jurisdiction where for the present the said prisoner or fugitive abideth shall forthwith graunt such a warrant as the case will beare for the apprehending of any such person, and the delivery of him into the hands of the officer, or other person who pursues him And if there be help required for the safe returneing of any such offendor, then it shalbe graunted to him that craves the same he payinge the charges thereof.

9. And for that the justest warrs may be of dangerous consequence especially to the smaler plantations in these united Colonies, It is agreed that neither the Massachusetts Plymouth Connecticutt nor New Haven, nor any of the members of any of them, shall at any tyme hereafter begin undertake, or engage

themselves or this Confederation or any part thereof in any warr whatsoever (sudden exegents with the necessary consequents thereof excepted which are also to be moderated as much as the case will permitt) without the consent and agreement of the forenamed eight Comissioners or at least six of them, as in the sixt Article is provided: And that no charge be required of any of the Confederats in case of a defensive warr till the said Comissioners have mett and approved the justice of the warr, and have agreed upon the summ of money to be levyed, which summ is then to be payd by the severall Confederates in proportion according to the fourth Article.

10. That in extraordinary occations when meettings are summoned by three Majestrates of any Jurisdiction, or two as in the fift Article If any of the Commissioners come not due warneing being given or sent It is agred that foure of the Comissioners shall have power to direct a warr which cannot be delayed and to send for due proportions of men out of eich Jurisdiction, as well as six might doe if all mett: but not lesse then six shall determine the justice of the warr or allow the demaunds or bills of charges, or cause any levies to be made for the same

11. It is further agreed that if any of the Confederates shall hereafter break any of these present Articles, or be any other wayes injurious to any one of thother Jurisdictions: such breach of agreement, or injurie shalbe duly considered and ordered by the Commissioners for thother Jurisdictions, that both peace and this present confederation may be entirely preserved without violation.

12. Lastly this perpetual Confederation and the severall Articles and agreements thereof being read and seriously considered both by the generall Court for the Massachusetts and by the Comissioners for Plymouth Conectacutt and New Haven were fully allowed and confirmed by three of the forenamed Confederates namely the Massachusetts Conectacutt and New Haven Onely the Comissioners for Plymouth haveing no Comission to conclude, desire respite till they might advise with their Generall Court, whereupon it was agreed and concluded by the said Court of the Massachusetts and the Comissioners for the other two Confederates That if Plymouth Consent, then the whole treaty as it stands in these presente Articles is and shall continue firme and stable without alteration: But if Plymouth come not in: yet the other three Confederates doe by these

presents confirme the whole Confederation and all the Articles
thereof: onely in September next when the second meeting of
the Comissioners is to be at Bostone, new consideration may be
taken of the sixt Article which concernes number of Commissioners for meeting and concluding the affaires of this Confederation to the satisfaction of the Court of the Massachusetts,
and the Comissioners for thother two Confederats, but the rest
to stand unquestioned.

In testimony whereof the Generall Court of the Massachusetts by their Secretary and the Comissioners for Conectacutt
and New Haven have subscribed these presente Articles this
xixth of the third month commonly called May Anno Domini
1643.

At a meeting of the Commissioners for the Confederation held
at Boston the seaventh of September, It appeareing that the
Generall Court of New Plymouth and the severall Towneships
thereof have read considered and approved these Articles of
confederation, as appeareth by Comission from their Generall
Court beareing date the xxixth of August 1643 to Mr. Edward
Winslow and Mr. William Collyer to ratifye and confirme the
same on their behalf wee therefore the Comissioners for the
Mattachusetts Conecktacutt and New Haven doe also for our
severall Governments subscribe unto them.

JOHN WINTHROP Governor, Massachusetts
THOMAS DUDLEY
GEORGE FENWICK
THEOPHILUS EATON
EDWARD HOPKINS
THOMAS GREGSON

APPENDIX B

Articles of Confederation, 1672
(*PCR*, X, 346-51)

WHERAS wee all came into these partes of America with one
and the same end and aime, viz: To advance the Kingdome of
ourLord Jesus Christ; and to Injoy the Liberties of the Gospell
in puritie with peace; And wheras in our settleing by a wise
providence of God wee are further dispersed upon the sea coasts
and Rivers then was first Intended; soe that wee can not according to our desire with conveniency comunicate in one Government and Jurisdiction; and wheras wee are compased with
people of severall Nations and strange Languages; which heerafter may prove injurious to us and our posteritie and forasmuch
as the Natives; have formerly comited sundry Insolencyes; and
outrages upon severall Plantations of the English; and have
severall times combined themselves against us; and seing by
reason of our distance from England (our deare native Countrey) wee are hindred both from that humble way of seeking
advice and reaping those comfortable fruites of protection which
wee might otherwise well expect; wee therfore doe accoumpt in
our duty; as well as safety To enter into a confeaderation for
mutuall healp and succor in all our future concernments; that
as in Nation and religion; soe in other respects; wee be and continew one; according to the tenure and true meaning of the
Insuing articles;

    1. WHERFORE it is agreed and concluded by and between
the parties or Jurisdictions above named and they doe Joyntly
and severally by these presents agree and conclude that they
all bee, and henceforth be called by the name of the united
Collonies of New England;

    2. The said united Collonies for themselves and theire pos-
terities doe Joyntly and severally heerby entere into a feirme
and perpetuall League of friendshipp and amity; mutuall advise
and succor upon all Just occasions; both for preserveing and
propagateing the truth and liberties of the Gospell; and for

theire owne mutuall safety and welfare, provided Notwithstanding, that the power of determination of an offencive Warr
properly soe called (soe as to engage the Collonies therin)
shalbe in the severall Generall Courts of the aforementioned
Confeaderates

3. It is agreed that the Plantations which att present are or
heerafter shalbe settled within the Lymetts of the Massachusetts shalbe for ever under the Government of Massachusetts;
and have peculiar Jurisdiction amongst themselves as an Intire
body; and that Plymouth and Conecticott each of them in all
Respects; have the like peculiare Jurisdiction; and Government
within theire Lymetts; according to theire Respective Letters
Pattents from his Majestie, provided that noe other Jurisdiction
shall heerafter be taken in as a distinct head or member of this
Confederation; nor shall any other Plantation or Jurisdiction in
present being and not alreddy in Combination or under the
Jurisdiction of any of these Confeaderates, Joyne in one Jurisdiction; without the consent of the severall Generall Courts of
the above named Confeaderates;

4. It is alsoe agreed that for the manageing and concluding
of all affaires proper to and concerning the whole Confeaderation; not excepted against in these articles) two Comissioners
shalbe chosen by and out of each of these three Jurisdictions,
viz: two for the Massachusetts two for Plymouth and two for
Conecticott; being all in Church fellowship with us) whoe shall
bringe full power from theire Generall Courts; Respectively, to
heare examine and weigh and determine the same; But if these
six Comissioners when mett; shall not all agree yett it is concluded that any five of the six agreeing shall have power to
settle and determine the case in controversye but if five doe not
agree; That then such propositions with theire Reasons (soe
farr as they have bine debated; be sent and Refered to the
severall Generall Courts; and if by all the said Courts there be
a Concurrance in the matter soe Refered; then to be accordingly
procecuted by all the confeaderats and all theire Members;

5. It is further agreed that the Comissioners for the united
Collonies shall meet but once in three yeers except in cases
extreordinary; which meetings shall ever be on the first Thursday in September and that the next meeting after the date of
these presents shalbe att Plymouth which shalbe accoumpted
the first meeting; the second att Boston the third att Hartford

the fourth att Boston the fift att Hartford; and soe the meeting wilbe but once in fifteen yeers att Plymouth and double soe often in the other Collonies if in the mean time some middle place be not found out and agreed on which may be comodious to all;

6. It is further agreed that att each meeting of these six Comissioners whether ordinary or extreordinary they may chose theire Presedent out of themselves; whose office and worke shalbe to take care and direct for order and a comly carrying on of all proceedings in the present meeting; But hee shalbe Invested with noe such power; by which hee may hinder the propounding or progresse of any business or any way cast the scales otherwise, then in the present articles is agreed;

7. It is alsoe agreed that the Comissioners for this Confeaderation heerafter att theire meetings whether ordinary or extreordinary, as they may have Comission or oppertunitie may consult of an propose to the severall Generall Courts, to be by them allowed; and established, such orders in Generall cases of a Civill Nature wherin all the plantations are Interested; for preserveing peace amongst themselves; and prevented (as much as may be) all occasions of warr and differences with others; as about the free and speedy passage of Justice in each Jurisdiction; to all the Confeaderates equally; as to theire owne; Receiveing of those that Remove from one plantation to another; how all the Jurisdictions may carry it towards the Indians that they neither grow Insolent nor be Injuried without due satisfaction Least warr breake in upon the Confeaderates through such miscarriages; It is alsoe agreed that if any servant Run away from his master into any other of these Confeaderated Jurisdictions; That in such case upon the certificate of one Majestrate in the Jurisdiction out of which the servant fled or upon other due proffe; the said servant shalbe delivered, either to his Master or any other that persues and bringes such Certificate or proffe; and that upon the escape of any prisonor whatsoever or fugative; for any criminall cause; whether breakeing prison or giting from the officer or otherwise escapeing upon the Certificate of one Majestrate of the Jurisdiction out of which the escape is made, that hee was a prisoner or such an offendor att the time of the escape; The Majestrates or some of them, of that Jurisdiction where for the present the said prisonor or fugative abideth; shall forthwith Graunt such a warrant as the

case will beare for the apprehending any such person; and the delivering of him or her into the hand of the persuer and if healp be required it shalbe graunted, hee paying the charge thereof;

8. It is further agreed that for the disposeing of the Indian stocke for the future the Choice of the Comissioners in the severall Collonies; being anually as formerly; The Comissioners of the Massachusetts with such others as shalbe present or any three of the Comissioners Meeting yeerly att Boston or else-where as they shall agree; and att the usuall time; They may doe any acte for the manageing and ordering of that affaire; as though all the Comissioners were present; and what they shall doe heerin they shall keep a true Record thereof; and transmitt the accoumpt of the same from time to time to the trianuall meeting of the Comissioners;

9. It is agreed alsoe by these Confederates That the charge of all Just warrs whether offencive or defencive upon what parte or member of this confeaderation soever they fall; shall both in men provisions and all other disbursements be bourne by all the partes of the Confederation; in different proportions according to theire different abillities: viz: that the Rule for proportioning men; and Raiseing of monyes for the defraying of such charges; as may from time to time arise; upon any warr defensive or offencive begun and carried on according to the articles of confederation; shalbe as followeth; The Massachusetts one hundred; Plymouth thirty Conecticott sixty; and this Rule to continew for fifteen yeers next coming after the begining of the meeting of the Comissioners, to be held att Plymouth in September next; and then if any one or more of the confead-erates shall apprehend the abovesaid proportion to be unequall; that then matters shalbe againe considered; by the Comissioners and what they shall agree upon shalbe presented to the severall Generall Courts for theire acceptance and confeirmation; each Jurisdiction or plantation being left to theire owne Just course and custome of Rateing themselves; and people and that accord-ing to the different charge of each Jurisdiction and Plantation; The whole advantage of the warr if it please God soe to blesse theire Indeavors; whether it be in Lands goods or persons shalbe proportionably devided amongst the said confederates;

10. It is further agreed that if any of these Jurisdictions or any Plantation under them be invaded by any enimie whomso-

ever; upon any notice or request of any three Majestrates of
that Jurisdiction soe Invaded; the rest of the Confeaderates without any further meeting or expostulation, shall forthwith send
aide to the Confederate in danger but in different proportions:
viz: The Masachusetts one hundred men sufficiently armed for
such a service and expedition Plymouth thirty men soe armed
and provided and Connecticott sixty men soe armed and provided; or any lesse number if lesse by required; according to
this proportion but if such confeaderate in danger may be supplyed; by the next confeaderate not exceeding the Numbers
heerby agreed; they may crave healp theire and seeke noe
further for the present; the charge to be bourne by the severall
Collonies according to theire proportions abosesaid and att
theire returne to be victualled and supplyed with powder and
shott (if theire be need) for theire Jurney by that Jurisdiction
that Imployed or sent for them; but in any such case of sending
men for present aide whether before or after such order or
alteration; It is agreed that att the meeting of the Comissioners
for this Confederation; the cause of such warr or Invasion be
duely considered; and if it appeer that the fault lay in the parties
soe invaded that then that Jurisdiction or plantation make Just
satisfaction both to the Invaders whom they have Injuried; and
beare all the Charges of the warr themselves without requireing
any allowance from the Rest of the Confederates towards the
same

11. And for that the Justest warr may be of dangerous consequence especially to the smaller plantations in these united
Collonies; It is agreed that Neither the Massachusetts Plymouth
nor Conecticott nor any of the members of any of them shall
att any time heerafter begin undertake or engage themselves or
this Confeaderation in any warr whatsoever (suddaine exegen-
cyes; with the nessearie consequences therof excepted; which are
alsoe to be moderated as much as the case will permitt) without the consent of the severall Generall Courts of the united
Collonies

12. It is alsoe agreed that incase of any suddaine exegensies
or other waighty occations requireing the meeting of the Comissioners before the ordinary time, The Governor or any three
Majestrates of any of the Confederate Jurisdictions may summon a meeting of the Comissioners; brieffly signifying the occation therof and the time and place of the meeting which shalbe

accordingly attended by the Comissioners of all the Confeaderate Jurisdictions; and when mett they may adjourn to any other time or place as they shall see meet

13. It is alsoe agreed for settleing of vagabonds and wandering persons removeing from one Collonie to another to the disatisfaction and burthen of the places where they come as dayly experience sheweth us; for the future It is ordered that wher any person or persons shalbe found in any Jurisdiction to have had theire abode for more then three monthes and not warned out by the authoritie of the place; and incase of the neglect of any person soe warned; as abovesaid to depart; if hee be not by the first oppertunitie that the season will permitt sent away from Constable to Constable; to the end that hee may be returned to the place of his former aboad; every such person or persons shalbe accoumpted an Inhabitant where they are soe found; and by them governed and provided for as theire condition may require and in all such cases the Charge of the Constables to be bourne by the Treasurer where the said Constables doe dwell

14. It is agreed that if any of the Confeaderates shall heerafter breake any of these present Articles or be in any other way Injurious, to any of the confederat Jurisdictions such breach of agreement or injury shalbe duely considered and ordered by the Comissioners for the other Jurisdictions; that both peace, and this present Confeaderation may be preserved without violation;

WHERAS in the former Articles agreed upon May the 29th 1643 [should be the 19th O. S.] for the united Collonies above named New haven is therein Mensioned and was owned as a distinct Confeaderate and is by these Included and Concluded as one with Conecticott, the aforesaid union shall alwaies be Interpreted as by theire owne Consession and not otherwise;

NOW whereas for many years past upon divers good Considerations there was a Confeaderation agreed upon by the antient English Collonies under his Majesties Authoritie in New England for mutual healp support and defence, as alsoe for the better Maintaining his Majesties Interest against any opposition or Incursion of the barbarous Natives and others as appeereth by articles that were agreed upon in the yeer 1643 and are upon Record to be seen wherby the said Collonies have bin soe united as have proved very benificiall to all his Majesties subjects in these partes for theire peace and securitie; and wher-

as the severall General Courts of the said Collonies have seen
cause to renew the said Confeaderation; with some Nessessary
alteration and addition to the said Articles as is more fully
expressed in the Articles above written; and alsoe whereas the
Generall Court for the Massachusetts Collonie by theire Commission dated in Boston in August 1672 have nominated Thomas Danforth Esquire: and Major William Hawthorne Esquire
theire Commissioners Investing them with full power and authoritie to signe ratify and confeirme; the above Recited articles
of Confeaderation; And in like Manor the Generall Court held
att Plymouth June the fift 1672 have Nominated Thomas
Prence Esquire and Major Josias Winslow Esquire Investing
them with like power; and the Generall Court of Conecticott
Collonie; held att Hartford May the 9th and June the 26th
1672 have in like Manor Nominated John Winthorpe Esquire
and James Richards Esquire Investing them with like power;
The above said Commissioners being Assembled att Plymouth
September the fift 1672, have read and examined these above
written Articles, doe according to theire said Commissions; and
by vertue thereof Clearly and absolutely Rattify and Coneirme
the same: for the Reestablishing of a perpetuall Confeaderation
between the above named Collonies; as was the declared Inten-
sions of the former Articles; In Confeirmation wherof, the Commissioners above named; by the authoritie Graunted unto them
from theire several General Courts; and in theire Name and
sted, have heerunto Subscribed theire hands In Plymouth September the fift 1672.

    JOHN WINTHORPP (jr.)
    JAMES RICHARDS
    THOMAS PRENCE
    JOSIA WINSLOW
    THOMAS DANFORTH
    WILLIAM HAWTHORN

MEETINGS OF THE COMMISSIONERS OF THE UNITED COLONIES

Below are listed the official meetings, regular and extraordinary, of the Commissioners of the United Colonies. Such get-togethers of several of the Commissioners, for administering the funds for the "Indian Worke" or treating with Cromwell's commissioners in 1654 (Frothingham lists this as a regular meeting, which, however, was not an official meeting of the Commissioners of the United Colonies) are not included. Triennial meetings were adopted in 1672. There were no meetings during the Dominion period, and the meeting of 1689 did not fall into the triennial sequence because of the interruption in New England government from 1686-1689. Intercolonial conferences involving Commissioners of the United Colonies (e.g., the N.Y. Congress of 1690) are likewise not here considered as meetings of the Confederation.

Month, Year	Place	President
Sep., 1643	Boston	John Winthrop
Sep., 1644	Hartford	Edward Hopkins
July-Aug., 1645*	Boston	John Winthrop
Sep., 1645	Boston	John Winthrop
Sep., 1646	New Haven	Theophilus Eaton
July, Aug., 1647*	Boston	Thomas Dudley

(the above meeting was considered sufficient for the year)

Sep., 1648	Plymouth	William Bradford
July, 1649*	Boston	Thomas Dudley

(as in 1647, no regular meeting)

31 Aug. 50

Sep., 1650	Hartford	Edward Hopkins
Sep., 1651	New Haven	Theophilus Eaton
Sep., 1652	Plymouth	
April, 1653*	Boston	John Endecott
May-June, 1653* (continuation)	Boston	Simon Bradstreet
Sep., 1653	Boston	Simon Bradstreet

Sep., 1654 ....Hartford ...Theophilus Eaton
Sep., 1655 ....New Haven .Theophilus Eaton
Sep., 1656   Plymouth   William Bradford
Sep., 1657 ....Boston .....Simon Bradstreet
Sep., 1658 ....Boston ....John Endecott
Sep., 1659 ....Hartford ...John Winthrop, Jr.
Sep., 1660 ....New Haven .Francis Newman
Sep., 1661 ....Plymouth ....Thomas Prence
Sep., 1662 ....Boston ......Daniel Denison
Sep., 1663 ....Boston .....Simon Bradstreet
Sep., 1664 ....Hartford ...Simon Bradstreet
Sep., 1667 ....Hartford ......William Leete
June, 1670 (for proposing new Articles only)
Sep., 1672 ....Plymouth ....Thomas Prence
Aug., 1673* ....Hartford ......William Leete
Sep.-Dec., 1675—Jan., Apr. '76 Boston ....Thomas Danforth
Sep., 1678 ....Hartford ......William Leete
Aug., 1679* ....Boston .....Thomas Danforth
Sep., 1681 ....Boston ....William Stoughton
Sep., 1684 ....Hartford ......Robert Treat
Sep., 1689-Dec., 1689 ......Boston .....Thomas Danforth

*Extraordinary sessions

THE COMMISSIONERS OF THE UNITED COLONIES

(Thumbnail Sketches)

Below are brief sketches identifying the fifty-eight men who were appointed Commissioners or substitute Commissioners of the United Colonies from 1643 to 1691. The letters after the names indicate the colony represented, and less obvious abbreviations are: G.-Governor; DG.-Deputy Governor; Asst.-Assistant; Dep.-Deputy. For further information, besides the few available biographies, one may consult the various New England genealogies, such as those sketches found in the publications of the New England Genealogical Society.

ALLYN, JOHN: (C) born in England; settled at Hartford, where he was town clerk from 1659-96; his ability as a clerk was put to use for the Colony, being Secretary of Connecticut from 1663 to 1695, with the exception of two years; an assistant of the Colony for many years after 1657; rose in the militia to the rank of Colonel; member of Andros's Council, 1687; Commissioner or substitute Commissioner, 1673-1686, every year except when none was chosen in 1685; d. November, 1696.

ALLYN, MATTHEW: (C) first settled at Cambridge in 1635, but soon removed to Hartford and finally Windsor; Dep. from Windsor from 1648-1657; Asst. from Conn. from 1658-1666, incl.; served on the War and Militia Committees for Windsor, and served as a commissioner in various capacities to settle boundary disputes; father of John Allyn (above); Commissioner, 1660 and 1664; d. 1671.

ASTWOOD, JOHN: (NH) in 1643, a Dep. from Milford to the N. H. Gen. Ct.; 1646, 1653, 1654, Asst. for the Colony; Commissioner, 1648, 1649, 1652, and 1653; d. 1654.

BRADFORD, WILLIAM: (P) b. in Austerfield, Eng., bapt. 1607; came to N. E. on the Mayflower; author of the *History of Plimouth Plantation*, succeeded Carver as Gov., which office he held until his death, except for three years; Commissioner, 1647-49, 1652, and 1656; d. May, 1657.

BRADFORD, WILLIAM, Major: (P) son of William Bradford (above); Dep. from Plymouth, 1656-7; Asst., 1658, the first of twenty-four consecutive years; DG. from 1682 until arrival of Charter in 1692, except when a member of the Andros Council; a member of the orthodox faction which opposed Hatherly and Cudworth; commanded the Taunton troops in King Philip's War; wounded at the Narraganset Swamp Fight, carrying a musket ball in his body for the rest of his life; Commissioner, or substitute Commissioner, 1673-8, 1680-4, 1686; d. 20Feb-1704.

BRADSTREET, SIMON: (M) b. in Hobling, Eng., March, 1603; educ. at Cambridge, A.M., 1624; came to N. E. in the Winthrop fleet of 1630; settled at Cambridge, later resided at Andover and Salem; Secretary of the Colony from 1630-1643; one of the assistants of the Mass. Bay Co. in Eng. in 1629; married a daughter of Commissioner Thos. Dudley; an Asst. for 48 consecutive years until 1678; G., 1679-86, and after Andros, 1689-92; his wife Anne Bradstreet, was a poet of renown and author of "The Tenth Muse" (d. 1672); Commissioner, 1644, 1648-61 (longest consecutive term of the Commissioners); Commissioner or alternate Commissioner, 1663-4, 1669-72, 1674-5, 1677—a total of 24 years; d. at the age of 94, March, 1697.

BROWN, JOHN: (P) traveled in Low Countries where he became familiar with the Pilgrims; came to Plymouth and removed before 1646 to Rehoboth; also a founder of Swansea; from 1636 on was an Asst. for 17 years; returned to Eng. before 1659 and became the steward of Sir Harry Vane; came back to Plymouth about 1661; left large estate; d. 10Apr62. Commissioner 12 consecutive years, 1644-1655.

BULKELEY, PETER: (M) major of the Mass. militia; resided at Concord; Dep. 1673-6—Speaker during the last year; an agent

to Eng. to defend Mass. against accusations from the heirs of
Gorges and Mason; Asst. 1678-1684; Commissioner, during the
final years of the Confederation, 1682-4; d. 24May88.

COLLIER, WILLIAM: (P) before coming over, 7 years a member of the Adventurers for New Plymouth, felt he had to come
to New World to share in the hardships as well as the profits;
married a daughter of Commissioner Prence; Asst. 28 years between 1634-1665; before the Confederation had visited with
Bradford at Boston in 1634 about the Hocking incident; Commissioner for the first meeting in 1643 only; d. 1670.

COOKE, ELISHA: (M) a physician, but better known as a politician; married a daughter of Commissioner Leverett; Dep.
1681-3; Assist. 1684-6; a member of the Mass. Council of Safety
during Revolution of 1689; colonial agent to Eng., 1690-1 with
Oakes and Mather; judge of the Province of Mass, 1701; G.
upon death of Stoughton; Commissioner or alternate Commissioner during twilight of the Confederacy, 1682-4 and upon its
attempted revival in 1689—left post of Commissioner to become
the Mass. agent to Eng.; d. Oct., 1715.

CUDWORTH, JAMES: (P) came to N. E. about 1634; Dep.
1649-56; Assist. 1656-8; commanded as general of Plymouth
troops during King Philip's War; agent for the Colony in England and DG. in 1681; showed rare courage in opposing the
persecution of Quakers in Plymouth, and lost post of Commissioner on that account; Commissioner, 1655, 1657, 1678-9, and
1681; d. 1682.

CULLICK, JOHN: (C) served in the Pequot War, later became
a Captain; Dep. from Hartford 1644, 1646-7; Asst. 1648-57;
Secretary of Conn., 1648-50, 1652, 1654-57; Commissioner 1652-
3, 1655; d. Jan. 1663.

DANFORTH, THOMAS: (M) b. in Eng.; Dep. from Cambridge
1657-8; Assist. 1659-78; DG. 1679-86 and after the fall of Andros; Pres. for Maine 1680; 1692 judge of Sup. Ct.; Commissioner 1663-79, 1682, and rep. Mass. at the attempted revival
of the Confederation in 1689; d. November 5, 1699.

DAVY, HUMPHREY: (M) Boston merchant; came from London in 1662; Dep. from Billerica and later Woburn; Asst. 1679-86; second wife was widow of Commissioner James Richards of Hartford, and later moved there to take over the estate; Commissioner alternate only, 1679.

DENISON, DANIEL: (M) b. about 1612; married as did several of his brother Commissioners a daughter of Commissioner Dudley (Thos.); Dep. from Ipswich for 8 years beginning in 1635; Speaker 1649, 1651, 1652; commanded the artillery company in 1660; Asst. 1654-82; Commissioner 1654-7, 1659-62, and a substitute from 1671, 1673, 1674-5, 1679; d. 19Sep82.

DUDLEY, JOSEPH: (M) b. 1647, son of Commissioner Thos. Dudley; Dep. from Roxbury 1672-76; during King Philip's War one of the Commissioners to accompany Major Savage in an attempt to hold the Narragansets in line and also present at the Swamp fight; Asst. 1676, 1685; frequently chosen to treat with the Indians; Pres. of the colonies of Mass. and New Hamp. 1686; unpopular in New England because of his siding with the Andros government; imprisoned with Andros in Boston in 1689; then went to England, and for a while DG. of the Isle of Wright; returned to Mass. in 1702 as G.—until 1715; Commissioner 1677-81; d. 2Apr1715.

DUDLEY, THOMAS: (M) b. in Northampton, Eng. c. 1576; served under Henry IV of France at the siege of Amiens; came over in 1630 and an undertaker in the Mass. Bay Co.; resided at Charlestown, Cambridge, and finally Roxbury; DG., G., or Asst. all his life in Mass.; sided with the Winthrop party for the maintenance of the established church; father of Joseph Dudley (above); unlike Winthrop, however, wanted rotation of the governor's office; lived across street from John Eliot, the Indian Apostle for the Confederation, in Roxbury; Commissioner for the first meeting 1643, 1647, and 1649; d. July, 1653.

EATON, THEOPHILUS: (NH) b. in Stratford, Eng.; chief magistrate of New Haven 1639-42; G. of N. H. Col. 1643; had been an agent of King James at the Court of Denmark; DG. of the Eastland Company while in London; pursued merchant interests at New Haven; Commissioner from the first meeting to the time of his death in Jan., 1658.

ENDICOTT, JOHN: (M) b. about 1589; one of 6 original purchasers of the Mass. Bay from the Ply. Council in 1628; leader of 1st settlement at Salem; G. 1644, 1649, 1651-3, 1655-64; because of storm created by his cutting out the cross of St. George from the English flag, he was left out of the Assists. in 1635; military interests, headed unsuccessful expedition against Pequots in 1636; though an "eastern man" he got along with Winthrop, and in final years moved to Boston; Commissioner 1646-8, 1658; d. while G., 1665.

FENN, BENJAMIN: (NH) Dep. from Milford, 1653; Assist. 1654-8, 1661-4; Assist., Conn. Col., 1664-72; d. 1672. Commissioner 1661-3.

FENWICK, GEORGE: (C) came to Boston from Eng. in 1636, returned and came back with family in 1639 as an agent for Lords Say, Brook, et al.; head of this settlement at the mouth of the Connecticut until sold out to Conn. Col. in 1644; lured into the Confederation by being made a Commissioner from Conn. 1643-5; also an Asst. 1644-5, 1647, 1648; had been a lawyer in Eng.; on return became a member of Parliament and of the High Court of Justice which sentenced the King, but did not sit as such; sister married Commissioner Cullick; d. while Gov. of Berwick, 15Mar57.

GOODYEAR, STEPHEN: (NH) arrived New Haven in 1638; probably a London merchant; an Assist. in 1641 and DG. from 1643 to 1657; conducted the diplomatic correspondence of the Colony; of a retiring and unassuming nature; first to embark upon shipbuilding in the colonies; first to successfully open up a trade with the West Indies; Commissioner, 1645-7, 1650-1; went home in 1657 and d. in London, 1658.

GREGSON, THOMAS: (NH) came with Eaton and Davenport from London in 1637; active in the commercial interests of the Colony; Asst., 1643; agent for the Colony to Parliament, 1644; Commissioner, 1643-4; first Treasurer of the Colony;

sailed with George Lamberton on the so-called "Phantom Ship" in 1646 for London, which was lost at sea.

HATHERLY, TIMOTHY: (P) felt maker and merchant from London; came in 1623, but returned following year; returned to Plymouth in 1630; a leading partner of the Plymouth Company; a second journey to Eng., and returned in 1632; settled at Scituate; Asst., 1636-57 except 1638; a Treasurer of the Colony; sided with Cudworth against persecution of the Quakers; Commissioner, 1646, 1651; d. 1666.

HATHORNE, WILLIAM: (M) came to Dorchester in 1630; removed to Salem in 1636; Speaker of the House of Deputies in 1644-51; Asst., 1662-79; aggressive and independent, challenged the Boston cabal for control of the Colony; served as a major in King Philip's War and in the expeditions against the Eastern Indians; Commissioner or substitute Commissioner, 1644, 1650-3, 1669-73; d. 1681, age 74.

HAYNES, JOHN: (C) one of the original settlers at Hartford; Asst., 1637-8, 1642, 1648; first G. of Conn. in 1639, also in 1641 and alternate years (with Hopkins) until 1653; DG. alternate years when not G.; Commissioner, 1646, 1650; d. 1654.

HINCKLEY, THOMAS: (P) b. in England, 1618; came to N. E. about 1635; Dep. in 1647; Assist., 1668-79; DG., 1680; last G. of Plymouth, 1681-92 when Colony became part of Mass. —except during the Andros period; council of the Province named by King, member of; his daughter was baptized on day of the Great Swamp Fight, named Reliance; d. in Barnstable, 1706, 88 years old. Commissioner, 1672-84, 1686 and on revival of the Confederation.

HOPKINS, EDWARD: (C) came to N. E. in 1637 with Davenport and Eaton; married a daughter of Eaton; removed to Hartford, from where he became an Assist. of the Colony; G. in 1639 and alternated with Haynes in that post until 1654—went to England in 1652, and his final election as G. was *in absentia;* DG., 1643-53 in alternate years; Secretary of the Colony, 1639; pursued commercial interests in N. E. as he did in England; Commissioner, 1643-51; d. in England, 1657, aged 50 years, only

THE UNITED COLONIES OF NEW ENGLAND

a few days before Commissioner Fenwick; in final years served Cromwell's government in various capacities.

JONES, WILLIAM: (NH) b. 1624 in London, where he served as a lawyer; in N. E., married as did Hopkins a daughter of Commissioner Eaton; Asst., 1662-3; DG., 1664-7; Asst. Conn. Colony 1665-77; member of the Conn. Council of War, 1673, 1675-6; may have been son of one of the regicides, Col. John Jones, executed in 1660; Commissioner, 1664; d. 1706, age 82 years.

LEETE, WILLIAM: (NH and C) Dep. from Guilford, 1643-4; Secretary of New Haven Co., 1646; Assist., 1653-7; DG., 1658-60; G. of N.H., 1661-64; Asst. for Conn., 1665-7; DG. 1669-75; G. of Conn., 1676-82; member of Council of War (Conn.), 1673-6; Commissioner from N. H., 1655-64; Commissioner from Conn., 1667-8, 1672-3, 1678; d. while Gov. of Conn., 1683.

LEVERETT, JOHN: (M) b. in England, 1616; Dep. for a no. of years from 1651-1664 and Speaker, 1663-4; successor to Denison as major-general in 1663; Assist., 1665-71; DG. 1671-2; G. 1673-8; agent for Mass. in England, 1655-61; in the 1640's, captain of a foot company in England; back in N. E., appointed by Cromwell in 1653 to raise 500 volunteers for service against the Dutch; in 1676 knighted and created a baronet by Charles II for his part in King Philip's War; Commissioner or substitute Commissioner, 1667-70, 1672; d. 1679; grandson, John Leverett, became president of Harvard.

LUDLOW, ROGER: (C) merchant, an Assist. of the Mass. Bay Co.; came over in 1630 and settled at Dorchester; DG. of Mass., 1634; in 1635 removed to Windsor; frequently displayed his temper, which resulted in his removal to Fairfield in 1639 and to Virginia in 1654; accused of running off with town records to Virginia, but later vindicated; Commissioner from Conn., 1648, 1651-3; DG. of Conn., 1648; d. in Va.

MALBON, RICHARD: (NH) Dep. from town of New Haven to the Colony Gen. Ct., 1644-5; Assist., 1646; Capt. of militia, 1645; Treasurer of the Colony, 1643-5; thereafter ret. to England; served only as substitute Commissioner, 1643.

MASON, JOHN: (C) came to Dorchester, probably in 1632; Capt. in expedition, 1632, against pirates; Dep., 1635-6; removed to Windsor, 1637; commander of Conn. forces in Pequot War; Dep. from Windsor, 1637-41; Assist. for Con. Col., 1642-59, 1669-71; DG., 1660-8; Militia Committee, 1667-72; in later years resided at Saybrook and Norwich; vigorously claimed his lands in the Narr. Country belonged under Conn. jurisdiction; Commissioner, 1647, 1654-7, 1661; d. 1672, age 72.

MASON, SAMUEL: (C) son of John Mason (above); lieut. of Stonington Train Band; Assist., 1683-7; Commissioner on revival of Confederacy; d. 1705.

NEWMAN, FRANCIS: (NH) b. in England, came to New Haven in 1638; in his barn the constitution of N. H. Colony was drawn up, 1639; Dep., 1647, 1649-52; Assist., 1653-57; Secretary of Col., 1653-7; G., 1658-60; officer in military co., 1642-52; Commissioner, 1654, 1658-60; d. Nov., 1660.

NOWELL, SAMUEL: (M) unlike most of the Commissioners who were merchants or large landholders, trained for the ministry; resided at Charleston; chaplain of Mass. during King Philip's War on Conn. River maneuvers and Narr. fight; Assist., 1680; Treasurer of Col., 1685; went to England with I. Mather to secure Mass. Charter; Commissioner, or subst. Commissioner, 1682-6; d. in London, 1688.

PELHAM, HERBERT: (M) came to Cambridge in 1635; had been a lawyer in England and befriended the Mass. Co. in London; first Treasurer of Harvard College, 1643; Assist., 1645-9; returned to England in 1649; Commissioner, 1645-6; d. in England, July, 1673.

PITKIN, WILLIAM: (C) experience as a schoolteacher and lawyer in England; Dep. from Hartford and Greenwich, 1675-7; Treasurer, 1676; Agent to N. Y., 1676; Commissioner on revival of the Confederacy; d. Dec., 1694, age 58.

PRENCE, THOMAS: (P) came over in 1621 to Plymouth; removed to Duxbury, 1635; G. in 1634-5, 1638-9, 1657-72; Assist. when not G.; removed to Eastham, but returned to Plymouth;

Commissioner, 1645, 1650, 1653-4, 1656-8, 1661-3, 1668-72; d. May, 1673, age 72.

RICHARDS, JAMES: (C) Asst., 1664-5, 1669-77; Lt. of Conn. troops, 1664; commissioner to R. I., 1670-72; commissioner to Dutch naval commanders, 1673; member of Conn. Council of War, 1673-75-6; agent to England, 1675, 1677; commissioner to N. Y., 1677; Commissioner, or subst. Commissioner, 1669-72, 1674-7, 1679-80; d. 1680.

SMITH, DANIEL: (P) Asst., 1679-86; mem. of the Council under Andros; subst. Commissioner, 1682-4; d.—no date.

SOUTHWORTH, THOMAS: (P) Assist., 1652-3, 1657-69; militia lt. and capt.; Commissioner, 1659-61, 1664, 1667-9; d. Dec, 1669.

STOUGHTON, WILLIAM: (M) b. 1631 in England; settled at Dorchester; grad. from Harvard and attended Oxford in Eng.; for a time preacher in Eng.; upon return is noted for election sermon of 1668; entered politics; Assist., 1671-86; mem. of Andros's Council; Lt. Gov. under new charter and chief justice 1695 to 1701; agent with Bulkeley (both of whom had served as Comm. for the United Col.) for Mass. in London; acting G. when Gov. Phips recalled to London; though others were made scapegoats for the Witchcraft Delusion, his part in the affair, esp. as presiding judge of the witch trials, is probably the darkest of all; Commissioner, or subst. Commissioner, 1673-7, 1680-6; d. July, 1701.

TALCOTT, JOHN: (C) (Sr.) came in 1632 from London to Cambridge; removed with Hooker to Hartford; Dep. in first Court in 1637 until 1654-60; Treasurer of Conn.; Commissioner, 1656-8; often confused with his son, who did not use Jr. after his name (Palfrey in *Hist. of N. E.* considers father and son as the same person); d. 1660.

TALCOTT, JOHN: (C) (Jr.) son of the above; b. in England 1650; Dep., 1660-1; Assist., 1662-7; Treasurer of Conn., 1660-75, declined the position in 1676-7; commissioner to treat with N. H. Col. in 1663; also in 1663-4 commissioner to treat with various boundaries, e.g., N. Y., Mass., R.I.; mem. of the War Council of Conn., 1673; Commander-in-Chief of Conn. forces in King Philip's War (1676); Commissionei, 1662 3, 1669-77, 1683-4, 1686; d. July, 1688.

TREAT, ROBERT: (C) b. in England; Dep. from Milford to N. H. Gen. Ct., 1653-6, 1658; Assist. for N. H. Col. 1659-3, declined in 1664; Assist. for Conn. Col. 1664; Dep. from Milford, 1665; Major of N. H. County Troop, 1673; mem. of Conn. War Council, 1673, 1675-6; Commander-in-Chief of Conn. forces (1675); Commissioner, 1681-2; Gov. of Conn., 1683; mem. of Andros's Council; G. after overthrow of Andros for 15 years; d. July, 1710, age 88.

VAUGHN, WILLIAM: (Portsmouth, New Hampshire) came from England; a freeman under jurisdiction of Mass. in 1669; capt. of troops from the New Hampshire towns; a member of the council when N. Hamp. became a royal province in 1679; a loyal Mass. man, helped to bring the N. Hamp. towns back to Mass. after overthrow of the N. E. Dominion earlier had been dismissed as a member of the council; under the second provincial gov. again a member of the council and later Chief Justice of the Sup. Ct.; d. 1719; when Confederation revived in 1689 sat briefly as a Commissioner from the N. Hamp. settlements—the only person to sit as a member of the Confederation from outside of the prescribed confederate colonies.

WALLEY, JOHN: (P) b. in Eng.; first settled in Boston; removed to Barnstable in 1683; helped settle Bristol; Assist., 1684-6; mem. of Andros's Council and the Mass. Council under the charter; served under Phips in the expedition against Quebec in 1690; Sup. Ct., judge, 1700-11; Commissioner or subst. Commissioner, 1684-6 and upon the revival of the Confederation in 1689 chosen as Commissioner from Plymouth until 1691; d. January, 1712, age 68.

WEBSTER, JOHN: (C) came to Hartford in 1636 and Dep., 1637-8; Assist., 1640-54, 1657-9; DG., 1655; G., 1656; War Committee for Hartford, 1653-4; founded Hadley; as did Commissionei Oulliok, had dispute with the Hartford Church; Assist. in Mass., 1660; Commissioner, 1654; d. April, 1661.

WELLES, THOMAS: (C) Dep. from Wethersfield, 1657-61, 1675; Capt. of Wethersfield Train Band, 1670; mem. of Conn. War Council, 1675; Assist., 1658-9; Commissioner, 1649, 1659; d. 1660 or 1661. G. of Conn., 1655 and 1658; DG. in 1656 and 1659.

WHITING, WILLIAM: (C) Dep. from Hartford, 1637; wealthy merchant; Assist., 1641-7; Treasurer; 1641, 1643-5, 1647; Commissioner, 1647; lost at sea, 1647. (Elected, but did not serve as Commissioner.)

WILLIS, SAMUEL: (C) b. in England in 1632; married daughter of Commissioner Haynes; Assist., 1654-84; Commissioner to treat with N. H. Col. 1662-3 and for Mass. and R. I. boundaries, 1664; mem. of Conn. War Council, 1673; Agent to N. Y., 1676; Commissioner, 1661-2, 1664, 1667, 1668 (subst.) 1670-1; d. May, 1709.

WINSLOW, EDWARD: (P) b. in England, 1595; went to Leyden with the Pilgrims; came over on the *Mayflower;* and a signer of the Mayflower Compact; agent for the colonies in England; received a military commission from Cromwell; second to Bradford in Plymouth Colony for his literary output; Assist. to 1647, 1650; G. of Ply., 1633-4; 1636-7; 1644-5; Commissioner, 1643-4; d. at sea, May, 1655.

WINSLOW, JOSIAH: (P) son of the above; b. 1629; Assist., 1657-72; G., 1673-80; astute politician, took advantage of popular reaction against the harsh Quaker policy of Plymouth, which had turned Commissioner Cudworth out of office; general of the joint forces of the United Colonies against the Narragansetts in 1675; first native born governor of any Amer. colony; Commissioner, 1658-60, 1662-4, 1668-80; d. 1680.

WINTHROP, JOHN: (M) (Sr.) b. in England; studied at Cambridge Univ., and became a successful lawyer; as member of the Mass. Bay Co. helped to secure its removal to New England, and first G. of the Co. in N. E., and G. off and on until 1648; also frequently DG.; successfully held his own against all forms of insurgency, religious or political; Commissioner, 1643 and 1645; d. 1649; with Bradford, shares the honor of being the chronicler of early New England; as did his son, John, Jr., carried on a large correspondence.

WINTHROP, JOHN: (C) (Jr.) b. in England in 1606; educ. at Trinity College, Dublin; came to N. E. in 1631; agent for Mass. in 1635, and for Conn. to secure charter, 1660's, in Eng.; in 1646, founded New London; Assist. for Conn. 1651-6; G. of Conn., 1657; 1659-75; Commissioner, 1658-60, 1663, 1668-9, 1675; d. in 1676 while attending a session of the Confederation which had been prolonged into the spring to meet the war emergency; one of the most versatile men of the century—not only a man of political and landed interests, but gathered a considerable library, started several manufacturing enterprises, and made contributions to science in the colonies.

WINTHROP, WAIT-STILL: (C) son of the above; mem. of the Council under Dudley and Andros, and helped in their overthrow; appointed by the Mass. Council of Safety during the revolt against Andros as commander of the military forces; Assist. in 1692 only a few days before arrival of the Charter, and afterwards mem. of the Council of the Province; later chief justice; Comm., 1672, 1675-6; d. 1717.

BIBLIOGRAPHY

The seventeenth century affords the most restrictive area for American historical study because of the absence of American newspapers, a dependency upon London printers, and the ecclesiastical preoccupation of the literary mind of the Puritans. But, even in the seventeenth century, there are vast reservoirs of virtually unused material. Most of the valuable collections of papers for the period have been published at least in part. The complete publication of the Winthrop Papers now in progress by the Massachusetts Historical Society—at the time of writing this study as far as 1649, the year of the death of John Winthrop, Sr.—is perhaps to date the highlight in the reproduction of the sources for this period. Local records—deeds, local business records, etc.—though not pertaining to this study could shed a great deal of light on early New England local life or entrepreneurial history. Even the great collections, such as the remaining unpublished Winthrop Papers, Winslow Papers, and Miscellaneous Collection at the Massachusetts Historical Society or the voluminous manuscripts of the Massachusetts or Connecticut Archives still present a wealth of fresh material to the enterprising scholar.

The publication of the records of the New England colonies during the last century has greatly facilitated research in the seventeenth century. The inclusion of the Acts of the Commissioners of the United Colonies in the publication of the Plymouth Colony Records has been of real service, since most of the records of the Commissioners were hastily jotted down, often in shorthand, which makes the original script difficult to read. The Plymouth manuscript records are still in the Plymouth Registry of Deeds, in spite of the efforts to bring them into the Massachusetts Archives. The Massachusetts copy of the Acts of the Commissioners was presumed lost in the fire of 1747, and that of New Haven has also been lost. A very legible copy of the Acts, probably a copy from the original, may be found in the Connecticut Archives (Conn. Colony Records, Vols. 52-3).

Before the publication of the records of New Plymouth, 1855-61, the Acts of the Commissioners were printed in Hazard's *State Papers.* The appendices of Hazard's work provide a supplement to the later Pulsifer edition, as do the Appendices of Volume X of the Pulsifer edition, which bring in the additions to the Plymouth copy obtained by a comparison with the Connecticut copy. A misconception has been to assume that the Acts of the Commissioners contained in the colony records were complete. But miscellaneous records of the Confederation are scattered throughout the early papers, some of which have not been included in the published records of the Commissioners, and, added to the correspondence of the period relating to the Confederation, they give a different view of the Confederacy. For example, the extra-records of the Confederation show that the Confederation met almost continually for six months during King Philip's War and that the Confederation met briefly after the downfall of the Andros regime, none of which is shown in the official Acts of the Commissioners as they have been published.

The search for seventeenth century manuscript material is often a frustrating experience. There were many dead ends in the course of this study. The collections used for this study have been of a disproportionate value. In order not to mislead the student of the quantity of material in the following collections, those collections which yielded only one or two items of value will be marked with an asterisk (*), and those used which were reproductions of originals will be designated with (P).

Although a bibliography of secondary sources is not presented here, it should be remembered that a vast amount of primary material has been included in the various biographies and the town and colony histories—the most useful of these books have been mentioned in the footnotes.

A. *Manuscript Sources*

Boston Atheneum
    Miscellaneous Manuscripts, I and III(P)
Boston Public Library
    Miscellaneous Manuscripts
Columbia University Library
    Letter, Mather to Hinckley, 26Feb91(P)

Connecticut Historical Society
    Indian Deeds*
    States Papers (Narragansett Lands, R. I.)*
    Trumbull (Annie) Papers*
    Willys Papers
    Wolcott Papers*
Connecticut State Library
    Connecticut Archives
    R. C. Winthrop Collection
    John Talcott Memorandum Book(P)
Essex Institute
    Hathorne Papers*
Forbes Library
    Judd Transcripts*
John Carter Brown Library
    Stevens Transcripts (HBM State Paper Office)
Library of Congress
    Miscellaneous Correspondence of John Eliot in Various
    British Collections(P)
Massachusetts Historical Society
    Miscellaneous Papers
    Saltonstall Papers*
    New England and New York MSS
    Winslow Papers
    Winthrop Papers
Massachusetts State House
    Massachusetts Archives
New York Historical Society
    Miscellaneous Connecticut Papers*
New York Public Library
    Bancroft Transcripts, New England, 1603-83*
    Transcripts from Public Records Office, Great Britain,
    Revolution in N. E.*
    Letters and Papers of Roger Williams(P)
    Winthrop-Davenport Letters
    Emmet Coll.*
Pilgrim Hall
    Miscellaneous Documents(P)
Rhode Island State House
    Rhode Island Archives (Boundary, Treasury Docs.)*

Rhode Island Historical Society
> Miscellaneous Manuscripts*
> Peck Collection*
Yale University Library
> W. G. Lane Collection*
> Rabinowitz Collection*

B. *Unpublished Dissertations and Typewritten Material*

Butler, Eva, "Beginnings of Pequot Plantation" (with excerpts from New London Town Records), CHS.

Leach, Douglas E., 'The Causes and Effects of King Philip's War," Unpublished Harvard PhD Thesis, 1950, RIHS.

Hammelef, John C., "British and American Attempts to Co-ordinate the Defenses of the Continental Colonies to Meet French and Northern Indian Attacks," Unpublished PhD Dissertation, University of Michigan, 1955, Univ. Mcrflm.

Hansen, Harold A., "The Sound Trade and Anglo-Dutch Conflict, 1640-1654" (Baltic phases of Anglo-Dutch Conflict), Unpublished PhD Dissertation, UCLA, 1946-7.

MacFarlane, Ronald O., "Indian Relations in New England, 1620-1760," Unpublished Harvard PhD Dissertation, 1933 (Abstract).

Sharp, Morison, "The New England Trainbands in the Seventeenth Century," Unpublished Harvard PhD Dissertation, 1938.

Smith, Frank, "John Eliot and the Praying Indians" (Excerpts from), Dedham Historical Society.

C. *Records and Laws*

Arnold, James, (ed.). *The Fones Record*, Vol. I of *Rhode Island Colonial Gleanings*. Providence: Narragansett Hist. Pub. Co., 1894.

Batchellor, Albert S., (ed.). *Laws of New Hampshire*. Vol. I. Manchester, N. H.: 1904.

Boston Records, 1634-1660. Second Report of the Record Commissioners. Vol. VII. Boston: 1881.

Bouton, Nathaniel. (ed.). *Documents and Records relating to the Province of New Hampshire, 1623-86*. Provincial Papers. Vols. I and II. Concord and Manchester. 1867.

Brigham, William. (ed.). *The Compact of the Charter and Laws of the Colony of New Plymouth.* Boston: 1836.

Browne, William H. (ed.). *Archives of Maryland. Proceedings and Acts of the General Assembly of Maryland, 1684-92.* Baltimore: Md. Hist. Soc., 1894.

Case, J. Wickham. (ed.). *Southold Town Records.* New York: S. W. Green's Sons, 1882.

Public Records of the Colony of Connecticut. Vols. I-III edited by J. H. Trumbull. Vol. IV edited by C. J. Hoadley. Hartford: Brown and Parsons-Case, Lockwood and Brainard, 1850-68.

Davenport, Frances D. (ed.). *European Treaties bearing on the History of the United States and its Dependencies to 1648.* No. 254 of the Publications of the Carnegie Institution of Washington. Washington, D. C.: 1917.

Early Records of the Town of Dedham. Vol. IV. Dedham, Mass.: 1894.

Dexter, Franklin B. (ed.). *New Haven Town Records, 1662-84.* Vol. II. New Haven: New Haven Col. Hist. Soc., 1919.

Dorchester Town Records. Fourth Report of the Records Commission of Boston. Boston: Rockwell and Churchill, 1883.

Exemplification of the Judgment for Vacating the Charter of Massachusetts Bay. Endorsed by Pengry. *MHSC.* Fourth Series. Vol. II. Boston: 1854. Pp. 246-78.

Extracts from Records in the County of York. Collections of Maine Hist. Soc. Vol. I. Portland: 1831.

Fernow, Berthold. (ed.). *The Records of New Amsterdam, 1653-74.* 7 Vols. New York: Knickerbocker Press, 1897.

Green, Samuel A. (ed.). *Early Records of Groton.* Groton: 1880.

Harvard College Records. Part I, Corporation Records, 1636-1750. Vol. XV of *PCSM.* Boston: MHS, 1925.

MacDonald, William (ed.). *Select Charters of American History, 1606-1775.* New York: The Macmillan Co., 1899

Province and Court Records of Maine. Vols. I and III. Portland: Maine Hist. Soc., 1928 and 1947.

Records of the Governor and Company of Massachusetts Bay. Edited by N. B. Shurtleff. 6 Vols. Boston: William White: 1853-4.

Records of the Massachusetts Court of Assistants, 1630-92. 3 Vols. Boston: 1901-28.

The Charters and General Laws of the Colony and Province of Massachusetts. Boston: 1814.

Records of the Colony of New Haven. Edited by C. J. Hoadley.
2 Vols. Hartford: Case, Tiffany and Co., 1857-8.

Records of the Colony of New Plymouth. Vols. I-VI (edited by
N. B. Shurtleff). Vols. IX-XI (edited by D. Pulsifer). Boston: W. White, 1855-61.

Records of North and South Hempstead, L. I. Vol. I. Jamaica,
N. Y.: 1896.

Nourse, Henry S. (ed.). *The Early Records of Lancaster, Mass.*
Lancaster: 1884.

Orders in Council. 39 Charles II (1660) III. *Briefe for England
and Wales. MHSC.* Fourth Series. Vol. II. Pp. 283-4.

*Printed Laws of New England contrary or Disagreable to Laws
of England. Andros Tracts.* Vol. VII of the PPS. Vol. III. Boston: J. Wilson and Sons, 1874.

Records of the Colony of Rhode Island. Edited by J. R. Bartlett.
Vols. I-III. Providence: Knowles, Anthony and Co., 1858.

Street, Charles R. (ed.). *Huntington, L. I. Records.* Vol. I. Huntington: 1887.

The First Book of Records of the Town of Southampton, L. I.
Sag Harbor, N. Y.: 1874.

Records of the Town of Easthampton, L. I. Vol. I. Sag Harbor,
N. Y.: J. H. Hart, 1887.

Records of the Suffolk County Court, 1671-80. Vol. XXX of the
PCSM. Vol. III. Boston: 1933.

Whitmore, William H. (ed.) *The Colonial Laws of Massachusetts.* Reprints of editions of 1660 and 1672, with supplements through 1886. Boston: 1887-9.

Winship, George P. (ed.). *The New England Company of 1649
and John Eliot.* Vol. XXXVI of the PPS. Contains: *Records
of the Company, 1650-86; the Ledger, 1650-1660;* and *The
Record Book, 1656-86.*

D. Documents and Letters

The Andros Tracts. 3 Vols. (Vols. V, VI, VII of the PPS). Certain of these tracts are listed here individually—see separate
headings. Boston: 1868-74.

Baxter, James P. (ed.). *Documentary History of Maine. Baxter
MSS.* Second Series. Vols. IV-VI, IX. Portland: 1889-1907.

Birch, Thomas. (ed.). *The Works of Robert Boyle.* Vol. I. London: 1772.

The Boston Society Publication, 1677-8. Vol. VI. Boston: 1910.

British Royal Proclamations Relating to America, 1603-1783. Edited by Clarence S. Brigham. Vol. XII of the *Transactions of the Amer. Antiquarian Soc.* (1911).

Brodhead, John R. (ed.). Holland Documents. Vol. I of the *Colonial History of New York.* Albany: Weed, Parsons and Co., 1853. Vol. II. See entry under O'Callaghan.

Calder, Isabel M. (ed.). *Letters of John Davenport.* London: Oxford University Press, 1937.

Chapin, Howard M. (ed.). *Documentary History of Rhode Island.* Providence: Preston and Rounds Co., 1916.

The Clarendon Papers. Vol. II of the *NYHSC.* 1869.

Commager, Henry S. (ed.). *Documents of American History.* 5th ed. New York: Appleton-Century-Crofts, Inc., 1949.

D'Aulney and La Tour, *Papers Relative to the Rival Chiefs. MHSC.* Third Series. VII. Boston: Little and Brown, 1838. Pp. 90-121.

Danforth, Thomas. *Papers. MHSC.* Second Series. Vol. VIII. Boston: N. Hale, 1826.

Dexter, Franklin. (ed.). "Sketch of the Life and Writings of John Davenport." *Miscellaneous Historical Papers.* Contains a bibliography of John Davenport's writings. New Haven: 1918.

Dykes, D. Oswald. (ed.). *Source Book of Constitutional History from 1660.* New York: Longmans, Green and Co., 1930 .

Eames, Wilberforce. (ed.). *John Eliot and the Indians, 1652-57.* Letters to Johnathan Hanmer of Barnstaple, England. New York: 1915.

Eliot to Stiles. Letter of 1673. *MHSC.* First Series. Vol. X. Pp. 124-6.

Letters from Rev. John Eliot to Hon. Robert Boyle. *MHSC.* First Series. Vol. III.

Farnham, Mary F. (ed.). *The Farnham Papers, 1603-1688.* Vol. VII of *The Documentary History of Maine.* Portland: The Thurston Press, 1901.

Ford, John W. (ed.). *Some Correspondence between the Governors and the New England Company in London and the Commissioners of the United Colonies in America.* London: 1896.

Gardiner, Samuel R. (ed.). *The Constitutional Documents of the Puritan Revolution, 1628-1660.* Oxford: Clarendon Press, 1889.

Haynes, John to John Winthrop. Letter of 27Feb44. *MHSC.* Third Series Vol. I. Boston: Phelps and Farnham, 1825. Pp. 229-31.

Hazard, Ebenezer. (ed.). *Historical Collections consisting of State Papers.* Philadelphia: T. Dobson, 1794. Vol. II.

Hinckley, Thomas. *Papers.* Fourth Series. *MHSC.* Vol. V. Boston: 1861.

Hooker, Thomas to John Winthrop. Letter of Dec38. *CHSC.* Hartford: 1860. Vol. I. Pp. 2-15.

Hinman, R. R. (ed.). *Letters from the English Kings and Queens to the Governors of Connecticut with Answers Thereto.* Hartford: 1836.

Hough, Franklin B. (ed.). *Papers Relating to the Island of Nantucket.* Albany: 1856.

Hutchinson Papers. MHSC. Third Series. Vol. I.

Hutchinson, Thomas. *A Collection of Original Papers Relative to the History of Massachusetts Bay.* 2 Vols. Albany: J. Munsell, 1865.

James II. Commission of King James II to Sir Edmund Andros. 3Jun86. Vol. IV. No. 8. *Force Tracts.* New York: Peter Smith, 1947.

Jameson, John F. (ed.). *Privateering and Piracy in the Colonial Period: Illustrative Documents.* New York: The Macmillan Co., 1923.

Jenness, John S. (ed.). *Transcripts of Original Documents in the Archives relating to the Early History of New Hampshire.* New York: 1876.

Johnson, Amandus. (ed. and trans.). "Correspondence between Governor Johan Printz and Governor John Winthrop, 1643-44." *The Instruction for Johan Printz.* Philadelphia: Swedish Colonial Society, 1930.

Larabee, Leonard W. (ed.). *Royal Instructions to British Colonial Governors, 1670-1776.* New York: D. Appleton-Century Co., 1935.

Leisler Papers. Vol. I. of the *NYHSC.* 1868.

Massachusetts Historical Society Collections. Miscellaneous Letters. For letters not in collections nor listed separately in this bibliography (especially the various letters of the First Series, Vols. I, V, VI) see footnotes.

Mather, Cotton. *Diary, 1681-1708. MHSC.* Seventh Series. Vol. VII. Boston: 1911.

O'Callaghan, E. B. (ed.). *The Documentary History of New York.* 4 Vols. Albany: 1849-51.

——. (ed.). *Documents Relative to the Colonial History of New York.* Transcripts of London, Holland, and Paris Documents. 11 Vols. Albany: 1856-1861.

Pincheon Papers. MHSC. Second Series. Vol. VIII. Pp. 227-249.

Powicke, F. J. (ed.). "Some Unpublished Correspondence of the Rev. Richard Baxter and the Rev. John Eliot, 1656-82." Vol. XV of the *John Rylands Library Bulletin.* Manchester, England.

Rhode Island State Papers. MHSC. Second Series. Vol. VII. Boston: N. Hale. Pp. 75-113.

Richman, I. B. (ed.). *Harris Papers. RIHSC.* Vol. X. 1902.

Sainsbury, W. N. (ed.). *Calendar of State Papers.* Colonial Series. Papers found in the Public Records Office. Vols. IX 1893); VII (1889); and V (1880).

Sir Ferdinando Gorges and his Province of Maine. Edited by J. P. Baxter. Vols. XVIII and XIX of the *PPS.* 2 Vols. Boston: 1890.

Stiles Collection of published MSS. *Memoir of the Pequots. MHSC.* First Series. Vol. X.

Stock, Leo F. (ed.). *Proceedings and Debates of the British Parliaments respecting North America.* Vols. I and II. Washington, D. C.: Carnegie Institution, 1924-7.

Thurloe, John. (ed.). *A Collection of State Papers, 1638-60.* 7 Vols. London: 1742.

Toppan, R. N. and Goodrick, A. T. S. (eds.). *Edward Randolph: Documents and letters.* 7 Vols. *PPS.* Boston: 1898-1909.

Thwaites, Reuben. (ed.). *The Jesuit Relations and Allied Documents, 1610-1791.* Vols. XXXVI, LXII, LXIV. Cleveland: 1899-1900.

Trumbull Papers. MHSC. Fifth Series. Vol. IX. Boston: 1885.

van Laer, A. J. F. (ed. and trans.). *Correspondence of Jeremias van Rensselaer, 1651-1674.* Albany: 1932.

——. (ed. and trans.). *Correspondence of Maria van Rensselaer, 1669-89.* Albany: 1935.

Walker, Williston. *The Creeds and Platforms of Congregationalism.* New York: Charles Scribner's Sons, 1893.

Letters of Roger Williams. MHSC. Third Series. Vol. I. Pp. 123-8.

Whalley and Goffe. MHSC. Third Series. Vol. VII. Boston: 1838. Pp. 12-8.

Williams to Winthrop, Jr. Letter of Sep.19. *MHSP.* Second Series. Vol. III. Boston: 1888. Pp. 256-7.

Petition of Roger Williams to the General Court of Massachusetts. MHSC. Fourth Series. Vol. IV. Boston: 1858. Pp. 471-3.

Letters of Roger Williams. Edited by J. R. Bartlett. *The Narragansett Club Publications.* First Series. Vol. VI. Providence: 1874.

Williams, Roger, to the Commissioners of the United Colonies. Letter of Sep72. *MHSP.* Second Series. Vol. III. Boston: 1888. Pp. 258-9.

Winthrop Papers. 5 Vols. MHS. Boston: Merrymount Press, 1929-47.

Winthrop Papers. MHSC. Third Series, Vol. X; Fourth Series, Vols. VI and VII; Fifth Series, Vols. I and VIII.

Wraxall, Peter. *An Abridgement of the Indian Affairs, 1678-1751.* Edited and Introd. by C. H. McIlwain. ol. XXI of Harvard Historical Series. Cambridge: Harvard Univ. Press, 1915.

Willys Papers. Vol. XXI of *CHSC.* Hartford: 1924.

E. *Contemporary or Near Contemporary Writings*

Andrews, Charles M. (ed.). *Narratives of the Insurrections, 1675-1690. Original Narratives of Early American History Series.* Edited by J. F. Jameson. Vol. XVI. New York: Charles Scribner's Sons, 1915.

Bradford, William. *History of Plimoth Plantation.* Boston: Wright and Potter Printing Co., 1898.

Baxter, Richard. *A Holy Commonwealth.* London: 1659.

Bishop, George. *New-England Judged.* London: 1661 (Reprinted 1703).

Bulkeley, Gershom. *Will and Doom.* Introd. and notes by C. J. Hoadley. *CHSC.* Vol. III. Pp. 69-270.

Burr, George L. (ed.). *Narratives of the Witchcraft Cases, 1648-1706. Original Narratives of Early American History Series.* Edited by J. F. Jameson. New York: Charles Scribner's Sons, 1911.

Childe, John. *New-Englands Jonas Cast Up at London*. Vol. IV, No. 3 of *Force Tracts*. New York: Peter Smith, 1947.

Church, Benjamin. *The History of King Philip's War. Part I: Entertaining Passages Relating to Philip's War*. Part II: *The History of the Eastern Expeditions*. Vols. II and III of the *Library of New-England History*. Edited by H. M. Dexter. Boston: 1845-7.

Coles, Elisha. *A Practical Discourse of God's Sovereignty*. Newburyport: 1798 (1667).

Cotton, John. *A Treatise of the Covenant of Grace*. London: 1659.

——. *The Way of Congregational Churches Cleared*. London: 1648.

——. *The Bloudy Tenant Washed White in the bloud of the Lambe*. London: 1647.

Dankers, Jaspar and Sluyter, Peter. "Journal of our Voyage from New Netherland." *Memoirs of the L. I. Hist. Soc.* Vol. I. Albany: 1867.

Davis, Andrew McF. (ed.). *Several Tracts relating to the Fund. Colonial Currency Reprints*. Vol. XXXII of the *PPS*.

de Britaine, William. *The Dutch Usurpation: or, A Brief View of the States-General of the United Provinces towards the Kings of Great Britain*. London: 1672.

de Menou, Count Julius. *Notice of the Sieur D'Aulnay of Acadie*. Translated by W. Jenks. *MHSC*. Fourth Series. Vol. IV. Boston: 1858. Pp. 462-70.

de Vries, David. *Voyages from Holland to America, 1632 and 1644*. Edited by H. C. Murphy.

Drake, Samuel G. (ed.). *The Old Indian Chronicle*. Boston: 1867. A Collection of Rare Tracts published during King Philip's War. Contents: *The Present State of New-England* (1676); *A Continuation of the State of New England* (1676); *A new and farther Narrative* (1676); *A true Account of the most considerable Occurrences* (1676); *The War in New-England visibly ended* (1677); *News from New-England* 1676); *A farther brief and true Narrative of the late Warr risen New-England* (1676).

Easton, John. *A Narrative of the Causes which led to Philip's Indian War*. Edited by Franklin B. Hough. Albany: 1858.

Eliot, John. *The Christian Commonwealth. MHSC*. Third Series. Vol. IX.

Eliot Tracts. The title given to eleven tracts published between 1643-1671 in London. The first five tracts were published by individuals, the remainder by the Corporation. All were for the purpose of encouraging the missionary work in New England. They may be found in a number of American collections, e.g., the Lenox Collection of the NYPL; also reprinted in various places, e.g., *Sabin's Reprints.* See footnotes for individual listing.

Gardiner, Lion. *Relation of the Pequot Warres. MHSC.* Third Series. Vol. III. Cambridge: 1833. Pp. 131-60.

Gookin, Daniel. *Historical Collections of the Indians in New England. MHSC.* First Series. Vol. I. Boston: 1806.

——. *An Historical Account of the Doings and Suffering of the Christian Indians. American Antiquarian Society Transactions and Collections* (1836), Pp. 423-534.

Gorton, Samuel. Letter to Nathaniel Morton. 30Jun69. Vol. IV, No. 7 of *Force Tracts.* New York: Peter Smith, 1947.

——. *Simplicities Defense against Seven-Headed Policy.* Vol. IV, No. 6 of *Force Tracts.* New York: Peter Smith, 1947.

Hooker, Thomas. *The Soules Ingrafting into Christ.* London: 1637.

Hubbard, Rev. William. *The History of the Indian Wars in New England.* Vols. III and IV of Woodward's Historical Series. 2 Vols. Edited by Samuel G. Drake. Roxbury: 1845.

Hull, John. *Diary.* Vol. III of the *American Antiquarian Transactions* (1857). Pp. 109-316.

Intrusion of the Rhode-Island People upon the Indian Lands. Declaration of the Commissioners of the United Colonies. *MHSC.* Third Series. Vol. III. Cambridge: 1833. Pp. 209-10.

Johnson, Edward. *Wonder Working Providence of Sion's Saviour in New England. Original Narratives of Early American History* Series. New York: Charles Scribner's Sons, 1909. Also *MHSC.* Second Series. Vol. VII. Boston: 1826. Pp. 1-57.

Journal of the Life of William Edmundson, A. London: 1774.

Journal of Van Ruyven, Van Cortlandt and Lawrence, The 1663. Edited by J. F. Jameson. *Narratives of New Netherland.* Vol. VIII of *Original Narratives of Early American History* Series. New York: Charles Scribner's Sons, 1909.

Josselyn, John. *An Account of Two Voyages to New England, 1638 and 1663.* Boston: 1865.

Lincoln, Charles. (ed.). *Narratives of the Indian Wars.* Vol. XIV of the *Original Narratives of Early American History.* Edited by J. F. Jameson. New York: Charles Scribner's Sons, 1913.

Mason, John. *A Brief History of the Pequot War. MHSC.* Second Series. Vol. VIII. Introd. by T. Prince. Boston: 1826. Pp. 120-153.

Mather, Cotton. *The Life of Sir William Phips.* Edited by Mark Van Doren from the *Magnalia Christi Americana.* (1697). New York: Stratford Press, 1929.

——. *Magnalia Christi Americana.* Edited by Thomas Robbins and L. F. Robinson. Hartford: 1853-5. 2 Vols.

Mather, Increase. *A brief History of the War with the Indians of New-England.* Edited by S. G. Drake. Albany: J. Munsell, 1862.

——. *The Early History of New England.* Relations of Hostile Passages Between the Indian and European Voyages. Boston: S. G. Drake, 1864.

Mather, Richard. *Church-Government and Church-Covenant.* London: 1643.

Maverick, Samuel. *A Briefe Description of New England. MHSP.* Second Series. Vol. I. Boston: 1885.

Milton, John. *A treatise on civil power in Ecclesiastical Affairs.* London: 1659.

Miner, Sidney H. and Stanton, G. D. (ed.). *The Diary of Thomas Miner, 1653-84.* New London, Conn.: 1899.

Morton, Nathaniel. "New England's Memorial." *Chronicles of the Pilgrim Fathers.* Edited by John Masefield. New York: E. P. Dutton and Co., 1910.

Neal, Daniel. *The History of New-England to 1700.* 2 Vols. London: 1720.

New Englands First Fruits. London: 1643. Anon. Reprinted in *Sabin Reprints.* No. VII. Quarto Series. New York: 1865.

Norton, Humphrey, et. al. *New-England's Ensigne.* London: 1659.

O'Callaghan, E. B. (ed. and trans.). Donck, Adrian van der. *Remonstrance of New Netherland to the States General of the United Netherlands.* (1649). Albany: 1856.

Orr, Charles. (ed.). *History of the Pequot War.* Reprint of a contemporary account. Cleveland: The Helman-Taylor Co., 1897.

Pierson, Rev. Abraham. *Some Help for the Indians: A Cate-*

chism. Edited and Introd. by J. H. Trumbull. *CHSC.* Vol. III. Pp. 1-67.

Randolph, Edward. *Representation of the Bostoneers, 1680.* Hutchinson Papers. Vol. III. of the *PPS.* Vol. II. of Boston: 1865. P. 265.

——. *A short Narrative of my proceedings. Andros Tracts.* Vol. VII of the *PPS.* Vol. III. Boston: 1874.

Reasons for Conferring of Charters belonging to the several Corporations in New-England. Andros Tracts. Vol. VI of the *PPS.* Vol. II. Boston: 1869. Pp. 225-9.

The Revolution in New-England Justified. Vol. V, No. 9 of *Force Tracts.* New York: Peter Smith, 1947.

Savage, T. *An Account of the New Englanders against the French at Canada* (1691). *MHSC.* Second Series. Vol. III. Boston: 1815.

Sewall, Samuel. *Diary. MHSC.* Fifth Series. Vol. V. Boston: 1878.

——. *Letter-Book. MHSC.* Sixth Series. Vol. I. Boston: 1876.

Stuyvesant, Peter. "Report on the Surrender of New Netherland." *Narratives of New Netherland.* Vol. VIII of the *Original Narratives of Early American History.* Edited by J. F. Jameson. New York: Charles Scribner's Sons, 1909.

True Relation of the Late Battle Fought in New England, A Anon. *MHSC.* Third Series. Vol. VI. Pp. 29-43.

Underhill, John. *History of the Pequot War. WHSC.* Third Series. Vol. VI. Pp. 1-28.

Ward, Edward. *Boston in 1682 and 1699: A Trip to New England.* Edited by G. P. Winship. Providence: 1905.

Wheeler, Captain Thomas. *Narrative of an Expedition to the Nipmuck Country, 1675.* Printed in *An Historical Discourse.* Edited by Joseph Foot. West Brookfield: 1843.

Winthrop, John. *Journal.* Edited by James K. Hosmer. 2 Vols. New York: Charles Scribner's Sons, 1908. Also Savage, James (ed.). 2 Vols. Boston: 1853. The Hosmer edition is used, except when marked by an (S), indicating the Savage edition, in the footnotes.

Winthrop, Wait. *Some meditations concerning . . . pursuit of those barbarous natives in the Narragansett-Country.* (1675). Reprinted, 1721. Broadside facsimile. Boston: MHS, 1919.

INDEX

A

Abenakis, 118, 320ff, 350ff
Acadia, 91ff, 252, 381-2
Achaian League, 12
Adams, John, 378, 88n.
Adams, John Quincy, 77
admiralty jurisdiction, 74, 170,
219, 228n.
Agamenticus (Gorgeana) 42, 47n.
Agawam, see Springfield
Albany, 271, 282, 299, 304, 345,
341, 355ff
Albany Plan of Union (1754), 376-7
Alden, John, 26
Alfred, 80
Algonquins, 38, 118; Algonquian
tongue, 245
Allyn, John, 66, 312n, 332, 400
Allyn, Matthew, 74, 156n, 400
Anabaptists, 145
Andros, Edmund, 282, 314, 329,
339n., 345, 366, Ch. 14.
Anglican Church, 84, 214, 322
Antinomian controversy, 30, 103, 118
appellate jurisdiction 380
Appleton, Samuel, 287ff, 290ff
Arnold, Benjamin, 259n.
Articles of Confederation (1643),
Ch. 3, 41ff, 384ff
Articles of Confederation (1672),
72, Ch. 12, 222ff, 391ff
Articles of Confederation (1781), 53,
56, 376-7, 381
Aspinwell, William, 161
Astwood, John, 400
Atherton, Humphrey, 123, 125, 146,
193, 197n., 199n., 236-7
Atherton Company, 146ff, 323ff, 332
Averell, James, 236

B

Bacon, Andrew, 70
Baptists, 145, 152n., 155n.
Barbados, 158, 205, 221, 229n., 369n.
Bartholomew, Mr., 275n.
Baxter, George, 166, 176n.
Baxter, Richard, 255n.
Bay Psalm Book, 245
beaver trade, 30, 109, 160-9, 164;
also see fur trade

Bedford Flag, 83
Beers, Captain, 284
Bellingham, Richard, 176n., 276n.
Bermudas, 369n.
Bishop, James, 106-7
Blinman, Richard, 232
Block Island, 27
blockade, 237; also see John Youngs
Body of Liberties, 58, 86n.
Bossy, James, 70
Boyle, Robert, 244
Bradford, William, Sr., 25, 27, 30,
39, 55, 59, 197n., 398, 401
Bradford, William, Jr., 66, 280, 290,
311n., 321, 365, 401
Bradstreet, Simon, 59n., 66, 67, 165,
182, 188, 224n., 275n., 276n., 323,
332, 336, 337, 355-6, 373, 398-9, 401
Branford, 209, 233
Breda, Treaty of (1667), 95, 228n.
Bridges, Robert, 94
Brocklebank, Samuel, 298
Brookfield (Quabaug), 284,
301, 312n.
Brown, John, 59, 67, 139, 155n., 401
Bulkeley, Peter, 317, 401
Bull, Jeremiah, 327
Bumpus, Hannah, 268

C

Caleb, (Ind. name), 238
Call to the Unconverted, 247
Calvinists and Calvinism, 10-12,
15, 16
Cambridge (Newton), synods at, 30,
32, 40, 103ff, 245
Cambridge Platform (1648), 115n.
Cambridge Press, 248, 254
Canonchet, 302
Canonicus, 122
Cape Cod, 110
Carr, Sir Robert, 214, 217
Cartwright, George, 214, 217
Casco Bay, 152n.
Cassasinamon, 203ff, 235
Charles I, 213
Charles II, 77, 88n., 201, 207ff, 227n.,
271, 273, 275, 308n.
Charlestown, 40, 138, 170-1, 177n.
Child, Robert, 103

427

Church, Benjamin, 293, 304, 310n.,
345, 347-8
Civil War (English), 107, 382
Clarke, John, 149
Coddington, William, 43, 115n., 145
Cohasset River, 47n.
Collier, William, 41, 47n., 309, 402
commander-in-chief, 76, 93ff, 122ff,
169, 271, 285, 287ff, 290ff, 349, 357,
362, 364, 371n.
Commissioners of Customs, 316
Committee of States (1784), 20, 171
Committee on Trade and Plantations,
354
common law, 14
Congregationalism, 18, 32, 103, 249
Connecticut Charter, 149, 208, 219,
331ff, 336
conservatives and conservatism
(orthodox party), 31, 64, 66ff, 79-
80, 103, 251, 316, 328
Constitution (1787), 19, 49, 54, 376-8
Continental Congress, 38
Cook, George, 137
Cooke, Elisha, 154n., 336, 347, 353,
368n., 369, 402
Coopers Hall (London), 231
Corporation (The Society for the
Propagation of the Gospel in New
England, 1649, and The Corpora-
tion for Propagation of the Gospel
in New England and the parts ad-
jacent in America, 1662), 75, 76,
85n., 101, 104ff, 169, 201ff, 217,
266-7, 309n., 321-2, 364, Ch. 11
Corsicans, 83
Cotton, John, 16, 233, 374
Council for Trade and Plantations,
316
Council of Safety (1689), 347
covenants, Ch. 1; 47, 263
criminal law, 268
Cromwell, Oliver, 44n., 170-1, 177n.,
180, 185, 190, 198n., 249, 275, 319
Cross of St. George, 82, 84 (Flag)
Cudworth, James, 67, 251ff, 280,
373, 402
Cullick, John, 170, 249, 402

D

D'Ailleboust, Louis, 95

Danforth, Thomas, 66, 114n., 208,
240, 248, 265, 275n., 278n., 206,
290, 299, 328, 336, 341n., 364,
397, 402
Dankers, Jasper, 240
D'Aulney, Charles, 91ff
Davenport, Captain, 294-5
Davenport, John, 13, 15, 212,
225n., 374
Davis, William, 180, 228n., 278n.
Davy, Humphrey, 403
Deane, Thomas, 216
Dedham, 234, 255n.; Dedham Plain,
293
Deer Island, 244
Deerfield, 323
defensive war, Ch. 9; 286, 349
de la Tour, Charles, 91ff, 95;
Madame de la T., 95
Delaware Company, 159ff, 173
Delaware River, 158ff
Denison, Daniel, 155n., 181, 193,
197n., 199n., 271, 273, 293, 321,
399, 403
Denison, George, 147, 277n.
de Razilly, Isaac, 91
Dexter, Franklin, 264
Dixwell, John, 213
Dixy Bull, 25
Dominion of New England, Ch. 14.
Dongan, Thomas, 331
Dorchester, 26, 40
Dover, 352
Druillettes, Father Gabriel, 195-6,
240, 341n.
Dudley (Mass.), 258n.
Dudley, Joseph, 66, 103, 238, 293,
322, 328, 329-30, 337, 341n., 344,
347, 368n., 403
Dudley, Thomas, 13, 47n., 50, 59n.,
66, 174n., 390, 398
Duke of Hamilton, 327
Duke of York, 176, 206, 220,
282, 317ff
Dunster, Henry, 105, 116n.
Dutch Republic, 21n., 22n., 52n. see
United Provinces
Dutch Wars: (1652-4), 170, 380;
Chs. 8 and 9; (1664), 149, 218;
(1672-4), 271ff.

E

Earl of Warwick, 142
East Friesland, 80
East India Company, 80ff
Eaton, Samuel, 45n.
Eaton, Theophilus, 41, 53, 64, 73,
    161, 173n., 197n., 209, 390,
    398, 403
education, 105ff, 306; see
    Harvard College
Eliot, John, 76-7, 96, 104, 267, 309n.,
    321ff, 334, 341n.; Ch. 11.
Endicott, John, 27, 82, 87n., 213,
    398-9, 404
English Constitution, 14

F

Fairfield, 169, 189, 313n., 380
Falmouth, 349
Faneuil Hall, 71
Fenn, Benjamin, 404
Fenwick, George, 36, 41, 46n.,
    47n., 390
flag, origins of, 79ff
Flushing (L. I.), 176n.
Franklin, Benjamin, 88n., 377-8
The Freeman's Oath, 245
Frontenac, Count, 354
Fugill, Thomas, 41
the "Fund," 257n.
Fundamental Orders, 37
fur trade, 91ff, 270, 355;
    see beaver trade

G

Galloway's Plan of Union, 377
Gay Head tribe, 233
*General Laws and Liberties of
    Mass.*, 216
Gibbons, Edward, 59n., 76, 122,
    199n., 125, 129, 193
Glover, 176n.
Glorious Revolution, 382, Ch. 14.
Godefroy, Jean, 96, 97
Goffe, William, 213, 285
Gold, Nathan, 356
Good Hope, Fort of, 176n., 46n.,
    157ff, 162-3
Goodyear, Stephen, 41, 66, 82, 173n.

Gookin, Daniel, 67, 75, 224n., 236-7,
    242-3, 256n., 257, 267, 275n., 278n.,
    321ff, 342n.
Gorges, Ferdinando, 29, 40, 101,
    152n., 317, 325, 363
Gorton, Samuel, 14, 102, 137ff
Gortonists, 136ff
governor-general, 29, 44n., 93, 142,
    314ff, 329ff
Grafton (Mass.), 258n.
Gravesend, 176n.
Great Harbor (Edgartown), 233
Greeks, 12
Green, John, 154n.
Green, Samuel, 245-6, 248, 259n.
Greenwich, 209, 219
Greenwich Bay, 166, 179
Gregson, Thomas, 41, 161, 173n.,
    175n., 390, 404-5
Guilford, 46n., 209, 233

H

Hadley, 284-5, 290, 302, 303
Half Way Covenant, 249
Hampton Court Palace, 83, 251
Hanseatic League, 12-3
Harrington, James, 15
Hartford, Treaty of (1650), 145,
    165ff, 179, 219-20
Harvard College, 105ff, 131, 270,
    238, 339n.
Hassamesit, 252, 321
Hatfield, 287, 323
Hatherly, Timothy, 38, 252, 373, 405
Hathorne, William, 59, 64, 67, 114n.,
    182, 188, 197n., 265, 275n., 373,
    397, 405
Haynes, John, 33, 36, 41, 126
Henchman, Daniel, 166, 284, 303
Herrman, Augustine, 88n.
Hinckley, Thomas, 64, 251-2, 286,
    322, 324, 368n., 405
Hingham, 39-40, 47n., 268
Hobbes, Thomas, 15
Holden, Randall, 154n.
Holland, 14, 206, 271, 222
Holyoke, Capt., 303
Hooker, Thomas, 13, 15, 17, 34-6,
    46n., 90
Hopkins, Edward, 30, 41, 47n., 65-6,
    116n., 125, 130, 175n., 398, 405-0

Hopkinton (Mass.), 258n.
Hudson Valley, 162, 219-20, 357
Huntington (I. I.), 206
Hutchinson, Anne, 42, 110
Hutchinson, Edward, 284
Hutchinson, Elisha, 345

I

impost duties, 108, 163, 179, 182, 221
Indian Bible, 321ff; Ch. 10
The Indian Grammar begun, 247
Indian Language, 245
Indian Primer, 247
"Indian Worke", chs. 10-15
internal improvements, 105
Ipswich, 284, 290
Iroquois Confederacy, 97, 118, 205,
    268ff, 321, 355; see Mohawks
Israelites, 12, 198n., 235

J

Jamaica (L. I.), 176n.
Jamaica (W. I.), 177n., 229n.
James I, 80
Jesuits, 93ff.
Johnson, Marmaduke, 245, 248,
    259n., 277n.
Jones, John, 66
Jones, John Paul, 80
Jones, William, 209, 406
Judges' Cave, 213

K

Keayne, Captain, 25
Kennebec River, 26; trading post,
    44n.
Kieft, William, 46n., 159ff
King, Rufus, 374, 378
King Philip, 13, 238-9, 268ff,
    311n.; Ch. 13
King Philip's War, 204, 243-4, 253,
    270, 314ff, 320, 459-50; Ch. 13.
King's commissioners, 149ff.; Ch. 10
King's Province, 149ff, 270, 325ff,
    333, 340n.; see also Narragansett
    Country
Kittery (Me.), 152n.

L

Lamberton, George, 41, 158ff
Lancaster, 300

Lanoy, P. D., 356
Leete, William, 64, 154n., 209, 312n.,
    399, 406
Leisler, Jacob, 355ff
Leverett, John, 81-2, 123, 133n., 170,
    180, 197n., 228n., 274, 276n., 278n.,
    293, 303, 312n., 316, 406
Leveridge, William, 232
Leyden, 13
liberalism, 64, 154n., 170, 209,
    262, 312n.
liquor regulation, 234, 236
Littleton (Mass.), 258n.
Livingston, Robert, 355
Locke, John, 15
The Logic Primer, 247
London, 208-9, 232, 245, 253,
    322, 327
London fire (1666), 241
Long Parliament, 231
Long Island, 42, 145, 168ff, 175n.,
    196n., 204, 206, 209, 220ff, 229n.,
    232, 261, 268, 272-3, 274
Long Island Indians, 128, 130, 188,
    193ff, 199n., 204
Long Island Sound, 24, 82, 166, 203
Lords of Trade, 316ff, 350
Lothrop, Captain, 284
Lovelace, Francis, 268
Ludlow, Roger, 33, 46n., 169, 177n.,
    197n., 406

M

Maine, 42, 240, 261, 319ff, 347ff,
    352ff, 363
Malbon, Richard, 406
Marlboro (Mass.), 258n.
Martha's Vineyard, 145, 232,
    233ff, 267
Maryland, 339n., 347, 355, 356-7
Mason, George, heirs of, 317
Mason, John, 28, 123, 133n., 140,
    170, 177n., 407
Mason, Samuel, 346, 407
Massachusetts Charter (1691),
    314ff, 363
Massasoit, 281
Mather, Cotton, 51, 314, 363-4, 374
Mather, Increase, 345ff, 353, 369n.,
    374, 381
Maverick, Samuel, 207-8, 217

Mayhew, Experience, 233ff, 255n.
Mayhew, Thomas, Sr., 76, 232
Mayhew, Thomas, Jr., 232ff
Mendon, 284
Miantinomo, 120ff, 202ff, 205, 380
Middlesex County (Mass.), 83,
 200n., 234
Milborne, Jacob, 359
Milford, 209, 212
Milton, 302
Milton, John, 15, 248, 259n.
Mohawks, 97, 119, 125, 128, 204, 205,
 268, 282, 286, 302, 304, 312n., 323,
 346, 355, 362
Mohawk Valley, 357
Mohegans, 28-9, 75, 232, 235, 267-8,
 280ff, 298-9, 303, 380
Monaco, 83
Montauks, 268
Montreal, 361ff
Mosely, Captain, 284, 293, 295
Mount Hope, 280ff, 305, 315, 323,
 327, 340n.
Mystic and Mystic River, 27,
 141, 147ff

N

Nantucket, 258n.
Narragansett Bay, 225n., 250
Narragansett country, 140ff, 234,
 290, 311n.; see King's Province
Narragansetts, 27, 75-6, 118ff, 137,
 202ff, 380; Ch. 13.
Nassau, Fort, 161
Natick, 234ff, 258n., 270, 321
Navigation Acts and Acts of Trade,
 165, 168, 216, 315-6, 318ff
Neponset, 234
New Amsterdam, 38, Ch. 8
New-England's Ensigne, The, 252
New-England Judged, 252
New Hampshire 42, 46n., 152n., 249,
 281, 319ff, 345ff, 352ff, 366, 368n.
New Jersey, 245
New London, 141, 277n., 290, 298
Newman, Francis, 180, 209, 225n.,
 399, 407
Newman, Robert, 41, 64, 154n.
Newton (L. I.), 176n.
New York, 271ff, 282, 315ff, 320,
 345ff, 378n., Ch. 15

New York Conference (Congress),
 1690, 315
Niantics, 27, 75, 119, 124, 127, 130,
 140, 194ff, 198n., 253, 290
Niantic Country, 326
Nicolls, Richard, 214, 217, 218, 220
Ninigret, 128, 130, 188ff, 199n., 296
Nipmucks, 118, 156n., 281, 283ff, 302
Nipmuck Country, 243, 258n.,
 284, 300
Nonantum, 234
Northampton, 302
North Attleboro, 303
Norwich (Conn.), 290
Nowell, Samuel, 407

O

offensive war, 58; Chs. 9, 12
Oldham, John, 27
Oliver, James, 294
Orange, Fort, 158
Orangian flag, 81ff
Osgood, H. L., 77, 345
Oxford (Mass.), 258n.

P

Palfrey, J. G., 264
Parliament, 14, 102, 104, 142ff, 168,
 228n., 335
patronage, 237, 330
Patuxet, 302, 327
Pawcatuck, 148; P. River, 150
Pawtuxet and P. River, 137ff
Peirce, Capt., 261n., 301
Pelham, Herbert, 407
Penn's Plan of Union, 376
Penobscot, 94
Pequots, 27ff, 97, 104, 128, 131, 203ff,
 235ff, 267ff, 281, 303, 321ff
Pequot Country, 107, 116n., 139ff,
 194, 206, 278n.
Pequot War, 109, 118, 120, 140, 148,
 306; Ch. 2
Peskeompscut, 302
Pessacus, 124-5, 128
Pettasquamscut, 294
Peter, Hugh, 92, 158, 231
Phips, Sir William, 345, 359-60, 362,
 370n., 371n.
Pierson, Abraham, 232-4, 235, 245

Pilgrims, 14ff
pine tree shilling, 99
piracy, 232
Piscataqua, 23, 37
Pitkin, William, 245, 346, 356, 407
Pocock, John, 154n.
Pocasset Swamp, 283
Pocomtucks, 118, 198n., 202ff, 284, 302, 303
Pokanokets (Wampanoags), 118, 269ff; Ch. 13
Poland, 83
Ponkapoag, 234, 238
Popham, 137
popular party (Mass.), 373
Port Royal, 95, 358-60
Portsmouth (N. H.), 352
Prence, Thomas, 154n., 165, 216, 251, 265, 397, 399, 407-8
Prentice, Capt., 294, 342n.
Presbyterianism, 103
Printz, Johan, 159ff
privileges and immunities clause (Const.), 377
privateering, 170, 176n.
Privy Council, 46n., 207, 317, 327, 354, 363
Protectorate, 382
Providence (R. I.), 42, 102, 124, 251, 290, 293
Putney debates, 15
Pynchon, John, 284, 287, 323-4
Pynchon, William, 33, 74, 108-9

Q

Quakers, 67, 103, 234, 244, 249ff
Quebec, 95ff, 355, 357, 360, 362
Quebec Council, 96
Quinnipiacs, 118, 234-5, 244
Quiripis, 245
quo warranto proceedings, 318, 328, 331

R

Randolph, Edward, 316ff, 350; Ch. 14
Rawson, Edward, 49-50, 70, 74, 104, 218, 239-40
regicides, 213ff, 226n., 285, 317

regulatory measures, 98-101
Rehoboth, 73, 283, 290
religious policy, 103
Restoration, 177-8, 207, 331-2, 341, 257n., 365, 382
Richards, James, 34n., 70, 265, 286, 289, 305, 312n., 322, 397, 408
Romans, 12
Roman Catholics, 10
Ross, Betsy, 80
Rousseau, Jean Jacques, 375
Rowley, 298
Roxbury, 40, 230, 234, 240
royal commissioners, 212ff; see king's commissioners

S

Saco Indians, 320
Sacononoco, 137
Salem, 320
Saltonstall, Richard, 92, 154n.
Sanford, Peleg, 324
Sassacus, 128, 135n.
Sassamon, John, 238, 270, 281
Savage, Thomas, 283, 301
Saybrook, 36, 41, 46n., 107ff, 140, 282
Schenectady, 355
Schuyler, Peter, 355
Scituate, 39, 47n.
Scott, John, 220
Scott, Sir Walter, 213
secession, 57; Ch. 9; 210
Seconets, 269
Sedgwick, Robert, 170
Seekonk, 107, 293
Senate (U. S.) and Senators, 377-80
Sequasson, 125-6
Sewell, Samuel, 323, 345, 356, 358
Shawomet, see Warwick
Shepard, Thomas, 166n.
slavery, 70, 126, 134n., 256n., 294-5, 320, 339n.
Smith, Richard, 293
smuggling, 272
Smith, Daniel, 408
Some Helps for the Indians, 245
Southampton, 278n.
Souther, Nathaniel, 74
Southertown, 147, 273
Southold, 46n., 189, 196n., 209

Southworth, Thomas, 228n., 408
Springfield, 33, 39, 74, 108ff, 117n., 284ff, 301
Stamford, 46n., 166, 169, 189, 196n., 209
Stamp Act Congress, 80
Standish, Myles, 26, 38, 69, 123-4, 133n., 134n.
Stanton, Thomas, 75, 126-7, 147, 194, 202-3, 236, 245, 257n., 277n., 309n.; son, 257n.
Steele, John, 33, 70
Stonington, 297
Stoughton (Mass.), 258n.
Stoughton, William, 286, 317, 322, 330, 332, 336, 356, 364-5, 399, 408
Stratford, 272
Stuarts, 151, 217, 207, 221, 247, 261, 282, 314, 317, 329-30, 332, 335, 354, 365, 368n., 382
Stuyvesant, Peter, 163ff, 179ff
Sudbury, 302
Suffolk County (Mass.), 83, 145, 352
Supreme Court (U. S.), 380
Swansea, 270, 280ff
Swedes, 53, 158ff
Swiss Cantons (Confederation), 12, 198n.

T

Talcott, John, Sr., 156n., 408
Talcott, John, Jr., 273, 275n., 303-4, 312n., 321, 332, 408-9
Taunton, 59n.
Tewksbury (Mass.), 258n.
Thomas, William, 69
Three County Troop Flag, 83
Tower, Lawrence Phelps, 79-80, 83, 84
Triennial Act (Parliament), 215
Tripartite Treaty (Hartford—1638), 29, 38, 120-2, 124
Treat, Robert, 289-90, 295, 320, 332, 346, 359, 399, 409
Tudors, 80
Turner, Nathaniel, 158-9
Turner Falls, 302
Tyng, William, 59n.

U

Uncas, 120ff, 204, 267, 298

Underhill, John, 28, 134n., 162, 169, 196n., 176n.
Union of Utrecht, 13
United Provinces of Netherlands, Ch. 1; 80ff
Usher, Hezekiah, 76, 232
Uxbridge (Mass.), 258n.

V

Vagabond Act of 1661 (Mass.), 253
vagrancy, 266, 268, 320, 338n.
Vane, Henry, 27
Van Cortlandt, Stephanus, 340
Varkens Kill, 158ff
Vaughn, William, 353, 409
veto powers, 189, 363
Vice President (U. S.), 379

W

Wadsworth, Samuel, 302, 332
Waldron, Richard, 320
Walley, John, 346, 357-8, 362, 368n., 370n., 409
Wamesit, 321
War Department (U. S.), 59n.
Warwick patent, 36, 140, 153n.
Warwick, 120-1, 137ff, 290
Washington, George, 383n.
Watertown, 40, 284
Webster, John, 409
Weld-Peter Mission, 231
Welles, Thomas, 46n., 410
Westerhouse, Mr., 164, 166, 175n.
West India Company, 81
Wethersfield, 44n.
Whalley, Edward, 213
Wharton, Richard, 345
Wheeler, Thomas, 284
Whitfield, Henry, 233
Whiting, William, 65, 86n., 126, 410
Wickford, 150, 293-4, 297, 327
Willard, Simon, Jr., 349
Willard, Simon, Sr., 194ff, 200n.
Willett, Thomas, 166
William III, 335
Williams, Roger, 26, 35, 102, 122, 124, 127, 136ff, 204, 223n., 234-5, 252, 270, 278n., 306, 308n.
Willis (Wyllis), Samuel, 156n., 276n., 312n., 410

Winslow, Edward, 25, 29, 38, 41, 47n., 50, 66, 76, 104, 123, 139, 160, 168, 230ff, 390, 410
Winslow, John, 96
Winslow, Josiah, 66-7, 143ff, 154n., 155n., 205, 253, 265, 269, 275n., 285-6, 290ff, 317, 320, 397, 410
Winthrop, Fitz-John, 273-4, 357ff
Winthrop, John, Sr., 15, 26, 31, 50, 66-7, 73-4, 90, 92-5, 137, 160ff, 390, 398, 410-1

Winthrop, John, Jr., 66-7, 107, 134n., 140ff, 177n., 205, 208-9, 252, 267, 278n., 286, 300, 308n., 311n., 312n., 373, 397, 399, 411
Winthrop, Wait, 66, 289, 312n., 336-7, 339n.
Woodstock (Mass.), 258n.
Worcester, 258n.

Y

Youngs, John, 204, 223n.

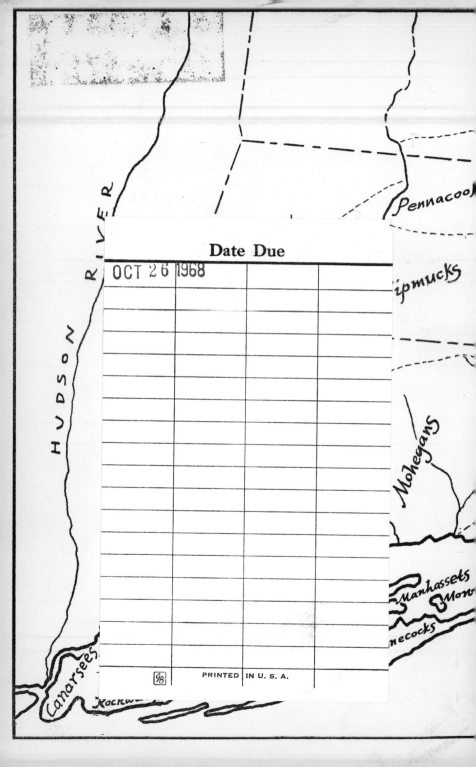

HUDSON RIVER

Pennacoo

ipmucks

Mohegans

Manhassets

Mon

necocks

Canarsees

Rockw